The study of behavioral decision making has recently expanded into the area of accounting and auditing. This branch of research seeks to understand the cognitive processes that govern such necessary functions as the pricing of products and services, evaluating corporate performance, granting credit to prospective borrowers, and investing in financial securities.

In *Judgment and Decision-Making Research in Accounting and Auditing,* editors Robert and Alison Ashton present and review more than 20 years of research in decision-making science. The book analyzes the judgments that business managers, investors, auditors, and creditors make daily. It considers the assets and liabilities of applied decision making and makes suggestions for future research.

Cambridge Series on Judgment and Decision Making

Judgment and decision-making research in accounting and auditing

Cambridge Series on Judgment and Decision Making

The purpose of the series is to convey the general principles of and findings about judgment and decision making to the many academic and professional fields to which these apply. The contributions are written by authorities in the field and supervised by highly qualified editors and the Publications Board. The series will attract readers from many different disciplines, largely among academics, advanced undergraduates, graduate students, and practicing professionals.

Also in the series:

Inside the Juror: The Psychology of Juror Decision Making
Edited by Reid Hastie

Psychological Perspectives on Justice: Theory and Applications
Edited by Barbara A. Mellers and Jonathan Baron

Judgment and decision-making research in accounting and auditing

Edited by

Robert H. Ashton and Alison Hubbard Ashton

Duke University

CAMBRIDGE
UNIVERSITY PRESS

Published by the Press Syndicate of the University of Cambridge
The Pitt Building, Trumpington Street, Cambridge CB2 1RP
40 West 20th Street, New York, NY 10011-4211, USA
10 Stamford Road, Oakleigh, Melbourne 3166, Australia

First published 1995

Printed in the United States of America

Library of Congress Cataloging-in-Publication Data

Ashton, Robert H.
Judment and decision-making research in accounting and auditing / Robert H. Ashton, Alison Hubbard Ashton.
p. cm.
Includes bibliographical references (p.).
Romanized record.
ISBN 0-521-41844-5
1. Accounting—Decision making—Research. 2. Auditing—Decision making—Research. 3. Managerial accounting—Research. I. Ashton, Alison Hubbard. II. Title.
HF5657.A77 1995
657′.01′9—dc20 95-1537
CIP

A catalog record for this book is available from the British Library

ISBN 0-521-41844-5 Hardback

Contents

Contributors

Alison Hubbard Ashton *Fuqua School of Business, Duke University*

Robert H. Ashton *Fuqua School of Business, Duke University*

Joyce Berg *Department of Accounting, College of Business Administration, University of Iowa*

John Dickhaut *Department of Accounting, Carlson School of Management, University of Minnesota*

Michael Gibbins *Department of Accounting, Faculty of Business, University of Alberta*

Barry Lewis *Department of Accounting, College of Business and Administration, University of Colorado*

Robert Libby *Johnson Graduate School of Management, Cornell University*

Laureen A. Maines *Fuqua School of Business, Duke University*

Kevin McCabe *Department of Accounting, Carlson School of Management, University of Minnesota*

William F. Messier, Jr. *Fisher School of Accounting, College of Business Administration, University of Florida*

Michael D. Shields *School of Accountancy, Fogelman College of Business and Economics, University of Memphis*

Ira Solomon *Department of Accountancy, College of Commerce and Business Administration, University of Illinois*

Robert J. Swieringa *Financial Accounting Standards Board, New Canaan, CT*

William S. Waller *Department of Accounting, College of Business and Public Administration, University of Arizona*

S. Mark Young *School of Accounting, University of Southern California*

Series preface

The Society for Judgment and Decision Making first collaborated with Cambridge University Press in 1986, with the publication of *Judgment and Decision Making: An Interdisciplinary Reader,* edited by Hal R. Arkes and Kenneth R. Hammond. As the editors stated in their introduction, "judgment and decision making are of critical importance, and the fact that it is possible to study them in a scientific, empirical manner is a new and exciting event in the recent history of science" (p. 1). The decade of the 1980s witnessed the flowering of the area of human judgment and decision making. The founding and expansion of the Society was one feature of this growth. At the same time, there has been an explosion of research and teaching in departments of psychology, economics, and schools of business, engineering, public policy, and medicine, with significant practical contributions through applied research and consulting in public and private institutions.

The Arkes and Hammond *Reader* was successful as an outline of the core ideas and approaches of the field and an illustration of the impressive range of useful applications. The Society, with Ken Hammond's encouragement, recognized the potential for a series of books to provide an educational and intellectual focus for the continued growth and dissemination of judgment and decision-making research. Each book in the series will be devoted to domains of practical or theoretical interest, offering an accessible presentation of the best new ideas and empirical approaches from the field of judgment and decision making.

The Publications Committee is pleased to proffer this volume. Accountants have long recognized that they are in the business of providing information to decision makers. As early as 1966, a committee of the American Accounting Association defined accounting as "the process of identifying, measuring, and communicating economic information to permit informed judgments and decisions" (*A Statement of Basic Accounting Theory,* p. 1). Accountants supply information to investors, creditors, and government regulators, as well as managers inside the firm, who rely upon this information for critical operating and strategic decisions. Accountants also perform audits, assuring decision makers that information is as accurate, timely, and useful as possible. Increasingly, accountants operate in a complex global business environment, with rapidly evolving information technology and increasing scrutiny of accounting regulation. Accountants must comprehend and manage the uncertainty and risk inherent in their professional activities while maintaining their role as facilitators of economic decision making. Thus, accounting is an ideal proving ground for the theories and insights of judgment and decision making. We expect this volume will entice researchers from the two fields into a productive dialogue.

Don K. Kleinmuntz, Chairman
for the Publications Committee

Preface

This book describes the current state of judgment and decision-making research in the field of accounting and auditing and suggests possible directions for such research in the future. It is part of the "shelf-of-books" series of the Society for Judgment and Decision Making. The purpose of the series is to consolidate much of what is known in the field of judgment and decision making, and to make this knowledge accessible to a wide range of readers. Consistent with this broad goal, this particular book is intended to play two different roles for two different audiences.

The first audience is accounting and auditing researchers who are active, or might wish to become active, in this research area – particularly younger members of this group, such as new faculty and doctoral students. For this audience, the book is intended to provide state-of-the-art coverage of judgment and decision-making research in accounting and auditing and to set the stage for further work over the next several years. Consequently, each chapter contains a wealth of material about what currently is known in the particular area covered in the chapter *and* the authors' opinions about this area (what it contributes to knowledge, where research should or should not go from here, etc.). In this respect, the book seeks to document the development of the field to date, to provide some coherence to a diverse and fragmented research literature, and to influence future research directions. We hope it will be a significant positive force in shaping the production of future knowledge on judgment and decision-making issues in accounting and auditing.

The second audience for the book consists of scholars who work outside the immediate field, including judgment and decision-making researchers at both the basic and applied levels, and accounting and auditing researchers whose work derives from nonjudgmental paradigms. For this audience, the book is intended to help explain what judgment and decision-making research in accounting and auditing is all about, why judgment and decision-making topics in this field are important, and how research in accounting and auditing relates to judgment and decision-making research defined more broadly. We suspect that many researchers have more difficulty appreciating the relevance of judgment and decision-making research in accounting and auditing than in other applied areas (such as marketing or medicine). We hope this book will help inform our judgment and decision-making colleagues outside our immediate field.

To facilitate the production of a high-quality book, we held two conferences at the Fuqua School of Business at Duke University. The first was an informal "summer camp" involving only the authors of the various chapters. Rough drafts were presented to share ideas and generate new ones about the content of each chapter, to assess the current status of the various parts of the field, and to coordinate among ourselves the issue of who was to cover what in the various chapters. The second was a more formal symposium at which the completed chapters were presented. The attendees consisted mainly of judgment and decision-making researchers in accounting and auditing and in the underlying disciplines. After this event was held, the chapters were revised extensively to incorporate the many ideas generated at the symposium. The result is a set of chapters that feature an excellent blend of breadth and depth in their coverage of the principal streams of judgment research in accounting and auditing.

Robert H. Ashton
Alison Hubbard Ashton

Acknowledgments

Projects of this scope are not possible without the support and encouragement of many people. We would like to recognize our indebtedness to several individuals who, directly and indirectly, enabled this book to be written. These include the KPMG Peat Marwick Foundation and its personnel, and several scholars in both the judgment and decision-making field and in accounting and auditing. Our principal debt, however, is to the authors who contributed chapters to the book. We solicited from the authors the best, most thoughtful work they could produce. They not only answered our call, but graciously tolerated our (not-too-successful) efforts to produce the book in a timely fashion.

A generous grant from the international accounting and auditing firm of KPMG Peat Marwick, through its foundation, enabled two conferences to be held at Duke University at which all the chapters were presented and discussed. KPMG Peat Marwick's record of support for a broad range of fundamental and applied research in accounting and auditing is unsurpassed. The firm has not only supplied funding, data, and professional subjects to many researchers, but also has been open to implementing insights and results provided by research. Tim Bell, Bob Elliott, Bernie Milano, and John Willingham have played especially significant roles in providing both the overall support and the support for this particular effort, and they deserve our deepest gratitude.

We are indebted to Ken Hammond who, as president of the Society for Judgment and Decision Making, first proposed the "shelf-of-books" series and encouraged us to produce a volume for it. We also are grateful to the Society's publications committee that approved the concept for the book (John Carroll, Don Kleinmuntz, and Jim Shanteau). We are especially grateful to Don Kleinmuntz, who provided extensive comments on earlier drafts of all chapters and played a significant role in shaping the book.

Our debt extends to many judgment and decision-making researchers whose published work has strongly influenced the development of the allied work in accounting and auditing. At the risk of omitting some researchers whose work has been influential, we want to explicitly recognize ten scholars in the underlying discipline: Robyn Dawes, Ward Edwards, Hillel Einhorn, Baruch Fischhoff, Robin Hogarth, Daniel Kahneman, Sarah Lichtenstein, John Payne, Paul Slovic, and Amos Tversky. Many of these individuals not only have contributed by virtue of their own research, but also in more personal ways, including providing comments on working papers, speaking at accounting and auditing workshops and seminars, informal conversations at J/DM and Bayesian conferences, and general encouragement and support for judgment researchers in accounting and auditing. Above all others, these comments describe Hilly Einhorn, whose death in 1987 left a void in the judgment and decision-making community that will long be felt by both basic and applied researchers.

Established scholars in accounting and auditing have provided equally strong encouragement and support for judgment and decision-making research. Again at the risk of omitting some individuals to whom our field is indebted, we want to mention Jake Birnberg and Nick Dopuch. Both have been strongly involved in judgment and decision-making research in accounting and auditing – as researchers, editors, supporters, and critics – from the earliest days to the present. We are grateful to them.

Finally, we wish to take this opportunity to recognize John Willingham. Since completing one of the earliest "behavioral accounting" dissertations at Ohio State University in 1963, John has been both a researcher and a leader in the efforts to merge research with practical concerns. After 15 years as an academic researcher and teacher (during which he also coauthored an innovative textbook on auditing), John became a partner in Peat Marwick Mitchell & Co. (now KPMG Peat Marwick) in 1978, where until 1993 he played a critical linchpin role between the practical and academic sides of our profession. John was extremely influential in his firm's efforts to implement the results of judgment and decision-making (and other) research, and he channeled the firm's research support to productive uses in the academic community. At the same time, he continued to do research, with both academic and practical aims. In 1993, John returned to academe at the University of Texas at Austin. Our field has benefitted greatly from John Willingham's many contributions, and our debt to him is significant.

Part I
Overview

1

Perspectives on judgment and decision-making research in accounting and auditing

Robert H. Ashton and Alison Hubbard Ashton

Introduction

Fundamental research in judgment and decision making has significantly influenced research in several applied fields including medicine, law, public policy, and business. Applied research results increasingly have been put to practical use. One of the disciplines within business that has been heavily influenced is accounting and auditing. Applied judgment research in accounting and auditing has proliferated during the past 20 years, as the importance of descriptive research and the role of experimental methods have been more fully appreciated and more researchers have been trained in core disciplines such as cognitive psychology and Bayesian inference and decision making. During that time, the field has undergone several important shifts in emphasis, and undoubtedly will continue to evolve in the future. It is that evolution that we wish to capture and influence in the chapters of this book.

To set the stage for the chapters that follow, this introductory chapter encompasses three main topics. The first section provides a broad description of both accounting and auditing *practice* and the evolution of judgment and decision-making *research* in these fields. The purpose of this section, which is written primarily for readers outside of accounting and auditing, is to provide some perspective on the judgment tasks and research approaches that have attracted accounting and auditing researchers. The next section previews the chapters in this book, all of which provide excellent descriptions of past and current research and extremely thoughtful discussions of future research avenues. It provides a quick glimpse into each of these insightful chapters. The final section centers around several prominent research themes identified in the various chapters. Some of these themes appear in all or most of the chapters, while others appear in only a few chapters. By collecting these themes in this introductory chapter, and by adding our own perspective to those provided by the chapters' authors, we try to give the reader a sense of the issues and opportunities that face judgment and decision-making research in accounting and auditing today.

Judgments and decisions in accounting and auditing

Accounting and auditing are distinct but related fields from both a research and a practical standpoint. Together, they provide critical information for economic judgments and decisions. Accounting is traditionally divided into managerial accounting, which involves information generated by organizations and used *internally*, and financial accounting, which involves internally generated information that is communicated *outside* the organization. Auditing, in contrast, is an independent review and attest function performed by independent accounting firms. Together, managerial accounting, financial accounting, and auditing have a significant impact on the financial economy by facilitating the intra- and interorganizational flow of investment and the orderly operation of the capital markets.

In this section of the chapter, we first describe the practice of managerial accounting, financial accounting, and auditing, paying special attention to the types of judgments and decisions that are important in those fields. Following this, we comment on several features of accounting and auditing tasks that tend to distinguish them from generic judgment and decision-making settings. Finally, we describe the general nature of research in accounting and auditing, with special emphasis on the phases through which judgment and decision-making research has evolved.

Accounting and auditing practice

Managerial accounting provides information to decision makers who are managers and executives of organizations, including both profit-seeking organizations such as corporations and not-for-profit organizations such as universities and municipalities. Managerial accounting information is used in planning and controlling the costs of operations, reporting on the profitability of products and activities, and formulating overall firm policies. Decisions based on managerial accounting information determine the allocation of financial resources both inside and outside the specific organization. Typical decisions involve, for example, the quantities of products to be produced by the firm, the introduction of new product lines, location of new manufacturing or sales facilities, acquisition of new business entities, pricing of products and services offered to customers, and performance evaluation of individuals and organizational subunits.

While managerial accounting information is provided to parties who are internal to a specific organization, *financial accounting* information is supplied by the organization to a variety of external parties such as investors, creditors, financial analysts and other financial advisors, suppliers, customers, labor unions, and regulatory authorities. The two primary classes of external users are current and potential investors and creditors (and their advisors). Investors buy and sell equity securities (stocks) of corporations; they consist of individual "nonprofessional" investors, professionals who provide investment advice to others (called "sell-side" analysts), and professionals who manage investment portfolios for institutions such as insurance companies and pension funds (called "buy-side" analysts). Creditors provide financial capital to organizations in many forms ranging from bank loans to debt securities (bonds); principal external parties from this perspective are bank loan officers and bond-rating agencies. Like financial analysts, the latter are professionals who provide advice to others.

The information supplied to external parties relates to the financial condition, financial performance, and cash flows of the firm for current and prior years; its main purpose is to assist external parties in predicting these variables in the future. Because financial accounting information is generated and disclosed by managers of particular organizations, who typically have significant incentives to portray the results of their stewardship favorably, and because external users have only limited access to such information via other channels, an extensive set of measurement and disclosure rules for financial accounting information is mandated by regulatory bodies in both the public sector (most notably the Securities and Exchange Commission) and the private sector (most notably the Financial Accounting Standards Board). Thus, in contrast to the provision of managerial accounting information to internal users, significant constraints exist on the form and content of financial accounting information that is communicated to external users. One of the most important of those constraints is the requirement of an independent *audit*.

The principal vehicle by which an organization's financial accounting information is communicated to investors, creditors, and other external parties is a set of financial statements that are part of a company's "annual report." The annual report also contains information other than financial statements, the most important of which is an *auditor's report* prepared by a firm of certified public accountants (CPAs) that is independent of the reporting organization. The CPA firm provides an independent review and attest service by examining the reporting firm's financial statements, related disclosures, and underlying systems and records to assess whether the financial statements are presented in accordance with "generally accepted accounting principles" as promulgated by the Financial Accounting Standards Board (and with the concurrence of the Securities and Exchange Commission).

Both the audit *process* and the *output* of that process are replete with important judgments and decisions. The audit process entails judgments about the amount and type of evidence to collect, the extent to which such evidence is credible, and the actions that should be taken in response to the evidence that has been collected and evaluated. The ultimate output of an audit is an independent opinion (i.e., judgment) about whether the company's financial statements are "free of material misstatements." To the extent the financial statements are judged *not* to be free of material misstatements, the confidence of investors and creditors in the reporting firm's disclosures will be undermined, with associated negative effects on the firm's ability to raise additional debt or equity capital. Similarly, other parties such as suppliers, employees, and labor unions will react negatively to auditors' judgments that a firm's financial statements contain material misstatements, and regulatory agencies may impose significant penalties on such companies. Thus, auditing is a critical professional service from the standpoint of both individual companies and the financial economy in general.

Distinguishing features of accounting and auditing tasks

At their most basic or generic level, the judgment tasks and settings of accounting and auditing resemble those of any domain. However, a number of features tend to distinguish accounting and auditing tasks from those in generic settings. Four such features relate to (1) the multiperiod/multiperson nature of the judgments and decisions, (2) enormous financial (and other) consequences involved, (3) the presence of markets, and (4) important institutional considerations (also see Libby, 1990).

First, many judgments and decisions in accounting and auditing are made in multiperiod/multiperson settings. Decisions such as the pricing of products and services, investing in equity securities of corporations, and evidence collection and evaluation in auditing are not made on a one-shot basis by an individual working in isolation. Instead, such decisions typically have recurring effects over several time periods, often have to be "re-made," and often must take into account the preferences and beliefs of others. The multiperiod/multiperson nature of accounting and auditing tasks brings to the forefront many important considerations for applied decision making. For example, their multiperiod nature emphasizes an approach to decision making that is sequential and iterative, while their multiperson nature significantly increases the accountability requirements on the decision maker.

Second, the tasks and settings of accounting and auditing tend to have financial consequences that often are enormous in magnitude. Consider, for example, the financial consequences of a pension fund manager's "bad" choice of which stocks and bonds to include in the fund's investment portfolio. Life-or-death consequences – like those associated with some judgments in medical and legal domains – do not exist. However, the high stakes of accounting and auditing judgment tasks are not limited to financial outcomes, but involve important "human" consequences as well. In the pension fund case, adverse financial consequences for the fund can translate into important lifestyle consequences for individuals whose future retirement income is partially determined by the fund manager's choices. In managerial accounting settings, a manager's opportunities for promotion and professional development – and, ultimately, his or her career path – can be affected by periodic performance evaluations based in part on managerial accounting information. In auditing, a report attesting that an organization's financial statements are "free of material misstatements" when they subsequently are found *not* to be free of material misstatements can have serious reputational consequences for the auditors who were directly responsible for the report.

Accounting and auditing decisions also have "secondary" consequences that extend to parties other than those who are most immediately affected (e.g., the retirees, managers, and auditors in the above scenarios). For example, if a bank loan officer decides to stop the liberal credit terms that historically have been extended to a particular business firm, this can affect not only the firm itself but its employees, suppliers, customers, and others.

A third important feature of accounting and auditing judgment settings is the critical role played by various markets that mediate the ultimate consequences of decisions made by individuals or groups. An excellent example is the market in which a company's equity securities are traded, such as the New York Stock Exchange. The existence of such a market induces a form of competition among individual decision makers that can result in strategic decision behavior, thus adding a significant layer of complexity to the decision-making process. Naturally, the role of markets in accounting decisions is a reflection of multiperson considerations, as described earlier, since the effect of accounting information on market prices is caused by the interactions of many individuals.

Finally, accounting and auditing judgment tasks are embedded in pervasive institutional settings. An organized stock exchange is one such setting but there are many others – including organizational structures, professional societies, and networks of regulatory agencies – that somehow must be taken into account by decision makers. For example, the decisions of individual auditors are made in settings that involve (1) the presence of other members of the audit team, including peers, subordinates, and superiors; (2) the existence of a market for audit services in which other independent auditing firms compete for audit clients; (3) a strong professional society (the American Institute of Certified Public Accountants) that formulates professional standards and enforces a code of professional responsibilities; (4) a regulatory environment involving massive government agencies such as the Securities and Exchange Commission, the Federal Trade Commission, and the Federal Home Loan Bank Board; and (5) a legal environment involving increasingly frequent lawsuits against auditors alleging fraud or negligence in the performance of the audit, which can result in large financial losses for which insurance is becoming increasingly difficult to obtain. Such a setting imposes enormous constraints and risks that influence judgments made throughout an audit.

Markets, institutions, financial consequences, and multiperiod/multiperson issues are some of the features that distinguish judgments and decisions made in the applied fields of accounting and auditing from those made in generic settings. Other applied fields no doubt have their own features that distinguish them from generic settings, and perhaps from other applied settings. On the other hand, commonalities likely exist among the various applied fields in which judgment and decision making are practiced (and researched). Such commonalities could perhaps be used to effectively link the research in one applied field to the practical issues of other applied fields. In many applied fields (such as accounting and auditing, medicine, law, and engineering), perhaps the key distinguishing feature is the professional nature of both the judgments and the judgment settings. The professional aspects of several applied fields may serve not only to distinguish research in those fields from generic research, but also to link the research results of such fields to each other. The professional nature of accounting and auditing judgment tasks, and of the contexts and settings in which they are embedded, is a central topic throughout the various chapters of this book.

Accounting and auditing research

Prior to the mid-1960s, research and scholarship in accounting consisted largely of a priori research based on implicit assumptions about both the functioning of capital markets and the objectives and decision processes of investors, creditors, and managers of organizations. Virtually all of the research was in the areas of managerial accounting and financial accounting, and it typically was directed at developing measures of the "true" economic performance of managers and business firms. Little research attention was directed toward auditing during this time.

Accounting scholarship changed dramatically in the mid-1960s from heavy reliance on a priori reasoning to the construction and evaluation of formal models of accounting phenomena and the application of empirical methods designed to understand the effects of accounting practices on the firm's reported performance and the market's evaluation of the firm. During the first few years of contemporary accounting research, the modeling and empirical analyses largely were driven by an economic conception of accounting decision makers. In much of the research, decision makers were assumed to be perfectly rational economic actors with unlimited cognitive abilities who were infinitely sensitive to variations in accounting information and who used such information to maximize their own subjective well-being or utility. While this world view provided important insights that were missing from the earlier era, it largely omitted real people from accounting's research domain. Judgment and decision-making research in accounting began to appear in this economics-based setting in the mid-1960s. Its roots were in both practice and policy issues and in the theories and methods that underlie generic research in judgment and decision making.

Phases of judgment and decision-making research in accounting and auditing

Since the mid-1960s, judgment and decision-making research in accounting and auditing has evolved through three phases. The research of the mid-1960s to the early 1970s was inspired mostly by practice and policy issues. In managerial accounting, it focused on the impact of control systems and budgetary standards on the performance of employees who were subject to their control. In financial accounting, it focused on the types of information to supply to external decision makers and on how best to measure and disclose that information. In auditing, it focused on how to perform audits more effectively and efficiently and how best to report audit results to external users. For the most part, researchers' attempts to address such issues during this time period occurred before they had a clear sense of the theories and methods of generic judgment and decision-making research.

In the second stage, from the early 1970s to the mid-1980s, theories and methods to guide the research were imported from the underlying literature in judgment and decision making. Much of the research emphasis in this period centered on constructing linear models of individual decision makers, evaluating the extent to which individuals' judgments and decisions departed from the prescriptions of normative models, such as expected-utility theory and Bayes theorem, and investigating reliance on judgment heuristics and the various biases to which that reliance could lead. While the development of the field during this period was influenced by the work of several researchers from the underlying disciplines, the most significant influences were several papers by Paul Slovic and Sarah Lichtenstein (especially Slovic and Lichtenstein, 1971) and by Amos Tversky and Daniel Kahneman (especially Tversky and Kahneman, 1974).

In many ways, this was a period in which judgment and decision-making researchers in accounting and auditing learned and practiced existing theories and methods, and these same theories and methods often were a major point of emphasis in our more "applied" studies. This phase of judgment and decision-making research in accounting and auditing has been reviewed extensively, e.g., by Libby (1981), Ashton (1982), and Birnberg and Shields (1989).

Since the mid-1980s, the research focus has shifted from documenting the shortcomings of human judgment in accounting and auditing settings to understanding (and reducing or eliminating) those shortcomings. The use of process-tracing techniques to describe the decision processes underlying choice in richer detail than is possible with analyses based on linear modeling is one example (e.g., Biggs and Mock, 1983). Another is exploration of alternatives to the Bayesian model of belief revision (e.g., Ashton and Ashton, 1988).

A major shift of this period has been from viewing the decision maker as a passive converter of inputs to outputs to viewing the decision maker as a diagnostician, especially in the auditing domain; the related roles of knowledge and memory in decision making have been emphasized and new models have emerged to guide the research (e.g., Libby, 1985). Various papers by Hillel Einhorn and Robin Hogarth heavily influenced these developments (e.g., Einhorn and Hogarth, 1981, 1985). More recently, researchers have begun to focus on ways of controlling or "debiasing" the errors, inconsistencies, and biases identified by the earlier research, particularly with mechanical decision aids of some type and, again, especially in auditing (see Ashton and Willingham, 1989).

Other recent research has responded to criticisms of judgment and decision-making research. Such criticisms typically concern variables that were omitted from earlier research in accounting and auditing settings, e.g., variables related to economic or organizational aspects of decision making that often are ignored (or at least downplayed) in generic judgment and decision-making settings but are likely to be extremely important in settings of interest to accounting and auditing research. Examples include financial incentives, feedback about the results of previous decisions, various accountability mechanisms, domain-specific experience and knowledge, and the impact of markets on decision-making processes and outcomes.

In short, the range of theories, methods and variables that are studied today is much broader than before, and today's studies are richer than those of earlier years. Several sources provide reviews of this most recent phase of judgment and decision-making research in accounting and auditing, as well as commentary about the types of shifts in emphasis that have occurred (e.g., Ashton et al., 1988; Libby, 1990; Hogarth, 1991, 1993; Gibbins and Jamal, 1993; Libby and Luft, 1993).

A preview of the chapters

The chapters in this book analyze these and other influences on judgment and decision-making research in accounting and auditing, and they suggest many directions for future research in the field. While broad-ranging, the coverage in each chapter is not exhaustive but reflects the authors' judgments about where the field stands today and where many of the gains are likely to be realized in the future. Each chapter focuses on a substantive area of inquiry – generally, subfields within managerial accounting, financial accounting, or auditing – instead of on a particular methodological approach. This choice is purposeful and is intended to encourage future research that puts problems before paradigms.

Two chapters examine managerial accounting topics. Waller focuses on "decision-facilitating" aspects of managerial accounting, while Young and Lewis focus on "decision-influencing" aspects (see Demski and Feltham, 1976). Briefly, the decision-facilitating role of managerial accounting information refers to the predecision provision of information to reduce uncertainty, while the decision-influencing role refers to the postdecision provision of information for monitoring the performance of an individual or subunit. Research focusing on decision-facilitating aspects declined during the 1980s, while that focusing on decision-influencing effects increased.

Waller

Waller (Chapter 2) seeks to rejuvenate research on managerial accounting's decision-facilitating effects by advocating that decision research in managerial accounting return to a behavioral-economics foundation. The behavioral-economics approach, with its roots in the early work of March and Simon (1958) and Cyert and March (1963), is concerned with the empirical validity of the assumptions that neoclassical economic theory makes about human behavior, with the actual processes (instead of the "as if" fiction) that produce decision behavior, and with the implications of empirical results for revising economic theory to improve its predictive and explanatory power.

Waller focuses on three decision areas that often have been studied in behavioral decision research in managerial accounting: (1) the choice of alternative information systems for communicating information to internal decision makers, (2) cost-variance investigation decisions, and (3) product-pricing decisions. The first area derives largely from the decision-theoretic notion that managerial accountants should consider the costs and benefits of alternative information systems they could supply to decision makers, while the latter two areas consider the choice of particular types of information that might be supplied for particular decisions. In each of these areas, Waller describes a set of existing studies that have attempted, in their own way, to bridge the gap between economics-based and psychology-based approaches to decision making. More importantly, he analyzes how these studies have fallen short of bridging that gap effectively, and how research in each area would differ – providing a richer and more effective integration of the economics- and psychology-based approaches – if the studies had been conducted from an explicit behavioral-economics foundation.

Young and Lewis

Young and Lewis (Chapter 3) note that questions about the decision-influencing aspects of managerial accounting information center on the effects of incentives on the decisions of subordinates within control systems. Against this background, they examine the experimental "incentive-contracting" research in managerial accounting. Incentive-contracting research concerns the design of incentive systems or contracts that motivate employees to meet or exceed budgeted performance levels. Such performance levels are established in part with managerial accounting information, and incentives can be used to reward the attainment of, or to penalize the failure to obtain, a particular standard. Incentive-contracting research tries to gain insights into decision making in managerial settings by combining aspects of normative principal-agent theory (e.g., Demski and Feltham, 1978) with aspects of descriptive research in industrial sociology (going back, for example, to Roy, 1952, 1954).

Young and Lewis analyze two major categories of incentive contracting research: (1) the effects of incentives on the self-selection of employees who possess different skill levels and on their subsequent performance of a task, and (2) incentive aspects of participation in standard setting, and its effects on budgetary slack formation and performance. Analogous to Waller's call for a return to behavioral-economics foundations for addressing managerial accounting's decision-facilitating role, Young and Lewis argue that future research on its decision-influencing role could profit from the incentive-contracting literature's "cycling back" to its roots in industrial sociology. Note that both Waller's and Young and Lewis's prescriptions for future research would involve going beyond the typical laboratory experiment on individual judgment that has been the focus of almost all research to date. Specifically, Waller advocates greater use of market settings, while Young and Lewis advocate greater reliance on field-study methods.

Maines

While Waller and Young and Lewis focus on the effects of managerial accounting information on internal decision makers, the next chapter focuses on the effects of financial accounting information that is supplied to decision makers outside the organization. Maines (Chapter 4) examines research conducted at the level of the individual investor or creditor – including intermediaries in the financial-reporting process who advise investors and creditors, such as financial analysts and bond raters. Two major types of studies are examined: (1) those in which subjects are modeled in an input–output fashion (e.g., by regression) or whose decision processes are studied at a more micro level (e.g., by process-tracing methods); and (2) those that manipulate the form, type, or amount of information supplied to external decision makers, as well as information portrayed by alternative accounting methods. Studies in the first category can be distinguished by the extent to which the researcher attempts to "get inside the black box" between decision inputs and outputs, while studies in the second category can be distinguished by the practical or policy-oriented issue that motivated the particular study (e.g., what information to supply to external decision makers).

Maines discusses the implications of financial accounting judgment and decision-making research for improving financial decision making, e.g., via the use of models and composites of individual decision makers and the provision of feedback about past decisions. She also discusses the lack of impact of this research on policy decisions concerning the form, type, and amount of information to supply to external decision makers. She suggests possible reasons for this lack of impact that relate to insufficient attention to incentives, accountability, and, particularly, market mechanisms that condition the financial decision making environment. Historically, the inability of individual-level decision researchers in financial accounting to link their results with the role of market forces in investment decision-making has been a major reason for the relative lack of interest in this research area. Maines, however, sees some reasons for optimism concerning an increased emphasis on financial accounting judgment and decision-making research at the individual-investor level, and she explicates some important roles that such research can play.

Berg, Dickhaut, and McCabe

Berg, Dickhaut, and McCabe (Chapter 5) explore the complex issue of individual versus aggregate behavior. The authors develop a framework for understanding (and researching) various topics in this important area. The principal focus of the chapter is captured in its first sentence: "To what degree do individual decision biases affect aggregate behavior?" In posing this question, the authors recognize that "aggregate behavior" occurs in a broad range of settings of interest to accountants, from simple two-person production (agency) and bargaining situations to complex market settings with many actors.

The framework consists of (observable) exogenous environmental attributes of aggregate settings and (unobservable) endogenous behavioral dynamics. The authors propose that seven attributes distinguish individual from aggregate decision-making settings (and aggregate settings from each other): (1) multiple players, (2) differences in choice sets, (3) payoff interdependency, (4) observability of others' actions or information, (5) communication, (6) contracting, and (7) order of play. It is argued that one or more of these seven attributes must determine whether individual biases affect aggregate behavior. The authors also propose that certain behavioral dynamics (such as anticipation of others' actions, conflicts of interest, norms of behavior, and followership) provide the causal links between these attributes and an individual's decision behavior in aggregate settings. The framework is illustrated by analyses of several prominent research streams from the agency, bargaining, and experimental markets literatures.

Experimental economics methods are a central focus of this chapter. By using such methods to manipulate the various attributes that distinguish individual and aggregate settings, one can study not only the persistence of individual biases in the aggregate, but also their elimination or exacerbation. Berg, Dickhaut, and McCabe also point out that aggregate settings can create additional biases that are not observed in individual settings (e.g., fairness and anticipation of the behavior of others). Moreover, the costs of biases potentially can be measured in experimental settings and the interplay of the individual and the aggregate can be observed. In contrast, standard archival-data-based *empirical* methods that often are applied in aggregate settings are ill-suited for such purposes because of the difficulty of controlling for confounding variables.

Solomon and Shields

The next three chapters concern auditing. In an ambitious chapter that opens this section of the book, Solomon and Shields (Chapter 6) provide a broad discussion of the pervasiveness of judgment and decision-making issues in auditing that serves as a common foundation for the subsequent chapters by Libby and by Messier. Solomon and Shields review the voluminous research on judgment and decision making in auditing, organizing their review along three dimensions: (1) theoretical frameworks that have guided the research (policy capturing, probabilistic judgment, heuristics and biases, cognitive processes, and multiperson information processing); (2) judgment and decision-evaluation criteria that have been employed (cue usage, self-insight, accuracy, consensus, stability, and consistency); and (3) the substantive phase of the audit process investigated (from the initial orientation in which a general strategy for the audit is devised to the choice of the audit report type to issue). They also draw attention to important activities that precede and follow the audit proper – e.g., the choice of an organizational structure and audit strategy that impact on the environment in which judgments and decisions are made, and the potential need to "recall" previous audit reports when new information comes to light – activities that typically are ignored by audit-judgment research. Among other things, their review makes clear the areas in which research results in auditing agree, and disagree, with the results of generic research on judgment and decision making.

Solomon and Shields provide a wealth of recommendations for future research. At least three of those broad recommendations are relevant for research in financial accounting and managerial accounting as well: (1) the need for an expanded set of both theoretical frameworks and judgment/decision-making evaluation criteria; (2) the importance of understanding and analyzing the task and a greater emphasis on task/auditor interaction instead of simply viewing the auditor as a generic information processor; and (3) a proposed shift in emphasis from laboratory to field-based research.

Libby

Libby (Chapter 7) examines the critically important roles that knowledge and memory play in audit judgment. Working from the premise that a complete understanding of audit-judgment performance will require significant emphasis on knowledge and memory issues, Libby describes a model of knowledge acquisition and its impact on judgment performance. While elements of this model have been researched in auditing settings by Libby and others for several years, the present explication is a particularly comprehensive and integrative treatment of this rapidly growing area.

The model focuses on experience, ability, and knowledge as principal determinants of audit judgment performance. It proposes that experience and ability jointly determine knowledge, and that knowledge, along with the direct effect of ability, determines performance. Libby offers operational definitions of the model's variables – experience, ability, knowledge, and performance – and he delineates some of their major dimensions. More importantly, he examines the links between four pairs of these variables: experience and knowledge, ability and knowledge, knowledge and performance, and ability and performance. These four links provide a basis for (1) clarifying the focus (and evaluating the contributions) of many existing studies of audit-judgment performance, (2) suggesting research directions for the future, and (3) possibly resolving various "open issues" in audit-judgment research (e.g., the circumstances under which knowledge differences will result in performance differences). The model is especially valuable for the perspective it provides on audit-judgment research that ranges from investigations of specific links between variables (e.g., Frederick, 1991) to broader psychometric analyses of multiple links (e.g., Bonner and Lewis, 1990).

Messier

The chapter by Messier (Chapter 8) focuses on research issues related to the development and use of decision aids by audit practitioners. Messier reviews the types of decision aids that have been developed for audit practice, often with the involvement of academic researchers. This development has been stimulated in part by competitive and regulatory pressures on auditors to provide more efficient and effective audits. Simple deterministic algorithms, decision-support systems, and expert systems are discussed, and features of audit tasks that are most likely to make them good candidates for one or more of these types of decision aids are analyzed.

Messier also reviews the (relatively little) research that has been reported on the effects of audit-decision aids, and he discusses potential effects of such aids – on both individual auditors' judgments and the auditing firm itself – that have not yet been studied. He proposes future research on the effects of audit-decision aids and on various issues involved in their practical development. He also focuses on the critical area of decision-aid implementation. For example, drawing an analogy with the clinical versus statistical prediction controversy in psychology (e.g., Dawes et al., 1989; Kleinmuntz, 1990), he notes that while research in auditing strongly suggests the superiority of the statistical approach for many tasks, few audit practitioners have embraced it. Thus, Messier highlights the key role of the implementation process and the importance of research questions related to implementation.

Gibbins and Swieringa

The final chapter, by Gibbins and Swieringa (Chapter 9), provides a comprehensive and thoughtful "wrap-up" to the book. Much of the chapter's focus is on (1) the specific tasks that are studied by judgment and decision-making researchers in accounting and auditing, and (2) the broader contexts or settings in which those tasks are embedded. The authors suggest that by tending to ignore individual differences among subjects, researchers have focused much more on tasks and settings than on the people who actually make accounting and auditing judgments. As a consequence, they suggest, the existing research in accounting and auditing may reveal as much about the task as about the subjects who perform it. They also observe that while the tasks of interest are complex, subjective, and potentially entail substantial costs of judgment errors, our experimental studies "take the laboratory to the participants," expecting them to respond as they do in their natural settings. However, since we provide subjects with a simplified representation of the natural tasks they face – without such basic and pervasive task features as decision aids or consultation possibilities – we run the risk that our subjects will behave differently in the experimental tasks than in the natural environment (also see Winkler and Murphy, 1973).

Gibbins and Swieringa call for increased attention to the economic, organizational, and professional contexts in which accounting and auditing tasks are embedded. They discuss several *economic* forces (including markets for equity and debt securities and for auditing services) that need to be better incorporated into experimental studies, and they argue for the increased use of economic models to make predictions that are tested by experimental studies. They also suggest that *organizational* factors at both the group and firm level – such as power, status, organizational policies, and promotion – should be better incorporated into future research. They note that recent studies of audit structure and accountability are two exceptions to the tendency to ignore organizational factors. Finally, they observe that judgment researchers in accounting and auditing have tended to ignore the fact that our subjects typically are members of a *profession* and are subject to legal, professional, and ethical standards that may significantly condition their judgment processes and outputs.

Gibbins and Swieringa conclude with observations on several issues that are pertinent to judgment and decision-making research in accounting and auditing today. For example, given the dual objective of contributing to both scholarship and practice, they discuss (1) the existing links between accounting/auditing judgment and decision-making research and accounting/auditing research that is based on other paradigms, and (2) the impact of judgment research on accounting and auditing practice. Concerning the first issue, they observe that the impact of judgment and decision-making research on other paradigms is much weaker than the impact of other paradigms on judgment and decision-making research; they argue that this imbalance potentially could be overcome by joint development of theory with other paradigms and by corroboration of judgment and decision making results with nonexperimental research methods (e.g., interviews and archival analysis). Concerning impact on practice, they observe that judgment and decision making researchers have done little to exploit their ability to create, control, and manipulate laboratory situations and variables in order to analyze "what if" questions. Instead, our research tends to examine practical issues *after* they happen, instead of providing predictive advice to practitioners.

Prominent research themes

The foregoing chapter summaries reveal that many important themes appear in this book. Some are pervasive themes that cut across several chapters (and subfields of research). Others appear in only a few chapters, or perhaps in just a single chapter (raising the question of why they are *not* of interest in other subfields). Each chapter features themes that are considered important by its author(s), who were, of course, sought for this book because they are well qualified to identify and comment on important themes in their areas of expertise. This section of the chapter brings together many of the other chapters' themes – and provides some comments of our own – in order to develop additional perspectives for the field as a whole. The various themes are grouped into four broad areas: (1) judgment tasks, (2) judgment performance criteria, (3) scope of analysis of the research, and (4) debiasing judgments in professional settings.

Judgment Tasks

It is clear from the chapters in this book that judgment and decision-making research in accounting and auditing has focused on a relatively small number of tasks. In managerial accounting, contract selection tasks (patterned after Chow, 1983) and, to a lesser extent, product pricing tasks have been popular. In financial accounting, bankruptcy/loan default prediction tasks and, to a lesser extent, stock price prediction tasks have been studied extensively. In auditing, the tasks of internal control evaluation, analytical review, extent of detailed testing, going concern assessment, and choice of audit report type have attracted significant research interest.

This list of tasks reveals that the research is heavily concentrated in *auditing*. This is not surprising, at least in hindsight, given the accessibility of cooperative subjects and the availability of data and financial support from auditing firms during the past 15 to 20 years. The research in auditing, as a whole, leads that in managerial accounting and financial accounting – not only in terms of quantity, but also in maturity, depth of analysis, and relevance to practical concerns. In auditing, we have explored more fully the "black box" that connects judgment inputs with associated outputs; we have studied more extensively the role of experience and knowledge in audit judgment; and we have considered in greater depth ways of "debiasing" audit judgments, including both developing audit decision aids of various types and researching their effects.

Although auditing generally leads managerial accounting and financial accounting in terms of research attention and accomplishments, there are areas in which the opposite is true. While all three subfields have emphasized *laboratory* studies of *individual* decision makers, managerial accounting probably has done a better job than auditing of incorporating organizational perspectives, and financial accounting has done a better job of addressing decisions made in aggregate (market) settings and decisions made over multiperiod time horizons.

Research in all three subfields has tended to avoid many of the critical issues that face auditors and users of accounting information. In saying this, we do not mean to suggest that traditional tasks such as internal control evaluation, product pricing, and bankruptcy prediction are unimportant. We believe, however, that such tasks are fundamentally different from, say, the assessment of the legal liability implications of audit practice, the introduction and use of new manufacturing technologies, and the choice of the form and content of accounting disclosures to external parties, to name a few.

It is natural, of course, to concentrate initially on research topics that are most tractable, given the existing level of development of a subfield and its dominant research methods. However, continued pursuit of a small set of favored topics may result in diminishing returns over time, for both the field as a whole and the individual researchers who pursue them. At present, we would appear to be much closer to such a state in auditing than in either managerial or financial accounting.

The counterargument to this line of reasoning is that sustained progress toward understanding an important judgment or decision will be hampered by skipping around from field to field (or from topic to topic within a field); there is, of course, merit in this counterargument. We suspect, however, that many of the greatest opportunities for substantial impact in the future are likely to exist more in managerial and financial accounting than in the types of topics traditionally studied in auditing.

Considering the judgment tasks that have received relatively little attention is one useful way of characterizing the existing research. A related way is to focus on the types of subjects that largely have been omitted from the research. To the extent that managerial accounting and financial accounting tasks have been downplayed in favor of auditing tasks, then, naturally, corporate managers and investors and investment advisors have been downplayed as subjects. However, Young and Lewis (Chapter 3) suggest that new manufacturing practices and the growing impact of national culture on manufacturing performance may result in increased attention to managers as subjects. Similarly, Maines (Chapter 4) argues that capital markets based research showing market prices to be influenced by judgment errors and biases and empirical research on analysts' earnings forecasts may boost interest in research on investors and investment advisors (also see Schipper, 1991).

If we look beyond auditors, managers, and investors and creditors, it is clear that very little research has been reported using other subject groups who are regularly engaged in important accounting-related judgments and decisions. For example, there is virtually no research on the judgments and decisions of *internal* auditors, in spite of the voluminous research on external auditors. And very little judgment research has focused on the preparers (as opposed to the users) of external accounting information or on the members of accounting or auditing standard-setting bodies. A small amount of work in these areas has appeared – such as Plumlee (1985) and Bailey (1990) on internal auditors, Gibbins and Mason (1988) and Gibbins et al. (1990) on preparers, and Joyce et al. (1982) and Kinney (1986) on standard setters – but nothing resembling a critical mass of results has formed. Somewhat more research has been reported on the judgments of individual taxpayers and professional tax preparers, but has been spread across a wide array of substantive tax-related tasks (see Ashton, 1994). Like those in managerial and financial accounting settings, the opportunities for judgment research to make important contributions in these and other "underresearched" areas could be substantial.

Regardless of whether future research examines traditional tasks and subjects or nontraditional ones, the authors of the chapters in this book argue strongly for increased analysis and understanding of both the task and task/decision-maker interactions. It is not sufficient, in professional domains like accounting and auditing, to simply view the decision maker as a generic information processor (also see Smith and Kida, 1991). Task analysis is needed to understand a task's information requirements, and task/decision-maker interactions must be considered to fully appreciate the subject's role in the task. While the importance of the judgment task has long been a topic of comment by researchers, it is especially critical in applied, professional domains.

A final perspective on judgment tasks that is found in many of the chapters concerns the insights that potentially can be gained by employing "what-if" tasks in applied judgment research (also see Swieringa and Weick, 1982). While much of the existing concern with applied research tasks in professional domains centers on whether they adequately mirror the "real world" tasks of interest, at least in terms of their most crucial features, an exciting and underexploited role that judgment research tasks can play is to represent "potential real worlds" that do not currently exist but could be created.

For example, judgment research on individual investors could examine the impact of additional possible disclosures that are being *considered* by the Financial Accounting Standards Board (see Maines, 1994 and Chapter 4 in this volume). Kinney and Uecker (1982) did essentially this in their study of two alternative risk-assessment methods that were being considered by the Auditing Standards Board. As another possibility, experimental markets research could examine the impacts – on both individual- and aggregate-level variables – of alternative institutional arrangements, e.g., alternative market structures, that do not currently exist in the natural environment (see Chapter 5). Just as the standard experimental methods of judgment and decision-making research can effectively control and manipulate existing variables and settings, they also can be used to create alternative variables and settings for investigation. Such an orientation would make our research more *pro*-active and less *re*-active, and could lead to significant achievements in shaping important phenomena of interest. At the very least, judgment and decision-making researchers should be better able to analyze "what if" questions than are researchers who rely on other paradigms (see Chapter 9).

Judgment performance criteria

Another important theme in many of the chapters is the measurement of the performance of subjects in any particular judgment task. Two aspects of judgment performance arise in those chapters: (1) the appropriate criteria for evaluating judgment in applied, professional settings; and (2) the development of models of judgment performance.

Traditionally, the favored criterion for evaluating judgment performance in accounting and auditing has been ex post accuracy, or the correspondence of the judgment to some relevant environmental event. Since the use of a strict accuracy criterion is seldom feasible in applied tasks, several agreement-based surrogates for accuracy have been employed extensively. These include agreement with a statistical norm, with recognized experts in the task, and with other decision makers exposed to the same information set. Unfortunately, the strong focus on accuracy- and agreement-based performance measures may cause us to ignore other dimensions of performance that are extremely important in professional settings.

In discussing performance criteria for *auditing* judgments, both Solomon and Shields (Chapter 6) and Libby (Chapter 7) point to audit efficiency as a valuable criterion that deserves greater research attention. In addition, Solomon and Shields suggest that auditing researchers should consider the criterion of "evidence marshalling and justification" to support previously made judgments (see Emby and Gibbins, 1988). Such performance criteria would seem to be equally relevant in managerial accounting and financial accounting settings, although they seldom have been discussed in those fields.

Broadening our conception of relevant performance measures may entail recognizing different performance criteria for different judgment tasks or subtasks, as suggested by Libby (Chapter 7). It may also entail recognizing that the most relevant performance criteria for professional decision makers – and for the firms that employ them – can change dramatically over the decision makers' careers. For example, over a professional's career, success in the broad area of external development (e.g., securing new clients) might gradually replace technical proficiency or expertise as a major performance criterion in auditing and financial analysis settings. Moreover, avoiding legal liability problems may be a crucial performance criterion for more senior decision makers in auditing, as well as for corporate managers who must decide what information to disclose voluntarily to external parties. Incorporating performance measures such as these into judgment and decision-making research will be much more difficult than continuing to rely on accuracy- and agreement-based measures. Broader performance measures are likely to be required, however, to achieve the full potential of judgment research in professional settings.

Related to the choice of judgment-performance measures is the broader issue of achieving expert performance or expertise in professional judgment tasks. Research in financial accounting and auditing has addressed expertise issues, while research in managerial accounting has not. In financial accounting, the research generally has been limited to process-tracing studies that compare "novice" versus "professional" financial analysts' processing of accounting information in investment contexts. The research in auditing has been far more extensive and has involved a variety of research methods. Indeed, in the auditing setting the model relating experience, ability, and knowledge to judgment performance described by Libby (Chapter 7) focuses on the *development* of expertise in audit judgment.

The model described by Libby appears to be generally relevant for understanding judgment performance and expertise development in *any* applied field, not just in auditing. Indeed, essentially the same model was proposed by Schmidt et al. (1986) and applied to four military jobs (armor crewman, armor repairman, supply specialist, and cook). In spite of such broad applicability, the model does not seem to have influenced the research in either financial accounting or managerial accounting. However, Maines (see Chapter 4) suggests some reasons that internal memory, which underlies certain components of the model, might play a greater role in investment decision making than in auditing. The model might also be useful for refining the typical approaches to the skill and effort variables that are so central to experimental studies of incentive contracting (see Young and Lewis, Chapter 3). Some aspects of the model already have begun to appear in the literature on tax-related decision making (e.g., Marchant et al. 1991; Bonner et al. 1992).

Scope of analysis of the research

Another theme that is apparent in these chapters is the shift to a broader scope of analysis in the research of the past few years. Solomon and Shields (Chapter 6) describe the relation between the underlying generic research and the applied research in auditing as shifting from a "borrow and transfer" tradition to a "contrast before transfer" approach. Thus, the focus has changed from emphasizing the similarities between generic and applied judgment tasks to emphasizing their differences or "distinctive features" (see, e.g., Libby, 1990; Smith and Kida, 1991; Bonner and Pennington, 1991). This is a central part of "understanding the task," as discussed earlier.

Emphasizing distinctive features of accounting and auditing tasks may help researchers not only to have a clearer sense of which variables to manipulate, control, and measure in experimental studies, but also to understand better the differences in results that often surface between generic and accounting/auditing studies: Examples of such differences are less susceptibility to the overconfidence and confirmation biases, greater sensitivity to base-rate and source-reliability information, greater consensus and configural information processing, better calibration, and more weight placed on negative than on positive information.

A critical feature of shifting to the "contrast before transfer" approach has been the inclusion of *incentives* into what previously had been almost a "purely cognitive" approach to judgment issues in accounting and auditing (see, e.g., Ashton, 1990; Awasthi and Pratt, 1990; Libby and Lipe, 1992). While it has long been understood that a complete picture of judgment and decision-making performance in accounting and auditing will require significant concern with both economic and social incentives, as a field we have been slow to incorporate incentives into our research. It seems apparent, however, that judgment performance in professional settings is determined by the *joint* effects of cognition and incentives. The experimental methods of judgment research, with their facility for creating, controlling, and manipulating relevant variables, should place us in a unique position – relative to other accounting research paradigms – to disentangle the effects of cognition and incentives on judgment performance.

The inclusion of economic and social incentives in judgment research is shifting research away from the "individual-in-isolation" model that was dominant earlier. A critical question at this juncture is how existing research findings – based largely on the individual-in-isolation model – will be altered as the scope of analysis is expanded to include the impact on judgment and decision making of the economic and social incentives inherent in work groups, organizations, professions, and markets. Currently, the field is paying greater attention to the (economic) incentives inherent in market settings than to the (economic and social) incentives inherent in groups, organizations, and professions. Perhaps this is due to our historically-stronger intellectual ties to economics than to sociology or other "macro-behavioral" traditions.

Even in market settings, however, almost all of the attention has centered around equity markets in financial settings as opposed to, say, labor markets in managerial settings or the market for audit (or related) services. However, the focus on equity markets has served to emphasize not only the multiperson nature of many judgments in accounting and auditing, but also the multiperiod aspects of such judgments. Both Waller (Chapter 2) and Young and Lewis (Chapter 3) note the emergence of multiperiod experiments in managerial accounting settings, but this does not appear to be happening in auditing.

While recent studies have begun to include economic incentives, market forces, learning opportunities, and organizational routines such as accountability requirements and review processes in the scope of judgment research, such inclusions often have been on a one-variable-at-a-time basis. Little research has simultaneously addressed two or more such variables, along with their possible interactive effects, although it is clear that many such variables (and others) jointly characterize natural decision settings. Waller's (Chapter 2) suggested shift toward a "behavioral economics" perspective in managerial accounting, and Berg, Dickhaut, and McCabe's (Chapter 5) framework for understanding aggregate decision effects may hold considerable promise in this regard. Waller (1994) has recently outlined a behavioral-economics approach to research in auditing.

While the scope of the research has broadened recently, it has not systematically addressed many of the contemporary issues that are being embraced by businesses (and by business schools) today. Two examples are the impact on decision making of modern manufacturing practices and cross-cultural information-processing differences (but see Young and Selto (1991) and Chow et al. (1991) for some beginnings). Another example is the impact of information technology on decision making. Future researchers may wish to pay greater attention to such issues, given the strong pressures toward accountability and relevance that characterize both business and higher education today. With such pressures, the current tension between the relevance and the rigor of judgment research is likely to increase.

To the extent that the research continues to move beyond the individual-in-isolation model to encompass a broader set of economic, organizational, and professional forces, the research *methods* employed will need to become broader as well. While individual-level laboratory experiments seem certain to remain the dominant research method for the foreseeable future, an increased use of field-based methods will be required to effectively study issues such as disclosure in financial accounting settings, the use of new manufacturing practices in managerial accounting settings, and decision-aid implementation in auditing settings. Moreover, an increased use of experimental economics methods will be needed to study questions of aggregate behavior and the relation between individual and aggregate behavior.

Debiasing judgments in professional settings

Several chapters in this book discuss the shift that began to occur in the early 1980s from *documenting* judgment errors, biases, and inconsistences to *understanding* them. More recently, a further shift – toward the development of explicit debiasing techniques for eliminating or reducing the impact of errors, biases, and inconsistencies found in laboratory settings – has gained momentum. This latter shift is perhaps the strongest indication to date that the field is ready to address the difficult issue of applying research results to practice. However, virtually all of the recent emphasis on debiasing has occurred in auditing and, even there, only limited efforts have been reported.

Ironically, as research more fully incorporates the types of multiperson/multiperiod issues discussed earlier, the focus on explicit debiasing techniques might become *less* important. That is, for some biases, multiperson or multiperiod aspects of accounting and auditing settings may serve as "natural controls," so that explicit debiasing techniques are not needed (see Kennedy, 1993). For other biases, this is unlikely to be the case (see Kennedy, 1995). When natural controls *are* effective, research attention might be redirected toward understanding the mechanism(s) by which judgment biases are eliminated or reduced; some possibilities are the availability of additional information, structural features of multiperson or multiperiod settings, learning, and competition. When natural controls are *not* effective, researching explicit debiasing techniques may be extremely useful in applied, professional settings.

Like the other themes discussed in this section of the chapter, debiasing is likely to be a challenging direction for future research. First, there is the question of which judgment shortcomings *need* to be debiased. We mentioned above that some "natural debiasers" may be discovered as the scope of judgment research continues to expand to incorporate multiperson and multiperiod considerations. In addition, it could be found that the cost of simply tolerating judgment biases is so small in some settings that debiasing efforts are unwarranted (cf. Lewis et al. 1983).

Second, when the development and use of explicit debiasing techniques is potentially justifiable, there is likely to be a wide array of such techniques from which to choose: Some debiasers relate to the provision of new incentives (economic or otherwise); others relate to general education, task-specific training, or making available some type of decision aid (ranging from simple deterministic algorithms to expert systems); still others relate to restructuring the judgment *task* to make it more consonant with current incentives or with the decision maker's capabilities. Fischhoff (1982) provides an excellent framework for thinking about these and other types of debiasing alternatives.

Third, measuring the effectiveness of alternative debiasing techniques is likely to be at least as complex an issue as measuring unaided judgment performance. Both accuracy- and agreement-based effectiveness measures could be relevant, as could efficiency-based measures. And the relative cost (financial and nonfinancial) of developing and using alternative debiasing techniques must be considered. Moreover, the positive effects of certain debiasers could be offset by (perhaps unanticipated) negative effects (see, e.g., Kachelmeier and Messier, 1990).

In general, the performance of the various debaising techniques, including decision aids, should be evaluated by the same criteria that are employed to evaluate unaided human judgment. Ashton and Willingham (1989) elaborate on this notion. Of course, as the criteria for evaluating unaided judgment become broader, so should the criteria for evaluating judgment-debiasing techniques. Ultimately, the choice of the most appropriate debiasing technique in a particular setting must derive from an understanding of the *cause* of the judgment bias. Arkes (1991) provides an excellent framework for linking judgment biases to underlying causes and to particular types of debiasers.

Finally, the implementation of decision aids and other debiasers amid the politics and power structures of real organizations is likely to be a difficult issue, to say the least. However, the most practical aims of judgment and decision-making research in applied fields like accounting and auditing cannot be fully achieved without implementation of the specific products, or at least the general implications, of the research. When the evaluation and implementation of debiasing techniques is considered, the distinction between research (discovering new knowledge) and development (putting existing knowledge to practical use) tends to become blurred. The roles for research *and* development have been the subject of occasional commentaries in our field – at least in auditing (Kaplan, 1977; Ashton, 1981b; Ashton and

Willingham, 1989). While the focus of this book is on research, none of the chapters addresses research for research's sake alone; instead, the desire to "make a difference" in real decisions is one motivation that underlies each chapter. We think this desire will, and should, be an important influence on future judgment and decision-making research in accounting and auditing.

Conclusion

Issues involving judgment tasks, performance criteria, scope of analysis, and debiasing techniques have played central roles in the evolution of judgment and decision-making research in accounting and auditing. At the risk of oversimplifying, the research of two decades ago reflected a somewhat narrow range of research topics, research methods, and theoretical perspectives, and a relative isolation from other accounting research paradigms and from the practical concerns of accountants and auditors. Today's research, in contrast, features a much broader range of topics, methods, and perspectives, various connections to other accounting research paradigms, and, in the case of auditing, considerable influence on practice (Bell and Wright, 1994). The challenge of the field today – to paraphrase Gibbins and Swieringa's (Chapter 9) final paragraph – is to identify important topics and to apply rigorous research methods to them in ways that preserve the technical, organizational, economic, and institutional features that make them important to the accountants and auditors who perform them and to the people who rely on the results.

Acknowledgment

We are indebted to Laureen Maines and Ira Solomon for helpful comments on an earlier version of this chapter.

Part II

Judgment and decision-making research involving users of accounting information

2

Decision-making research in managerial accounting: Return to behavioral-economics foundations

William S. Waller

Introduction

There is a long-existing gap in accounting research, something like the Grand Canyon, between economics-based and psychology-based perspectives. The gap was originally delineated by a pioneering behavioral accounting researcher (Caplan, 1966, 1971) and recently found intact by nonbehavioral surveyors (Burgstahler and Sundem, 1989). Like all empirical phenomena, the gap has a cause and an effect. The cause of the gap is psychological. It is a hard-wired fact that accounting researchers and doctoral students have information-processing limitations; they must specialize to attain a measure of academic competence. The effect of the gap is economic. Intellectual resources are allocated among institutional positions, e.g., university faculty and editorial boards, in a manner that perpetuates and enlarges the gap. Will this pattern continue? The pessimist may cite recurrent observations of fresh doctoral students quickly fixing their thinking on either economic or psychological bases, but not both. Alternatively, the optimist may see hope in the same observations of malleable doctoral students. Things may change, the gap may be crossed, but only if (some) accounting researchers broaden their perspective and training.

Like the Grand Canyon, one should not attempt to cross the economics–psychology gap in a single leap. A more reasonable plan is to start on one side, slowly work one's way down to deeper levels, and then find a path up the other side. Further, unless one is thoroughly familiar with both sides, it is best to stick to established trails, despite the switchbacks. Fortunately for accounting researchers, there already exists a network of trails connecting the sides of the economics–psychology gap. These trails were blazed by Simon (1982), March (1988), and their colleagues in the area known as "behavioral economics." Behavioral economics generally is concerned with the empirical validity of assumptions underlying neoclassical economic theory and, when the assumptions are empirically invalid, with the implications for explaining and predicting human behavior and the operation of economic institutions.

Although early work in behavioral economics (March and Simon, 1958; Cyert and March, 1963) had a significant impact on early work in behavioral accounting (for a review see Birnberg and Shields, 1989), the impact slackened by the 1970s. Perhaps this outcome was due to the rapid growth and dominance of behavioral accounting studies adopting the lens model and Bayesian paradigms (e.g., Barefield, 1972; Dickhaut, 1973; Ashton, 1976). Whatever the reason, it was *not* the stagnation of behavioral economics. On the contrary, the area has developed enormously since Caplan (1966) originally drew from it. The field has produced many books (e.g., March and Olsen, 1976; Liebenstein, 1976, 1987; Gilad and Kaish, 1986; Kaish and Gilad, 1991; Thaler, 1992) and countless articles in economics and management journals (see References and any issue of *Journal of Economic Behavior and Organization, Journal of Behavioral Economics,* or *Administrative Science Quarterly*). In addition, elementary concepts of behavioral economics, such as "bounded rationality," have been incorporated into major theories on a variety of topics including economic organization (Williamson, 1975, 1985) and economic change (Nelson and Winter, 1982).

The agenda of behavioral economics overlaps significantly with those of other areas familiar to many readers of this book, especially behavioral decision research (Bell et al., 1988) and experimental economics (Smith, 1991). For example, experimental tests of expected-utility theory and variants at the individual level (Kahneman and Tversky, 1979; Chew and Waller, 1986; Camerer, 1989) and experimental tests of relations between individual behavior and market phenomena (Camerer, 1987; Camerer et al., 1989) may be reasonably classified in all three areas. Similarly, a 1985 conference at the University of Chicago on the behavioral foundations of economic theory combined contributions from behavioral economists, behavioral decision researchers, and experimental economists, among others (Hogarth and Reder, 1986). Despite much common ground, overlap among the areas is less than complete. Behavioral decision research includes many studies that involve psychological theory deeply but economic theory only superficially, if at all (Payne et al., 1992). The tests of experimental economics typically involve predictions from neoclassical economic theory, without reliance on psychology (Cox and Isaac, 1986). The distinctive orientation of behavioral economics is elaborated in the next section.

This chapter has two purposes: to take a look back at past decision research in managerial accounting, and to take a look forward to the prospect of building a research program in managerial accounting on behavioral-economics foundations. Regarding the first purpose, the chapter's (selective) review of experimental studies is intended to give readers, including those with little or no accounting background, an understanding of the issues examined and methods employed by researchers in this area of behavioral accounting. An unfortunate conclusion is that, with the possible exception of studies on pricing decisions, the area is at a standstill. The conclusion is unfortunate for two reasons. First, many decision-related, intrafirm policy issues are discussed at length in managerial-accounting textbooks without the benefit of empirical evidence. Behavioral-accounting researchers can provide such evidence and potentially affect practice through pedagogic channels. Second, in contrast with the inert state of experimental research, an atmosphere of vitality and innovation pervades current managerial-accounting practice (Cooper and Kaplan, 1991). Practitioners are now running more experiments (of a sort) in their organizations than university researchers are running in their laboratories. Behavioral-accounting researchers can add value by producing systematic observations of the effects of alternative managerial-accounting information systems.

Regarding the second purpose, the chapter advocates the view that, at least with respect to decision research in managerial accounting, the potential benefit of a return to behavioral-economics foundations is great. As the review shows, past experimental studies in managerial accounting have tried to integrate economic and psychological concepts. In each case, however, the integration is lacking in some way: (1) the study merely documents differences between actual behavior and that predicted by an economic model, providing no insight into the causal role of psychological processes; (2) the study contains no theory as to why specific accounting-information systems emerge to help economic decision makers cope with their cognitive limitations; (3) the study employs an economic model that, for the purpose at hand, is flawed on a priori grounds; or (4) the study's "integration" consists of nothing more than the loose use of economic jargon. A return to behavioral-economics foundations would produce richer and more meaningful integrations which eventually may offer an alternative basis for accounting research, a basis that fuses economics and psychology.

Before proceeding, a brief account of managerial accounting for readers unfamiliar with the discipline is in order. The function of managerial accounting is to provide useful information to organizational decision makers, primarily managers, whose actions determine the allocation of resources within their organization and, to a lesser extent, outside their organization. Managerial decisions for which accounting information may be relevant include product prices, types and quantities of inputs and outputs, and control of decentralized operations. To be effective, managerial accountants must consider the benefits and costs of alternative information systems, i.e., methods for measuring transactions or events and communicating the measurements to decision makers. Such information systems may be seen to have two broad effects: decision facilitating and decision influencing (Demski and Feltham, 1976). Decision facilitating refers to the predecision provision of information that resolves some uncertainty, e.g., the expected unit cost of production at a given output quantity. Decision influencing refers to the postdecision provision of information about the performance of an organizational subunit or employee. When used in conjunction with a properly designed schedule of rewards and penalties, anticipation of such postdecision information provides incentives that influence the decisions of employees whose performance is being evaluated. The decision-facilitating and decision-influencing effects are not independent. For example, a product-line manager's request for specific predecision information (e.g., expected product cost) may be driven by the specific postdecision information (e.g., product-line profit) to be used in his or her performance evaluation. Despite such dependence, researchers and textbook writers often treat the effects separately. In like manner, this chapter mainly focuses on research dealing with managerial accounting's decision-facilitating effects, while the chapter by Young and Lewis (Chapter 3) focuses on research dealing with decision-influencing effects.

The remainder of the chapter is organized as follows. The first section outlines the behavioral-economics perspective. The second through fourth sections review and critique experimental studies on three important managerial-accounting issues: information-system choice, cost-variance investigation decisions, and pricing decisions. For each issue, one or two studies are described in detail, and the approach taken is evaluated from a behavioral-economics perspective. The final section provides some concluding remarks.

Behavioral economics

As with behavioral accounting, mention of behavioral economics often evokes the following sort of question: Since all of economics involves behavior, what is *non*-behavioral economics against which behavioral economics may be contrasted? A starting point for an answer lies in the assumptions about human behavior that underlie neoclassical economic theory (Simon, 1987a). Individuals are assumed to act *as if* they maximize expected utility.[1] That is, an individual's preferences are taken as given, consistent, and representable in the form of a utility function. An individual knows a priori the set of alternative actions and chooses the action with the highest utility or expectation thereof. When uncertainty exists as to the actions' consequences, an individual can assess the probability distribution corresponding to his or her knowledge. When new information may be collected from the environment, an individual knows the information's possible content and can assess, in accord with Bayes' theorem, the probability distribution conditioned on the conjunction of such content and his or her prior knowledge. Against the backdrop of neoclassical economic theory, behavioral economics addresses three related questions: (1) When examined directly, what is the empirical validity of neoclassical theory's assumptions about human behavior? (2) What are the actual processes producing such behavior? (3) Given answers to the above, how should neoclassical theory be revised to improve its predictive and explanatory power?

There is an old debate in economics regarding the scientific relevance of the empirical validity of a theory's assumptions (for a thorough discussion see

Blaug, 1980). Friedman (1953) espoused the view that an economic theory is purely an instrument for prediction and that the realism of its assumptions is largely irrelevant.[2] Although not clearly distinguished by Friedman (1953), the irrelevance-of-assumptions thesis has at least two variations. First, any theory's assumptions must abstract from the complexity of empirical phenomena, and most social scientists would readily concede that assumptions are necessarily unrealistic in this sense. Second, an economic theory's assumptions may be unrealistic by contradicting an understanding, based on intuition or cognitive psychology, of what the human mind is capable. Friedman (1953) illustrated this variation with the "billiard player" example, which it is worthwhile to quote here at length:

> Consider the problem of predicting the shots made by an expert billiard player. It seems not at all unreasonable that excellent predictions would be yielded by the hypothesis that the billiard player made his shots *as if* he knew the complicated mathematical formulas that would give the optimum directions of travel, could estimate accurately by eye the angles, etc., describing the location of the balls, could make lightning calculations from the formulas, and could then make the balls travel in the direction indicated by the formulas. Our confidence in this hypothesis is not based on the belief that billiard players, even expert ones, can or do go through the process described; it derives rather from the belief that, unless in some way or other they were capable of reaching essentially the same result, they would not in fact be *expert* billiard players. It is only a short step . . . to the economic hypothesis that under a wide range of circumstances individual firms behave as if they were seeking rationally to maximize their expected returns . . . and had full knowledge of the data needed to succeed in this attempt (p. 21).
>
> Now, of course, businessmen do not actually and literally solve the system of simultaneous equations in terms of which the mathematical economist finds it convenient to express this hypothesis, any more than . . . billiard players go through complicated mathematical calculations. . . . The billiard player, if asked how he decides where to hit the ball, may say that he "just figures it out" but then also rubs a rabbit's foot just to make sure; and the businessman may well say that he prices at average cost, with of course some minor deviations when the market makes it necessary. The one statement is about as helpful as the other, and neither is a relevant test of the associated hypothesis (p. 22).
>
> Confidence in the maximization-of-returns hypothesis is justified by evidence of a very different character. This evidence is in part similar to that adduced on behalf of the billiard player hypothesis – unless the behavior of businessmen in some way or other approximated behavior consistent with the maximization of returns, it seems unlikely that they would remain in business for long. Let the apparent immediate determinant of business behavior be anything at all – habitual reaction, random chance, or whatnot. Whenever this determinant happens to lead to behavior consistent with rational and informed maximization of returns, the business will prosper and acquire resources with which to expand; whenever it does not, the business will tend to lose resources and can be kept in existence only by the addition of resources from outside. The process of "natural selection" thus helps to validate the hypothesis – or, rather, given natural selection, acceptance of the hypothesis can be based largely on the judgment that it summarizes appropriately the conditions for survival (p. 22).

In sum, the example reflects three key points: (1) the purpose of theory is prediction, period, and the rationality assumption is useful for prediction; (2) the usefulness of the rationality assumption is unaffected by its lack of coherence with accepted facts about cognitive limitations or by direct inquiry into actual decision processes; and (3) the rationality assumption is further justified by analogy with evolutionary theory, in that only maximizers survive an economic system's selection process. This variation of the irrelevance-of-assumptions thesis has been invoked, implicitly or explicitly, as support for the maintained hypothesis of maximizing behavior in countless applications of neoclassical economic theory over the last four decades.

Behavioral economists reject the irrelevance-of-assumptions thesis. Indeed, they base their research agenda on the opposing view that an economic theory's assumptions should be put to direct empirical test (Simon, 1987a). The following concerns about the thesis are frequently voiced in the behavioral-economics literature.

First, prediction is not the only purpose of theory. Another purpose is explanation, especially explanation in terms of the causal process producing the outcomes that are the object of prediction (e.g., Harre and Secord, 1972). Causal explanation facilitates a distinction between genuine and spurious correlation, interpretation of anomalies with respect to theoretical predictions, formulation of policy for improving the process, and conveying knowledge about how the world works. Viewed strictly as a component of neoclassical economists' engine for prediction, the rationality assumption serves no explanatory role beyond the as-if gloss, whether or not the engine generates correct predictions (Nagel, 1963). When economists try to lever a stronger explanatory role for the rationality assumption from the theory's predictive success, the assumption is effectively converted from an insulated, theoretical term into an empirical hypothesis that can and should be put to direct test. Such leverage also runs the risk of logical fallacy, i.e., given A (rationality assumption) implies B (predicted behavior), B does *not* imply A.

Second, knowledge of economic actors' internal properties may moderate predictions about their behavior, especially in complex and unstable environments. To use Simon's (1959) metaphor, suppose the task is to predict the behavior of a liquid when poured into a bowl with an irregular shape. If the bowl were held motionless, then predicting the liquid's resting position would require little knowledge of internal properties. The assumption that the force of gravity will minimize the height of the liquid's center of gravity, coupled with a specification of the bowl's shape, is sufficient for prediction. Alternatively, if the bowl were shaken, or if the prediction were to focus on the liquid's behavior prior to the resting position, then more knowledge of internal properties would be required (e.g., is the liquid water or molasses?). Similarly, predicting the equilibrium behavior of a perfectly adaptive individual in a stable environment requires knowledge of only his or her goal and the environment.[3] But predicting an individual's preequilibrium behavior or behavior in a complex, unstable environment requires more knowledge of internal properties. A fortiori, when a possible divergence between an individual's subjective representation and the objective environment is admitted, a possibility admitted by expected-utility theory (Savage, 1954), knowledge of internal properties is indispensable for prediction.

Third, knowledge of actual decision processes is important in its own right. Simon (1976a, 1978a,b, 1986) has stressed the distinction between the economist's notion of substantive rationality and the psychologist's notion of procedural rationality. Substantive rationality pertains to behavior that is appropriate for achieving given goals under given environmental constraints. The production quantity that maximizes profit, given cost and demand curves, is substantively rational (regardless of the actual procedure used to choose the quantity). Procedural rationality pertains to the effectiveness, given limited computational capacity, of the procedure used to choose actions. A chess player's heuristic for rapidly dismissing many unproductive moves and focusing on a few promising candidates is procedurally rational, relative to completely enumerating and evaluating all possible moves. For simple settings in which substantively rational behavior is obvious, procedural rationality is unimportant. For complex settings, however, in which the procedural demands of a "complete" analysis (Demski, 1980) would greatly exceed computational capacity, procedural rationality is paramount. Behavioral economists contend that most real-world settings fall into the latter category and that a reasonable starting point for explicating procedural rationality is to describe systematically the actual processes of individuals who make decisions in such settings.

Fourth, the conclusion that only maximizers survive an economic system's selection process is generally inconsistent with evolutionary theory (Simon, 1983). Darwinian theory proposes that evolution consists of the combined processes of variation, the generation of new life forms, and selection – preservation of life forms that are well-adapted to the environment. These processes do not guarantee that survivors are maximizers. To be selected, a life form first must be generated, and maximizers may never emerge. In the struggle for a particular niche, the survivor must merely beat the competition and generally does not need to maximize ("survival of the *fitter*" is more apt than "survival of the *fittest*"). Also, life forms may survive by identifying and exploiting new niches. Survival depends on the system of niches and its elaboration over time, not just competitive advantage. Further, when selecting life forms with a short-run competitive advantage, evolution is myopic. In a complex or unstable environment, "local" maximizers may fail to be "global" maximizers; climbing the local hill is a sure route to the top of the world only if there is one hill. Moreover, under uncertainty, evolution may select against maximizing behavior.

Taking an example from psychological research on probability matching, suppose subjects are asked to guess whether a red or green light will illuminate, where $P_{\text{red}} = 0.70$ and $P_{\text{green}} = 0.30$. A maximizer would always guess red. In contrast, subjects typically are suboptimizers, guessing red 70% of the time and green 30% of the time. Suppose further, ignoring Human Subjects Committee restrictions, the reward for being correct is survival and the penalty for being wrong is extinction. If the green light were to illuminate, some suboptimizers would survive, while all maximizers would become extinct. Finally, even if it were true that only as-if maximizers survive, finding out what the survivors actually did to survive seems to be a worthwhile scientific pursuit.

Rejecting the irrelevance-of-assumptions thesis, behavioral economists examine the empirical validity of neoclassical economic theory's assumptions, produce descriptions of actual decision processes, and suggest revisions in theory to accommodate such descriptions. Much of this effort falls under the rubric of "bounded rationality," a general term denoting rational choice given the decision maker's cognitive limitations with respect to both knowledge and computational capacity (Simon, 1987b). Specific theories of bounded rationality are developed by contrasting the neoclassical notion of substantive rationality and the psychological notion of procedural rationality, where the latter encompasses descriptions of actual decision processes. For example, instead of assuming that an individual knows a priori the set of alternative actions and chooses the action with the highest expected utility, behavioral economists propose a theory of search for alternatives including a stopping rule that involves "satisficing" (i.e., choosing the first alternative that exceeds an acceptability threshold) rather than maximizing (Simon, 1955, 1956, 1976b). Instead of assuming that an individual can assess the probability distribution corresponding to his or her knowledge, behavioral economists propose a theory of heuristics for dealing with uncertainty in nonprobabilistic ways (Simon, 1957). Instead of assuming an individual's preferences are given, consistent, and representable as a utility function, behavioral economists propose a theory of preference formation and change (March, 1978). All such theories are derived from empirical knowledge of human thought and choice processes.

Simon (1959, p. 253) posed the question: "How much psychology does economics need?" For the reasons discussed above in connection with the irrelevance-of-assumptions thesis, behavioral economists persistently respond with the answer: "More than we have seen in the past." Despite the ever-expanding scope of neoclassical economic theory (e.g., Becker, 1976; Eggertsson, 1990), there is evidence that many economists who are closer to the mainstream agree with the behavioral economists' answer. One indication is that Simon was the 1978 Nobel laureate in economics "for his pioneering work on decision-making processes in economic organizations." A more telling indication is the substantial effort expended by theorists to extend neoclassical theory in ways that accommodate the results of behavioral economics research; examples include extensions of expected utility theory to accommodate costly information and the emergence of agency theory to accommodate intrafirm conflict and coalition formation (March and Sevon, 1988). Naturally, behavioral economists take issue with the extensions' specifics, especially retention of the rationality assumption (Simon, 1979). But the continuing debate is best not seen as a struggle for survival between competing theories. Rather, the overall process of tension and accommodation between neoclassical and behavioral economists may be seen to produce a richer system of intellectual niches capable of sustaining both kinds of life forms.

Information-system choice

A major contribution to managerial accounting thought in the 1970s was the decision-theoretic explication of the notion that managerial accountants must consider the benefits and costs of alternative information systems (Feltham, 1972; Demski and Feltham, 1976; Demski, 1980). The explication was based on the assumption that a decision maker can correctly specify a complete decision model, $\{A,S,P,U \mid K\}$, where A is the set of alternative actions, S is the set of states of nature over which the decision maker has no control, P is his or her subjective probability distribution over states, U is his or her utility function over the outcomes that result from pairs of actions and states, and K is his or her knowledge at the time of specification. As used here, "correctly specify" does not imply that the decision model and objective environment correspond perfectly; rather, it implies that $\{A,S,P,U \mid K\}$ is the decision model that would result if the cost of analyzing K were zero.[4] In the absence of additional information processing (which is equivalent to a null information system), the decision maker would select the action that maximizes expected utility:

$$\begin{aligned} E(U \mid a^*) &= \max E(U \mid a), \\ &= \max \textstyle\sum U(s,a)P(s), \end{aligned} \tag{1}$$

where a and s are members of A and S, respectively. Relative to the baseline of Eq. (1), one may evaluate the effects of alternative information systems, N, which map unobservable states into observable signals, Y. Let n designate an available information system. For each possible signal from n, one computes:

$$P(s \mid y,n) = \frac{P(y \mid s,n)P(s)}{P(y \mid n)} \tag{2}$$

and

$$\begin{aligned} E(U \mid a^*,y,n) &= \max E(U \mid a,y,n), \\ &= \max \textstyle\sum U(s,a,n)P(s \mid y,n). \end{aligned} \tag{3}$$

Eq. (2) indicates that the role of new information is to revise the decision maker's subjective probabilities, via Bayesian conditionalization. Eq. (3) indicates that the benefits of n result from its signals' impact on a^*, and its cost is reflected as an argument of $U(\ldots)$. Folding back over the set of possible signals,

$$E(U \mid n) = \sum E(U \mid a^*,y,n)P(y \mid n). \tag{4}$$

Thus, acquisition of n is worthwhile to the decision maker, in the context of $\{A,S,P,U \mid K\}$, if and only if $E(U \mid n) > E(U \mid a^*)$. Extensions of this basic model introduce the role of managerial accountant by separating the choices of n and a. That is, the managerial accountant as "information evaluator" selects n so as to maximize his or her own expected utility, taking into account the impact of n's signals on the decision maker's choice of a. The accountant's choice is:

$$\begin{aligned} E(U_i \mid n^*) &= \max E(U_i \mid n), \\ &= \max \sum P_i(y \mid n) \sum E(U_i \mid a, y,n) P_i(a \mid y,n), \end{aligned} \tag{5}$$

where i designates the accountant's viewpoint and $P_i(a \mid y,n)$ represents the accountant's belief about the impact of y on a.

The decision-theoretic view of managerial accounting produced a flurry of experimental studies around 1980. The original piece was by Uecker (1978), who examined the issue of whether managerial accountants (actually student subjects) select from among alternative information systems as if they apply the above model of information evaluation. Recognizing the importance of the last term in Eq. (5), Uecker (1978) manipulated the (simulated) decision maker's strategy for choosing actions given signals and observed whether the manipulation affected subjects' information-system choices. A detailed description of the method and findings is presented next.

Comparable to early behavioral decision research within the Bayesian paradigm (for reviews see Slovic and Lichtenstein, 1971; Rapoport and Wallsten, 1972), the experiment operationalized alternative information systems as sample sizes (drawn from a binomial population) and the systems' signals as observed sample proportions. Each subject performed 40 trials for each of two simulated decision makers, without knowing in advance either the number of trials or a decision maker's strategy for choosing actions given signals. At the beginning of each trial, an urn was randomly selected from a set of ten urns. Subjects were told that each urn contained 100 black or white marbles and that the number of black marbles was 90 in two urns, 70 in four urns, 50 in three urns, and 30 in one urn. This information indicated the prior probability distribution over possible states of nature, i.e., the proportion of black marbles in an urn. Subjects also knew that the decision makers were simulated, held identical priors, faced identical payoffs, and maximized expected value.

Each subject's task was to specify the size of a sample, 0 to 50, to be drawn with replacement from the selected urn. A computer program drew a sample of the specified size and displayed the sample results to the subject. The simulated decision maker processed these results and predicted the state of nature. The prediction constituted the decision maker's action choice. When the prediction was correct, the subject won \$0.50 minus \$0.01 times the sample size. When the prediction was wrong, the subject lost \$0.50 plus \$0.01

times the sample size. Each subject was provided an initial stake of $3.00. Ultimately, each subject took home the greater of his or her cumulative net winnings or $1.50. The experiment took about an hour to complete.

The simulated decision makers differed with respect to their rules for processing the sample results. One decision maker was a Bayesian whose revised probabilities conformed to Eq. (2), while the other's revised probabilities were "conservative" relative to Eq. (2), specifically, a power function (0.25) of Bayesian posteriors. The order of decision-maker types was varied over subjects. The optimal sample size was 16 for the Bayesian decision maker, with expected subject pay of $0.0543 per trial, and 24 for the conservative decision maker, with expected subject pay of –$0.0319 per trial. Overall, expected subject pay given optimal responses was $0.896.

Subjects' performance was measured in three ways. First, for each subject, the Spearman rank correlation was computed for (1) the absolute difference between the specified and optimal sample sizes on each trial for a given decision maker, and (2) the number of trials. A significant negative correlation would indicate convergence on the optimal response over trials. The results contrarily showed that the mean correlation was not significantly less than zero. Second, for each subject, the absolute difference referred to above was averaged for a given decision maker, and the effect of decision-maker type on mean absolute difference was assessed over subjects. Mean absolute difference was significantly lower for the Bayesian decision maker than for the conservative decision maker, which indicates less error in subjects' sample sizes for the Bayesian decision maker. Third, for each subject, the specified sample size was averaged for a given decision maker, and the effect of decision-maker type on the mean sample size was assessed over subjects. Mean specified sample size was significantly lower for the Bayesian decision maker (x = 16.9, s = 6.1) than for the conservative decision maker (x = 19.4, s = 6.6). Consistent with the second result, subjects' responses on average were much closer to the optimal sample size for the Bayesian decision maker. In his discussion, however, Uecker (1978, p. 181) emphasized the first result, which implied "an inability of accountants to learn the most desirable information system for a decision maker."

Four subsequent studies used similar experimental tasks and settings. Uecker (1980) examined the effects of informing subjects in advance about the decision maker's strategy for choosing actions given signals. The main result was that such knowledge had no effect on task performance or improvement therein over trials. Hilton et al. (1981) studied the relation between an information system's accuracy (i.e., sample size) and its perceived value.[5] Subjects had an opportunity to purchase a sample of preset size at a stated price. Over trials, it was possible to impute from each subject's information-purchase decisions a vector of monetary demand values corresponding to a vector of six sample sizes (5, 10, . . . , 30). Overall, mean demand values were very close to optimal (i.e., expected-value-maximizing) responses. However, when the data were split into three groups based on common response patterns, only one group was close to optimality; the other groups either severely overvalued or undervalued the samples. In a closely related study, Hilton and Swieringa (1981) examined the relation between initial uncertainty, as reflected in prior probabilities, and the demand value of sample information. Overall, mean demand values differed significantly from optimal responses. When the data were split into three groups based on common response patterns, one group overvalued (undervalued) the smaller (larger) samples, while the other groups consistently overvalued the samples to varying degrees.

Finally, Hilton and Swieringa (1982) examined the relation between "decision flexibility," i.e., the size of the decision maker's choice set, and the demand value of sample information. In the experimental setting, optimal information value was monotonically increasing in decision flexibility, which was operationalized by varying the set of allowable predictions regarding the proportion of black marbles in the selected urn. For example, at the lowest level of flexibility, the decision maker was constrained to predict either of two proportions, even though the state set contained six possible proportions. On average, subjects' demand values differed significantly from the optimal responses. When the data were split into three groups, one group's values were directionally correct but lower than optimal, a second group's values were directionally correct but higher than optimal, and a third group's values were directionally incorrect as well as overvaluing the information. Comparing the last three studies, the task of discerning the relation between information value and accuracy was apparently much easier than that of discerning the relation between information value and either initial uncertainty or decision flexibility.

The contribution of the experimental studies on information-system choice was their innovative attempt to integrate economic and behavioral approaches. At the time, many authors voiced the need for integrating normative and descriptive models in accounting (e.g., Mock and Vasarhelyi, 1978; Hilton, 1980; Sundem, 1981), and the above studies answered the call. However, general statements about such integration require clarification (Waller and Jiambalvo, 1984). On one view, there is no line between microeconomics and behavioral science; integration is a nonissue. For example, expected utility theory may be seen as a descriptive or positive theory of individual behavior (Schoemaker, 1982). This is not the view underlying the above studies, which consistently interpreted expected-utility theory as normative. On another view, psychology is in the core of behavioral science, while economics is at or beyond the periphery. Adopting this view, the extent to which economics and psychology are integrated in the above studies is limited to Uecker's (1980) observation that subjects used an anchoring-and-adjustment heuristic when specifying sample sizes. Finally, claims to integration cannot rest on the use of experimentation, which is not unique to behavioral science (e.g., Smith, 1991). Instead, integration in the above studies amounts to describing subjects' performance in terms of conformance to or deviation from a normative model, much like pre-1970 behavioral decision research, which was decidedly light on psychological content (Pitz, 1970). Documenting such conformance or deviation was only a starting point for developing a behavioral theory of information-system choice. Given the absence of related research since 1982, it was arguably not the best starting point.

A behavioral-economics approach would differ from that of the above studies along the following lines. Recognizing that a managerial accountant's knowledge and computational capacity are limited in comparison with the complexity of the choice problem, a behavioral-economics approach would seek to develop a model of procedural rationality. Instead of using a model of substantive rationality as a baseline for empirical descriptions, a behavioral-economics approach would contrast the model's underlying assumptions with the kind of information evaluation that can be done by a boundedly rational accountant for whom the cost of analysis is greater than zero. For such an accountant, it may not be feasible to specify the sets of actions, states, and outcomes that are relevant to a decision maker. The accountant may be unable to specify his or her own utility function over outcomes, much less a decision maker's utility function. The accountant may be unable to specify the set of available information systems without introducing the option of searching the environment. For a given information system, the accountant may be unable to work through the possible effects of its signals on a decision maker's action choice, especially when the decision maker also may receive predecision information from other sources. Further problems arise from the typical requirement that a managerial accounting information system must serve more than one decision maker in more than one context.

Interestingly, some of the complications due to costly analysis were recognized by the accounting researchers who originally proposed the decision-theoretic view of information evaluation (Demski, 1980). They referred to such complications as "simplifications" with respect to a complete model and stressed that the role of information in simplified analyses may extend far beyond probability revision. Ironically, the "simplifications" discussed by economics-based researchers may be seen as more relevant to a behavioral theory of information-system choice than the experimental studies done by behavioral accounting researchers.

This is not to say that the experimental studies are irrelevant to such a theory. Although the experimental tasks and settings were abstractions of those faced by managerial accountants, they were nonetheless highly complex. To illustrate, consider Table 1, which uses the parameters in Uecker (1978) to compute the expected value of a sample size of four, given a Bayesian decision maker (and the use of paper, pencil, hand calculator, and table of cumulative binomial distributions). Of course, the computations for larger sample sizes would require more steps, and incorporating uncertainty about decision-maker type would add a layer of complexity. It is inconceivable that subjects could employ a calculative procedure similar to that in

Table 1. *Expected value computation for sample size of 4, using parameters from Uecker (1978).*

						Decision maker's choice			
y	s	$P(s)$	$P(y \mid s)$	$P(s,y)$	$P(s \mid y)$	90B	70B	50B	30B
0B	90B	0.20	0.0001	0.000	0.00	$.46	−$.54	$.54	−$.54
	70B	0.40	0.0081	0.003	0.07	−.54	.46	−.54	−.54
	50B	0.30	0.0625	0.019	0.41	−.54	−.54	.46	−.54
	30B	0.10	0.2401	0.024	0.52	−.54	−.54	−.54	.46
		1.00		0.046	1.00	−.54	−.47	−.13	−.02*
1B	90B	0.20	0.0036	0.001	0.01	$.46	−$.54	−$.54	−$.54
	70B	0.40	0.0756	0.030	0.20	−.54	.46	−.54	−.54
	50B	0.30	0.2500	0.075	0.51	−.54	−.54	.46	−.54
	30B	0.10	0.4116	0.041	0.28	−.54	−.54	−.54	.46
		1.00		0.147	1.00	−.53	−.34	−.03*	−.26
2B	90B	0.20	0.0486	0.010	0.04	$.46	−$.54	−$.54	−$.54
	70B	0.40	0.2646	0.106	0.42	−.54	.46	−.54	−.54
	50B	0.30	0.3750	0.113	0.44	−.54	−.54	.46	−.54
	30B	0.10	0.2646	0.026	0.10	−.54	−.54	−.54	.46
		1.00		0.255	1.00	−.50	−.12	−.10*	−.26
3B	90B	0.20	0.2916	0.058	0.19	$.46	−$.54	−$.54	−$.54
	70B	0.40	0.4116	0.165	0.54	−.54	.46	−.54	−.54
	50B	0.30	0.2500	0.075	0.25	−.54	−.54	.46	−.54
	30B	0.10	0.0756	0.008	0.02	−.54	−.54	−.54	.46
		1.00		0.306	1.00	−.35	.00*	−.29	−.52
4B	90B	0.20	0.6561	0.131	0.53	$.46	−$.54	−$.54	−$.54
	70B	0.40	0.2401	0.096	0.39	−.54	.46	−.54	−.54
	50B	0.30	0.0625	0.019	0.08	−.54	−.54	.46	−.54
	30B	0.10	0.0081	0.000	0.00	−.54	−.54	−.54	.46
		1.00		0.246	1.00	−.01 *	−.15	−.46	−.54

*−$.02 × .046 − $.03 × .147 − $.10 × .255 − $.00 × .306 − $.01 × .246 = −$.0333.

Table 1 within the allotted time, regardless of their incentives.[6] Despite Uecker's (1978) pessimistic conclusion, subjects on average performed remarkably well under the circumstances, at least for the Bayesian decision maker. Careful explanation of how subjects coped with the complexity of the experimental task and setting may shed light on how managerial accountants cope with the complexity of their choice problem.

Besides critically examining underlying assumptions, a behavioral economics approach would attempt to incorporate observations of actual information-system choice in practical settings. Unfortunately, access to field data has been historically limited for managerial accounting researchers.

During the last decade, however, a number of practical cases providing "thick" descriptions of information-system choice have been produced (Cooper and Kaplan, 1991). Although inadequate for theory testing purposes, such descriptions may be useful in early phases of theory development (Swieringa and Weick, 1982). For example, consider John Deere Component Works (JDCW). This case illustrates a change from a volume-based costing system to an activity-based costing (ABC) system. Under the old system, manufacturing overhead was divided into three cost pools and applied to various products based on associated volume measures. For example, machine-related overhead was assigned at the rate of $27.56 per machine hour; a product consuming 0.31 machine hour would be assigned a cost of $8.54. Under the ABC system, manufacturing overhead was divided into seven cost pools and applied to products based on associated "cost drivers," i.e., activities or transactions that presumably cause costs in the pool to be incurred. ABC systems are widely touted as providing more accurate product-cost information than traditional systems do (see Brinker, 1990). The change was precipitated by JDCW's poor showing in its cost-based bidding on new orders. It lost bids on high-volume products that could be produced efficiently and won bids on low-volume products that were relatively inefficient. Did JDCW's managerial accountant work through the new system's effects on action choices (i.e., bids) and related outcomes prior to implementation? The case presents detailed cost and bidding data on a sample of 44 products (13 won, 31 lost). Although not done in the case, an analysis of these data allows one to determine the hypothetical outcome under the ABC system: lost orders would include the original 31 plus seven of those previously won (Morris and Noreen, 1991). The case does not permit computations of profit under the actual and hypothetical bidding outcomes. Nevertheless, the ABC system apparently did not provide information that significantly facilitated bidding decisions. Indeed, JDCW soon switched to another bidding approach that was not based on cost. If managerial accountants do not work through the specific effects of an information system's signals on action choices, what process do they use? A model of procedural rationality that assumes a boundedly rational managerial accountant is more likely to give a satisfactory answer than is a model of substantive rationality that assumes a utility maximizing information evaluator.

Cost-variance investigation decisions

Many managerial accounting issues may be seen as variations on the theme of information-system choice. One variation is the provision of cost-variance information for managers' control decisions. In applying the "management by exception" principle, managerial accountants design information systems that consist of (1) setting a budget, standard, or target in terms of an accounting variable (e.g., cost, profit, or return on investment) that reflects the performance of an organizational subunit; (2) measuring the realized value of the accounting variable; and (3) reporting the difference or "variance" to the manager responsible for controlling the subunit. Upon receipt of the variance report, the manager must decide whether the variance is significant enough to trigger an investigation that diagnoses and, when necessary, corrects its cause. Such variance information is decision facilitating with respect to the responsible manager's investigation problem. Alternatively, the same information is decision influencing with respect to the manager's subordinate when the latter has incentives to achieve a favorable variance (see Chapter 3 by Young and Lewis). Such systems are common in decentralized organizations and are used at many levels including production lines or cells, plants, and divisions.

In the late 1960s and 1970s, managerial-accounting researchers produced a variety of quantitative models intended to solve the variance investigation problem (for reviews see Kaplan, 1975; Demski and Kreps, 1982). A typical formulation expressed the problem in Bayesian terms (cf. Lewis et al., 1983). Let a_1 denote the decision to investigate, a_2 the decision not to investigate, s_1 the state of an "in-control" process, s_2 the state of an "out-of-control" process, and y a variance report from an information system, n. The manager would investigate if and only if:

$$\begin{aligned} &E(U \mid a_1,y,n) > E(U \mid a_2,y,n), \\ &\textstyle\sum U(s,a_1,y,n)P(s \mid y,n) > \sum U(s,a_2,y,n)P(s \mid y,n). \end{aligned} \tag{6a}$$

Simplifying, let $c_1 = U(s_2,a_2,y,n) - U(s_2,a_1,y,n)$, the opportunity cost of not investigating when the process is out of control, and $c_2 = U(s_1,a_1,y,n) - U(s_1,a_2,y,n)$, the opportunity cost of investigating when the process is in control. In these terms, the manager would investigate if and only if:

$$\frac{P(s_1 \mid y,n)}{P(s_1 \mid y,n)} > \frac{c_1}{c_2}, \tag{6b}$$

where

$$\frac{P(s_1 \mid y,n)}{P(s_2 \mid y,n)} = \frac{P(y \mid s_1,n)}{P(y \mid s_2,n)} \times \frac{P(s_1)}{P(s_2)}. \tag{7}$$

As with the complete analysis discussed in the previous section, the role of accounting information is to update the manager's prior odds into posterior odds, via Bayesian conditionalization. Extensions of this basic model have taken into account factors such as future period consequences of operating out of control and multiple processes with related costs (e.g., Magee, 1977).

As a complement to the modeling efforts, behavioral-accounting researchers have conducted numerous experiments using similar formulations of the investigation problem. Magee and Dickhaut (1978) found that subjects' cost-control heuristics (i.e., cost thresholds that trigger investigations) were affected by alternative compensation plans. Brown (1981) manipulated various parameters of the normative model (i.e., presence or absence of distributional information, overlap between in-control and out-of-control distributions, and opportunity-cost structures) and observed the effects on subjects' performance in terms of overall cost efficiency, among other criteria. A main result was that the difference between subjects' and optimal performance was not large, ranging from 4% to 9% of total costs given optimality (see also C. Brown, 1983). Lewis et al. (1983) used verbal protocol analysis to infer subjects' control heuristics and, through a long-run simulation, compared the consequences of employing such heuristics with the normative model's total costs. The results were very similar to those of Brown (1981, 1983). Employing a novel method whereby subjects could pick the desired variance information from an "information board" (i.e., a large cardboard with envelopes containing reports of specific variances), Shields (1983) examined subjects' "demand" for such information and its relations to judgment accuracy and consensus. Finally, Waller and Mitchell (1984) found that subjects' choice of an information system was affected by the significance of the investigation problem to the firm and the structure of their compensation plan. The Lewis et al. (1983) study is described in detail below.

Lewis et al. (1983) presented a framework for evaluating human judgments and prescribing decision aids, along with an experiment that demonstrated some aspects of the framework.[7] The framework is quite interesting. Its basic point is that the preconditions for prescribing decision aids go beyond documenting suboptimal human performance vis-à-vis a normative model. In addition, the researcher should assess the opportunity cost and, when the cost is significant, the cause of suboptimal performance. To elaborate, suppose the researcher has identified a normative model applicable to the problem at hand. Next, the researcher needs to consider whether the decision maker's goal, cue set, and strategy for cue combination, match those of the model. If not, then the researcher needs to assess the opportunity cost of the divergence. When the cost is high, the researcher's prescription should depend on the source(s) of the divergence, e.g., use of checklists or fault trees is appropriate when the divergence involves cue sets.

In the experiment, each of ten subjects assumed the role of a production supervisor responsible for controlling the costs to produce a precision-tooled part on a new machine. The machine's operating state was either in-control or out-of-control, with known prior probabilities. In either state, unit weight (the control variable) was normally distributed with a known mean and standard deviation. The mean was higher for the out-of-control state. At the start of a period, each subject received a report on mean weight from a random sample.[8] If the subject investigated and the state was out-of-control, then the machine was reset to the in-control state where it remained for the rest of the period. If the subject did not investigate and the state was out-of-control, it would remain that way until an investigation was made in a subsequent period. After seven periods, each subject was informed of changes in the process with respect to costs and prior probabilities, and the task was repeated for another five periods. That is, the opportunity-cost structure and prior probabilities were jointly manipulated on a within-subject basis, with the order of treatments varied over subjects.

The authors audiotaped the subjects' verbalizations concurrently with task performance and analyzed the transcription to classify subjects by their control heuristics. Eight subjects were classified as using a "control chart" heuristic whereby a threshold was set between the in-control and out-of-control means; if the reported unit weight exceeded the threshold, then an investigation was made (cf. Magee and Dickhaut, 1978). One subject used an anchoring-and-adjustment heuristic and one subject acted on an expected-value basis. Subjects did not appear to change their heuristics in response to changes in the process parameters. Given the experiment's results, the authors ran simulations over 5,000 periods for each treatment level to evaluate the performance of a "control chart" heuristic, with a threshold equal to the in-control mean plus one standard deviation, against a normative model [Eq. (6b)]. Overall, the opportunity cost associated with the heuristic was 4% or 9%, depending on treatment parameters, of the total costs under the normative model. Viewed from the authors' framework, the simulation results indicated that the relatively low opportunity cost would not justify prescribing a decision aid for this problem.

From a behavioral-economics perspective, the approach taken by Lewis et al. (1983) is a step in the right direction: away from merely documenting suboptimal human performance and toward describing actual decision processes. Indeed, the authors' framework suggests an agenda for behavioral-economics research in managerial accounting. Over the last two decades, countless studies in psychology and applied areas have demonstrated how the use of simplified cognitive processes, or heuristics, may produce systematic errors vis-à-vis normative models. The studies typically open with the following sort of statement: "In general, these heuristics are quite useful, but sometimes they lead to severe and systematic errors" (Tversky and Kahneman, 1974, p. 1124). In such studies, errors are the relevant phenomena, and heuristics are central to cognitive explanations of them. Lewis et al. (1983) rightly argued that researchers must consider the errors' consequences, i.e., the opportunity cost of using heuristics in specific settings, before prescribing correcting mechanisms. From a behavioral-economics perspective, it might be further argued that *non*-errors, i.e., conformance to normative models, also constitute relevant phenomena. Given that limits on knowledge and computational capacity compel humans to use heuristics in complex settings, why do they nevertheless generally perform so well? Do nonerrors result from the interaction of heuristics and contextual variables including economic institutions? Will the same heuristics, when used in conjunction with alternative economic institutions, lead to "severe and systematic" errors? Pursuing such issues would take behavioral-accounting researchers beyond decision aids to examinations of how economic institutions moderate the effects of heuristics and, obversely, how individuals' bounded rationality contributes to the emergence of particular economic institutions.

Before conducting further research on the cost-variance investigation problem, however, it is important to consider whether the Bayesian model, as presented earlier, is really applicable in this setting. Three limitations of the model are relevant to this discussion. First, as suggested earlier, the process subject to control may partly consist of humans who are reactive to characteristics of the control system, e.g., the variable(s) measured by the information system and the manager's investigation rule (Demski and Feltham, 1978). In such strategic settings, it is inappropriate to talk of prior probabilities for in-control and out-of-control states independently of the investigation rule. Second, in field settings, it is unlikely that a manager's information sources would be confined to a managerial accounting report. For example, a plant manager may walk through the production facilities and chat with machine operators before picking up a cost-variance report. If the parallel information systems and their signals cannot be specified in advance, then the normative status of Eqs. (6a), (6b), and (7), is upset.[9] Third, the manner in which control problems are represented in practice is changing. For example, there are frequent references to goals such as "total quality control," "zero inventory," and "continuous improvement" in the professional literature. Taken literally, such expressions suggest that the prior probability of the out-of-control state equals one, and *no* new information can change such extreme beliefs within the Bayesian model. At a minimum, the set of states requires reformulation to be consistent with current management practice.

Pricing decisions

In a single-product, short-run setting where knowledge of demand and (economic) cost functions is complete and certain, pricing decisions are trivial: find the price that equates marginal revenue and marginal cost. In other settings, however, where knowledge about demand or cost is incomplete and uncertain, where the price variable is only one element of a marketing strategy, where the firm makes multiple products whose demand and cost functions interact, or where long-run considerations such as entry by new competitors are important, pricing decisions are more complex. To cope with such complexity, prices often are set by using heuristics such as cost-plus pricing: an initial price equals accounting cost per unit plus a profit markup, where accounting cost may include full cost (i.e., variable and fixed) or just variable cost (Hall and Hitch, 1939; Kaplan et al., 1958). Because this heuristic does not explicitly incorporate demand and thus seems at odds with the marginal-pricing rule, the early observations of cost-plus pricing by Hall and Hitch (1939) sparked considerable debate among economists and led to various attempts at reconciling theory and practice (Machlup, 1946; Friedman, 1953). Although it can be shown that cost-plus and marginal pricing are mathematically equivalent under certain conditions (e.g., Nicholson, 1983), a more plausible reconciliation is that "flexible" cost-plus pricing (i.e., an initial cost-based price is subject to adjustment over time as market conditions dictate) is a useful trial-and-error approach to maximizing profit when demand is initially unknown. Nevertheless, questions about the relative effects of cost and demand on prices continue to attract the attention of economists using various empirical methods (for reviews see Coutts, 1987; Dorward, 1987). Questions about the relation between costs and prices also have attracted the attention of behavioral accounting researchers, who have focused mainly on the effects of full versus variable costing, another variation on the theme of information-system choice.

Ashton (1976) employed a lens-model approach to assess whether subjects' pricing decisions were sensitive to changes in costing systems. Each subject set prices for 60 hypothetical products using three uncorrelated cues: unit cost, demand elasticity, and competitor responsiveness. For each of four experimental groups, the costing system (full or variable) was manipulated on a within-subject basis after the first 30 products' prices had been set, with the order of systems varied over subjects. Subjects starting with variable costing (full costing) also were told that the change in systems would result in less (more) useful cost information due to the inclusion (exclusion) of unit fixed cost. The other between-subject variable was the extent of information about the change in systems, i.e., presence or absence of a statement about the target correlation for cost and prices. Two more groups, using either full or variable costing for all 60 products, were added for control purposes; for these groups, the unit costs for products 1–30 were defined in the same way for products 31–60.

For each subject, a regression model of his or her prechange pricing policy with respect to the three cues was constructed over the first 30 products. For the last 30 products, differences between a subject's actual prices and predicted prices based on his or her prechange policy were computed. The average absolute difference divided by average predicted price (to scale for differences in subjects' prices) was used to measure a subject's sensitivity to the change in costing systems. The results showed that the difference measures were significantly higher for the experimental groups than for the control groups, which suggests sensitivity to the change in systems. However, the distribution for the experimental groups was positively skewed, with nearly one-half of the subjects having difference measures comparable to those of the control groups. Further, based on a median test, the difference measures did not vary among the four experimental groups.

In a critique of Ashton (1976), Libby (1976c) expressed concerns about the confounded manipulation of costing-system change and stated usefulness, and about differences in cost data for the experimental and control groups. Responding to Libby's (1976) concerns, Swieringa et al. (1979) replicated Ashton's (1976) study, isolating the manipulation of costing-system change and holding constant the cost data over groups. Swieringa et al. (1979) found that subjects who experienced a costing-system change adjusted their information processing more than the control groups did. Also, such adjustments were moderated by the extent of information about the change, but not in the predicted direction. Subjects who received some or considerable additional information about the change adjusted their information processing less than subjects who did not receive this information. In another replication using somewhat older subjects with more exposure to accounting, Dyckman et al. (1982) reported similar results.

Not to be left out of the stream of replications and extensions of his earlier work, Ashton (1981a) used the same pricing task in a study that linked the lens-model approach and decision-theoretic view of information evaluation. Employing lens-model criteria (i.e., matching and consistency coefficients), Ashton (1981a) evaluated subjects in the role of information evaluator for decision makers whose pricing policies varied in terms of predictability. The nature of feedback also was manipulated. The results indicated that subjects were able to acquire and apply knowledge of the decision maker's policy and that such ability was moderated by the decision makers' predictability but was unaffected by the feedback manipulation.

Finally, in the only recent development in this area of behavioral accounting, Hilton et al. (1988) took an alternative approach to the pricing decision, an approach that falls close to that of behavioral economics. In their experiment, Hilton et al. (1988) tested predictions from Lere's (1986) model of cost-based pricing (see also Dickhaut and Lere, 1983). Lere (1986) recognized that, when a decision maker's knowledge of marginal cost is limited, accounting cost may be an efficient surrogate. In the model, the decision maker sets a price using a heuristic that consists of the following steps: (1) the decision maker suggests a price, p, to the accountant; (2) the accountant determines the expected quantity demanded at that price, $E[q(p)]$, and reports back the accounting cost per unit, c; (3) the decision maker evaluates the accounting cost against:

$$c = \frac{E[pq'(p) + q(p)]}{E[q'(p)]}; \tag{8}$$

and (4) the process iterates until Eq. (8) is satisfied.[10] The extent to which this heuristic approximates marginal pricing depends on whether the accountant reports full or variable cost, in conjunction with the type of demand function, nature of cost function, and the decision maker's risk preference. Given a linear, deterministic cost function (the demand function may be stochastic or deterministic), variable costing induces better prices, i.e., heuristic-based prices that are closer to marginal prices, than full costing does. Given a linear, stochastic cost function (and deterministic demand function), variable costing induces better prices for risk-neutral decision makers, while full costing induces better prices for risk-averse decision makers. Given a nonlinear cost function, full costing always induces better prices.

In the Hilton et al. (1988) experiment, subjects set prices on each of 12 trials, two trials for each of six experimental treatments reflecting the conditions of Lere's (1986) predictions. On a given trial, each subject was told the demand function, if deterministic, or possible demand functions, if stochastic. Each subject also was told whether the cost function (used by the accountant to compute cost per unit) was linear or nonlinear, and whether it was deterministic or stochastic, but the subject did not see the actual cost function. Each subject specified the type of costing system, variable or full, to be used throughout the trial; he or she then had up to ten iterations (receive a cost report, set a tentative price, and so on) to set a final price for the trial. Finally, each subject received an ex post report of demand, revenue, cost, and profit for the trial. The results provided only limited support for Lere's (1986) predictions. Subjects' prices differed significantly from heuristic-based prices. They also differed significantly from marginal prices, but not in a pattern consistent with Lere's (1986) predictions. Subjects, especially those classified as risk-averse using a separate measure, generally preferred full over variable costing.[11] In a related study involving a quantity rather than pricing decision, Turner and Hilton (1989) reported stronger support for the heuristic proposed by Dickhaut and Lere (1983 – see note 10). Similar to Hilton et al. (1988), Turner and Hilton (1989) found significant divergences from optimality and a tendency for risk-averse subjects to prefer full costing.

Market competition is an equivocal term in economics. Analogous to the distinction between procedural and substantive rationality at the individual level, market competition may refer to an economic process or its product. Although the two senses of competition are acknowledged by virtually all economists, there are diametrically opposed views as to whether the object of economic analysis should be the process or product. The dominant view of neoclassical economic theory emphasizes competition-as-product, e.g., equilibrium prices and resource allocation under perfect competition (Stigler, 1957, 1987). This is the view reflected by Friedman (1953), who focused theoretical attention strictly on predicting equilibrium outcomes and expressed positive disregard for the actual processes causing the outcomes. Accordingly, the received theory is a theory of price competition that cannot explain price formation (Roberts, 1987). The opposing view emphasizes competition-as-process. Hayek (1948, p. 94) provided an early statement:

> [T]he modern theory of competition deals almost exclusively with a state of what is called "competitive equilibrium" in which it is assumed that the data for the different individuals are fully adjusted to each other, while the problem which requires explanation is the nature of the process by which the data are thus adjusted. . . .
>
> [C]ompetition is by its nature a dynamic process whose essential characteristics are assumed away by the assumptions underlying static analysis.

Although the competition-as-process view often is identified with the so-called Austrian school (Kirzner, 1973, 1979), it is germane to a variety of economic analyses (Schumpeter, 1976; Nelson and Winter, 1982; Demsetz, 1982; Langlois, 1986; Loasby, 1990). Clearly, the competition-as-process view also is consistent with behavioral economics. But recall that the behavioral economics approach proceeds by way of contrast with, and thus is intrinsically linked to, neoclassical theory. Such linkage suggests a kind of complementarity in which behavioral economics, including relevant contributions from behavioral accounting, can provide an account of price formation missing from the received theory.

Unfortunately, the competition-as-process view is absent from past behavioral accounting studies on pricing decisions. Although the stream of studies beginning with Ashton (1976) included variables representing market conditions (i.e., indexes of demand elasticity and competitor responsiveness) in subjects' cue sets, the authors reported minimal analyses of the variables' effects, relative to those of cost information. More importantly, the authors examined subjects' pricing decisions in static settings (except for changes in costing systems), without regard to naturally occurring feedback, i.e., reactions of customers and competitors to price offers made in the context of a specific market institution. If cost-plus pricing is to be motivated as an efficient, trial-and-error heuristic, then experimenters need to place subjects as price makers in dynamic, laboratory market settings with appropriate feedback and incentives. The most recent studies (Hilton et al., 1988; Turner and Hilton, 1989) have attractive features including recognition of bounded rationality with respect to marginal cost and appropriate incentives. However, the studies are anchored on heuristics whose trials and errors iterate within the firm between decision maker and accountant, rather than in market settings. The studies also maintain the assumption that demand is known, exactly or as a probability distribution. Relaxing substantive rationality assumptions in a piecemeal fashion has the advantage of increased realism without complete loss of tractability. Offsetting disadvantages include tasks that are curious hybrids (part marginal analysis, part simplified analysis) and the need to produce experimental measures of properties such as utility-based risk preferences, which exist in the theory but not in subjects (March and Shapira, 1987, 1992). As a more radical alternative, behavioral accounting researchers might take a page from Friedman (1953): just as descriptions of actual processes may be seen as largely irrelevant for predicting outcomes, as-if maximizing models may be seen as largely irrelevant for describing actual processes.

Concluding remarks

As the review suggests, experimental research on managerial accounting's decision-facilitating effects reached its highpoint in the early 1980s. Since that time, activity in the area has decreased significantly, at least relative to experimental research on managerial accounting's decision-influencing effects (see Young and Lewis, Chapter 3). In an attempt to rejuvenate the area, this chapter has advocated a return to behavioral-economics foundations. To summarize, behavioral economics is distinguished by its concern with the empirical validity of assumptions (especially the as-if maximizing assumption) underlying neoclassical economic theory, its emphasis on describing and assessing the procedural rationality of the actual processes producing economic outcomes (as opposed to a limited focus on the outcomes' substantive rationality), and its working through the implications for explaining the operation of economic institutions, revising neoclassical theory, and formulating public policy (Simon, 1987a).

For accounting researchers, a return to behavioral-economics foundations is likely to produce several related benefits. First, they would be exposed to a thought-provoking literature that examines in depth the implications of individuals' cognitive limitations, or bounded rationality, for decision making in *economic* settings. Many readers of this book are familiar with the literature in cognitive psychology on judgment and decision making (e.g., Kahneman et al., 1982). The latter literature also examines in depth the implications of cognitive limitations for decision making, but often with a more general orientation using generic tasks and settings rather than specific economic decision tasks and settings. Past attempts by behavioral accounting researchers to apply cognitive psychology's general orientation to accounting problems frequently have been met with the criticism that key economic conditions were missing. Any such deficiency is less likely for accounting research, which is grounded on behavioral economics foundations.

Second, there is increased pressure on accounting scholars at many universities for improved integration of research and teaching. The behavioral-economics literature emphasizes the need to incorporate systematic observations of actual decision processes, at least in the abstract form of "stylized facts" (e.g., cost-plus pricing), and of the institutional setting in which such processes unfold. A direct benefit of incorporating such observations would be more relevant research questions and experimental designs. Another benefit would be a richer knowledge base for the accounting scholar as teacher. At a minimum, conveying knowledge about actual decision processes and institutional detail to students would be an improvement over the advice: "Whatever you do, act as if you maximize something!"

Third, as stated in the introduction, for those accounting researchers who see a gap between economics-based and psychology-based research and who think the gap should be crossed, behavioral economics provides a network of trails for the trek. In light of behavioral accounting researchers' historical interest in cognitive and social psychological processes, they may have a comparative advantage in examining economic processes that involve boundedly rational individuals, relative to researchers whose thinking has been dominated by equilibrium models and substantive rationality assumptions. Reading the behavioral-economics literature may prompt the former to exploit their advantage, addressing issues such as the role of managerial accounting information systems in the competitive process of price formation (Sevcik et al., 1995).

Finally, a potential return to behavioral-economics foundations is not limited to research on managerial accounting's decision-facilitating effects. Other candidates include the role of financial accounting information systems vis-à-vis individual investors and capital markets, and the structure of audit tasks within public accounting firms. Perhaps most promising would be research based on behavioral-economics foundations that examines the *interaction* of managerial accounting's decision-facilitating and decision-influencing effects. When the next book of this sort is compiled in a decade or so, the idea of dividing research on the decision-related effects of managerial accounting into two chapters may be unthinkable.

Notes

1. The as-if qualifier is important because it is seen by many economists to warrant their lack of concern about the actual processes producing behavior.
2. Friedman (1953) presented his instrumentalist view in the context of the distinction between normative and positive economics; his primary concern was that economic policy should be properly informed by economic science. In subsequent discussions of this view, the positive aspect has been the focus of attention, while its linkage with the normative aspect has received less emphasis.
3. There are exceptions. In many two-person games, where each player's goal is clear and the environment is stable, neoclassical economic theory nevertheless predicts multiple equilibria (Kreps, 1990). Consistent with the behavioral-economics perspective, introducing knowledge of players' internal properties may help to resolve such ambiguity.
4. Brown and Lindley (1982) discussed current knowledge in the context of decision analysis:

   > The decision-maker will be referred to as a *subject, S. S* is characterized at any given point in time by a psychological field, which comprises the totality of his cognitive processes, experience, memory, or indeed anything which may be actually or potentially in his mind. We are, of course, particularly interested in those parts of *S*'s psychological field which may bear on his judgment of probability, utility, or choice. Usually *S* will only consider part of his psychological field but may extend this part by including extra material. Such an extension will be referred to as "digging" in his psychological field (p. 120).

   The assumption that the cost of analysis is zero implies that the decision maker faces no constraint when "digging" in his or her psychological field, and the assumption of a complete analysis implies that anything worth mining from the field is reflected by the model, $\{A,S,P,U \mid K\}$.
5. Hilton et al. (1981) motivated their study in part by noting a shortcoming in the experimental procedures used by Green et al. (1967) and Snapper and Peterson (1971). In the latter studies, each subject played the dual role of information evaluator and decision maker, and inferences about a subject's performance as information evaluator assumed the optimality of his or her performance as decision maker. This assumption and inferences based thereon are subject to question. Thus, in addition to clarifying the function of managerial accounting, separating the roles of information evaluator and decision maker contributed a methodological refinement of past behavioral decision research on information evaluation.
6. Regarding incentives, not only was expected pay relatively low (less than $1.00 per hour), subjects also faced a "flat-top maxima" situation, i.e., expected payoffs were insensitive to a broad range of sample sizes (see Fig. 1 of Uecker, 1978).
7. The topic of decision aids has received far more attention in auditing than in managerial accounting (see Chapter 8 by Messier).
8. The sample size was not told to subjects (see Appendix A of Lewis et al., 1983). However, the authors' description of the random generator in the text indicated a sample size of one.
9. This is a general and serious limitation in the Bayesian representation of information-system choice. Recall that a decision maker's model, $\{A,S,P,U \mid K\}$, is conditioned on his or her knowledge, K, at the time of specification. Similarly, his or her probability assessments are conditioned on K, such that $P(s \mid y,n)$ is more accurately, though awkwardly, stated as $P(s \mid K,y,n)$. If, between the time of model specification and receipt of a signal from a given information system, the decision maker's knowledge may change in a manner that cannot

be specified in advance, then a preposterior analysis of the information system's value unravels (for discussions see Shafer, 1985; Waller and Mitchell, 1991).

10. Dickhaut and Lere (1983) offered a similar, though simpler, heuristic whereby the decision maker evaluates the accounting cost by focusing on changes in profit.
11. Hilton et al. (1988) classified subjects as risk-averse or risk-neutral using a statistical procedure that fit utility functions to subjects' responses to a postexperimental instrument involving ten hypothetical gambles.

3

Experimental incentive-contracting research in management accounting

S. Mark Young and Barry Lewis

Introduction

Research on the effects of incentives on judgment and decision making has been conducted in a variety of contexts including memory and attention (Craik and Tulving, 1975; Nilsson, 1987), judgment (Arkes et al., 1986; Wright and Aboul-Ezz, 1988; Camerer, 1987), choice (Grether and Plott, 1979), learning (Hogarth et al., 1991), and goal setting (Locke and Latham, 1990). The questions addressed by experimental research in management accounting on incentives are most closely related to those studied in the goal-setting literature. However, management accounting research differs from the goal-setting literature in experimental contexts and the types of incentives studied.

Research in management accounting centers primarily on how incentives affect decisions made by employees (usually subordinates) within control systems (see Waller, Chapter 2, for discussion of a wider range of decisions within the management accounting domain). A control system consists of a work standard or series of work standards against which employees are evaluated (Hopwood, 1976; Lawler and Rhode, 1976). For instance, in manufacturing contexts, production is broken down into specific work standards such as the number of units of product that an individual or division produces. Once the task is performed, feedback is provided to suggest reasons why performance occurred at a particular level and the ways in which it can be improved. Often incentives are tied to standard attainment to provide motivation and to reduce the amount of feedback required to affect behavior.

Over the last decade, managerial accounting researchers have investigated incentives that encourage attainment of a standard or penalize failure to achieve a standard. While some well-known incentive schemes such as piece rate and fixed fee schemes have been studied (as in the goal-setting literature), the management accounting literature has been innovative in testing the effects of incentives derived from economic theories of behavior such as budget-based schemes. This body of work is now commonly referred to as the incentive-contracting literature.

This chapter will review the literature in the following manner. In the next two sections, influences on the development of the literature are discussed, followed by a description of a central economic theory – the agency model. The two major topics that have dominated research are then presented and critiqued. The final section summarizes the chapter and suggests new directions for research.

Development of the literature

The development of the incentive-contracting literature can be traced to two major influences. The first is the work of industrial sociologists from the Chicago school of sociology (see Bulmer, 1984), such as William Whyte (1955) and Donald Roy (1952; 1954), who investigated the effects of piece-rate incentives, difficulty of work standards, and group norms on individual and group behavior in industrial settings. These studies influenced early accounting research, including Stedry's (1960) work on standard setting, Becker and Green's (1962) theoretical paper on participation in setting the budget, and Ronen and Livingstone's (1975) paper on expectancy theory and standard difficulty. A second significant influence was the introduction of the theory of agency into the accounting literature by Demski and Feltham (1978). Agency theory made more explicit the role of incentives and their effect on motivation and performance through the development of analytical models of behavior.

These two influences are overlapping. For example, the industrial sociology studies took place in manufacturing settings and many of the agency examples occur in traditional manufacturing contexts (see Baiman, 1982). Also, both literatures focus on the effects of various forms of incentives, but invoke different research traditions. For instance, the industrial sociology studies primarily use inductive field research methods while agency research relies mostly on deductive analytical techniques.

However, the differences in research methods have provided insights and synergies for researchers seeking an integration of the two literatures. While the field work involved with the industrial sociology studies makes them compelling, it is difficult to determine clearly the effects of incentives on human behavior and performance due to the descriptive nature of field research and the inability to observe the desired variation. On the other hand, agency theory provides a rigorous framework and precisely specified theories regarding the effects of various types of incentive contracts, but under restrictive assumptions about human decision making and behavior. The studies reviewed in this paper are attempts to combine insights from the descriptive behavioral studies with variables from agency theory to form a framework for incentives research in managerial accounting settings.

The two major influences described above have led to incentive-contracting research in two major categories: (1) the effects of self-selection and incentive contracts on performance, and (2) participation in standard setting and incentives and their effects on behavior and performance. The two topics have been investigated primarily in single superior–single subordinate production settings. In the next section, an overview of the agency model is presented.

The agency model – a brief introduction

As mentioned earlier, empirical studies of the effects of different forms of incentives have been influenced strongly by agency theory. The agency model is a normative model of the employment relationship between two parties, a principal (employer or superior) and an agent (employee or subordinate), both of whom are expected-utility maximizers (Ross, 1973). A more detailed and technical presentation of the agency model can be found in Baiman (1982, 1990), and Levinthal (1988). The principal employs the agent to perform a task. Both are assumed to have the same information and beliefs about the state of nature (the environment) prior to determining their employment contract. Typically, the principal is either risk-averse or risk-neutral and maximizes consumption, while the agent is strictly risk-averse and has disutility for effort. The basic agency problem is modeled in a single-period setting.

Both parties are part of a larger labor market and the agent has a reservation wage, which if not met by the principal, will cause him or her to leave the firm. Individuals act in their own best interest and assume that all other parties do the same. The principal wishes to design a contract and monitoring system that takes advantage of the agent's self-interested behavior. Further, the principal cannot observe directly the agent's action choice. The solution to the agency problem is self-enforcing (perfectly Nash) and the set of feasible contracts are pareto optimal (one party's expected utility is maximized subject to the other party receiving not less than some clearly specified level of utility).

Several issues presented in the agency model have been pursued in empirical work. One relates to informational asymmetries between the principal and the agent. Arrow (1985) discusses two types of asymmetries that he calls "hidden information" (or adverse selection) and "hidden action" (or moral hazard). A hidden-action problem arises because the principal cannot directly observe the agent.

Hidden-information problems, or problems relating to the principal's inability to observe an employee's skill, have given rise to one aspect of adverse selection called the "self-selection" problem. As employers cannot observe skill level prior to contracting, one solution to the self-selection problem is to offer prospective employees their choice of contracts and to let them reveal their skill level by the type of contract they select. Another solution is to allow agents to participate with the principal by communicating their private information to the employer. Interestingly enough, the goals of the studies that are reviewed in this paper are not to test the agency model per se. There has been some confusion and controversy in the literature over this point. As illustrated above, agency theory is intended to be both a normative and descriptive theory of human behavior. However, in order for the theory to be descriptive, researchers have to accept the many "as-if" assumptions underlying the model, including expected-utility theory. Since expected-utility has been largely rejected as a descriptive theory of individual behavior by many judgment and decision-making researchers testing agency theory directly is problematic.[1] Thus, the position of incentive-contracting studies has been to merge agency and behavioral variables into descriptive, testable models without imposing any of its restrictive behavioral assumptions.

Self-selection and incentive contracts

Chow's (1983) experiment was the first in accounting to investigate empirically the effects of compensation contracts on performance. Basing his research on Demski and Feltham (1978), Chow varied two levels of job tightness or difficulty (average versus tight) and three types of assigned-compensation schemes (fixed pay, piece-rate, and budget-based).[2] Controlling for skill with a pretest performance measure, Chow found main effects for both tightness (a tight standard led to higher performance) and compensation (the piece-rate incentive dominated the other two). Interactive effects of compensation and standard tightness on performance were not found.

Chow (1983) also studied the effects of individuals' self-selecting the kind of incentive scheme under which they desired to work. Additional subjects were assigned to two new cells that employed tight and average job standards. But this time subjects were permitted to select their form of compensation either from a fixed or budget-based pay scheme. Risk attitude was assessed using conventional two-stage lotteries. The piece-rate incentive used earlier by Chow was not included as an option because of the small sample of available subjects.

Using pretest performance as a skill measure, subjects with higher skill levels chose the budget-based scheme whereas those with lower skill levels chose fixed pay, as hypothesized. Risk attitude did not affect compensation-scheme choice. A final hypothesis predicted that subjects who could self-select their compensation scheme (comparing those in the fixed and budget-based cells only) would outperform those whose scheme was assigned. Controlling for skill level, results showed that under average standard difficulty only those in the budget-based condition with self-selection outperformed those in the assigned condition; no differences in performance were found for those in the fixed-incentive conditions. When standard difficulty was tight, the ability to self-select and the type of compensation scheme had no significant effects.

Chow's (1983) innovative paper is a significant contribution to management accounting research and it set the tone for much of the work to follow.

Subsequent studies were inspired by the following methodological choices and tradeoffs. First, hypothetical payoffs were used, based on each student subject's performance on a computer punch card decoding task (Forward, 1969; Rockness, 1977). Subjects were to act as if they were being paid in each condition, leaving open the possibility of different results if real payoffs had been used. Chow did not try to assess the motivational effects of the hypothetical payoffs in postexperimental questionnaires. A second issue relates to the way that average and tight standards were defined. Chow defined them based on the pretest performance of all subjects. An average standard was 24 cards per half hour, while a tight standard was 0.67 standard deviations above the average, or 27 cards per half hour. Thus, a subject with an extremely high pretest score could have been assigned a "tight" standard, but the subject's pretest performance could have exceeded this standard. Thus, the subject might not perceive the standard to be tight and the desired motivational effect would not obtain. Further, no manipulation checks of any independent variables were done to assess whether subjects understood the conditions in which they had been placed.

Third, the definition of skill and the fact that it is not distinguished from effort are problems that still have not been addressed well in the literature. Since Demski and Feltham's (1978) analytical paper clearly distinguishes skill and effort, combining them into a single measure confounds measurement and testing. Fourth, the amount of pretest time also did not seem adequate to ensure that all learning had been driven out of the task, and learning could have occurred during the performance periods.

Finally, several competing models of behavior regarding individual motivation and performance exist, including goal setting, agency theory, and expectancy theory. Thus, distinguishing between skill and effort is important if one is basing tests on the agency model, but may not be of major concern if one is testing other kinds of theories.

In an extension, Waller and Chow (1985) focused exclusively on the self-selection and effort problem and included a controllability filter[3] to remove from measured performance factors that were not controllable by subjects. The design varied state uncertainty (presence and absence), a controllability filter (present versus absent) and two levels of standard (moderate and high).[4]

Waller and Chow allowed subjects to choose from eleven combinations of contracts of the form:

$$p = f + b(x - s), \qquad \text{if } x > s \tag{1}$$

or $p = f$ if $x \le s$, where p = a worker's total pay; f = fixed pay; b = a bonus parameter; x = actual performance and s = standard performance.

State uncertainty was operationalized by having a "no uncertainty" group, who were told that the number of letters per card (using the same task as Chow's) was ten, and an "uncertainty" group, who were given a probability distribution over the number of letters per card (ranging from 4 to 15). The controllability filter (CF) groups were told that their performance would be measured in terms of number of *letters* decoded correctly, while the no-controllability filter (NCF) group were told that performance would be measured in terms of the number of *cards* decoded correctly. Thus the uncertainty associated with any particular card was reduced.

Skill, which Waller and Chow called performance capability (a skill–effort variable) and defined as pretest performance, was assessed with 4 minutes of familiarization and 15 minutes to do the pretest. The standards were set in the following way: A moderate standard was 110 letters per 15 minutes based on the pretest for the CF group and 11 cards per 15 minutes for the NCF group. A high standard was 150 letters (the 86th percentile) for the CF group and 15 cards for the NCF group.

Waller and Chow found some support for a positive correlation between performance capability (assessed in the same manner as Chow) and the performance incentives in the contracts that workers selected. Those with low performance capability selected contracts with minimal performance incentives whereas high performance capability subjects selected contracts with maximal performance incentives. They also found that in the presence of state uncertainty (and assuming worker risk aversion), the correlation between performance capability and performance incentives in the contract selected was higher when a controllability filter was present.

This study shares some of the same problems as Chow (1983). The confounding of skill and effort still persists. One improvement over Chow is that subjects were compensated in this experiment. Further, the operationalization of the controllability filter was cleverly done given the state-uncertainty variable.

Shields et al. (1989) studied the effects of a controllability filter (present versus absent), and the self-selection between a piece-rate and a standard-based compensation contract. The task in this study requires the translation of triplets of numbers into alphabetic characters. Subjects were pretested for performance capability and then selected one of two performance-contingent compensation contracts before state revelation (how many alphabetic characters were required to count as one unit of measured performance).

The controllability filter resembled that of Waller and Chow (1985). A piece rate was paid for each sheet completed without the controllability filter and another rate for each alphabetic character with the controllability filter. The standard-based contract had a fixed portion plus a bonus per unit for performance in excess of the standard. With the controllability filter the standard was set in terms of alphabets that counted as one unit of performance and a bonus paid for each alphabet in excess of standard. For those subjects without the controllability filter the standard was set in terms of 16 answer sheets.

Shields et al. (1989) hypothesized that in the presence of state uncertainty an individual's choice of a performance-contingent compensation contract is a three-way interactive function of the presence/absence of a controllability filter, risk preferences, and performance capability. A second hypothesis was that the relationship between an individual's actual work effort and his or her expected work effort when selecting a contract is a joint function of the realized state and the presence or absence of a controllability filter.

Results indicated that regardless of the state, subjects whose contracts included a controllability filter performed at about the same level as they had expected at the time they selected their contracts. Those without a controllability filter who experienced an adverse state (a large number of alphabetic characters for each unit of performance) still performed at about the same level as their prior expectations even though their marginal pay per unit of effort was substantially reduced. Those in the no-filter condition who had a favorable state significantly outperformed their expected levels.

Dillard and Fisher (1990) used Waller and Chow's (1985) task and tested hypotheses relating to perceived fairness and performance in both single-period and multiperiod settings. As in Waller and Chow (1985), subjects selected compensation schemes based on their skill level, with high-skill subjects selecting budget-based schemes. Subjects who were allowed to select their schemes perceived significantly more fairness than those in the assigned groups. Changing incentive schemes during the study produced mixed results on performance, subjects changing from fixed pay to budget-based showed significant increases in performance as did subjects changing from fixed pay to being able to self-select their scheme.

MBAs were allowed two 15 minute training periods with no pay. Dillard and Fisher used the second training period as their measure of skill. Similar to Chow (1983), standards were based on average performance of the entire group of subjects. Subjects were either assigned or were allowed to select their compensation contracts from three of the schemes that Waller and Chow (1985) devised; one scheme was strictly budget-based, one was budget-based with a fixed component, and the other was strictly fixed pay. There were two measured performance sessions. At the beginning of the second session, subjects were either told to switch to a different incentive scheme or were able to choose a different scheme.

The length of Dillard and Fisher's training period to assess performance capability may reduce the problem of learning on the task. Testing hypotheses relating to fairness is also an interesting direction for research. However, although fairness was assessed using a single seven-point Likert scale, construct validity could not be assessed for the measure. Changing from one type of compensation scheme to another also presents an interesting direction for research.

Shields and Waller (1988) also extended Waller and Chow (1985) by allowing subjects to act as employers (who could design the form of contracts) or employees (who could choose any contract offered by an employer). Shields and Waller's first hypothesis replicated Waller and Chow (1985), positing a positive association between worker's performance capability and the standard-based performance incentives in the contracts they choose. This hypothesis was supported, although the correlations were low. The authors observed that little learning occurred and that employers relied heavily on standards when designing incentive contracts.

Shields and Waller also hypothesized that average pay would be lower for workers choosing contracts with a controllability filter, ceteris paribus. This hypothesis was supported, but the test was done only in the second market, where 23 workers chose contracts with and 19 chose contracts without a controllability filter. The third hypothesis was that employers use a "win-stay/lose-shift" strategy for revising their employment contract offers from period to period. This hypothesis was also supported.

The incentive scheme and task were the same as in Waller and Chow (1985). Employees were given two 5 minute trials under a fixed-fee contract to see how well they could perform. The second trial performance was used as a measure of performance capability (PC) – a skill and effort preference variable. Five periods were used including a precontracting, preliminary contracting, and three main contracting periods. Of the 110 subjects, 12 played employers and 43 played workers in each of two markets.

This ambitious experiment links this area of research more closely with that conducted in the experimental-economics framework in which markets are created (Smith, 1982). Another significant contribution is that subjects acted as employers *and* employees, and they designed and selected contracts. Thus, the experiment extends some of the results from nonmarket settings and provides some results in a market setting.

In contrast to the other studies reviewed in this section, Baiman and Lewis (1989) were not interested in performance effects. Limiting the scope of their experiment to contract selection, they illustrated some potentially useful techniques for testing agency-related issues in the laboratory. In particular, they tested an agency assumption that the form of a contract is not a relevant consideration in contract selection. That is, no conceptual difference exists between an agent's truthfully reporting his or her skill level and receiving a contract that is optimal for that level on the one hand, and simply choosing among contracts designed to be optimal for different skill levels on the other. Specifically, they tested the hypothesis that more subjects will be willing to misrepresent their skill levels as rewards for so doing are increased. Their results supported the descriptive validity of the agency formulation of the contract-selection process.

Baiman and Lewis (1989) is reviewed here largely for methodological reasons. They created a laboratory experiment that controlled for skill, risk and effort preferences, and private information, and they demonstrated that agency-derived pareto optimal contracts based on those controlled variables can effectively screen agents as predicted by the agency model. The simplicity of the laboratory environment made possible the experimental controls. Subjects merely inserted a preprogrammed diskette into a PC and chose from a series of contracts. The program randomly generated an output based on information about the skill level of the subject, and it computed the compensation earned by the subject based on the output achieved and the contract selected.

Skill was operationalized as the probability of achieving a high level of output. The skill of each subject was thus an assigned variable and was private information of the agent. No effort was involved in the task of producing output. It is important to note that the simplicity of their environment merely allowed Baiman and Lewis to show the conceptual separation of skill and effort. Finally, risk preferences were controlled by inducing subjects to behave as if they were risk-neutral. This was achieved by having all contracts reducible to a simple lottery involving some probability p of earning \$10 and a complementary probability $(1-p)$ of earning \$3.75. The result of this design is that the expected utility of any contract is a linear function of the probability of winning the \$10 payoff.

The Baiman and Lewis (1989) paper reinforces the notion that contract selection addresses a "hidden information" problem as discussed earlier. Contract selection is one way an agent has of communicating information (about skill or other relevant inputs) to the principal. Another way is to disclose the information directly after the principal has precommited to offer optimal contracts based on the level of information provided. The agency-theoretic equivalence of these two forms of communication tends to blur the distinction between the research on incentives and contract selection and the research on participation (which is reviewed in the next section of this chapter).

A paper by Waller and Bishop (1990) highlights how closely the two areas are becoming. In this study, unit managers have private information about the current-period productivity potential of their own units as measured by the ratio of outputs to inputs (p-ratios). A central manager allocates the firms' inputs based on unit managers' reported p-ratios. The central manager's goal is to allocate scarce inputs to the most productive units in order to maximize firm profits. In many instances, however, unit managers may be individually better off by having more inputs (if, for example, their compensation were based only on unit profitability), thus providing an incentive for overstating their own p-ratios. The problem is to develop an incentive scheme that encourages truthful reporting by unit managers. While this study is closely related to the incentive-contracting experiments discussed above, it is also closely related to both the participation issue (since direct communication between principal and agent can affect resource allocation) and to the budgetary slack issue (since misrepresentations by the agent can divert firm resources to less productive uses).

A popular incentive scheme to alleviate/mitigate the problem of allocating resources to competing units involves a compensation scheme that bases a unit manager's rewards on both the performance of the manager's unit and the performance of the other units in the firm. The scheme used by Waller and Bishop (1990) is one proposed by Groves (see Groves, 1973; Groves and Loeb, 1979). In two related experiments, Waller and Bishop compared the Groves scheme to a unit-profit scheme and a unit-profit-plus-penalty scheme that penalized below-budgeted output. In the first experiment, overall firm profits were lower and there were more misrepresentations by unit managers under the unit-profit scheme than under the other two schemes. While the unit-profit-plus-penalty scheme resulted in the fewest misrepresentations, it did not result in lower firm profits than the Groves scheme. Note that number of misrepresentations does not necessarily translate into suboptimal allocations because competing managers who misrepresent in the same way will not affect the allocation.

The only incentive for managers to overstate the *p*-ratio in the first experiment was related to compensation for performance relative to budget. In the second experiment, however, an additional incentive was provided by allowing managers to "consume" extra resources by selling allocated inputs directly for cash instead of using them in a productive activity. This aspect of the design was intended to simulate managers' personal consumption in a way analogous to spending firm resources on manager perquisites. Waller and Bishop found that the unit-profit-plus-penalty scheme was significantly better than the Groves scheme in preventing consumption by managers.

While this paper, like others, suffers from the ad hoc nature of the contracts used it is important because it expands research on incentive-contracting issues beyond an emphasis on skill to include a more general notion of hidden information. It also forms a bridge to other lines of research on allocation problems such as transfer pricing.

Chalos and Haka (1990), in a study similar in many respects to Waller and Bishop (1990), specifically examined the effects of different incentive schemes in a transfer-pricing context. Chalos and Haka compared divisional-incentive schemes and mixed-(firm and division)incentive schemes in a negotiated transfer-pricing setting. They were interested in both the equity of the outcomes, as measured by differences in profits across divisions, and the maximization of firm profits. In a bilateral bargaining task, pairs of subjects playing roles of managers in buying and selling divisions negotiated transfer prices for three components manufactured by the selling division. Each subject was given a schedule of division profits under each of five pricing alternatives for the three components. Another independent variable was the existence and nature (certain versus uncertain) of an external market for the three components.

A comparison of Waller and Bishop (1990) and Chalos and Haka (1990) yields two striking observations. First, despite their conceptual similarity, there is virtually no overlap in the underlying literature cited by the two sets of authors. While Waller and Bishop motivate their work by the incentive literature and related experimental tests, Chalos and Haka motivate theirs by the literature on bargaining and transfer pricing. Second, the results of the two studies are similar: Mixed-incentive schemes, developed specifically to motivate division managers to consider overall firm profitability, are not as effective as incentive schemes based solely on divisional performance. This finding across two distinct settings should generate additional research to examine the general conditions under which it holds.

General comments on contract-selection research

This line of research has produced some provocative results. The most consistent finding is that individuals with high skill levels select budget-based incentive schemes when given a choice between piece rate and fixed pay. Other variables, such as the effects of risk preferences, have been hypothesized but either not tested directly or measured poorly.[5]

Perhaps the most significant contribution, however, has been the attempt to incorporate and operationalize agency variables into experiments. For instance, Waller and Chow's (1985) method of operationalizing controllability filters in experiments is highly innovative. Further, many experiments have required elaborate procedures (beginning with Chow, 1983) and a very good sense of timing requiring a good deal of skill to execute.

Yet, as in any new area of research, there are some difficult questions that have not been adequately addressed. Several limitations impede our ability to make strong inferences from these studies. First, being able to separate the skill and effort variables would advance the experimental literature by not only providing a methodological advance, but also a greater consistency with the agency literature. This is a daunting task, as economic definitions of effort (or actions that create disutility) may not correspond directly with psychological notions such as mental effort.

Another advance would be to develop a more explicit understanding of the currently used experimental tasks. In addition, a greater variety of tasks are needed; presently, the task used in this line of research by Chow (1983) has both cognitive and physical elements that have not been clearly separated. Understanding the nature of tasks from both a cognitive and physical perspective could help link this line of research to the literature in judgment and decision making. Longer learning periods for the task also need to be included, so that learning will not confound experimental results. Further, sound experimental procedures, e.g., manipulation checks, need to be used, and debriefing questions relating to subjects' overall understanding of aspects of the design should be posed to obtain more information about the efficacy of procedures used.[6]

Another limitation involves comparisons of different types of contracts or different forms of the same contract. In the agency model, contracts are developed endogenously and the focus is on finding an optimal set of contracts given the parameters of the problem. In some instances, certain types of contracts are superior to others and within types some parameterizations dominate others. However, as mentioned above, experimental studies generally have compared contracts on an ad hoc basis. While these studies can suggest that a particular contract elicits better performance in a particular situation than some other particular contract, the results do not necessarily generalize to broader classes of contracts or situations.

The paper by Baiman and Lewis provides some guidance for this line of research by carefully side-stepping around the skill and effort issue and by using agency-derived contracts. Their approach might be used to replicate some of the previous studies to observe whether similar results obtain. Another direction for research is to conduct basic research on the skill and effort problem that can disentangle the two experimentally. Such an advance would make the testing of agency models much cleaner and more precise.

Participative budgeting and incentives

Within a control system, superiors may not always know where to set a standard for motivational purposes and thus may rely on subordinates' participation in standard setting. Research has centered on participation due to claims about its benefits, such as increased motivation, job satisfaction, and performance. However, a second reason for interest in participation has been the conflicting findings in the literature (Locke and Schweiger, 1979; Shields and Young, 1993). For instance, while many studies report increases in job satisfaction, the evidence is mixed regarding increases in performance. Recently, the literature on participation has begun to focus on both the psychological antecedent conditions under which a subordinate would be most likely to respond positively to participation, and on the psychological outcomes that in turn would affect performance (see Shields and Young, 1993).

Private information and the creation of budgetary slack

In the early 1980s the focus of participation research turned to a different aspect of participation. Rather than looking at outcome variables such as job satisfaction, agency and experimental researchers began examining how subordinates could contribute to the firm via participation.

One major contribution that subordinates can bring to participative budgeting is their knowledge of both local conditions and their abilities to perform necessary tasks. Agency theorists have labeled this knowledge "private information." Superiors value this private information, as sharing it through the participatory process may benefit both the firm and the individual by improving productive efficiency and risk sharing (Baiman, 1982). Experimental researchers also suggested this idea (Hopwood, 1976; Locke and Schweiger, 1979; Locke, Saari, Shaw and Latham, 1981), but agency theorists were the first to study explicitly the effects of private information (Baiman, 1982).

From the superior's point of view, if a subordinate has private information and participates in standard setting he or she can create budgetary slack whereby subordinates either build excess resources into the budget or knowingly understate their production capabilities. In either case, the building of slack has been suggested by the Soviet incentive (Weitzman, 1976) and agency literatures (Baiman and Evans, 1983), and empirically verified in field studies in the accounting literature (Schiff and Lewin, 1970).[7]

Young (1985) reported a laboratory experiment in a production context that studied the effects of information asymmetry between a subordinate and a superior on slack. Young found that risk-averse subjects built in more budget slack than nonrisk-averse subjects, and that subjects whose information was known by management felt greater social pressure not to misrepresent their performance capability when given a chance to participate in selecting their own work standard. Further, there was a negative correlation between felt social pressure and the amount of slack in the standard selected. Thus, the social-pressure variable mediated the relationship between information asymmetry and slack. Subjects were divided randomly into two groups, one in which information asymmetry existed and one in which it did not. Information asymmetry was operationalized as whether the subordinate had private information that the superior did not have about his or her performance capability on a toy-construction task.

Subjects were trained in a construction task and were then asked to see how well they could perform. During this period subjects were paid a flat fee. To create state uncertainty, the experimenter would interrupt the production process and tell subjects to cease working due to downtime. Subjects were then asked to provide their best estimate of how many toys they could produce given two minutes of downtime.

Slack was defined as the subject's best estimate minus the standard selected in the presence of the superior. While incentives were not manipulated in the experiment, all subjects faced the same incentive scheme:

$$C = K_1(A) - K_2\,|\,(S-A)\,|, \tag{2}$$

where A = actual production, S = the standard, and C = total compensation; K_1 and $K_2 > 0$ and $K_1 = K_2$.

Thus, subjects are induced to produce no more than the standard they selected, because they are not any better off monetarily if they exceed the standard; if they produce less than the standard selected they will be penalized monetarily. Since slack is defined as the best estimate of production minus the standard selected, keeping K_1 and K_2 equal prevents subjects from adding another layer of complexity to the measurement of slack by considering alternative weighting of these parameters. If this were the case, then the slack measure would be confounded through the weighting choices.

Manipulation checks for information asymmetry were successful as was a test of subject understanding of the incentive scheme. Young used a single-item measure of risk preferences and social pressure. Thus, no construct validity could be assessed. Similar to the contract-selection studies, performance capability was a combination of skill and effort.

Waller (1988) extended Young (1985) by manipulating two incentive schemes based on Weitzman (1976), a slack-inducing and a truth-inducing scheme, and he investigated their efforts on slack. Waller hypothesized that both risk-neutral and risk-averse subjects would create slack under the slack-inducing scheme, and that when a truth-inducing scheme is introduced, the decrease in slack is greater for risk-neutral subjects than for risk-averse subjects. As predicted, under the slack-inducing scheme, similar amounts of slack were created by risk-neutral and risk-averse subjects. When the truth-inducing scheme was introduced, however, the slack created by risk-neutral subjects was reduced significantly, whereas that created by risk-averse subjects changed very little.

Waller used the technique developed by Berg et al. (1986) to control risk preferences. He measured effort preferences with two questions. Slack was measured as the difference between each subject's self-estimated performance and their chosen budget. Waller used the decoding task developed earlier by Chow (1983) in this experiment. The state variable was operationalized as the size of the alphabetic groups to be decoded. Subjects worked for three periods under different incentive schemes. In the first period, subjects practiced without pay. Then they worked under a piece-rate scheme, earning points for every symbol group correctly decoded. Points were related to the probability of winning $1 at the end of each period (see Berg et al., 1986 for more details). Subjects also wrote down their estimated performance capability. In the second period, a budget-based, slack-inducing scheme was used and standards were set participatively. Following this the state was determined by spinning a probability wheel. In the third period, parameters were changed to a budget-based, truth-inducing scheme. Manipulation checks were successful for the incentive manipulations and mixed for the risk-preference manipulation.

The incentive schemes had the following forms:

$$\begin{aligned} B &= B' + b(y'' - y') + a(y - y''), \qquad \text{if } y \geq y'' \\ &= B' + b(y'' - y') + c(y - y''), \qquad \text{if } y < y'' \end{aligned} \tag{3}$$

where, B is the worker's actual bonus; y is actual performance; B and y' are tentative bonus and budget levels, respectively, set by the manager; y'' is the budget level as revised by the worker via participation, and a, b, and c are reward/penalty coefficients specified by the manager prior to participation such that $0 < a < b < c$.

The slack-inducing scheme occurs when the above equation's reward/penalty coefficients are $0 < b < a < c$. The truth-inducing scheme occurs when the coefficients are $0 < a < b < c$. Risk-neutral subjects had the induced utility function $U(B) = B$, and the risk-averse subjects had the induced function, $U(B) = -e^{-0.006B}$.

Waller's experiment was innovative in his use of the Berg et al. (1986) method of controlling risk preferences and in the experimental design involving a within-subject change in compensation scheme. Further, it extends

Young (1985) by expanding the range of compensation schemes, avoiding the problem of penalizing overfulfillment of the chosen standard.

Chow et al. (1988) extended Waller (1988) by manipulating two types of incentive schemes and the presence or absence of a superior/subordinate information asymmetry. However, they did not find evidence that slack is lower under the truth-inducing pay scheme than under the slack-inducing pay scheme as hypothesized. They did find a marginally significant result for the interaction between pay schemes and information asymmetry. When there was an information asymmetry, slack was lower under the truth-inducing scheme, but with no asymmetry there was no significant difference in the amount of slack.

Chow et al. (1988) did not find performance differences using the truth-inducing or slack-inducing pay schemes as hypothesized. Finally, under information asymmetry, performance was higher under the slack-inducing scheme, but only slightly higher under the truth-inducing scheme with no asymmetry. All of the above hypotheses were tested using ANCOVA with performance capability as a covariate, as this variable may have an effect on slack.

Subjects were assigned randomly to these conditions and performed the task developed by Chow (1983). A short practice period was used. The information asymmetry condition was accomplished by having subjects determine their own performance and placing all decoding sheets in an envelope that he or she kept. The no-information asymmetry condition involved a research assistant assessing the subject's performance. The incentive scheme was the same as that used in Waller (1988) except that the parameters were slightly different, with the truth-inducing scheme $a < b < c$ and $b < a = c$ for the slack-inducing scheme.

This paper did not incorporate state uncertainty into the experiment and risk preferences were not assessed. Manipulation checks were successful for the information asymmetry variable, but only marginally so for the incentive scheme. The method and prior criticisms of earlier papers on incentive contracting still hold.

Chow et al. (1991a) studied the effects of compensation schemes and a "ratchet" on budgetary slack and performance in a multiperiod experiment (Weitzman, 1980). A ratchet, according to Berliner (1956), operates such that once a new level of performance has been reached, the next standard or target under which a subordinate works cannot be reduced below that level but is raised above it.

Chow et al. (1991a) found that slack was lower under the truth-inducing rather than fixed-pay-plus-bonus scheme, but that the anticipation of a ratchet had no effect on slack production controlling for effort preference. When an actual ratchet was imposed, slack was reduced and the reduction was smaller under the truth-inducing scheme. Using performance capability as a covariate, another finding was that subjects tended not to exceed the standard when a ratchet is present. Finally, while it was predicted that performance would be lower in the presence of a ratchet and the fixed-pay-plus-bonus scheme, this hypothesis was not supported.

Using a very similar method to Chow et al. (1988), 55 subjects were assigned randomly to four experimental cells – two levels of compensation scheme, truth-inducing or fixed pay, plus bonus and the presence or absence of a ratchet. In addition, all subjects had private information about their performance capability that management did not have. There was no state uncertainty in the experiment.

For subjects in the ratchet condition the following rules had to be met. If subject's output equalled the self-set standard the next period's standard could not be below the current standard. If output was greater than the self-set standard then the next standard had to be the previous standard plus 85% of the difference between the previous standard and output for that period. Finally, if output was less than the standard then the next period's standard could be reduced by 85% of the difference between the previous standard and the output.

Subjects trained for 10 minutes on the decoding task and were paid $1. These sheets were exchanged among subjects and they graded each other's answers. Effort preference was assessed using a single 11-point scale. Subjects set their own standards and their expected production. A 10 minute production period was given and once again subjects exchanged answer sheets. Two more production periods were used. A single manipulation check question assessed influence in the standard setting. This paper is significant in that it has begun to move research into a multiperiod context.

In a follow-up paper, Chow et al. (1991b) extended their previous paper, this time under state uncertainty. The same experimental design was used. Budgetary slack was found to be lower under the truth-inducing scheme than under the fixed scheme. The presence of a ratchet reduced slack in the second and third production periods. However, no effects of risk preference and pay scheme were found.

Controlling for performance capability, both expected and actual performance were predicted to be lower under the truth-inducing scheme, but this was not borne out. Again, risk preferences played no role; however, expected performance under the ratchet was lower for the fixed-pay-plus-bonus scheme than for the truth-inducing scheme. Actual performance was not affected by the ratchet. Finally, job satisfaction was not different under either incentive scheme, but was higher when the ratchet was absent.

Overall, both of these papers by Chow et al., have provided a new direction for research in participative budgeting. Refinements in the experimental methods will aid our understanding of multiperiod effects of participation and incentives.

Kren and Greenstein (1991) varied three factors – the presence or absence of budget-based incentives, participation (yes/no), or level of monitoring (high/low). Subjects performed a task, iteratively, in which they had to solve an equation that determined the optimal production quantity so that net income for the firm would be maximized.

Kren and Greenstein found support for hypotheses that the strategy they used to solve the equation was positively correlated with performance, as was effort level. The presence of incentives caused more effort on the task, but did not affect strategy. Participation affected strategy, but not effort, and monitoring was positively related to more effort. Strategy was measured as the absolute value of the difference between a subject's first estimate of Q, or quantity to solve the equation, and the optimal value. Effort was the number of iterations that the subject attempted in order to solve the problem.

Both the effort and strategy variables seem to need refinement in this experiment, as the two measures seem to be confounded. For example, a subject could be lucky and guess a value of Q that was close to the optimal value. The authors would then interpret this as the subject having a better "strategy." Effort, on the other hand, was the number of trials needed to solve the problem. The relationship that Kren and Greenstein were hoping for was that a poor strategy would lead to more effort; however, one could imagine that simply by guess-work or luck a subject could start off with a poor strategy and guess the optimal solution. This would imply that a poor strategy led to lower effort. Finally, the monitoring manipulation was checked and found to be successful.

Chalos and Haka (1989) used Chow's decoding task in an experiment that varied favorable and unfavorable state information, relative subordinate skill information for the superior (individual skill information versus individual skill information plus distributional informational for all subjects), and participation versus imposition of the standard.

Participation did increase firm and manager returns across symmetric favorable and unfavorable states of nature. Further, returns to both firm and manager were higher with participation than imposition under the unfavorable state. Firm returns decreased with participation with a favorable rather than an unfavorable state, but the opposite was true for imposition. The manager's payoff in a favorable state improved significantly. Low-ability managers also were found to provide more effort on the task and firm returns increased significantly with relative managerial skill signals.

A favorable state was operationalized as more cards with a favorable skew towards the median of the distribution and unfavorable was defined as more cards toward the high end of the distribution. Skill was pretest performance and the manipulation involved whether managers received only individual skill information, or individual skill information and the minimum and maximum values for all subjects and average performance.

One difficulty with this study is the operationalization of firm and manager returns. The superior received two points for each card coded correctly by the subordinate; however, the subordinate worked under a budget-based scheme. Under this specific scheme the subordinate earned 36 points if he or she hit the standard, and zero points otherwise. Since subjects could participate in setting the standard, the incentive scheme encouraged them to choose a low standard. In addition, they would lose points if they coded cards incorrectly.

This study highlights the problems associated with using ad hoc compensation schemes in participative budgeting research. There is no theoretical basis for the kind of point system that was used or for the setting of payoffs to the superior and subordinate.

General comments on this branch of research

This line of research is not as closely linked to the agency literature as the first branch. While much of the research focuses on the information-asymmetry variable, there is less of a tie to specific agency models such as Demski–Feltham (1978). Instead, many studies tested variations of Weitzman's incentive scheme and found them to induce the kind of behavior hypothesized.

The overall findings are that information asymmetry can provide subjects an incentive to misrepresent how well they can perform, probably due to lack of social pressure to reveal the information. Risk aversion causes subjects to create more slack and truth-inducing and budget-based contracts also can reduce slack. Another contribution of this research is that slack has been documented directly as a result of participation in the budgeting process. Until these studies, evidence of slack was largely anecdotal. Another variable had also been assessed in prior survey studies – the propensity to build in slack. This variable relates more to intentions rather than action.

This direction for research will also improve as more advanced experimental procedures are developed. Limitations of most of this work are similar to those of the contract-selection literature reviewed earlier and are related to the separation of skill and effort and the selection of parameters for compensation schemes. One recent development, however, is the trend toward multiperiod experiments as exemplified by Chow and colleagues. In addition, a recent paper by Young et al. (1993) studied participation in a workgroup context under intragroup-cooperative and intergroup-competitive conditions. This paper used both a daily truth-inducing incentive scheme and a bonus payment for the best performing groups. Results supported hypotheses relating to intergroup competition, but not intragroup cooperation. The motivation for this paper was derived from site visits to manufacturing firms employing workgroup structures and similar types of incentive schemes.

General comments and some new directions for research

General comments

The literature on incentive contracting has focused on two major topics – contract selection and participation. The literature has developed hybrid theories that incorporate behavioral and economic variables into models that have been experimentally tested. For the most part results seem to be consistent with the hypotheses tested. However, it is clear that the literature is still in its infancy and that there are many ways in which research can be improved, especially regarding experimental design and experimental techniques. Perhaps the greatest contributions of this literature, to date, has been the advancement of previous behavioral research by incorporating agency variables such as private information, risk preferences and truth-inducing incentives, and the development of innovative experimental procedures.

The incentive-contracting literature has also enriched our understanding of control-system design and the role that incentives and participation play in the standard-setting process. Finally, researchers in judgment and decision making may find this literature of interest, especially if they are concerned with incorporating economics-based incentives such as truth-inducing schemes into their research designs.

Some new directions for research

Within management accounting research on incentives there appear to be at least three new directions for research. First, two papers have begun to address the issue of relative-performance evaluation (Chow and Haddad, 1991; Frederickson, 1992). Relative-performance evaluation is a process in which the performances of individuals are compared. In particular, a paper by Frederickson (1992) extends an economic model of relative-performance evaluation by incorporating the notion of social influence to test hypotheses related to the effects of profit sharing versus relative performance-evaluation contracts and common uncertainty on effort. While the results of the experiment were mixed, the paper is a strong attempt at moving the incentive-contracting literature into a new context.

Second, some researchers are beginning to study decision making in control contexts (Awasthi and Pratt, 1990; Luft, 1992). Awashi and Pratt (1990) studied how incentives affect effort related to the application of certain types of decision rules and Luft (1992) investigated how the framing of an incentive as a bonus or penalty affected compensation-system choice. Some research in progress (Bonner et al., 1993) is attempting to link incentive research across areas of judgment and decision making. Bonner et al. are conducting experiments in which subjects perform a mental arithmetic task for very long periods of time under differing forms of incentives. Results of this research should provide insights into prior research that has used only brief performance periods and primarily physical tasks in their experimental designs.

Finally, there is a return to the field to study how new manufacturing and service practices are changing management control system design (see Kaplan, 1983, Young and Selto, 1991, and Young, 1992, for reviews of field research). Insights from the field have informed the initial development of laboratory studies focusing on two main topic areas – the effects of new manufacturing practices (such as just-in-time manufacturing) on standard setting and control-system design (Young et al., 1988; Young et al., 1993) and the impact of national culture and incentives on manufacturing performance (Chow et al., 1991). A relevant aspect for incentive-contracting research relates to how new business practices are affecting the design of compensation schemes. For instance, as many manufacturing firms are reorganizing operations to focus on workgroups, group-incentive systems such as profit and gainsharing plans are becoming popular (Kaplan, 1983; Young and Selto, 1991). The effects of these types of schemes can be studied both in the field and the lab.

As we begin to study the effects of incentives in teams, two issues should be considered. First, experiments with multiple subordinates in teams should be conducted over multiple periods. Though the literature on small group behavior is well developed and has been discussed in management accounting research for over 30 years, very little empirical research has been undertaken (Becker and Green, 1962). Second, theories of the effects of incentives other than agency theory will probably become more relevant as we move to new contexts. Consistent with the movement to teams, gainsharing incentive mechanisms represent a largely unexplored area of research.

The return to the field by management accounting researchers and others in business disciplines after a number of years of absence should yield insights that can be used to advance our understanding of the effects of incentives on control-system design. In this manner, the incentive-contracting literature in management accounting will cycle back to its roots in industrial settings.

Acknowledgments

We acknowledge the financial support of the KPMG Peat Marwick Foundation, the University of Southern California, and the University of Colorado. We thank Bob Ashton, Sarah Bonner, Jake Birnberg, Don Kleinmuntz, Joan Luft, and Frank Selto for providing written comments. We also benefitted from very productive discussions with participants at conferences at Duke University on earlier drafts of this chapter.

Notes

1. Chapter 5 by Berg, Dickhaut, and McCabe discusses a different literature in which more direct tests of the agency model have been conducted.
2. In a "bang-bang" contract, standard attainment is rewarded with a large payment while failing to make the standard brings a much smaller reward.
3. A controllability filter is any mechanism that helps to remove uncertainty in the environment from playing a role in an employee's performance evaluation. A flexible budget, or one where actual performance is compared to a predetermined standard, is the most common example of a controllability filter.
4. The design was not fully crossed, as two cells (no state uncertainty and moderate and high standards) were not used due to the lack of relevance of controllability filters when there is no state uncertainty.

5. Selto and Cooper (1990) offer a number of ways of controlling risk attitude in experimental settings.
6. Only Shields et al. (1989) and Dillard and Fisher (1990) performed manipulation checks.
7. Slack had been discussed earlier by a number of researchers including Cyert and March (1963), Schiff and Lewin (1970), and Onsi (1973). However, experimental research on this topic only began in the early 1980s.

4

Judgment and decision-making research in financial accounting: A review and analysis

Laureen A. Maines

Financial reporting provides information about business enterprises that is useful for the decisions of individuals and groups external to businesses, including investors, creditors, suppliers, customers, labor unions, financial analysts, and regulatory authorities (Financial Accounting Standards Board, 1978). The types of information included in financial reports, as well as accounting methods used to generate this information, are governed by bodies such as the Securities and Exchange Commission and the Financial Accounting Standards Board. Although the information is primarily historical, its main purpose is to help decision makers predict future cash flows that will be generated by a business. Thus, financial reporting provides information for "risky" decision making, i.e., decisions in which outcomes are not known with certainty.

Since the 1960s, accounting researchers have used theories and methods from cognitive psychology, particularly the judgment and decision-making literature, to examine decision-making issues in financial reporting. Studies in this area have individuals make judgments and decisions about businesses using accounting information. Some studies employ an experimental method in which one or more variables, such as the amount of information, differ between groups of subjects to determine the effect of these variables on judgments and decisions. Other studies provide all subjects with identical information and either model subjects' judgments or study the process by which judgments are made.

The goal of this literature is to understand how information provided to external users of financial reports is used in judgment and decision making. The primary decision makers studied are investors and creditors, both of whom provide financial resources to businesses with the expectation of obtaining a return on this investment. Using an input–process–output framework for decision making, the studies in this area can be segregated into two categories. One type of study focuses on the first component of this framework, decision inputs, examining how specific types and characteristics of accounting information affect users' judgments and decisions. The second type of study examines the second and third components, decision processes and the resulting judgments and decisions. Studies in this area investigate whether findings from the judgment and decision-making literature, such as decision makers' use of heuristics, provide insight into investors' and creditors' decision processes and outputs.

This chapter is organized in four sections. First, investment and credit decisions are described, along with the individuals making these decisions and the environment in which the decisions are made. The next two sections summarize the literature on investment and credit decisions. The first examines research on decision processes and outputs, and the second focuses on accounting information used as inputs to judgments and decisions.[1] Studies on investment and credit decisions are presented jointly in each section, since similar issues are examined in both areas. Contributions of this research to the fields of judgment and decision making and accounting are discussed in the final section, along with suggestions for future research.[2]

Investment and credit decisions

Investment decisions

Investment decisions concern the purchase or sale of corporate securities, typically via an organized stock market such as the New York Stock Exchange.[3] Since returns on corporate stock are obtained in the form of dividends and appreciation in a stock's price, investment judgments include predicting future dividends and changes in stock price, as well as assessing the uncertainty (risk) of these returns. Although many methods exist for making these judgments, accounting information is most important to "fundamental analysis," which uses economy, industry, and firm-specific information to make investment decisions. Prediction of a corporation's future earnings is part of fundamental analysis, since net earnings represent income remaining to shareholders after current claims of employees, suppliers, and creditors have been met.

Investors vary in their degree of knowledge and experience and the purpose for which their investment decisions are made. Three primary categories of investors are individual nonprofessional investors, professional financial analysts who manage investment portfolios for institutions such as insurance companies and pension funds (termed institutional investors or "buy-side" analysts), and professional financial analysts and stockbrokers who aid less sophisticated investors by making buy/sell recommendations and earnings forecasts (termed "sell-side" analysts).

Several characteristics of the investment environment are noteworthy. First, the magnitude of financial resources involved "raises the stakes" of these decisions relative to many other types of decisions. Second, the presence of an organized stock market may induce aspects of a zero-sum game into investment decisions if investors view themselves as competing with other market participants. Finally, the institutional environments in which professional investors operate place particular types of incentives on these decision makers. For example, the fact that brokerage firms generate revenue from brokering buy/sell transactions may influence financial analysts' stock recommendations and earnings forecasts. In addition, analysts' access to private information from the management of a corporation may depend on their buy/sell recommendation for the corporation's stock. Finally, fiduciary responsibilities that professional investment advisors have toward their clients induce aspects of justification and accountability in their decision environment.

Credit decisions

Credit decisions involve determining the amount and terms of loans made to businesses, ranging from small bank loans to large debt issues in the bond market. The prediction of future cash flows is necessary to assess the probability that the loan principal and related interest will be repaid. An important judgment in this area is the likelihood that a business will experience financial distress (including bankruptcy) and fail to make interest or principal payments as scheduled. Financial ratios, which express the relation between various financial statement items, often are used to assess the likelihood of default. For example, a loan officer may want to assess a firm's ability to repay a one-year loan. The current ratio, defined as current assets (assets that will be converted to cash within a year) divided by current liabilities (liabilities that are due within a year) can be used to assess whether the firm will have sufficient resources to repay the loan in a year.

Credit judgments and decisions are made by bank loan officers and bond raters. Loan officers are responsible for granting bank loans and determining their terms, such as amount, interest rate, and repayment schedule. Bond rating companies (e.g., Moody's Investors Service) provide guidance to current and potential bond investors by evaluating the likelihood that corporations will fail to make interest and principal payments required by the bond agreement. This default risk is expressed by placing bond issues in one of several categories, ranging from "smallest risk of default" to "largest risk of default."

Decision makers in the credit area are professionals who may be subject to specific incentives associated with their organizational positions. For example, one interesting institutional characteristic is the use of review committees in both bond rating and loan granting decisions.

Decision processes and outputs

Researchers have studied three issues related to investors' and creditors' decision processes and related outputs. The first area uses the lens model

(Brunswik, 1952) to model individuals' judgments and compare the accuracy of these judgments to that of linear statistical models. A second area focuses on several aspects of the judgment process. This area (1) compares process models of human judgment with linear statistical models, (2) compares the decision processes of novices to those of professionals, (3) investigates strategies used to make choices among alternatives, and (4) examines the role of judgment heuristics and related biases in the decision processes of investors and creditors. Finally, the third area studies issues related to multiple decision makers.

Linear models of judgments and decisions

The methodology associated with the lens model represents an individual's judgments or decisions as a linear function of informational cues used to make the judgments or decisions (see Meehl, 1954 and Goldberg, 1968 for seminal studies in this area and the Committee on Accounting Valuation Bases, 1972, Ashton, 1974c, 1975, and Libby, 1975b for papers that introduced the use of the lens model in accounting contexts).[4] This model does not attempt to mirror the actual judgment process, but simply provides a representation of the relation between a judgment and the information used to form this judgment. Lens-model research in financial accounting has focused primarily on investment decisions, including stock price change predictions, buy/sell decisions, and evaluations of security risk. Four basic issues have been addressed: the degree of linearity and configurality in judgments, how different pieces of information (cues) are weighted in arriving at the judgment, the comparison of the accuracy of decision makers' judgments to that of predictions from bootstrapping and environmental models, and the use of the lens model as feedback to decision makers.

Linearity of judgment. Decision makers often believe that their decision processes involve complex information-evaluation and integration strategies. For example, they may explicitly state that their evaluation of one piece of information depends on the specific value of another piece of information, which suggests configural or interactive information processing. However, much decision-making research finds that judgments can be represented as a simple linear combination of cues.[5] In the financial-accounting area, studies of investors' judgments also have found them to be represented well by linear models (Ebert and Kruse, 1978).

In these studies, the mean correlation between subjects' judgments and their predicted judgments from a linear bootstrapping model (R_s) ranges from 0.43 to 0.98. These results are consistent with 12 lens-model studies in other decision contexts reviewed by Camerer (1981), in which R_s ranged from 0.41 to 0.91, with a mean of 0.74.[6] Even studies that report fairly low values for R_s typically do not find evidence of significant nonlinear processing (Wright, 1979), with the exception of Slovic (1969) and Schepanski (1983) who found several significant informational interactions in studies of stock brokers' investment decisions and loan officers' credit decisions, respectively.

Cue weighting. Studies also have examined subjects' self-insight into how they weight information by comparing weights assessed by a subject (subjective weights) with cue beta-weights from the subject's bootstrapping model (objective weights). The correlation between subjective and objective weights varies considerably between studies. For example, Wright (1977a,b) and Mear and Firth (1987a) found relatively low self-insight on the part of their subjects (correlations of approximately 0.30 to 0.52), while Savich (1977) found substantial self-insight (mean correlation of 0.92). Slovic et al. (1972) reported that students in their study had greater self-insight than did professional stockbrokers (mean correlations between subjective and objective cue weights of 0.79 and 0.34, respectively), suggesting that professionals' decision processes are more automatic than those of novices.

While most studies in this area do not report the correlation between weights from subjects' bootstrapping models and cue weights from the environmental model (i.e., the matching index, *G*), Wright (1979) noted a mean correlation of 0.46 for students' predictions of stock price changes and Mear and Firth (1987a) reported a mean of 0.29 for analysts' stock return predictions. These correlations are below the mean matching index of 0.61 for the 12 lens model studies in nonaccounting contexts cited by Camerer (1981), although the matching index correlations varied greatly between the studies reported in his paper, with a range of 0.02 to 0.94.

Judgment accuracy. The lens paradigm also has been used to compare the accuracy of human judgment about investments (r_a) with that of environmental models (R_e) and bootstrapping models of the decision maker (r_b). In general, results are consistent with those of other studies in the judgment and decision-making area, although the values for R_e, r_a, and r_b in financial accounting studies typically are less than the means of 0.64, 0.33, and 0.40, respectively, for nonaccounting studies reported in Camerer (1981). The superiority of environmental models and bootstrapping models of individuals over human judgment is confirmed in financial accounting studies, with a mean difference between the accuracy of environmental models and humans of 0.31 and a mean difference between the accuracy of bootstrapping models and humans of 0.04.[7] Individuals were more accurate than linear models of their judgments in only one study (Libby, 1975a, 1976a,b).

Studies have investigated two possibilities for models' superior accuracy over humans: suboptimal choice of information and failure to combine information appropriately in reaching a judgment. In a study of loan default prediction, Abdel-khalik and El-Sheshai (1980) used four types of information choice and combination methods to examine this issue: (1) human selection of information/human combination of information, (2) human selection/bootstrapping model of human combination, (3) human selection/environmental model combination, and (4) model selection/environmental model combination. The first two combinations resulted in equal accuracy (62.5% of the companies accurately predicted as default/nondefault firms), while the third was only slightly more accurate (67.5% accuracy). Since the fourth method was significantly better (90.6% accuracy), the authors concluded that the difference in accuracy between people and models is attributable to poor information choice by people. This result is counter to suggestions from earlier lens-model studies that the comparative advantage of people is in choosing rather than combining information.

Lewis et al. (1988) reported a similar study using a bond rating task. In addition to the four pairs of information selection and combination examined by Abdel-khalik and El-Sheshai (1980), they examined two additional pairs: model selection/human combination and model selection/bootstrapping model of human combination. While results of one experiment reinforced the conclusions of Abdel-khalik and El-Sheshai (1980), a second experiment using a cross-validation approach for the environmental model found that all six combinations of information selection and combination were approximately equally accurate. Lewis et al. (1988) concluded that humans select and use cues which have predictive validity across many different companies rather than choosing differential information that is relevant for only one specific firm.

Lens-model feedback. The lens paradigm has been used to examine the effects of feedback on subjects' judgments. Kessler and Ashton (1981) examined the effect of feedback on students' ability to predict bond ratings over four trials. Four types of feedback were used: (1) outcome feedback only, (2) outcome feedback plus the correlation between each cue and the subjects' bond rating (cognitive feedback), (3) outcome feedback plus the correlation between each cue and the actual bond ratings (task properties feedback), and (4) all three types of feedback (lens-model feedback). Using a correlational accuracy measure, the results indicated that subjects who received task properties and lens-model feedback improved the accuracy of their predictions over the four sessions, while those who received outcome feedback or cognitive feedback did not. Kessler and Ashton (1981) suggested that task properties and lens-model feedback improved subjects' predictions by allowing them to match their cue weights more closely to those of the environmental model.

In summary, the results of lens-model studies in financial accounting correspond very closely to results of lens-model studies in other decision contexts. These studies find that investors' and creditors' judgments are represented well by a linear model, which typically is more accurate in its predictions than the investor or creditor. This conclusion must be tempered by the results of Lewis et al. (1988) who found that decision makers are as accurate as bootstrapping and environmental models if an out-of-sample, cross-validation approach is used. Finally, research in this area has confirmed that the lens model can be an effective feedback tool for improving judgment accuracy.

Decision processes

Linear models versus process tracing models. Process-tracing models use verbal protocols or subjects' descriptions of their decision processes to form a decision-tree representation of this process, with nodes representing cues considered in the judgment and related branches representing decisions associated with specific values of the cues. Cue importance in process-tracing models is measured by the frequency with which cues are mentioned and the order in which cues are processed.

Larcker and Lessig (1983) and Selling and Shank (1989) compared the ability of linear statistical models to predict human judgment with that of process-tracing models. In addition, they examined the correspondence of measures of cue importance in linear statistical and process-tracing models. The studies found that both models exhibited predictive validity, with Larcker and Lessig (1983) finding that process-tracing models were better at replicating human judgment in a stock selection task and Selling and Shank (1989) finding linear models to be better at replicating judgments in a bankruptcy prediction task. Larcker and Lessig (1983) found measures of cue importance in process-tracing models to be significantly correlated with standardized coefficients from subjects' linear models; however, Selling and Shank (1989) found little convergence between measures of cue importance in process-tracing and linear models. Given these conflicting results, Selling and Shank (1989) suggested that additional research is needed on the assessment of cue importance.

Novices versus professionals. Researchers have used verbal protocols to trace the process by which investment judgments and decisions are made in order to study differences between professional and novice investors' information-search patterns and their evaluation of hypotheses regarding the financial condition of a company. This research has the potential to discover factors that influence both the accuracy of judgments and the efficiency with which the judgments are made. Two major differences between the information-search patterns of professional analysts and students have been observed. First, students typically search through information in the order in which it is presented, while professionals' search appears to be guided by a mental "checklist" (Bouwman, 1982; Bouwman et al. 1987). This checklist contains conditional questions that cause the professional analyst to skip back and forth in the information presented depending on the answers to these questions. Jacoby et al. (1985) also found that use of a mental checklist to guide information selection improves analysts' ability to choose high-return stocks.

A second difference between professionals and novices is that novices search for information that is expected to confirm their current hypothesis about the financial condition of the company, while professionals keep several potential hypotheses in working memory and search for information that has the potential to contradict and distinguish among these hypotheses (Bouwman, 1982; Biggs, 1984; Anderson, 1988). As noted by Anderson (1988), incorporating both hypothesis-consistent and -inconsistent data does not guarantee greater accuracy, but does tend to be associated with fewer errors (Einhorn, 1980).

Choice strategies. Several strategies for making choices among multiple alternatives have been identified in the judgment and decision-making literature, including additive compensatory, additive difference, elimination-by-aspects, and conjunctive strategies.[8] Several studies have examined the use of these choice strategies in investment and credit decision making. Biggs (1979) documented the use of all four strategies by analysts who chose among five companies on the basis of earnings power. The analysts had good insight into their own strategies, since the strategies identified by Biggs from subjects' verbal protocols typically matched subjects' responses to a questionnaire about their decision process.

Two studies using traditional experiments have investigated the use of different choice strategies. Biggs et al. (1985) examined the effect of task size, measured by number of choice alternatives and dimensions, and the similarity of dimensions between alternatives on the use of different choice strategies in a loan task. As the number of dimensions and choice alternatives increased, more bank officers used noncompensatory strategies, such as conjunctive and elimination-by-aspects strategies, to make decisions. However, the number of subjects using compensatory strategies, such as additive-compensatory and additive-difference strategies, increased as dimensions became more similar between alternatives.

Paquette and Kida (1988) investigated the effect of different choice strategies on professional analysts' decision time and accuracy in a bond rating task. Each subject was required to use one of three choice strategies (additive-compensatory, additive-difference, elimination-by-aspects) to choose the company with the highest bond rating from a set of two to nine companies. For larger sets of alternatives, the elimination-by-aspects method required less time to reach a decision with no loss in accuracy. Thus, the authors suggested that elimination-by-aspects may be the best strategy for combined efficiency and effectiveness.

Heuristics and biases. Several studies have examined whether heuristics and their related biases are found in investors' and creditors' judgment processes. Johnson (1983) investigated whether students use the representativeness heuristic when forming bankruptcy probability judgments.[9] Subjects assessed the similarity of each firm to prototypical financial profiles of bankrupt and nonbankrupt companies and then estimated the probability that each firm was bankrupt. Since Johnson found that subjects' average probability of bankruptcy corresponded closely to their similarity judgments, he concluded that the representativeness heuristic played a major role in bankruptcy assessment.

One bias related to the use of the representativeness heuristic is that individuals tend to ignore the population base rate of the event in question when making likelihood judgments. For example, if bankruptcy judgments are made by the representativeness heuristic, individuals will likely overstate the number of bankrupt companies in a sample, since the actual percentage of companies exhibiting signs of bankruptcy is very low. The effect of base rates on bankruptcy prediction has been an intensely examined issue, with studies producing conflicting results.

In Johnson's (1983) study, information on the base rate of bankruptcy affected probability judgments only when the company's financial profile was judged as not similar to either the prototypical bankrupt or nonbankrupt profile. Casey (1980a; 1983) and Casey and Selling (1986) also found that telling loan officers the frequency of bankruptcies in their sample had no effect on the loan officers' predictive accuracy. However, both Houghton (1984) and Houghton and Segupta (1984) found the accuracy of bankruptcy predictions to be affected by differential base rates. In Houghton (1984), subjects who were provided with actual sample frequency of bankruptcy averaged 75% predictive accuracy compared to 65% accuracy for subjects who did not receive frequency information. Houghton and Segupta (1984) placed subjects in two groups with different sample frequencies of bankruptcy (33% and 50%) but did not provide them with information on the frequency of bankruptcy in the sample. Subjects in the 33% bankrupt group were more accurate than those in the 50% bankrupt group (84% versus 73% accuracy), suggesting that loan officers' judgments were influenced by the empirically low base rate of bankruptcy for businesses.

To examine these conflicting results, Hite (1987) performed a meta-analysis of bankruptcy prediction studies and found a positive effect of disclosing the relative frequency of failure in the sample on subjects' predictive accuracy. However, in a later study, van Breda and Ferris (1992) specifically tested whether the increase in accuracy was due to telling subjects about the sample base rate or due to how representative the sample base rate was to environmental base rates. They found that only the representativeness of the sample affected the accuracy of default prediction. Although not conclusive, results in this area suggest that loan officers are influenced by population base rates when making bankruptcy predictions.

Moser (1989) studied the effect of output interference and the availability heuristic on investors' earnings predictions.[10] Subjects generated reasons for and against the earnings of Apple Computer increasing more than 5% in the subsequent year. Two orders of reason generation were used: positive reasons followed by negative reasons, and negative reasons followed by positive reasons. Moser found that order affected the net (positive – negative) number of reasons generated. After generating the reasons, subjects judged the probability that earnings would increase by more than 5%. Since these assessments were affected by the net number of reasons generated, Moser concluded that the differential availability of reasons had an effect on subjects' probability judgments.

Finally, Buchman (1985) examined the hindsight bias in a bankruptcy prediction task.[11] Subjects who received outcome information about the actual occurrence or nonoccurrence of bankruptcy were not able to disregard that information when asked to estimate the probability of bankruptcy for each firm, even though they were specifically requested to do so.

In summary, studies indicate that many of the findings in the judgment and decision-making literature also apply to investors' and creditors' decision processes. For example, investors and creditors appear to use many of the heuristics identified in the judgment and decision-making literature, suggesting that their judgments are subject to biases associated with the use of these heuristics. In addition, consistent with findings in the judgment and decision-making literature, investors and creditors change their choice strategies depending on the demands of the task (see Payne et al. 1992 for a review of literature in this area). Finally, research indicates that the decision processes of professionals differ from those of novices both in the type of information searched for and the order in which it is processed.

Multiple decision makers

Research has examined multiple decision makers in both noninteractive and interactive settings. Studies in the first area investigate whether combining the judgments of multiple decision makers into a composite judgment affects decision accuracy. Judgments are aggregated by either averaging individual judgments that are made on a continuous scale (such as stock price predictions) or choosing the outcome preferred by the majority of decision makers when judgments are made on a dichotomous scale (such as bankruptcy predictions). Research has found that composite judgments are more accurate than both individual judgments and judgments from bootstrapping models of individual judges. In many cases, composite judgments are as accurate as those from environmental models (Libby, 1976a; Zimmer, 1980). Libby and Blashfield (1978) observed that most of the increase in accuracy comes from combining three judges, with the addition of more judges to the composite resulting in only very small increases in accuracy.

Chalos (1985) found that the bankruptcy predictions of interacting loan officer committees were more accurate than either predictions of individual loan officers or those from an environmental model. Investigating this issue further, Chalos and Pickard (1985) found that the increased accuracy of groups was due to greater consistency in their decision making, with no differences found between groups' and individuals' ability to select and weight pieces of information. Libby et al. (1987) compared the accuracy of bankruptcy predictions of interacting groups of loan officers to the accuracy of a composite prediction formed from loan officers' judgments. Whereas interacting groups were as accurate as their composite on average, whether a group outperformed or underperformed its composite was found to be a function of variation in the performance of groups' members and the ability of members to recognize differential expertise in the group. Thus, studies in this area support the use of both noninteractive and interactive groups to improve investment and credit decision making.

Decision inputs

Corporations provide financial information in many forms, including written reports, press releases, and individual or group discussions with users of financial information. The primary written report is the annual report, which consists of three financial statements (income statement, balance sheet and cash flow statement), notes to the financial statements, which include supporting schedules, and the audit opinion of an independent certified public accounting (auditing) firm. In addition, the annual report often includes management's discussion of financial results and graphical summaries of financial information. Since the accounting profession determines both the types of information presented in financial statements and the methods used to calculate the specific numbers, the profession wants to understand how different types and characteristics of information affect judgment and decision making. Four aspects of information that have been examined in accounting research are summarized in this chapter: (1) the inclusion of specific types of information in financial reports, such as the current cost of assets; (2) the use of different accounting methods to portray financial information (e.g., use of the first-in, first-out method of recording cost of sales versus the last-in, first-out method); (3) the amount of information presented; and (4) the form in which information is presented (e.g., graphical versus numerical presentation).

Types of accounting information

Accountants are interested in how different types of information provided to investors and creditors influence their judgments and decisions. Studies in this area have focused on quantitative financial information, qualitative information, and financial forecasts provided by management to the investment community.

Financial information. Since the accounting profession has a major impact on the information provided in accounting reports, it is interested in how specific types of accounting information affect decisions of users of these reports. Studies address this issue by either examining the types of information used by investors and creditors to make decisions or using experiments to investigate the effect of one specific type of information on decisions. In the first category, studies have found a large degree of individual variation in analysts' preferred information for making investment decisions (Slovic, 1969; Mear and Firth, 1990). However, earnings and sales appear to be used by most analysts to make investment decisions. For example, Pankoff and Virgil (1970) found that financial analysts in their study purchased earnings and sales information more often than other types of information. Mear and Firth (1987b) also found sales growth and profitability to be important for analysts' predictions of stock returns. Other accounting information found to be relevant for investment risk and return judgments includes liquidity ratios, information on lines of business, return on investment, and leverage (Frishkoff et al., 1984; Mear and Firth, 1988).

The accounting profession often considers requiring additional financial information in corporations' annual reports. An example is the inclusion of supplemental information on the current cost of certain financial statement items.[12] Several studies have examined the effect of current cost information on investment decisions. Heintz (1973) and McIntyre (1973) examined the effect of three types of financial information (historical cost only, current cost only, and both historical and current cost) on students' investment decisions. Neither study found differences that could be attributed to differences in historical versus current cost information.[13] In contrast, other studies have found decreased decision accuracy due to the use of combined historical and current cost information. For example, Dickhaut (1973) examined the effect of a joint historical/current cost information system versus a historical cost system on students' and executives' judgments of whether a stock's price would increase or decrease. In his experiment, both the students' and executives' probability judgments deviated more from the normative Bayesian posterior under the joint information system than under the single historical cost system. Enis (1988) gave investors either historical cost data or both historical cost and current cost data and found that the joint data set resulted in decreased accuracy of both nonprofessional and professional investors' predictions of stock price changes.

Studies have examined the addition of other types of information in financial statements, including uncertainty information (confidence intervals for numbers in financial statements) and information on human resources. Oliver (1972) and Keys (1978) found no difference in loan officers' credit decisions between loan officers who received confidence interval statements and those who received traditional (point-estimate) statements. Birnberg and Slevin (1976) suggested this result may be due to skilled financial statement users knowing the approximate precision of financial statement information from past experience. In the area of human resources, both Elias (1972) and Hendricks (1976) found that the inclusion of information on historical costs of recruiting, training, and personnel development affected subjects' decisions about stock investments. Acland (1976) also found that information on the sociopsychological aspects of human resources, such as employee morale, influenced financial analysts' investment decisions.

With the exception of studies on human resources, this research provides little support for the inclusion of additional information in financial statements, since it typically finds either no effect or detrimental effects of providing decision makers with additional information. The detrimental effects associated with adding information may be due to subjects' unfamiliarity with the new information, inconsistency in decision making caused by trying to reconcile conflicting sets of information, or inability to process more information. Although Heintz (1973) provided some support for the first explanation, a systematic investigation of these reasons has not been performed.

Qualitative information. Corporations' annual reports contain information other than the financial statements, notably the auditor's report and management's discussion of financial results. Certified public accountants examine the financial records of a corporation to assess whether financial statements are free of material misstatement and are prepared in accordance with generally accepted accounting principles. Auditors can issue several different types of audit reports, depending on the outcome of their examination. Research on the auditor's report has focused on the perception of the message conveyed by different reports and the effect of different audit reports on investment and credit decisions.[14]

Libby (1979b) found that bankers' perceptions of the messages conveyed by different audit reports were very similar to the perceptions of auditors. In contrast, Houghton and Messier (1991) found differences between auditors' and bankers' perceptions of qualified or modified audit reports, with auditors viewing these reports as more negative than bankers. The reports investigated by Houghton and Messier differed from those used by Libby, as the required wording of the reports changed in the intervening time period. Bailey (1981) investigated how different audit reports affect financial analysts' perceptions of the source of the financial statements (management versus auditors) and the credibility of management. He found that different audit reports have no effect on either the perceived source of financial statements or the perceived credibility of management. However, Bailey et al. (1983) found that wording changes proposed by the Auditing Standards Board shifted readers' perceptions of responsibility for financial statements from auditors toward management. These studies suggest that the messages conveyed by the audit report to users of these reports are highly dependent on the specific wording of the report.

Estes and Reimer (1977) found no significant differences between the amount loan officers were willing to lend a business with an unqualified (clean) audit opinion and one which had an audit opinion that was qualified for a technical departure from an accounting principle. Libby (1979a) and Houghton (1983–84) also concluded that whether an audit report is qualified or unqualified has no effect on lending decisions. However, a study using financial analysts as subjects found that analysts placed a 10% higher per share value on the stock of a firm with an unqualified opinion than on the stock of a firm which was identical in every respect except that it had received an audit opinion that was qualified for a technical departure from an accounting principle (Estes and Reimer, 1979).

Johnson et al. (1983) examined the effect on bankers' loan decisions of different levels of financial statement examination by auditors. Auditors can have three possible levels of association with financial statements of non-public clients: compilation, review, and audit, with the extent of auditors' work and responsibility increasing from compilation to audit. Johnson et al. (1988) found no difference in loan amount or interest rate for the different types of reports, although loan officers perceived audited financial statements to be less likely to contain clerical errors and fraud than compiled or reviewed statements. Pany and Smith (1982) also found that audited financial statements are viewed as more reliable than statements not subjected to auditor involvement.

Two studies examined the effect of management's discussion of financial results on investment decisions. Hofstedt (1972) investigated whether subjects' predictions of future earnings per share were affected by the consistency/inconsistency of the president's comments with the past trend of earnings per share. He found that both M.B.A. students and business executives made less extreme earnings per share forecasts when the president's comments were inconsistent with the past trend of earnings per share than when they were consistent. Kaplan et al. (1990) examined how different types of reasons given in the president's letter for poor financial results affected students' predictions of future firm performance and investment decisions. The results indicated that a president's letter that justified management's decisions or discussed changes made to alleviate problems resulted in greater expectations of improved performance than letters that explained poor results as due to uncontrollable external factors or those that provided no explanation.

In summary, research generally indicates that different types of audit reports have little effect on decisions, possibly because users presume the financial statements are free of material misstatements and little information is contained in the report beyond that in the financial statements. In contrast, management's discussion of operations does appear to affect the judgments and decisions of investors. These studies indicate that investors may be influenced by managements' letters even though a related line of literature finds that managements' letters typically contain self-serving attributions, with favorable results attributed to management actions and unfavorable results attributed to external, uncontrollable causes. See Bettman and Weitz (1983) and Staw et al. (1983) for further details of this research.

Financial forecasts. Although financial reports provide primarily historical information, some corporate managers also disseminate forecasts of financial variables, such as sales and net income. Danos et al. (1984) found that the degree of optimism or pessimism in a forecast, relative to the past earnings trend, differentially affected professional bond raters' probability distributions for the rating of a corporation's bond. The provision of management forecasts, along with the reasonableness of the underlying assumptions, also affected bank loan officers' probabilities of granting a loan (Danos et al., 1989). In contrast, Johnson and Pany (1984) found that the degree of optimism in management's earnings forecasts relative to historical earnings trends did not affect loan officers' decisions to grant a loan, although it did affect their perception of the forecast's accuracy. These studies suggest that forecasts are used by professionals in credit decisions, although they do not necessarily result in different decisions than would have been made without forecasts.

Alternative accounting methods

Financial reporting permits the use of different accounting methods to portray financial transactions.[15] Since most methods affect the time period in which costs are shown as expenses in the income statement, the use of different accounting methods causes differences in net income (revenues – expenses) during a particular time period, but typically does not affect cash flow.[16] Thus, these methods should not influence investment and credit decisions that depend only on cash flows.[17]

Research on the effect of different methods on investment decisions has produced conflicting results. Barrett (1971) found that the use of different accounting methods for corporate investments had no effect on financial analysts' estimates of the market value of a corporation's stock, as long as supplemental financial information produced using the method not used in the financial statements was provided to analysts. However, Dyckman's (1964) subjects placed different values on the stocks of two companies that differed only in inventory-valuation method.[18] Although his subjects were provided with information that would allow them to convert the data from one method to the other, they did not appear to use this information in their decisions. Jensen (1966) and Abdel-khalik and Keller (1979) also found differences in financial analysts' stock valuations due to the use of different inventory methods. Finally, Dopuch and Ronen's (1973) subjects failed to consider the tax benefits of the last-in, first-out inventory method when allocating a fixed amount between two stock investments. In their study, students generally were either indifferent between the two investments or they preferred the stock with the larger net income even though this firm had a smaller cash flow due to larger tax payments.

Research in this area suggests that at least some decision makers succumb to "functional fixation" and are unable to "see through" the use of different accounting methods for the same transaction.[19] This result seems particularly pronounced with students, although it also has been found with professional financial analysts. Providing supplemental financial data using the alternative method appears to mitigate functional fixation, although simply providing data that can be used to convert from one method to another does not appear to help.

Amount of information

The amount of information required in corporations' financial reports has increased dramatically over time. Much of this additional information is footnote explanations of numbers shown in the financial statements. Following studies in the judgment and decision-making literature which show that the quality of judgments does not necessarily improve as additional information is provided to decision makers (Oskamp, 1965), accounting researchers have examined whether increasing investors' and creditors' "information load" affects their judgments and decisions.

Casey (1980b) used three levels of information load in a bankruptcy prediction study with bank loan officers. One group of loan officers received only financial ratios, a second group received ratios and financial statements without footnotes, and a third received ratios and financial statements with footnotes. The last two groups were significantly more accurate in their bankruptcy predictions than the first group. In addition, the second group of subjects took less time to make their predictions than the third group, indicating increased efficiency without loss of accuracy. In contrast, Iselin (1991) found no difference in accuracy due to changes in the amount of information in a bankruptcy prediction task in which information load levels were similar to the first two levels of Casey (1980b).

Other studies examine whether the degree of aggregation in financial statements affects judgments and decisions, where information aggregation refers to the degree of numerical detail in the three financial statements. For example, should each type of expense be shown on a separate line item in the income statement or should several expenses be combined into a broader expense category? Abdel-khalik (1973, 1974a) examined the effect of three aggregation levels on loan officers' bankruptcy judgments and loan decisions. He found that aggregation affected loan decisions only for the firms in his sample that had defaulted on loans, with disaggregated data resulting in lower loan amounts and higher probabilities of default than aggregated data. In addition, loan officers spent more time making decisions and were more internally consistent in their judgments with less aggregated data. Harvey et al. (1979) found that financial analysts in their study considered less aggregated statements more useful; however, the effect of aggregation on investment decisions was inconclusive, since the degree of aggregation affected analysts' recommendations for only one of the two investments in the study.

Two studies investigated the issue of information aggregation by examining the effect of additional disclosures that break down company performance by industry or geographic region on investor's decisions. Stallman (1969) found that disclosure of separate industry performance for conglomerate corporations reduced the influence of past stock price performance on stock selection decisions, while subjects in Doupnik and Rolfe (1989) were more confident in their assessments of a stock's risk with disaggregated data on geographic performance than with only aggregated data.

The effect of redundant information on judgments and decisions is related to information load, since additional information provided to decision makers typically is correlated with the information already provided. In a study by Belkaoui (1983–84), loan officers who received redundant information made more accurate bankruptcy predictions than those who received only a basic set of diagnostic cues, even though the redundant cues did not increase the predictive ability of a statistical model of bankruptcy prediction. The loan officers who received redundant cues also were more overconfident in their judgments, which is consistent with the finding that decision makers typically do not take redundancy of information into account when assessing the expected accuracy of their judgments (Maines, 1990).

In summary, research examining implications of the amount of information provided to users has produced conflicting results. These conflicts may be due to the fact that some studies, particularly in the area of information load, have not controlled whether the additional information was "informative," i.e., whether it had the potential to improve decision making. In addition, studies typically have not assessed whether additional information was actually used by decision makers. Chewning and Harrell (1990) addressed this issue by using a model of decision makers to determine information usage. As the number of (uncorrelated) pieces of information (cues) increased, some subjects in their experiment used more cues, as indicated by the number of significant coefficients in a regression of their judgments on the cues, while for other subjects the number of significant cues used either remained the same or decreased as information was added. Moreover, the consistency of an individual's judgments, as well as the consensus among subjects, was higher for the first type of subject than the second type, suggesting that the use of more information may improve the decisions of some individuals. The question of what individual characteristics are associated with effective use of large amounts of information remains unanswered.

Form of information presentation

Accounting research has examined the form in which information is presented by comparing both the effectiveness of standard numerical presentation to different types of graphical presentations and examining different types of numerical presentation. Two studies have examined the use of graphs in investment judgments. DeSanctis and Jarvenpaa (1989) found that the use of graphs resulted in more accurate predictions of sales and expenses relative to the use of numerical information. Davis (1989) examined the effect of different types of graphics (bar charts, line graphs, pie charts, and tables) on the accuracy and decision time of judgments about financial variables. He found a significant interaction between the form of presentation and type of judgment for both accuracy and decision time and concluded that it is inappropriate to consider the best form of presentation without considering the particular judgment in question.

Moriarity (1979) examined the accuracy of students' and practicing accountants' bankruptcy judgments for merchandising companies using either financial ratios or schematic faces (Chernoff and Rizvi, 1975) in which different facial features represented different ratios and the specific shape and size of each facial feature was determined by the specific value of each ratio. He found that both students and accountants using schematic faces made more accurate judgments than those using financial ratios, and that subjects using the faces were more accurate than a bankruptcy prediction model based on discriminant analysis. However, Altman (1983) argued that Moriarity used a model that had been developed for manufacturing firms that was not appropriate for his sample of merchandising firms. After applying an industry-specific model to Moriarity's sample, Altman found that the model was more accurate than Moriarity's subjects.

Stock and Watson (1984) reported experiments similar to those in Moriarity (1979) using a bond rating task. In one, subjects who received schematic faces were more accurate at detecting changes in corporations' bond ratings than subjects who received numerical financial information and ratios. A second experiment found no difference between the judgments of subjects using schematic faces, subjects using both schematic faces and bond rating predictions from a discriminant model, and predictions from the discriminant model.

Several studies have addressed the issue of whether different formats for numerical presentation of accounting information affect judgments. Klammer and Reed (1990) examined the effect of two forms of numerical presentation for the cash flow statement on the accuracy of bank loan officers' answers to various computational questions about cash flows and on their degree of consensus about granting a loan. Two formats currently are accepted for this statement: the "direct" method subtracts cash payments relating to operations from cash receipts to arrive at a net amount of cash generated from operations, while the "indirect" method adjusts accrual net income to arrive at the net amount of cash generated from operations. Information in other financial statements, footnotes, and supporting schedules can be used to convert the cash flow statement from one format to the other. The study found that the direct method resulted in more correct answers to the computational questions and greater consensus in the loan decision.

Studies have also investigated the effect of placing information in the footnotes to financial statements as opposed to the body of the financial statements. Wilkins and Zimmer (1983) found no difference between loan officers' judgments of the perceived ability of a company to repay debt between leases shown as a liability in the balance sheet from those disclosed only in the footnotes to the financial statements. In contrast, Harper et al.

(1987) noted that only 10.8% of their subjects included the pension liability in the calculation of the debt/equity ratio when the liability was disclosed in the footnotes, compared to 68.3% of the subjects who did so when the pension liability was included as a liability in the balance sheet. Corroborating this finding, Sami and Schwartz (1992) found that loan officers' judgments about interest rates and probability of repayment were more conservative when the pension liability was included in the balance sheet than when it was shown only in the footnotes.

Research on presentation format holds promise for the greater effectiveness of graphical presentation compared to numerical presentation. In addition, studies indicate that the specific form of numerical presentation affects judgments and decisions. Unfortunately, studies in this area typically have not been guided by any theory to explain why or how different types of graphical or numerical presentation improve decision making. This concern has been raised by Kleinmuntz and Schkade (1993) regarding judgment and decision-making studies on information displays. In order to further this research, future research on presentation form needs to be grounded in the theory of how different displays affect cognitive processing.

Research contributions and future research directions

Research contributions

Contributions to judgment and decision-making research. Accounting research on judgments and decisions of investors and creditors has been at the forefront of several areas of judgment and decision-making research. For example, 3 of the 15 lens-model studies cited by Camerer (1981) were performed using investment or credit decisions, indicating that financial-accounting research composed a significant part of early lens-model studies. Studies examining differences between novices' and professionals' decision processes, decision makers' use of heuristics, and graphical versus numerical information presentation also are an integral part of judgment and decision-making knowledge.

A second contribution of accounting research on investors and creditors is the investigation of judgment and decision-making issues using professional decision makers in richer decision settings than often are studied in basic research. Most studies support the results and conclusions of the judgment and decision-making literature. Two examples are investors' use of heuristics such as availability (Moser, 1989) and the finding that bank loan officers change their choice strategies depending on the demands of the task (Biggs et al., 1985). However, some studies suggest that errors and biases found in abstract tasks do not always appear when professional decision makers are engaged in familiar tasks. For example, accounting studies have found that loan officers' bankruptcy judgments are sensitive to the base rate of bankruptcy. This result parallels more recent findings in the judgment and decision-making literature, which indicate that decision makers incorporate base rates into their judgments under some circumstances (Bar-Hillel, 1990).

Contributions to accounting research. Research on judgments and decisions in financial accounting has contributed to accounting knowledge by providing insight into how to improve the decisions of investors and creditors. For example, results of lens model studies suggest that a simple linear model of the decision maker can be used as a decision aid to improve judgmental accuracy. In addition, accounting research on composite judgments and group decision making indicates that the use of multiple decision makers also improves judgmental accuracy. Process-tracing studies find differences in the information processing of professional and nonprofessional investors that could have implications for training. The finding that heuristics are used in investment and credit decision making also could be integrated in training.

Much of the research in the decision-input area was intended to illuminate how accounting information affects investment and credit decisions, possibly with an eye towards influencing policy decisions on the amount and type of disclosure in financial statements. Unfortunately, three criticisms leveled against this research have limited its impact. First, studies on the same topic have produced conflicting results, preventing conclusive guidance for policy decisions. In addition, the experimental subjects and settings used in these studies often differ from those found in real judgment settings. Finally, accounting researchers have questioned whether policy should be influenced by research on individual decision makers. These criticisms are discussed below.

The literature review on decision-input studies revealed that results of similar studies often differ, making general conclusions difficult. For example, some studies on the use of current cost information found no differences in the judgmental accuracy of subjects who received historical cost information, current cost information, or both historical and current cost information, while others found decreased accuracy when current cost information was added to historical cost information. These conflicts preclude research from providing definitive advice to policy makers on issues such as the current debate on valuing marketable securities at current cost rather than historical cost. In many cases it is impossible to assess the cause of conflicts in these studies since many variables differ between studies. For example, conflicting results in the current-cost studies are difficult to interpret since there are differences in subjects (students versus actual investors), type of information provided (financial statements versus ratios), and the judgments and decisions required of subjects. Even more perplexing is the fact that differences are found between cases within a study (e.g., Harvey et al., 1979), indicating that the effect of different types of information depends on some unknown company-specific factor. Perhaps these results are not surprising given judgment and decision-making research that indicates that minor changes in the task affect judgment (Einhorn and Hogarth 1981); however, significant policy implications appear to be precluded.

The applicability of research results to real investment and credit decisions has been criticized on the grounds that studies often do not capture relevant aspects of these decisions. Two important factors cited are the use of student subjects and insufficient attention paid to institutional factors. While the use of student subjects does not necessarily render results devoid of implications for "real" judgments and decisions, there are often major differences between students and professionals in terms of knowledge, experience, and the degree of familiarity with judgments and decisions.[20] Many of the studies that explicitly examine differences between student and professional subjects (e.g., Dickhaut, 1973; Abdel-khalik, 1974b; Danos et al., 1984) have found differences between the judgments and decisions of these two groups. Institutional factors that are often ignored include accountability and incentives, both of which are likely to affect judgments and decisions. While the exact details of the environment do not, of course, have to be captured in an experimental study, the omission of the essence of environmental factors can inhibit the applicability of the study to real decisions.

The relevance of this research for investment decision making has also been questioned on the grounds that only market-level behavior is relevant for accounting policy. Griffin (1987) notes that accounting information affects the allocation of society's wealth in two ways. First, it directs resources to productive uses and, second, it allocates current wealth among individuals in the society. It is often argued that accounting should be concerned only with the first allocation since the second requires assumptions about preferences for wealth distribution which are outside the scope of accounting. Much of the first allocation process takes place in a market setting (i.e., the stock and bond markets) where market prices direct the flow of resources to productive uses.

The argument against research on individuals in favor of research on markets proceeds along two lines. First, since much of the research on types of accounting information and alternative accounting methods is not guided by any underlying theory, the primary purpose of this research is to document "facts", e.g., are judgments of investors influenced by changes in accounting methods? If accounting is primarily concerned with the allocation of wealth to productive uses, researchers argue that examining the stock market as a whole provides better factual answers to these questions than examining samples of individuals.[21]

In addition, it has been asserted that "errors" in judgment may be independent across individuals and will "wash out" in an aggregated setting and not affect market prices. If this phenomenon occurs, research on individual subjects will have little ability to predict the effect of accounting information on the market as a whole. Indeed, much of the capital-markets literature using stock price data finds that the market is "rational" in its reaction to accounting phenomenon, i.e., any individual "errors" in judgment are not reflected in market prices. However, recent research indicates that market prices can reflect "errors" in judgments, suggesting that some errors are systematic and will not "wash out" in an aggregated setting (Bernard and Thomas, 1989; Hand, 1990; Ganguly et al., 1994). Chapter 5 by Berg, Dickhaut, and McCabe in this book and Camerer (1992) discuss these issues in some depth.

Future research directions

Future research on judgment and decision-making issues. Although judgment and decision-making research on investors and creditors has contributed to both the accounting and judgment and decision-making literatures, additional research is needed to exploit the unique aspects and comparative advantages of decision making in accounting contexts. Future research can add to the judgment and decision-making literature by focusing on implications of institutional arrangements and decision-maker heterogeneity for judgments and decisions. Relative to other areas of judgment and decision-making research, accounting researchers have the advantage of access to professional institutional environments and subjects with varying levels of experience and knowledge. Settings in which financial decisions are made are rich in institutional details, such as the use of committees, accountability/justification, incentives, and feedback. Research has seldom incorporated these factors, leaving many important questions for future research. However, before future research on these issues can proceed, additional descriptive research is needed on the different types of investors and creditors and the institutional environments in which they operate. For example, there is little documentation of how analysts are evaluated, compensated, and trained. Clearly, these factors must be understood before research can investigate the implications of heterogeneity of users and institutional arrangements on judgment and decision making.

Potential questions for future research include how accountability created by the existence of review committees and boards of directors affects decision making. For example, does it lead to more careful processing of information, processing of more information, use of decision aids/models, or greater conservatism in decision making? Significant monetary incentives also characterize decisions in this area, due to both the amount of money involved in financial transactions and the fact that many decision makers are subject to specific incentives directly or indirectly through compensation contracts and performance evaluation practices. While studies suggest that incentives do not always improve decision-making (Ashton, 1990), future research on investors and creditors can examine how specific types of incentives affect their judgments and decisions. The existence of market settings for investment decision making provides an opportunity for examining the effect of "gaming" behavior of decision makers. For example, if professional analysts want to "beat the market," they have to predict the behavior of other market participants and take this behavior into account when making investment decisions. Future research can examine how these predictions and decisions are made and whether they are influenced by judgmental heuristics and biases.

Research on external users also has not thoroughly exploited the heterogeneity of users of financial reports. Although some studies have compared experienced decision makers to students (e.g., Abdel-khalik, 1974b; Anderson, 1988; Danos et al., 1984), more research is necessary to systematically identify differences between types of users of financial information and the effect of these differences on the efficiency and effectiveness of decision making. For example, the effect of experience on decision making could be addressed by examining the role of experience in memory processes. It is possible that memory plays a greater role in investment decisions than in auditing decisions, which is the primary arena in which memory has been studied in accounting.[22] It is likely that professional analysts do not use external memory devices, such as checklists, as much as auditors when making decisions, providing an enhanced role for internal memory. In addition, they typically have more varied experience than do auditors, since they may be involved in hundreds of investment/credit decisions within a single year, while auditors participate in only a few engagements per year. Thus, investment decisions may provide an excellent opportunity to study the effect of memory on decision making.

Future research on accounting issues. While judgment and decision-making research on investors and creditors flourished in the late 1960s and early 1970s, the lack of theory underlying much of this research and the introduction of stock price data bases resulted in a decline in this research in the late 1970s and 1980s. However, two factors have recently increased interest in judgment and decision-making research on investors. First, studies have found that market prices are influenced by systematic judgmental "errors" (Bernard and Thomas, 1990; Hand, 1990). This research has stimulated interest in the decisions of different types of investors, particularly nonprofessional investors. In addition, capital-markets research on earnings forecasts recently has started to examine issues relating to the analysts making these forecasts in order to understand better the properties of earnings forecasts. For example, Francis and Philbrick (1993) examine how analysts' forecasts are influenced by incentives, while Affleck-Graves et al. (1990) investigate whether biases in analysts' forecasts are caused by motivational or cognitive factors.[23]

Future judgment and decision-making research in accounting can further knowledge of investors' and creditors' decisions and how these decisions translate into market behavior. Judgment and decision making research may have an advantage over capital-markets research at examining "what if" types of questions, disentangling the effects of two or more factors on judgments and decisions, and examining underlying causes of findings in the capital markets literature. For example, if the Financial Accounting Standards Board is considering changing an accounting method or requiring additional disclosure, the impact of this change on investors' judgments could be studied using experimental methods. However, in order to understand "equilibrium behavior," flaws of past research indicate that future experiments should use experienced decision makers who are given sufficient practice at using the new methods or disclosures before the effects of these methods on their judgments and decisions are examined. In addition, laboratory market experiments can be coupled with individual experiments to assess the impact of the changes on market behavior.

Experimental methods also can be used to disentangle the effects of multiple factors on investors' and creditors' judgments and decisions. For example, financial analysts' forecasts of earnings are likely to be influenced by several factors, including cognitive biases, compensation arrangements, and the demands of other tasks they perform, such as making stock recommendations. Capital-markets research may be unable to examine the separate effects of individual factors since the actual forecasts used in this research are made under the influence of all factors. In contrast, experimental methods allow judgment and decision-making researchers to investigate the separate and interactive effects of factors.

Finally, judgment and decision-making research on investors can be used to examine underlying causes of findings in capital-markets research. For example, recent findings in the capital-markets literature indicate that investors may not fully incorporate the time series properties of quarterly earnings into their earnings forecasts (Bernard and Thomas, 1990). Evidence suggests that investors use earnings four quarters ago as their expectation of earnings, ignoring the quarter-to-quarter component of earnings. Research currently is in progress to determine whether this finding is due to cognitive factors, or whether institutional factors, such as the press reporting current quarterly earnings relative to quarterly earnings four quarters ago, is the cause of this finding (Hand and Maines, 1994).

Acknowledgments

I want to thank Robert Ashton and Alison Hubbard Ashton for many insightful discussions and detailed comments on this chapter. I also appreciate the comments of Joyce Berg, John Dickhaut, Michael Gibbins, John Hand, Don Kleinmuntz, Robert Libby, Kevin McCabe, William Messier, Don Moser, Patricia O'Brien, Katherine Schipper, Michael Shields, Ira Solomon, Ken Trotman, William Waller, John Willingham, and S. Mark Young. The research assistance of Daniel Wolf is greatly appreciated, as is financial support from the KPMG Peat Marwick Foundation and the Accounting Research Center at the Fuqua School of Business.

Notes

1. These sections are presented in the opposite order of the natural input–process–output sequence, since the studies on decision processes and outputs are more closely related to judgment and decision-making research than the decision–input studies.
2. See Libby and Lewis (1977), Libby (1981), Ashton (1982), Libby and Lewis (1982), Gibbins and Newton (1987), and Richardson and Gibbins (1988) for previous reviews of judgment and decision-making research in financial accounting.
3. Corporate securities include common and preferred stocks, which represent an ownership interest in a corporation, and corporate bonds, which are debt of the corporation. The discussion in this section focuses on stock investments, although it also applies to investors in corporate bonds. Individuals who rate the risk of bonds are discussed in the section on credit decisions.
4. As an example of the lens-model paradigm, assume that an investor is asked to predict the change in a stock's price over the next year (Y) using the current stock price (X_1), the average annual increase in earnings over the past five years (X_2), and dividend payments for the current year (X_3). The investor's judgment can be expressed as a linear equation, $Y = \beta_1 X_1 + \beta_2 X_2 + \beta_3 X_3 + \varepsilon$, where β_1, β_2, and β_3 represent the decision maker's weighting of each piece of information and ε is an error term. In addition to this "bootstrapping" model of human judgment, an "environmental" model can be estimated by regressing actual outcomes (e.g., actual stock price changes) on the same cues available to the decision maker. The insight conveyed by the lens model typically is summarized by correlations between pairs of variables, including r_a (the correlation between human judgment and actual outcomes), r_b (the correlation between predictions of the bootstrapping model of human judgment and actual outcomes), R_e (the correlation between predictions of the environmental model and actual outcomes), R_s (the correlation between human judgment and predictions from the bootstrapping model of human judgment), and G (the correlation between beta weights in the bootstrapping model and environmental model).
5. The fact that decisions can be approximated by linear models does not necessarily mean that decision processes are not configural. See Einhorn et al. (1979) for a discussion.
6. Camerer's review contains all lens-model studies published prior to 1981 for which sufficient information was available to calculate r_a and r_b. Three of the 15 studies in his review examined financial-accounting judgments (Libby, 1976a; Ebert and Kruse, 1978; Wright, 1979b). In this chapter, these three studies are excluded when computing lens-model statistics for Camerer's studies.
7. These statistics are based on results in Libby (1976a), Ebert and Kruse (1978), Wright (1979b), and Mear and Firth (1987b).
8. In this literature, a number of alternatives (e.g., stocks) are evaluated on several dimensions (e.g., earnings, dividends, risk) to arrive at a choice of one alternative. In the additive compensatory strategy, each alternative is separately evaluated on all dimensions to arrive at an overall "score" for that alternative. In the additive difference strategy, two alternatives are compared on each dimension and the differences between alternatives on each dimension are aggregated to arrive at the relative difference in scores. The elimination-by-aspects strategy requires a decision maker to choose a dimension and eliminate alternatives that do not possess this dimension. This process continues with other dimensions until only one alternative remains. Finally, in the conjunctive strategy, a decision maker sets certain cut-off points on each dimension, and eliminates alternatives not meeting one or more of these cut-off points.
9. Individuals who use the representativeness heuristic assess the likelihood of items belonging to a category by how similar the item is to the prototypical member of this category. For example, the probability that a certain person is an accountant would be assessed by how closely he or she resembles the image of a prototypical accountant.
10. Output interference implies that one's first thoughts about an issue inhibit later, possibly contradictory, thoughts about the issue. The availability heuristic suggests that probability judgments regarding the occurrence of an event are affected by the ease with which the event can be recalled.
11. The hindsight bias implies that actual outcomes will seem more plausible after they have occurred than prior to their occurrence, leading people in hindsight to believe that events were more predictable than they actually were in foresight.

12. Since financial statements are prepared on the basis of acquisition (historical) cost, assets and other financial statement items are shown at their original purchase price. From 1979 to 1986, large corporations were required to provide supplemental information on the current cost of certain financial statement items, such as plant and equipment. Some corporations still disclose this information voluntarily. This issue currently is being discussed again for certain balance sheet items such as marketable securities.
13. Heintz (1973) found differences in stock price predictions between the group that received both historical and current cost information and the other two groups in the early periods in his experiment. These effects greatly diminished in later periods after subjects became familiar with both sets of data.
14. See Strawser (1991) for a review of literature examining the effect of auditors' reports on users' decisions.
15. For example, there are several different depreciation methods that allocate the cost of equipment or buildings to expense over the life of the asset. The straight-line method expenses an equal amount each year, while accelerated methods expense larger amounts in early years of an asset's life, with correspondingly smaller amounts in later years.
16. One exception to this rule is the use of different inventory-valuation methods. Federal income tax regulations require that corporations that choose the last-in, first-out method of valuing inventory to determine their income tax liability also must use this method for financial reporting. In a period of inflation, the last-in, first-out method typically results in lower net income and a lower tax liability than the first-in, first-out method.
17. Different accounting methods may affect cash flows indirectly if they are used as a basis for contractual arrangements, such as compensation agreements or bond covenants, which influence the decisions and actions of management (Watts and Zimmerman, 1990).
18. Income taxes were excluded from the task in Dyckman's study so differences in stock prices cannot be attributed to the cash flow effects of these two methods.
19. The accounting literature borrowed the phrase "functional fixation" from psychological research where it was used to describe a phenomenon in which the prior use of an item in one function prevents the discovery of a different function for the object in a subsequent task. Ijiri et al. (1966) noted that a change in accounting method could cause functional fixation in accounting, since the use of the same term for an item (e.g., net income) might mask the fact that different methods were used to generate the item than were used in the past. Ashton (1976) provides an insightful discussion of how the functional fixation concept has been used in accounting to mean something very different from its original meaning in the psychology literature. For example, the original meaning of functional-fixation applied to a time series setting (use of the same object at two different periods of time), while accountants have often used it in a cross-sectional sense (comparison of two net income numbers from different companies in the same time period).
20. See Ashton and Kramer (1980) for a discussion of factors that may cause differences between decisions of student and nonstudent subjects and a review of early literature in accounting and business settings using both types of subjects. In addition, see Yates et al. (1991) for evidence showing that greater knowledge and experience does not always improve judgmental accuracy in investment decision making.
21. I thank Nick Dopuch and Jake Birnberg for these insights.
22. See R. Libby's chapter in this book (Chapter 7) and A. Ashton (1991) for discussions of the role of memory in auditing judgments.
23. See Schipper (1991) for on overview of research on financial analysts.

5

The individual versus the aggregate

Joyce Berg, John Dickhaut, and Kevin McCabe

Introduction

To what degree do individual decision biases affect aggregate behavior? This question was introduced, and "answered," in the accounting literature twenty years ago when Gonedes and Dopuch (1974) argued that market efficiency necessarily precluded any impact of individual bias on aggregate capital-market behavior (that is, price). We know now that this claim need not be true. Recent advances in both theoretical and empirical research open the door for the influence of individual bias on aggregate-level behavior in capital markets as well as other aggregate settings. Experimental methods enhance our ability to pinpoint when biases do occur, measure the cost of bias, and examine what factors extinguish biases. In this chapter, we review the historical development of the issue of individual and aggregate behavior and develop a framework to systematically advance our knowledge in this area.

Since no generally accepted theory linking individual behavior to aggregate level behavior exists, we develop a framework enumerating the observable factors that distinguish individual decision-making settings from aggregate decision-making settings. Since these factors transcend theoretical paradigms, they form the basis for dialog between those that draw theory from economics and those that draw theory from psychology. In the spirit of enhancing such a dialog, we use this framework to examine several streams of research, and begin to address how changes in observable factors affect aggregate behavior.

In examining these settings, we ask not only whether individual biases persist at the aggregate level, but also whether aggregate settings introduce "new" biases of their own.[1] We focus first on the two primary building blocks of aggregate settings: production (working together to determine the size of the output) and bargaining (deciding how joint output will be shared). Each of these can be captured in a relatively simple two-person setting, thus forming the smallest aggregate settings that we can investigate. We explore whether individual biases of illusion of control and hysteresis (a tendency to repeat past behavior) persist in a simple production setting (a two-person agency), and examine how observability of others' actions, communication, and the ability to write enforceable contracts affect these biases. In bargaining settings, we examine whether individual biases in cascaded inference appear at an aggregate level, and whether apparent "new" biases (fairness and errors in anticipation of others behavior) are robust to changes in observable characteristics such as order of play and observability. We then focus on more complex market settings, examining the impact of modifying choice sets (by introducing redundant securities) on apparent individual processing biases, the role of "anticipation" in stock market bubbles, and the role of observability in explaining the sunk-cost bias.

We conclude by focusing on ways of relating the work described here to other types of enquiry developed in this book.[2]

Historical development of the issue

Both Gonedes (1972) and Gonedes and Dopuch (1974) question the relevance of individual behavior research to aggregate market behavior. Gonedes (1972) argues that generalizing from individual to aggregate behavior is logically erroneous, stating:

> [A]chievement of a competitive solution (the establishment of competitive prices) is induced by the workings of the system as a whole, or *aggregate* market behavior, and not necessarily by individual "rationality." Rejection of this argument would seem to involve the familiar *Fallacy of Composition,* i.e., the argument that what is true for part is necessarily true for the whole. (Emphasis by Gonedes, page 17)

Gonedes and Dopuch (1974) strengthen this argument, arguing that lack of theoretical foundation coupled with the implications of capital-market efficiency lead one to conclude that individual biases cannot matter in understanding aggregate phenomena. Their paper relies heavily on the results of the time supporting capital-market efficiency, with market efficiency seen as prima facie evidence that individual biases are unimportant. They note:

> Even if these [lab/field] studies were based upon an explicit theory of resource allocation by individuals, it is still not apparent that their results would be pertinent to issues of reporting to capital market agents. To see this, consider the implications of capital market efficiency and competition in the market for information.
>
> Recall that the kind of efficient market considered there is simply a competitive market, a market within which each individual is a price-taker. Given this type of market, any generalizations made about the aggregate behavior of capital market agents on the basis of results from lab/field studies are extremely tenuous. Specifically, given an efficient capital market, studies of the behavior of particular types of investors (e.g., "average" investors or "financial analysts") are not likely to

lead to reliable generalizations about the relationship between the production of accounting information and capital market equilibrium. (pp. 105–106)

Skepticism also arose about whether processing biases should play any role in addressing policy issues such as the choice of appropriate accounting methods. Beaver (1973) argues that "the FASB must reconsider the nature of its traditional concern for the naive investor" (page 53), claiming that the naive investor is harmed not because he is naive but because firms' failures to fully disclose allow insiders to earn monopoly rents at the expense of outsiders.

These early pronouncements that information-processing studies could have nothing to say about accounting policy issues influenced research agendas. Few researchers attempted to relate information-processing studies to financial accounting issues after the Gonedes and Dopuch paper. However, Gonedes and Dopuch acknowledged that understanding individual behavior could be useful in managerial accounting and did not mention auditing and tax. Behavioral research flourished in these areas.

In retrospect, it is clear that there really was no reason for excluding these areas from the Gonedes–Dopuch critique, since all are multiperson settings and thus result in aggregate behavior that reflects the system as a whole. Yet, recent theoretical and empirical developments suggest that individual biases may affect even capital-market behavior.

Theoretical developments

The notion that market forces will eliminate individual biases predates its "discovery" in accounting literature. Frazer (1922) examines the development of magic and interprets the data as consistent with the hypothesis that poor practices die off with failure in repeated use (pp. 12–43 and 58–69). Alchian (1950) advances similar arguments in economics, describing the economy as an "adaptive" mechanism. The recent literature on evolutionary games has refined the notion of adaptivity, incorporating the idea that behavior depends on the historical fitness of strategies and modeling the rate at which certain types of behavior (strategy choices) will die out.

The claim that individual biases will not influence aggregate behavior is also supported by Ross (1976a,b) who shows that the "no unexploited arbitrage opportunities" condition leads to well-behaved prices (a linear pricing rule). Ross' arbitrage pricing theory has the appealing property that prices will be well behaved even if some agents are not "rational." Dybvig and Ross (1987) point out that "only a few rational agents are needed to bid away arbitrage opportunities, even in the presence of a sea of agents driven by 'animal spirits' " (p. 100).

However, other theorists document that the interaction of rational and quasirational (i.e., biased) agents can result in aggregate behavior that differs dramatically from fully rational equilibria. In a multiperson game-theoretic context, Kreps et al. (1982) document that cooperative solutions to a finitely repeated prisoner's dilemma game (a "nonrational" outcome) can result when rational (Nash) players believe that some portion of their opponents are not rational. Haltiwanger and Waldman (1985) demonstrate that when agents differ in their abilities to rationally form expectations, naive agents can disproportionately affect the equilibrium outcome. Perhaps more strikingly, similar results have been developed for competitive market settings. Akerlof and Yellen (1985) document that inertia (hysteresis) on the part of some market agents can significantly affect the market equilibrium while resulting in negligible losses to the "irrational" agents. Russell and Thaler (1985) show that the interaction of rational and quasirational agents in a competitive market can result in well-behaved prices that do not conform to rational-expectations equilibria.[3]

New evidence from capital markets

One of the greatest potential challenges to the position that information-processing biases cannot affect aggregate behavior has evolved from the literature on price anomalies in the capital market (see for example, Abarbanell and Bernard, 1992; DeBondt and Thaler, 1985, 1987, 1990; Bernard and Thomas, 1989; and Hand, 1990).[4] DeBondt and Thaler (1985) examine the hypothesis that individuals do not approximately use Bayes' theorem and consequently the market overreacts by overvaluing winners and undervaluing losers; this overreaction is reflected in lower returns for the winning portfolios and higher returns for the losing portfolios in later periods. Forming portfolios of New York Stock Exchange (NYSE) extreme performers (winners and losers) in a base period and examining the performance of such winners and losers in later periods, they document a returns effect consistent with the hypothesis. DeBondt and Thaler (1987) extend the study to show that these effects cannot be attributable to tax effects, size effects, or beta shifts (changes in risk).

Several studies have begun to ask whether biases can be detected in the behavior of decision makers who might not be price takers in the market. Lakonishok et al. (1991), examining the behavior of pension fund managers, conclude that fund managers appear to engage in window dressing, selling extreme poor performance stocks disproportionately, particularly in December.[5] DeBondt and Thaler (1990) study analysts' earnings forecasts, asking whether these forecasts are unbiased. They find that the relationships between forecasted changes in earnings and actual changes in earnings are too extreme.[6]

These empirical studies suggest that particular aggregate anomalies are consistent with failures of individual rationality. However, we get no real feel for the interplay of those biases as they are reflected in market prices, since the methodology does not allow us to examine the interplay of individual bias and market price behavior. To date we are in the position that Vernon

Smith has described as "trying to deduce the laws of electricity by listening to the radio play" (Smith, 1982, quote attributed to Guy Orcutt).

The role of experimental economics methodology

Experimental economics methodology overcomes this problem. In a laboratory economy, one can create a well-controlled aggregate setting and manipulate exogenous attributes of the setting, turning the "dials" to determine which factors eliminate, exacerbate, or create bias at the aggregate level.[7] One can even estimate the cost of the bias.[8] And, perhaps most importantly, in experimental economies one can directly observe the interplay of the individual and the aggregate.[9]

We now know that it is possible to generate anomalies in the laboratory that mimic phenomena we observe in real-world settings. Smith et al. (1988) document laboratory bubble–crashes (price above fundamental value, followed by sudden price drops) and Camerer and Weigelt (1991) document information mirages (price behaving as if information were released when it was not) in rather straightforward laboratory settings. Such failures of market efficiency are of interest to accountants, since they suggest a role for regulation (possibly disclosure or accounting policy) in an attempt to eliminate bubbles.

Lundholm (1991) also documents failures of market efficiency in an experimental market setting. He demonstrates that when traders are individually uncertain but aggregately certain about the state, market prices behave roughly the same as if the state were publicly revealed. However, when there is residual aggregate uncertainty about the state, prices do not behave in the same way as when the uncertain information is publicly revealed.

Forsythe et al. (1992) attempt to trace individual behavior to market-level phenomenon using their Iowa Political Stock Market technology (a market in which contract payoffs are determined by political election outcomes). They find that although many individuals appear to be biased (for instance, buying more Republicans at every price), these individuals do not appear to influence market price. Thus, in this market, while traders on average are biased, bias does not appear at the margin.

Exogenous environmental attributes and endogenous behavioral dynamics

Exogenous environmental attributes of aggregate settings

As a precursor to building a theory of how individual biases affect aggregate behavior, we specify *observable* exogenous environmental attributes that are present only in multiperson settings. Not only does the presence or absence of these factors differentiate multiperson from single-person settings, but the level of these factors also differentiates multiperson settings from one another. Since these attributes distinguish multiperson settings from individual decision-making settings, it logically follows that one or more of these factors must determine whether individual biases are manifested at the aggregate level. These attributes are: (1) multiple players, (2) payoff interdependency, (3) observability of others, (4) communication, (5) contracting, (6) order of play, and (7) differences in choice sets.

Multiple players. In aggregate settings, there must be more than one person. This number can vary dramatically, from simple two-person bargaining settings to large competitive markets. Early arguments about the relevance of individual biases for aggregate behavior hinge on the number of players being very large, so that each player is an atomistic part of the market and therefore a price taker. Recent theoretical work in economics has refined this idea by asking how many players it takes for markets to be competitive (Gresik and Satterthwaite, 1989).

The number of players differentiates monopoly, oligopoly, and competitive-market explanations of economic behavior. Work in experimental economics has documented that the interaction of this factor with order of play can result in strikingly different behavior. For instance, monopoly suppliers can only extract monopoly rents when the monopolist sets prices; when buyers set prices or double auctions are used to trade, the monopolist earns only competitive-equilibrium profits (Smith, 1981).

Differences in the choice sets. In aggregate settings, different players may have different roles. Such roles determine the choice sets and information sets available to each player. For instance, in a market such as the NYSE, the specialist has the right to set spreads and observe the order book; no other trader in the market has these privileges. In experimental markets, one can manipulate the degree to which these privileges are private to the specialist.

One can also manipulate the degree to which a player experiences other's choice sets. This can vary from no experience whatsoever, to reading about other's choices, to actually changing roles as the experiment progresses. Such manipulation would be manipulations of observability as defined below.

Payoff interdependency. In aggregate settings, one's payoffs can be dependent on the actions of others as well as one's own actions. Such interdependency has two dimensions: size of the effect and influence on one's strategy. When the number of players is small and output is defined by a joint production function, changes in others' actions can significantly affect one's share of the output. In other settings, such as large market settings, the effect of one person's actions on another's outcome may be negligible. Payoff interdependency can also be measured by the effect of one player's actions on another player's best course of action (strategy). A player's best course of action can be independent of others' strategies, so that while payoffs may vary with the others' actions, one's own best action choice does not depend on anyone else's (for example, the auditor always reconciles bank accounts, regardless of his beliefs about the auditee's honesty). Alternatively, best strategies can depend on what others do, so that knowing someone else's action could affect one's own action choice (for example, knowing that fraud took place, the auditor would extend his sample).

Observability of others' actions or information. In aggregate settings, there can be knowledge about the characteristics, information sets, and actions of other individuals. This might be minimal information, such as seeing the joint outcome of one's own actions together with all other actions (for example, a single market-clearing price), or more extensive information such as each person's individual characteristics, payoffs, bids, and offers. In economic models, information asymmetry (a condition in which one person has decision-relevant information that another cannot observe) is a crucial factor in determining behavior.

Feedback about the desirability of one's own actions is frequently confounded with the move to multiperson settings. These changes in the frequency or content of feedback can be isolated and manipulated independently of the multiperson setting to determine whether feedback difference alone can eliminate decision-making biases.

Communication. In aggregate settings, people can communicate. This communication can range from unverifiable and unenforceable statements to enforceable promises. Such messages are actions which in themselves do not directly affect outcomes; for example, a profit report that, except for a small out of pocket cost, does not directly affect the future cash flows of the company. However, the message can have an effect if it makes new actions available or if people take different actions based on the messages and those actions alter outcomes.

Contracting. In aggregate settings, people can enter into enforceable contracts with one another. These contracts can vary from simple agreements that involve sharing the output in a bargaining setting or delivering the object traded in an auction to rather extensive contingencies in insurance and production settings.

Order of play. In aggregate settings, participants may act at different times. This order of play could affect aggregate outcomes and hence whether individual biases are manifested at the aggregate level. Order of play may be an object of choice, such as the agenda for a meeting; while in other aggregate settings, order of play (such the ith player in an n-member game of Russian roulette) may affect the set of possible outcomes for the ith player.

Endogenous behavioral dynamics

We use the terms "dynamic" and "force" to designate proposed causal links between the exogenous environmental attributes of a setting and an individual's behavior within that setting. While such links may eventually prove to be erroneous, they serve as loose bases for organizing data. For example, notions of attraction existed prior to Galileo and Newton and, although incomplete, served as a basis for communicating ideas about the physical world.

Forces tend to be paradigm specific. When examining individual behavior, some social scientists might invoke forces such as attention and memory, while others invoke tastes and rationality. Forces particular to aggregate settings include but are not limited to anticipation of others' actions, conflict of interest, norms of behavior, and followership. These dynamics usually presume some complex web of unobservable features. For example, conflict of interest implies some notion of preferences, while followership and anticipation suggest a notion of common expectation, common goal, or common purpose. Norms of behavior include such phenomena as fairness and implicit rules of group behavior. While these forces themselves are not directly measurable or observable, they often serve as a basis for thinking about how we see particular institutions, and can be a basis for designing research to explore such institutions.

A move beyond a loose specification of forces to a specification of the dynamics of how exogenous environmental attributes give rise to particular phenomena is what we have in mind by "theory." Thus, a theory about how information-processing considerations are reflected in aggregate behavior must invoke one or more exogenous environmental attributes present in the aggregate (but not the individual) setting. For example, early attempts to explain why intransitivity of preference, observed at the individual level, would not be manifested in market settings assumed that markets made it possible to write contracts on the revealed preferences and therefore arbitrage intransitivities. This special feature of aggregate settings, the ability to enter into enforceable contracts, is crucial in making the arbitrage argument. Presumably, settings which do not admit such contracts would not eliminate intransitivity.

Claims that a market can discipline behavior through arbitrage or competitive forces (both endogenous dynamics) depend on one or more of the attributes that distinguish multiperson settings. Arbitrage depends on the ability to write enforceable contracts (attribute 5) and the ability to observe the arbitragee's choices (attribute 3). Market competitiveness depends on the number of players (attribute 1), observability of others' actions (attribute 3), and ability to send messages (attribute 4) in the form of acceptable prices. Similarly, the argument that people tend to hang onto losers (the sunk-cost phenomenon) not because of some underlying information-processing bias, but because of reputation effects, presumes an order of play (attribute 6), as well as some interdependency of payoffs (attribute 2).

In the rest of this chapter, we examine several streams of experimental research that bear on the role of individual bias in aggregate behavior. We explore whether illusion of control bias persists when enforceable contracts can be written on controllable and uncontrollable variables; the degree to which order of play and observability affect backward induction; and the degree to which failure of observability explains the sunk-cost phenomenon as compared with a psychologically based interpretation. In addition to examining whether certain biases persist in an aggregate setting, we also examine whether "biases" arise that are unique to aggregate settings. In our discussion of bargaining, we explore the role of fairness (a behavioral dynamic) in determining behavior in these settings. In our examination of market bubbles, we ask if followership (another behavioral dynamic) might account for these laboratory bubbles.

Production environments

Most settings of interest to accountants include a decentralized productive activity: an asset or action is entrusted to another with the understanding that it will be used to increase the output available for the parties to share. Such production environments introduce problems of coordination, control, and performance measurement. For instance, a publicly held corporation is a productive environment in which shareholders have delegated decisions on the day-to-day operation of the firm to professional managers. While the quality of the managers' performance affects the shareholders' welfare, shareholders cannot directly control or observe this quality.

Such unobservability poses no problem when the shareholders and the manager have identical goals.[10] However, while the shareholders can diversify their investment among many firms, the manager cannot, since much of his or her human capital is tied directly to the firm. Thus, preferences over particular courses of action that the firm could take will diverge. But, shareholders are not entirely helpless in the face of this conflict of interest. They have the ability to write enforceable contracts designating how the output of the firm will be shared. These contracts can be written on anything jointly observable and can be structured to influence the manager's behavior. The issue in these settings is how contracts are structured to most efficiently align the goals of the parties. A second issue – how gains to trade are apportioned among participants – is generally not addressed; one party (generally called the principal) is designated the residual claimant, while all others (the agents) receive exactly their market wage.[11]

Example

You and a colleague have decided to jointly purchase a house as an investment property, which you intend to hold for several years and then sell. You will provide most of the capital to purchase the house. Your colleague will reside in the house and provide both the funds and the effort to maintain it. You both know that while the final selling price of the house depends on economic factors beyond your control, the price is likely to be higher if the house is well maintained. How should you contract to split the proceeds of the house? Should you offer to pay your colleague a flat fee, a percentage of the selling price, or condition the split of profits on a local housing index?[12]

What exogenous environmental attributes distinguish this setting from a single-person decision-making setting? There are two players (attribute 1). The players have different choice sets (attribute 7): you choose the sharing rule, subject to your colleague's acceptance, and your colleague chooses the level of maintenance to provide. Payoffs are interdependent: you benefit from your colleague's residing in the house and maintaining it, and your colleague benefits from your contribution of capital (attribute 2). Some things are not observable to both parties: your colleague knows the care with which the house is maintained and whether selling price would have been higher had he conformed to your expectations about care, while you observe only the ultimate selling price (attribute 3). While you and your colleague will undoubtedly negotiate before reaching a contract, once the contract is signed very little other communication will take place (attribute 4). The profit sharing rule can be based on only jointly observable characteristics and forms an enforceable contract (attribute 5). Finally, there is an implicit order of play: your colleague moves last, maintaining the house knowing the profit sharing arrangement (attribute 6).

Theoretical overview

As Wolfson (1985b) points out, agency theory provides a theoretical framework for examining this setting. In the basic agency setting, the principal owns the right to a valuable production technology, and the agent supplies the input to this technology (his effort); neither party can generate output acting alone. Both parties are self-interested, meaning that they wish to maximize their own welfare. There is a conflict of interest: the principal, bearing none of the cost of effort, would prefer that the agent work as hard as possible; however, the agent, bearing the entire cost of the effort, will trade off his increased output share against the cost of his effort. Moreover, the agent's action cannot be perfectly observed by the principal either directly or indirectly through output; output, while correlated with action, is stochastic.

The sequence of events in this setting is as follows:

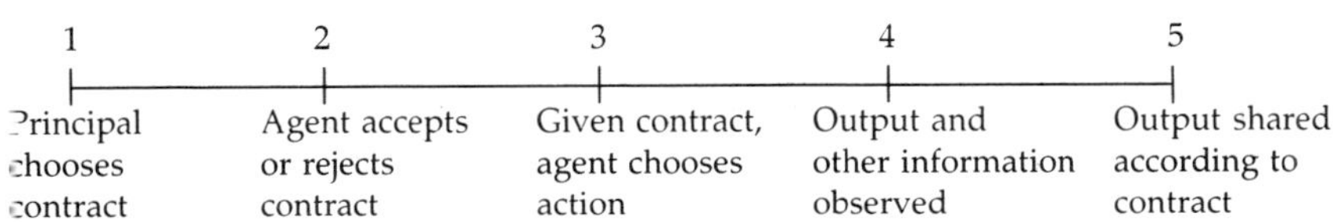

This setting consists of two major components: a contract-agreement stage in which one party (the principal) offers a contract and the other party (the agent) decides whether to accept or reject this contract (such a two-stage sequence is termed an "ultimatum game" in the economics literature), followed by a contract-fulfillment stage in which the agent chooses an action that influences the size of the output available to share. The economic solution to this problem is built on the concepts of self-interest and anticipation: in choosing their own actions, each party anticipates the other's actions based on the belief that others will act in their own self-interest. Formally, this anticipation process is termed "backward induction."[13] Applying backward induction to the basic agency setting, we see that once the contract has been accepted, the agent will choose the action that maximizes the agent's welfare conditional on the contract. Stepping backward, the agent, looking ahead to his own behavior, will decide whether or not to accept the contract. Stepping backward once more, the principal, looking ahead to the agent's behavior, will decide which contract maximizes the principal's welfare given the agent's behavior.

The general theoretical results are: (1) there is a deadweight loss associated with unobservability of action, and (2) any observable variable that contains information about the agent's action will decrease this deadweight loss and thus be valuable in contracting.[14] This second result means that even signals that are uncontrollable in an accounting sense (those where the manager's actions do not influence the distribution of the signal) can be valuable in contracting. In particular, when output is determined by both the manager's effort and some underlying economic condition, indices that reveal something about the underlying economic condition will be valuable even though they are not controllable.

In the example above, since the resident owner's action is unobservable, a flat-wage contract will provide no incentive to maintain the home. However, the resident can be motivated to maintain the home through an incentive contract that shares selling price between the resident and nonresident owners. Placing this selling price risk on the resident-owner provides incentive, but when the resident-owner is risk-averse it results in a deadweight loss: if costless perfect monitoring were available, both parties would be better off; since it is not, a second-best (risk-sharing) contract must be used. But, what risk-sharing contract? Both the resident's maintenance and the general price level for homes in the area will determine the selling price of the home. Thus, a local housing index, which reveals something about the general economic conditions influencing housing prices, is informative and should be written into the contract.

Recall that these conclusions are based on the behavioral forces of self-interest and backward induction. Other behavioral forces result in different predictions. For example, either unselfish devotion to the principal (altruism) or an ingrained work ethic would mitigate the problem of unobservability and reduce the deadweight loss; in the extreme, either of these forces would eliminate the conflict of interest and a flat-wage contract could be used in place of the second-best, risk-sharing contract. Under these conditions, there would be no need to contract on a housing index as in our example. Similarly, reputation (a behavioral force arising in a multiperiod setting) could also lead to a reduction in deadweight loss and less reliance on housing indices.

Evidence

Evidence from archival data about the predictive power of the agency model is mixed. Wolfson (1985a) finds evidence that contracts are written to mitigate the effect of unobservability in oil and gas tax shelters. However, Antle and Smith (1986) find only weak evidence that relative performance evaluation (that is, the incorporation of indices in contracts) is used in upper-management contracts, and Wolfson (1985b), investigating the shared housing contract described in the example, finds that local housing indices are *not* incorporated in the contracts. However, since these studies are conducted using real-world data, none can control for other variables that, according to the agency model, may legitimately counteract the importance of indices. Inability to control for important confounding variables precludes determining whether these results indicate behavioral departures from the agency model.

Experimental studies provide a means for controlling the environment well enough so that we can pinpoint when and why the agency predictions break down. The statistical relationships between signals and action are known to the experimenter and the set of available contracts can also be specified. The experimenter can even use a lottery reward mechanism that allows one to control for risk preferences (Berg et al., 1986).[15]

Berg et al. (1992) construct an experimental environment to investigate the predictive validity of the agency model. In these experiments, the ultimatum game aspect of contract selection is suppressed so that agents do not have the opportunity to reject contracts that meet their market wage. This allows the authors to examine the predictions of the agency model most closely related to production without confounding the investigation by introducing bargaining issues. They document that there is, in fact, a deadweight loss associated with unobservability of action, and that principals not only contract on output but do so in the most efficient manner available.[16] Backward induction appears to work quite well in these experiments. Principals anticipate the moral-hazard problem when it exists and contract around it. Whether or not backward induction will be successful when the ultimatum game aspect of the decision (that is, the accept/reject contract decision) is introduced is an open issue. As we will see in the next section of this chapter, backward induction breaks down in some ultimatum games; this may carry over to the agency setting as well.[17]

Varying observability. Berg et al. (1992) manipulate whether or not the principal can observe the agent's action. When action is observable, principals offer agents flat-wage (forcing) contracts (that is, a contract in which the agent only gets paid if the agent is observed to be working hard) and agents choose to work hard. This result is consistent both with the conjecture that the agent works hard because it is in his or her self-interest and with the conjecture that the agent's behavior is driven by altruism or work ethic. When action is not observable, however, principals do not offer the flat-wage contract, even though this contract results in the highest payoff to the principal if the agent chooses to work hard. These experiments provide evidence that self-interest, not altruism or work ethic, drive behavior in agency settings. If agents were altruistic when faced with the flat-wage contract, the agent could be no worse off than with any other contract available, and the principal would be better off. Yet, principals choose the flat-wage contract only when action is observable. In fact, in the few cases where principals experiment with a flat-wage contract in the unobservable action setting, agents shirk (acting in their own self-interest).

Berg et al. (1992) also investigate whether these results depend on the principal having direct experience with the agent's choice set. They conclude that they do not. Regardless of whether principals learn about the agent's choice set through reading about them or through direct experience, principals offer incentive contracts rather than flat-wage contracts when action is not observable.

Varying communication. The experiments described in Berg et al. (1992) do not incorporate any explicit communication between the agent and the principal; the principal does not explicitly tell the agent which action the principal prefers, nor does the agent make any claim about which action has been taken. If such communication were in place, social norms against misrepresentation (such as "fairness" or honesty) could mitigate self-interest. Baiman and Lewis (1989) investigate whether agents communicate opportunistically (i.e., act in their own self-interest) or whether they are reluctant to explicitly lie. In those experiments, subjects all play the role of agents and are asked to choose between three "employers": one offering a choice between two output-based contracts, one offering an output-based contract and requesting a specific agent type (so that the subject must misrepresent its type if this contract is chosen), and one offering a flat-wage contract. While subjects appear reluctant to misrepresent their type (i.e., they prefer to be truthful when the cost of honesty is negligible), introducing a small monetary advantage ($0.25) to misrepresentation induces that behavior. The authors conclude that communication-based and noncommunication-based contracts that are strategically (i.e., economically) equivalent are also behaviorly equivalent when agents are faced with nontrivial incentives to communicate opportunistically.

This result is also supported in Berg, Daley, Gigler and Kanodia (1990). In that paper, the authors examine the role of communication when principals can choose to contract on information reported to them by the agent.[18] Two sets of experiments are presented to examine whether subjects honestly report information regardless of the incentive to do so or whether truthful communication is contingent on incentive contracting. In the first set of experiments, agents' behavior is as predicted by theory, but contract choice (by the principal) is indistinguishable from random behavior. However, when payoffs are increased so that the loss associated with suboptimal contract choice is increased, subjects tend to choose contracts consistent with the agency model. There is some evidence that contract choice as a principal is conditioned on the subject's behavior in earlier stages of the experiment where they acted as agents. In particular, subjects that did not choose the predicted action in a single-person decision-making setting did not choose the predicted contract in a multiperson decision-making setting.

Varying contracting possibilities. Berg (1990) examines the interaction of controllability, prior experience, and informativeness in contracting. Three experiments are conducted: a benchmark that examines whether informative public signals are used as predicted by the agency model, a manipulation that isolates the impact of controllability, and a manipulation that isolates the effect of prior experience with a signal (a status-quo effect). All other features of the environment, including the subject pool and the reward mechanism, are held constant across experiments.

Controllability and prior experience significantly influence contractual choices in these simple settings. Observed behavior conforms to the predictions of the model only when the distribution of the signal depends on the agent's action (that is, the signal is controllable in the accounting sense) and the principal has no prior experience in which single-variable contracts are most profitable. In these settings, subjects appear to fully utilize nonredundant information. However, certain characteristics of the setting weaken the predictive ability of the agency model. When the signal is uncontrollable, the predictive ability of the informativeness criterion is seriously dampened: the signal tends not to be incorporated in the contracts. This result is the multiperson counterpart of the illusion of control bias reported in single-person decision-making studies (Langer, 1982).

When subjects have specific prior experience in which single-variable contracts are optimal, subsequent choices are biased toward single-variable contracts even though economic theory predicts that both output and index should be incorporated into the contract. This effect is a multiperson counterpart of framing effects documented in single-person decision-making settings (Tversky and Kahneman, 1987; Tversky and Sattath, 1979) and is consistent with subjects underutilizing nonredundant information (as reported in Schum and Martin, 1982 and suggested by data presented in Maines, 1990).

In addition to demonstrating that processing biases documented at the individual level extend to contracting biases at a multiperson level, these results reconcile apparent contradictions among evidence used to examine the predictive ability of the agency model. Experimental studies seem to provide strong support for the agency model. However, these experiments examine settings in which informative signals are also controllable (Berg, Daley, Dickhaut, and O'Brien, 1990; Berg, Daley, Gigler, and Kanodia, 1990). Similarly, Wolfson (1985a) reports relatively strong support for the agency model in a real-world tax shelter setting. However, Antle and Smith (1986), Wolfson (1985b), and Janakiraman et al. (1992) report weak support, at best, in examinations of naturally occurring settings in which the signals are uncontrollable and likely to have become available after some initial experience with contracting. These are precisely the characteristics that were found to compromise the performance of the informativeness criterion in the experiments discussed above.

Sequential bargaining environments

While production environments focus on how the size of the "pie" is determined, bargaining settings focus on the negotiation process that determines how participants will *share* a predetermined pie. Even organized markets such as the NYSE involve bargaining: bids and offers must converge to a trading price, and large block trades are completed off the floor in the "upstairs market," a network of trading desks that communicate electronically (see Schwartz, 1988).

> *Example*
>
> *A hardware store has been selling snow shovels for $15. During the night there is a large snowstorm, and customers are streaming into the store to buy snow shovels. Both the owner of the hardware store and the customers know that there are not enough snow shovels to meet demand, and that the fine for not shoveling the snow is $100. The owner needs to decide how to price the remaining snow shovels. What will he decide.*[19]

How are the seven exogenous factors that distinguish multiperson settings expressed in this setting? There are many players (attribute 1). The players have different choice sets (attribute 7): the owner chooses a price to post and the customers choose whether or not to buy. Payoffs are interdependent, since the hardware store's profit depends on the price charged and the number of buyers, whereas the buyers' disposable wealth depends on the amount spent on a snow shovel (attribute 2). Both the hardware store and the customers know each other's values for the shovels (attribute 3). No direct communication between the customer and the owner can take place; the customer can only accept or reject the owner's posted price (attribute 4). The owner's posted price forms the basis of an enforceable contract between the owner and the customer (attribute 5). Finally, the owner moves first by posting a price (attribute 6).

Theoretical overview

Conceptually, the snow shovel scenario can be modeled as a two-person sequential bargaining game. Economically, these are games in which the players must decide how to split a sum of money, bargaining takes place through a series of offers and counteroffers, and players are assumed to act rationally in their own self-interest (Stahl, 1972; Rubenstein, 1982). The ultimatum game, a special case with only one offer, most closely resembles our scenario. In this game, one player makes a proposal (how to split the money), and the other either accepts or rejects the proposal; no further negotiation takes place. The Stahl–Rubenstein model predicts that in the snow shovel scenario, the owner will post a price of $99.99. This prediction is attained through backward induction: both the owner and the customer know that paying $99.99 for the shovel is better than paying the $100 fine, and the owner, moving first, takes this into consideration.[20]

But, will players reach this solution? Behavior in the principal–agent experiments described above suggest that they will; in those experiments, the principal anticipated the agent's action and the agent acted in his own self-interest when choosing action. However, the ability to move to the end of the game and work backward through the tree is similar in procedure to multistage inference, where subjects must move to the end of a probability tree and correctly integrate backward. Since evidence exists that individual biases exist in multistage inference,[21] we may see similar failures of "rationality" in the sequential bargaining setting. Moreover, behavioral dynamics such as fairness and/or anticipation may cause failures in backward induction.

Evidence

A considerable number of experiments document just such "biases" and there is a well-developed literature attempting to pinpoint the causes of these distortions. Guth et al. (1982) study ultimatum bargaining using laboratory experiments. In these experiments, students were randomly assigned the role of first mover (player 1) or acceptor/rejector (player 2) and were randomly paired with an opposite type. Recall that the prediction in this setting is a proposal by player 1 to keep 99% of the reward and give 1% to player 2, and player 2 accepting this arrangement. With inexperienced subjects, the mean first round proposal was 65% for player 1, 35% for player 2; two of the 21 proposals were rejected by player 2. A week later, subjects played the game a second time, repeating their roles from the previous experiment. The mean proposal by these experienced subjects was 69% for player 1, 31% for player 2, with 5 of the 21 proposals rejected by player 2. Players do not behave as Stahl-Rubenstein predicts. Player 1 generally offers player 2 a share larger than 1%, and though there appears to be a first-mover advantage, proposals are much closer to a 50–50 split than the 99–1 split predicted by the economic model. Guth et al. conclude: "Our experimental results show that in actual life . . . subjects often rely on what they consider a fair or justified result. Furthermore, the ultimatum aspect cannot be completely exploited since subjects do not hesitate to punish if their opponents ask for 'too much'."

Prasnikar and Roth (1992) examine whether additional experience will lead to more extreme splits. Their results suggest that repeated observations are likely to lead to an even greater uniformity of offers around equal split.

Forsythe et al. (1989) attempt to disentangle "anticipation that player 2 might reject" from "fairness" – two forces hypothesized to drive observed behavior. They compare behavior in the ultimatum game to behavior in a game where player 1 simply determines the split (this game is termed the "dictator game"). Since player 2 does not get the chance to accept or reject, the dictator game controls for player 1's anticipation of player 2's actions. If, on the other hand, players have a preference for fair outcomes, then we would expect to see the same distribution of proposals in both games.

Forsythe et al. find that players 1 kept more on average in the dictator games than in the ultimatum games, and conclude that "the distribution of proposals in the ultimatum game cannot be fully explained by a taste for fairness among proposers" (p. 23). Roth (1991) notes, however, that one cannot eliminate anticipation as a force based only on these data. One still observes a concentration of equal splits in the dictator games and this is consistent with some subjects having a taste for fairness. If this is the case, then the existence of "fair-minded" players must be part of the expectations of all subjects, and the anticipation of fair players punishing unfair players can explain the tendency for fair offers in ultimatum games.

Hoffman et al. (1992) attempt to isolate the "fairness force" by requiring subjects to participate in a contest to assign the right to move first. Subjects were told that the winners of the contest had earned the right to this "definite advantage."[22] The contest entitlement did have a significant impact on offers, moving them closer to the Stahl–Rubenstein prediction. The authors conclude that the tendency toward equal splits is a result of anticipation, rather than a preference for equity.[23]

Varying observability. Binmore et al. (1985) also find that when subjects are inexperienced, the modal first-round proposal is an equal split. However, when subjects participate in a second game in which roles are switched (players 2 now act as players 1) the modal proposals are close to the predicted split. Thus, direct experience with player 2's choice set seems to matter.[24]

Harrison and McCabe (1992a) examine whether the ability to observe player 2's rejection rules, without explicitly playing the role of player 2, affects behavior in ultimatum bargaining. In their experiments, player 2 submits a minimum acceptable offer before seeing player 1's proposal. Both players know that this minimum acceptable offer will be used to determine whether player 1's proposal is accepted. In baseline experiments, where subjects see only their own choices, behavior is consistent with previous experimental results: there are a large number of near-equal splits and players 2 often reject offers that the theory predicts they should accept. However, when subjects observe both their own bargaining outcomes and the distribution of acceptable offers submitted by player 2, offers and accept/reject behavior converge toward the Stahl–Rubenstein prediction. Thus, increasing observability facilitates backward induction.

Harrison and McCabe (1992a) interpret the movement in acceptable offers as "free riding" by player 2: when player 2 observes that other players 2 are punishing asymmetric offers by players 1, he or she begins to act in myopic self interest, reducing the minimum acceptable amount so as to be more likely to consummate a trade. Other behavioral dynamics, such as followership, also account for the change in player 2 behavior. Player 2, observing that other players 2 reported lower minimum acceptable offers might mimic this behavior by lowering his or her own minimum acceptable offer. Data about individual behavior could be used to help disentangle which of these forces best explain the data. Followership suggests that a player 2 would be most likely to "follow" after seeing that his or her own strategy failed, whereas free-riding suggests that even players 2 with "winning" strategies would reduce their minimum acceptable offers in subsequent trials.

Hoffman et al. (1992) examine the impact of another type of observability: the ability of the experimenter to observe individual subjects' behavior. In other bargaining experiments, even though subjects were anonymous to one another, the experimenter could identify individual behavior. Hoffman et al. hypothesize that subjects, anticipating that their participation in future experiments depends on their behavior in the current experiment, modify their behavior. To test this hypothesis, they conduct a "double blind" dictator game (a game like the ultimatum game but in which player 2 has no choice but to accept), which guarantees the experimenter cannot observe individual's decisions. In these new experiments, only 2 of 36 splits were equal splits and 30 of the dictators either took everything or left the minimum possible.

Varying the order of play. The Stahl–Rubenstein model predicts outcomes in longer bargaining games where players make sequential counteroffers. An example of such a game is depicted in Table 1. In this example, there is a sequence of four offers – the first and third offers made by player 1 and the second and fourth offers made by player 2. The shrinking "pie" in subsequent rounds captures the idea that time is valuable, so that agreements that take longer are less valuable. Note that any split that is agreed upon in later rounds can be exceeded by agreeing earlier. For example, a round 2 agreement in which players agree to give player 1 $30 and player 2 $20 is dom-

Table 1. *Four-round bargaining game – backward induction predictions*

Round	Money	Proposal by:	Player 1 share	Player 2 share
1	$100	Player 1	$74	$26
2	$50	Player 2	$25	$25
3	$25	Player 1	$24	$1
4	$0	Player 2	$0	$0

inated by a round 1 agreement in which player 1 receives $55 and player 2 receives $45.[25]

The Stahl–Rubenstein model asserts that players will use backward induction and solve the problem as follows. If the game continues to round 4, each player receives $0. Now step backward one round. If the game continues to round 3, player 1 makes an offer knowing that the best player 2 can do by rejecting the offer is $0. Thus, player 1 need only offer $1 to player 2 and player 2, looking ahead, should accept. In round 2, player 2 must make an offer. Anticipating what will happen in round 3, player 2 will offer to keep $25 and give $25 to player 1, since this is better than the $24 player 1 can attain by waiting. Player 1, looking ahead, should accept. Finally, in round 1, player 1 must offer at least $26 to player 2 in order to entice player 2 to accept the offer. Player 2, anticipating how the future will unfold, should accept such an offer. Thus, the Stahl–Rubenstein solution to this problem is agreement in round 1, with player 1 receiving $74 and player 2 receiving $26.

Neelin et al. (1988) examine 2-round, 3-round, and 5-round games in which players do not change roles.[26] Data from the 2-round games is consistent with backward induction.[27] However, backward induction fails to predict behavior in 3-and 5-round games. Neelin et al. observe that the apparent theoretical fit in 2-round games may be an artifact of the experimental design: in 3- and 5-round games, first proposals tended to be the amount to which the pie would shrink if the game moved to the second round. Since this is also the predicted proposal in a 2-round game, behavior may be a manifestation of the rule "offer the second-round amount" and not a manifestation of backward induction.

Harrison and McCabe (1992a) observe that the incentive to agree to first-round proposals gives subjects little experience with later rounds of the bargaining game. They examine whether such experience affects behavior, by conducting an experiment in which subjects alternate between a three-round game and the imbedded subgame (the final two rounds of this three-round game). Subjects did not change roles during the experiment, but they were randomly repaired each period in order to minimize reputation effects (a possible endogenous force). In these experiments, behavior converges to the backward-induction prediction.

Johnson et al. (1991) use a process-tracing methodology to investigate whether observed failures to arrive at the Stahl–Rubenstein prediction could be attributed to individual processing biases.[28] In addition to observing proposals and accept/reject decisions, this methodology allows the researcher to track the sequence in which decision makers consider information about the amount of money to be split in each round. Results suggest that when subjects concentrate their attention on first-round payoffs, accepted proposals are near-equal splits. However, when subjects are trained in backward induction, they consider more information and do so in sequences consistent with backward induction; in this case, proposals and accept/reject decisions move toward the predicted split.

Market settings: Are markets informationally efficient?

Much capital-market research in accounting and finance has investigated whether markets are informationally efficient. And much of the accounting policy debate focuses on ways to improve market efficiency. Unfortunately, tests designed with real-world capital-markets data may not be powerful enough to detect inefficiencies. These tests focus on whether securities are priced right relative to one another, not whether they are priced right relative to each security's fundamental (intrinsic) value.

Example

You have been following the stock of a firm that has recently gone public. Several months ago, a great deal of "good" news was released on this company's product, causing prices to move up. Since then, the predictions made in the "good" news have not occurred but the price of the stock has continued to rise. You have been buying the stock all along and it has just risen above your estimate of its expected value. Analysts are still saying this is a good buy and it looks like the price could still rise significantly over at least the next six months. What should you do?

Theoretical background

Informational efficiency implies that all information available to market participants is impounded in price so that securities are "priced right" relative to their intrinsic value and risk. Only insiders could develop beneficial trading strategies based on their private information. However, as we have discussed above, recent theoretical advances suggest the possibility of securities trading at something other than fundamental value. These explanations seem to be reflected in anecdotes about trading behavior – many market traders claim that there is a market "psychology" that can lead to "bear" or "bull" markets independent of intrinsic value.

Evidence

A number of experimental studies, beginning with the work of Forsythe et al. (1982) and Plott and Sunder (1988), explore the informational efficiency of the market. Plott and Sunder examine the degree to which price conveys information when traders are differentially informed. They establish that it is possible to attain a rational expectations equilibrium in some settings, but not all. In particular, difficulties arise when residual state uncertainty exists, that is, when information eliminates some states but the underlying state is not known for sure. Lundholm (1991) explores this failure of market efficiency, demonstrating that when traders are individually uncertain but aggregately certain about the state, market prices behave roughly the same as if the state were publicly revealed. However, when there is residual aggregate uncertainty about the state, prices do not behave in the same way as when the uncertain information is publicly revealed.

Three strands of experimental research have documented systematic departures from intrinsic value. O'Brien and Srivastava (1990, 1993) document that while relative prices are correct, securities are not priced right relative to fundamentals. Smith et al. (1988) document laboratory bubble–crashes (price above fundamental value, followed by sudden price drops), and Camerer and Weigelt (1991) document information mirages (price behaving as if information were released when it was not).

Varying observability of others actions. Smith et al. (1988) study a double-auction market where long-lived assets with a commonly known probability distribution over future dividends are traded. The intrinsic value of the asset in any period is the expected dividend return for the remaining periods. In each period, subjects could either buy shares (paying cash), or sell shares (in return for cash); at the end of the experiment, subjects were paid their initial cash endowments, plus dividend earnings, plus capital gains, minus any capital loses. Typically, in an experiment such as this with inexperienced subjects, prices start below intrinsic value, quickly rise above intrinsic value (a bubble), and then stay above intrinsic value until late in the experiment when a crash occurs followed by trading (at a greatly reduced volume) near intrinsic value.

Why do these price bubbles occur? One force that may explain a bubble is "followership," the tendency for people to follow aggregate trends. Since prices rise from below intrinsic value, the initial trend of rising price may be due to excess demand based on fundamentals. However, once people see this trend and start to follow it, this behavior could cause prices to rise above intrinsic value. Smith et al. examine subjects' forecasts of next period's price and conclude that forecasts are highly adaptive and "bullish." In every experiment, the mean forecast of price for the next period was higher than the mean price in the current period. Furthermore, the forecasts missed the turning point completely.

Do price bubbles occur because of uncertainty in dividend return? Porter and Smith (1989) ran a series of 15-period asset markets where the dividend return on an asset was certain. They found that price bubbles occurred even when there was no uncertainty about the amount of future dividends. Thus, bubbles do not depend on individual uncertainty about returns.

Do price bubbles occur because of uncertainty about other traders' behavior? Smith et al. (1988) manipulate observability of other's behavior, by conducting experiments using experienced traders. When subjects participated in a second set of markets, price bubbles were smaller and collapsed sooner. When subjects participated a third time, bubbles were very small, with most trades occurring close to expected dividend return. An important aspect of these experience treatments is that subjects were told they were all at the same level of experience. These results suggest that prices follow intrinsic value when subjects gain greater common experience.

In these experiments, price bubbles can be interpreted as failures in backward induction. The experiments have known endpoints, so backward induction predicts that securities should trade at fundamental value.[29] Note that "fairness" does not seem to explain behavior in these experiments. Rather, subjects appear to believe that there are some quasirational individuals who will trade above expected value, and this belief is enough to support a bubble. When all traders know that other traders are rational (as in the thrice experienced experiments), bubbles tend to disappear.

Varying observability of other's information. Forsythe and Lundholm (1990) examine the informational efficiency of a laboratory economy with one-period-lived risky assets. Traders have diverse preferences over state outcomes (that is, for each state, traders' payoffs differ from one another) and are differentially informed about which states might occur. Although the market in aggregate is informed about the state that has occurred, each player is individually uncertain, knowing only that a particular state (of three) has not occurred. They find that when traders are experienced (that is, have participated in similar markets before) and have information about other traders' state payoffs, markets converge to the rational expectations equilibrium. And payoffs need not be experienced directly to attain the rational expectations equilibrium; making payoffs observable by including them in the instructions is enough. However, neither experience nor common knowledge of payoffs alone is sufficient to attain a rational expectations equilibrium. These results suggest that observability of both other's actions and other's information are necessary to achieve information efficiency.

In the Forsythe and Lundholm (1990) markets, all traders were aware that others were informed and that, aggregately, they had complete information about the state that had occurred. Camerer and Weigelt (1991) examine similar markets in which traders do not know whether others are informed. Each period, there is a 50% chance that half the traders will learn the true state. Thus, a trader knows only whether he or she was informed but cannot tell whether any other trader was informed. Information mirages, though not common, occur in these markets. In no-information periods, traders occasionally overreact to uninformed trades, resulting in price paths that mimic informed trade. However, these mirages occur in the early periods of the experiments; apparently, traders learn to use the speed of trade (a type of observability of other's actions) as an indicator of whether there are informed traders.

Varying the nature of contracts. O'Brien and Srivastava (1990, 1993) have conducted a series of studies in which it was possible, because of trading a multiplicity of securities, to initiate contracts that would exploit any arbitrage opportunities that might exist. They established that their price data was consistent with no-arbitrage pricing but did not meet the conditions of a rational expectations equilibrium in a two-period setting. In addition, they demonstrated that a standard test that would normally be expected to reveal informational inefficiency could not detect the failure of the rational expectations equilibrium, suggesting that there may be informational inefficiencies in real-world data that standard techniques cannot detect. O'Brien and Srivastava (1993) demonstrated put-and-call options can be designed that lead to informationally efficient prices. These securities were redundant with other securities in the market, but their reasonably simple structure allowed participants to exploit their individual information about state uncertainty.

The sunk-costs phenomenon in laboratory markets

Often, decision makers are faced with turning points in project continuation. Management accounting courses emphasize that marginal analysis is appropriate in these settings: one should ignore sunk costs and compare only future benefits and future costs. However, this approach seems to be counterintuitive; students frequently argue that sunk costs are appropriately incorporated in decisions. Moreover, the popular press is replete with instances where experts in the field appeal to sunk costs to justify or explain escalation. For example, Les Aspin, chairman of the House Armed Services Committee, was quoted as saying, "With $17 billion already invested in it, the B-2 is too costly to cancel." And in observing that a Shearson Lehman analyst, who had previously urged clients to buy America West Airline stock, failed to issue a sell recommendation until days before bankruptcy proceedings, "Heard On The Street" (*Wall Street Journal*, July 2, 1991) reports: "Wall street veterans say the Shearson saga isn't unique. All too frequently, they say, brokerage firms tend to be tardy in downgrading their opinion of a stock if its prospects turn sour after many of the firm's clients have been persuaded to buy it."

In addition to these public examples, many individuals report similar instances in their workplaces.[30] Indeed, there is even precedent for a "sunk-cost defense." The judge presiding over the Marion Barry trial ruled that the defense could have asked government investigators "whether they could have been biased because the government had put so much money into the case" (*New York Times*).

Example

About eight months ago you instituted a major project in which you made the case for the adoption of a new technology costing $20 million. Your main argument was that the new technology would make the company more competitive in the long run by reducing variable costs. The president of the company was impressed by your research and has suggested that you be named the new vice president of strategic planning in a year, when your predecessor retires. So far the company has spent $10 million on the new technology. The old technology is still being used for production. You have just learned that of the six companies who have adopted the new technology only one company has reduced its variable costs by 5%. By comparison, three companies who have instead overhauled their old technology (costing around $8 million) have decreased their variable costs by 10 to 30%. Should you advise your company to discontinue its investment in the new technology and overhaul the old equipment?

The example depicts a typical "sunk-cost" scenario. Current information suggests that the firm is better off treating the $10 million already spent as a sunk cost and overhauling their old technology. However, new attributes have been introduced by the addition of others who evaluate the decisions. First, people get to observe the decisions but not the information that guided them. Second, the order of play is important. Your decision is first, followed by a chance to change your decision, followed by a decision by someone else that will affect your income. Third, promotion is worth much more to you than your private return on the eventual outcome of the investment.

Theoretical background

If there is no conflict of interest, managers and the firms they work for should evaluate escalation decisions in the same way. If an incremental analysis indicates that future benefits outweigh future costs, then the project should be continued. Staw (1976) argues that individuals will tend toward escalation even when an incremental analysis indicates they should not – "self-justification" (a behavioral dynamic) causes individuals to act in ways that protect their own self-image. Staw (1976) argues that self-justification is a psychological need leading to a kind of "retrospective rationality," in contrast to the "prospective rationality" assumed in economic theory. This idea is extended to social settings, invoking "external justification" as an additional force driving people to attend to sunk costs.

Kanodia et al. (1989) provide an economic model in which the sunk-cost phenomenon arises as a result of purely rational behavior. This model introduces information asymmetry and a labor market that values "foresighted" managers. Since the market cannot observe whether a manager is foresighted or not, the market will attempt to assess this quality by examining the manager's past decisions. In particular, managers that switch projects are deemed to lack foresight since they did not properly anticipate the future in choosing projects. This gives rise to an incentive to manage one's reputation by ignoring new information and not switching. In this model the "sunk-cost" phenomenon is not an individual processing bias at all but, instead, the consequence of an individual's desire to maximize income!

Evidence

Staw (1976) uses a case-study methodology to examine self-justification and personal responsibility as explanators of escalation behavior. Subjects play the role of a corporate financial officer and allocate R&D funds to one of the operating divisions of the company. Half the subjects make an initial allocation to one of the two divisions, receive feedback on their decisions, and make a second allocation of funds. The other subjects do not make the initial allocation themselves but instead are told that it was made by another financial officer of the firm. Feedback is manipulated so that half of the subjects receive positive results on their initial decisions while half receive negative results.

Staw finds that subjects allocate significantly more money to failing divisions than successful divisions. Moreover, much more money is allocated to the chosen division when the subject himself, rather than another financial officer, makes the initial allocation. This data is consistent with Staw's hypothesis that a feeling of personal responsibility invokes self-justification behavior, in turn leading to increased commitment. Allocating more funds to the initial project is interpreted as retrospectively justifying the initial project.[31]

However, the data are also consistent with an asymmetric information explanation. Subjects may reasonably believe that in real-world settings the decision to allocate funds of such magnitude and importance would be entrusted only to persons possessing special information and foresight. Since the numerical data are public information and provide no means for discriminating between two alternatives under consideration, delegation of the task implies that financial officers have special insight not reflected in the numerical data. Given such as scenario, the reputation model predicts escalation. However, when the subject does not make the initial choice there is no longer any need to protect a reputation for foresight in making decisions and one would expect no escalation.

Varying whether there are multiple players. Berg et al. (1993) conduct laboratory experiments to examine the sunk-cost phenomenon, explicitly manipulating whether individuals are in a multiperson setting or not. In these experiments, subjects first participated in an individual decision-making setting, and then in an aggregate decision-making setting. In the individual-choice experiments, subjects were told they were project managers who must decide between two projects: one would have an 80% chance of a high return (and a 20% chance of a low return) and other would have a 20% chance of a high return (and an 80% chance of the low return), each project being equally likely to have the high return. Before choosing a project, each subject was randomly assigned a "type." Type 1 managers received an information signal revealing which project had the highest expected return; type 2 managers received no additional information about project returns. After a project was chosen, each subject learned which project had the highest expected return and had the opportunity to switch projects. After a final project choice was made, outcome was determined based on the chosen project's return distribution.

In the individual-choice setting, subjects' dominant strategy is to pick the high-return project if it is revealed in the initial information and switch to the high-return project if they had chosen the low-return project initially. Escalation rate is measured as the percentage of times subjects initially choosing the low-return project switched after receiving disconfirming information. Berg et al. report an average escalation rate of approximately 15% in the individual-choice settings.

After participating in the individual-choice settings, subjects then participated in an aggregate setting for 25 periods. This setting was identical to the individual decision-making setting with one exception: after project managers made their final project choices, they entered a labor market in which employers hired project managers. Half the subjects were assigned the role of employers while half the subjects remained project managers.

Employers earned the difference between the value of the project manager and the wage. Employers had private values, which were much higher for type 1 project managers (those that receive information "early") than type 2 managers (those that need to wait until after an initial choice is made to see which project has the highest expected return). Thus, employers should be willing to pay higher wages for type 1 managers than type 2 managers. Subjects participated in one of two information treatments: public or private information.

In the public-information setting, there is no information asymmetry – the market sees everything that the project manager sees. Employers bid for managers in a sealed-bid second-price auction for each manager. Once each employer submitted bids for each manager, the market cleared by matching the project manager to the employer with the highest bid for that manager. The wage the employer paid the manager was equal to the second highest bid for that manager. In the public-information case, employers knew the managers' types. As predicted, the experimental results show a much higher wage for type 1 managers. Furthermore, the escalation rate is 18%, not significantly different than the rate in the individual-choice task.

These results show that imbedding the individual in a social setting is not sufficient to produce the sunk-cost phenomenon. This evidence supports the information-asymmetry explanation of the phenomenon.

Varying observability of other's information. Berg et al. (1993) also manipulate observability in their experiments. In the private-information experiment, firms do not know who is a "good" manager; they see only the sequence of choices that the manager makes. However, switching projects provides a clear signal that one is a "bad" manager. Thus, the market wage for known "bad" managers should be lower than the market wage for other managers whose types are still uncertain. This wage pattern is observed in the private-information treatment. Since "reputation" force gives subjects an incentive to hide their type by not switching, so information asymmetry should result in a sharp increase in the escalation rate. This is exactly what the data show: in the private-information setting, the escalation rate is 54%. The data from these experiments suggest that information asymmetry is crucial in determining when sunk-cost behavior will occur.

Berg et al. (1992) conjecture that previous case studies investigating the sunk-cost phenomenon have implicitly manipulated observability when manipulating other variables of interest.[32] In the baseline condition of a case study designed to explicitly manipulate observability, subjects were told only that they had overlooked an important factor in making their decision. In the treatment condition, subjects were also told that a peer-review process was in place. The results showed a significant *increase* in escalation in the peer-review treatment. Berg et al. then conduct a second case study identical to the first except that subjects are asked about their perceptions of the information environment. In these experiments, escalation again increased in the peer-review setting. The postexperimental questionnaire revealed that subjects believed the information asymmetry was *greater* in the peer-review setting. This case study provides additional evidence that escalation increases with the degree of perceived information asymmetry, and that the reputation model presented in Kanodia et al. (1989) may provide a parsimonious explanation of the sunk-cost phenomenon.

Conclusion

To move from the individual to aggregate settings involves many observable differences. We have attempted to provide a common framework for researchers of any persuasion, including accountants, psychologists, and economists, to examine what it might mean for a decision-making bias to occur in an aggregate setting and, in particular, how biases might persist. We first enumerated seven factors that change when moving from an individual to an aggregate setting. We referred to these factors as "exogenous environmental attributes of aggregate settings." They include multiple players, differences in choice sets, payoff interdependency, observability, communication, contracting, and order of play. From a scientific perspective, these are the variables that can be manipulated to determine how individual behavior is altered in multiperson settings and whether some new type(s) of bias might emerge. Since different paradigms assume that different forces are at work when these attributes are changed, concentrating attention on manipulating these attributes rather than different opinions of what forces are at work is a useful way to structure the scientific effort. We examined how these attributes can be manipulated when considering various phenomena such as the illusion of control in agency settings, fairness in bargaining, the role of redundant securities and the formation of price bubbles in securities markets, and sunk-cost behavior.

One striking aspect of the results of these studies is that no unique answer exists about how aggregate factors impact on individual biases, suggesting the possibility of a rich set of future studies on this issue in accounting. It appears there are a large set of questions that may be examined by joining the framework suggested here with the questions raised and approaches reviewed in other chapters of this book. Interdisciplinary research efforts are likely to be especially fruitful.

Auditing

First, let's consider the area of auditing. We learn from other chapters that in general the auditing task is largely one of controlling audit risk, and that auditing is sequential in nature, requiring the processing efforts of multiple individuals who must interact in many different types of environments. We learn that there have been vigorous attempts to understand the processes by which auditors make choices, the ability of auditors to process probabilities, the role of experience, whether information processing is configural, and whether there is consensus in audit judgment. There are investigations into the abilities and performance of auditors and the degree to which the problem representations of experienced auditors differ from those of inexperienced auditors, the role of first- and secondhand encounters of audit knowledge, as well as the different abilities required by auditors, such as encoding, retrieval, and analysis. Finally, we see attempts to examine the conditions under which decision aids could improve the quality of the audit, and we learn that it is rather difficult to evaluate the performance of such decision aids.

Most of the work done in auditing is at the individual-choice level, and so one can ask whether the results will change when aggregate environmental attributes are brought into the setting. For example, do the problems that we elaborated with respect to backward induction in the bargaining setting (where there is sequential play) manifest themselves similarly in auditing settings when there are a large number of sequential activities performed by multiple individuals? To what degree do we see sunk-cost behavior emerge in auditing settings when, for example, an internal control feature is overlooked early in an audit? Is there a relationship between the idea of sunk cost and the recent savings and loan scandal? Is the degree of configural processing affected by the nature of the payoff interdependencies in the audit setting? Usually we find in simple game environments that responses are easily influenced by varying payoff interdependency, but we know little of how payoff interdependency might affect an auditor's ability to learn or to perform. Yet, in auditing environments the nature of payoff interdependency can vary greatly, ranging from the relationship of the junior auditor's payoff to his superior's to the interdependency of payoffs between two partners of a large audit firm.

To date, consensus among the judgments and choices of different auditors has often been used as a criterion for evaluating audit judgment. But what if we view consensus endogenously as a form of followership. Are there variables that can be manipulated (such as order of play and knowledge of other's performance) that would systematically affect the nature of consensus? Turning to probability assessments, is there a difference in an auditor's ability to assess the probability of a strategic versus a stochastic outcome? In considering audit effectiveness, for example, state uncertainty regarding the performance of competing technologies may be an issue, whereas in assessing detection risk, strategic uncertainty regarding the decision strategy of the client may be more fundamental.

Is "observation of others" likely to play a role similar to secondhand encounters as an experience variable, or is it more likely to affect a schematic representation in memory? What is the relationship between the degree of conflict of interest (interdependency of payoffs) and the nature of auditors' abilities? Does varying conflict of interest affect analysis but not encoding in an auditing setting? There are aspects of the auditing setting that may lead to reconsideration of some of the results cited in this chapter. For example, a choice point for an auditor may involve substantially more activity than a standard choice point in a game-theory-type environment. Is it possible that by changing the nature of the choice set at the decision nodes our conclusions with respect to bargaining might be altered? Will backward induction be altered?

In terms of decision aids, the approach in this chapter can be used to sketch a potential way of evaluating such aids. As we learn to work with more complex laboratory environments – especially the nature of the audit environment in which the auditor operates – it becomes easier to represent the notion of audit risk in the laboratory. When a number of factors are varied, we might envision something along the lines of a flight simulator. It then becomes possible to control the inherent risk and ask to what degree it is detected by existing methods, or to what degree a particular decision aid facilitates its detection.

External users

Research on the external user generally focuses on investment evaluations and loan decisions, and research has addressed how different inputs to such decisions may affect decision outcomes. At least two aggregate factors have the potential to contribute to knowledge in this area: observability of others' choices and payoff interdependency. For example, what occurs when the ability of the other party to manipulate the financial statements varies in the evaluation setting? Does it make a difference if there are other individuals competing to have companies use their funds? Is the nature of inferences about the probability of return affected by the nature of the competition for investment or by information in the environment? What transpires when the risk characteristics of the other participants are altered?

Internal users

In managerial accounting, the work on incentive contracting indicates a desire to do field research to find some additional characterizations of contracts. One often-raised question concerns the lack of similarity between contracts frequently observed in the real world and those studied in theory (and in some of the contracting experiments). What environmental attributes should be considered in going to the field? For example, degree of observability and conflict of interests seem to be natural factors to control for in researching characteristics of real-world contracts. But there may be more subtle issues. For example, in bargaining we found that certain preconditions or property rights had to be established by the first mover in an ultimatum game. Analogously, the explanation for differences between observed experimental contracts and observed field contracts may hinge on understanding the preconditions existing prior to contract offers.

Acknowledgments

This chapter would not be complete without our thanking the editors, Robert and Alison Ashton, for the opportunity to write this chapter and present our thoughts at two writers' conferences, and the participants, especially Don Kleinmuntz, for their efforts in improving our thinking. Their challenge has inspired us to think broadly about the relationship between the individual and the aggregate. We are excited by the advances in theory and methodology and the tremendous research opportunities that lie ahead.

Notes

1. In related work, Camerer and Kunreuther (1984) describe an experimental economics-based approach to linking individual and *market* behavior, suggesting specific market experiments to address whether biases documented at the individual level persist in simple laboratory

market economies. We focus on more general aggregate settings and also introduce the question of "new" biases that result from aggregate settings.

2. This chapter is not intended to be a comprehensive survey of the literature addressing individual bias and aggregate behavior. For examples of work addressing whether specific individual biases are extinguished by market forces, see Camerer (1987), Camerer et al. (1989), Duh and Sunder (1986), Grether (1980), Ganguly et al. (1994), and Knez et al. (1985). Camerer (1990) develops the notion of "behavioral game theory" (the systematic study of departures from normative game theory), suggesting that it is a natural successor to behavioral decision theory. See also Hogarth and Reder (1986) for a comparison of psychological and economic approaches.
3. Along similar lines, DeLong et al. (1991) demonstrate that noise traders (traders with erroneous beliefs about asset prices) can survive and dominate (amass more wealth than) rational traders. However, their model relies on noise traders who do not affect prices. Thus, there are information-processing biases in the market and the persons with these biases do not die out, but (by construction) there is no aggregate level impact.
4. There is a large literature on market anomalies. DeBondt and Thaler are among the first (and the few) who try to tie anomalies to specific individual biases. See also Thaler (1992).
5. Such behavior could indicate that pension fund managers themselves are "biased" or that fund managers believe that investors are "fooled" by this behavior.
6. While this paper suggests that analysts overreaction and stock price overreaction may be related, it does not empirically document such a link, and they do not specifically model what information analysts are overreacting to. Abarbanell and Bernard (1992) claim that the link may be more complex (and tenuous) than DeBondt and Thaler suggest. Abarbanell and Bernard document that analysts *underreact* to earnings and that extreme forecast reactions do not seem tied to movement in stock prices.
7. Camerer (1992) provides a survey of some of this research.
8. One unexploited area of experimental economics is its application to measuring the cost of bias. Since cost of bias will be institution and parameter specific, measuring these costs will require knowledge of the industrial-organization literature (to define the crucial features of the institution) and field study work to evaluate parameters.
9. For overviews of experimental-economics methodology see Davis and Holt (1993), Forsythe (1986), Plott (1982), Roth (1986, 1987, 1988), and Smith (1982, 1989, 1991). For discussion of applications to accounting see Berg et al. (1990), Davis and Swenson (1988), DeJong and Forsythe (1992), DeJong et al. (1985), and Smith et al. (1987).
10. Unobservability can cause a coordination problem even when goals are perfectly aligned. See, for instance, Jordan (1989) and Jordan (1990).
11. The issue in the agency literature is when information is valuable in contracting. Assumptions about how the gain to trade will be split is irrelevant in addressing this question, so nothing is lost by assuming that the principal receives all residual above the agent's market wage.
12. This example is based on Wolfson (1985b), who discusses shared home-ownership contracts as a special instance of generalized lease-or-buy problems.
13. The term "backward induction" is generally not used in the agency literature; instead, contract alternatives are limited to those that guarantee the agent's market wage (through an "individual rationality" constraint) and the term "incentive compatible" is used to convey the idea that the principal considers the agent's self-interest when designing a contract. We introduce the term "backward induction" here so that we can tie the agency literature to the literature on sequential bargaining discussed in the next section.
14. More precisely, a signal, y, is valuable if and only if it is informative. A signal, y, is informative if output, x, is not a sufficient statistic for the pair (x,y) with respect to the agent's effort.
15. This mechanism rewards subjects in units of experimental exchange, which are converted via a prespecified transformation function to a probability of winning a prespecified two-prize gamble. Subjects who conform to the transitivity, monotonicity, and compound lottery axioms will exhibit preferences that are linear in this probability. Thus, by introducing a concave transformation function, subjects will be induced to act as if risk-averse. The performance characteristics of this methodology is a topic of ongoing research (see Berg et al., 1992).
16. These experiments incorporate a limited contract set, suppress the ultimatum game aspect

of the setting by eliminating the agent's accept/reject choice, and use the lottery reward mechanism to control for difference in subjects' risk preferences.

17. Epstein (1992) contains evidence that can be interpreted as loosely consistent with this conjecture. He finds that introducing the opportunity to reject the contract in favor of a flat reward (the agent's market wage) reduces the predictive power of the agency model. In these settings, some principals offer suboptimal risk-sharing contracts, some agents fail to reject contracts when it is in their best interest to do so, and some reject contracts when it is not in their best interest to do so. However, behavior in these experiments appears not to have stabilized by the end of the experiments (period 10). This differs from results reported in Berg et al. (1992), where behavior did converge by period 10. This may be attributable to increased complexity in the Epstein experiments or a problem of payoff dominance. In some of the Epstein experiments, the payoff associated with choosing the predicted contracts and actions are not much larger than the payoffs associated with choosing suboptimal contracts.
18. In the Baiman and Lewis experiments, the contracts offered did not depend on the agents' behavior. The set of contracts was preselected and no principals actually existed, although subjects were told that the contracts had been specified by previous participants and that those participants' payoffs would be affected by the subject's choices. Subjects in the Berg et al. experiments consisted of both principals and agents, so that the contract offered depended on the principals' belief about agent behavior. The experiment consisted of many periods of the same choice task (with the same subject pairs), so that contract choice in later periods could be influenced by agent behavior in previous periods.
19. This example is a variation on one of the survey questions included in Kahneman et al. (1986), p. 729. Eighty-two percent of respondents indicated that raising the price of snow shovels was unfair.
20. To make this prediction, we are assuming that the customer does not escape the (physical) cost of shoveling by paying the fine. This will be the case if the city, after fining the customer for failure to shovel, lends the customer a shovel to shovel the snow. If the customer could escape this cost by paying the fine, then the maximum that the customer would pay for the snow shovel is the cost of the fine less the cost of shoveling.
21. For example, subjects appear to segregate (rather than integrate) information in decision making (Tversky and Kahneman, 1987).
22. See Hoffman and Spitzer (1982, 1985) for related work.
23. However, when Kachelmeier et al. (1991) extend the investigation of fairness to a market setting, they find that fairness affects market prices but the effect declines over time. This effect appears to be attributable to "fairness," not anticipation. See also Bolton (1991) for development and test of a bargaining model incorporating preferences for both absolute and relative payoffs.
24. This is the same type of experience that principals in many of the agency experiments had and might account for differences in subjects' ability to backward induct reported in these two literatures.
25. There are many such early agreements that would make both players better off. We use an equal split of the $50 lost by delay as an illustration only.
26. The sums of money in each round were as follows:

	Round 1	Round 2	Round 3	Round 4	Round 5
1.	$5.00	$1.25			
2.	$5.00	$2.50	$1.25		
3.	$5.00	$1.70	$0.58	$0.20	$0.07

For all three games the backward-induction solution predicts accepted first-round proposals around ($3.75, $1.25).

27. This differs from the results of previous ultimatum-game research. Binmore et al. (1988) point out that there are several differences between their study and the Neelin et al. study; among these is pretrial experience in a four-round bargaining game in the Neelin et al. study. Binmore et al. (1985) have established that experience can affect behavior; this may account for the results.
28. This research uses the "mouse lab" process-tracing technology, a PC-based application that

allows the researcher to record information about subjects' search patterns. For a more complete description of this methodology, see Johnson et al. (1988).

29. In addition to sequential bargaining experiments, backward induction has been examined in more complex environments. McCabe (1989) examines the behavior of fiat money (money with no intrinsic value of its own, but which can be used as a "store of value" for buying goods later). Backward induction predicts that there should be no trade, since in the last period money is worthless and subjects, realizing this, should refuse to accept money in any period. Though there is trading in early periods, McCabe finds that with experience trade collapses sooner and sooner.

    McKelvey and Palfrey (1990) find that backward induction also fails in a "centipede game" (a game in which players alternate choosing whether to end the game immediately, resulting in some payoff for themselves and a smaller payoff for their opponent, or to continue the game, increasing the total prize money). Backward induction predicts that the game should end in the first move. However, McKelvey and Palfrey find that only 7% of their 4-move games stopped after the first move.
30. Our awareness of such examples came from asking our management-accounting students, many of whom were in management positions at firms, to write about the tendency to escalate commitment to losing courses of action in their firms. The papers were written under the promise of anonymity regarding the names of the companies and persons involved.
31. The data are also consistent with what Staw calls the self-perception hypothesis. Under the self-perception hypothesis, the subject does not see the negative outcomes as really negative, but as necessary suffering that must accompany any truly meritorious initial choice. Staw argues that self-justification is a more credible explanation.
32. Technically, one can only manipulate perceptions in a case study. Therefore, whether or not observability was actually manipulated must be determined by means of a manipulation check. No such manipulation check was conducted in prior studies, so one cannot determine whether observability was manipulated in these studies.

Part III

Judgment and decision-making research involving auditors of accounting information

6

Judgment and decision-making research in auditing

Ira Solomon and Michael D. Shields

Introduction

This chapter has four interrelated objectives. One objective is to provide an overview and evaluation of the many studies published during the last 20 years in which experienced auditors formed judgments or made decisions while performing audit tasks. The second objective is to recommend issues for and approaches to future research. A third objective is to compare findings of the audit judgment/decision-making (J/DM) studies with nonaudit J/DM studies, thereby increasing nonaudit J/DM researchers' awareness of these audit studies. The fourth objective is to provide a common foundation for Chapter 7 by Libby on knowledge and memory in auditing and Chapter 8 by Messier on audit decision aids. Meeting these objectives, as discussed later, should enhance the accessibility of audit J/DM research findings, highlight boundary conditions of extant theories, focus future research on promising issues, identify profitable methods for future research, and stimulate J/DM theory construction and revision.

The remainder of this chapter is divided into seven sections. The next section defines auditing and the following one highlights the objectives of J/DM research in the audit context. In these sections it is noted that the audit J/DM studies we review have primarily sought to: (a) describe how and how well auditors make judgments and decisions, (b) prescribe how to improve audit J/DM, and (c) contribute to nonaudit J/DM knowledge. In addition, it is noted that the totality of audit tasks/contexts features make auditing both distinctive and a rich arena for developing and testing J/DM theories. These sections also introduce our characterization of audit J/DM as a function of the task/context, processor, and task/context-by-processor interaction. An overview of the history and foci of audit J/DM studies follows. Also included in this section is a brief discussion of prior papers that have reviewed audit

J/DM studies. A major theme is that the central features of audit J/DM research (issues, questions, theories, methods, and evaluation criteria) have mirrored the development of nonaudit J/DM studies as a consequence of audit researchers' employment of a "borrow and transfer" and then a "contrast before transfer" approach.

The next section focuses on the audit process and the key J/DM tendencies that pervade that process. Presentation of a three-dimensional organizational framework begins the discussion in the following section. The three dimensions are the stage of the audit process (e.g., planning audit procedures, evaluating evidence), the underlying theoretical framework (e.g., policy capturing, probabilistic judgment), and the J/DM evaluation criteria employed (e.g., accuracy, self-insight). These dimensions subsequently serve as the organizing principles for our review of audit J/DM research. The next section presents both an evaluation of the prior research and recommendations for future audit J/DM research. One trend noted therein is the recent movement away from modeling the auditor as a generic information processor to modeling auditor J/DM more in terms of the audit task and the task-by-processor interaction. Attendant with this trend is an increasing realization that it may be inappropriate to assume that auditors' J/DM goals can be satisfactorily characterized in terms of standard J/DM evaluation criteria like accuracy. The final section completes the chapter by noting that although most audit J/DM results are consistent with other J/DM results, there are four salient result departures that have potential to contribute to construction or revision of general J/DM theory.

Auditing defined

Auditing may be characterized as a process of appraising the validity of an assertion vis-à-vis specified criteria and reporting the findings to interested parties. In the U.S., financial-statement auditing is the most common form. The assertions to be appraised concern economic transactions into which an organization has entered, the criteria used to appraise the validity of the assertions are generally accepted accounting principles (GAAP), and the reports are issued by independent auditors (called Certified Public Accountants or CPAs) to interested parties such as current and prospective business owners, employees, lenders, and regulators. To illustrate, when a financial statement lists $1,000,000 of inventory, the organization is asserting, among other things, that the inventory exists, it is owned by the organization, and it is properly valued according to GAAP at $1,000,000. An auditor can appraise these assertions by performing procedures (e.g., observing employees counting the inventory) that produce evidence useful in determining the extent to which the assertions conform to the criteria. Ultimately, if the auditor concludes that the assertions in the financial statements conform to GAAP, he or she would issue a report communicating that message. Otherwise, the auditor would require an adjustment to the assertions or would issue a report indicating that the financial statements significantly depart from GAAP in describing the organization's economic transactions.

Judging and deciding are inherent in every phase of the audit process. For example, when focused on a specific financial-statement assertion and account balance (e.g., valuation of inventory), the auditor must *judge* the significance of the balance and assertion, how much risk there is of misstatement, how to best produce evidence to confirm or disconfirm this assertion, how much such evidence should be produced, and when during the course of the audit it should be produced. Subsequently, the auditor must evaluate the resultant evidence and form a judgment about its meaning. In concert with similar judgments for other accounts and assertions, the auditor then must integrate these findings and *decide* what to communicate to the financial-statement users (i.e., choose the audit report to be issued).

Audits can have wide-ranging foci and purposes within the U.S. economic system.[1] However, almost all audit J/DM research has been couched in the context of financial-statement auditing. Because the objective of this chapter is to review extant audit J/DM research, a sensible approach is to frame it in financial-statement auditing terms. It should be noted, however, that little, if any, of what follows is restricted to financial-statement (as opposed to other types of) auditing.

Objectives of audit J/DM research

Audit researchers have recognized for almost 20 years that the judgments and decisions inherent in auditing are amenable to scientific investigation. Like other fields of endeavor, the purposes of such investigation typically have been described as threefold: descriptive, prescriptive, and normative. That is, audit J/DM research is intended to *describe how* and *how well* auditors make judgments and decisions and to suggest how they can be *improved.* How audit judgments and decisions *should be made* also has been addressed by numerous studies. The focus of this chapter is studies that primarily have described auditor J/DM. To a lesser degree, normative studies also will be included.[2] Prescriptive studies, however, are excluded, as they are the focus of Messier's chapter on decision aiding *in this volume* (Chapter 8).

To this list of three audit J/DM research objectives we add a fourth and fifth objective: instruction/training enhancement and advancement of nonaudit J/DM knowledge.[3] The fourth objective recognizes that audit J/DM researchers are engaged in the acquisition of knowledge and that, once acquired, it may be transmitted to students in the university setting. One example is provided by the audit research on heuristics and biases that many educators have brought into the university classroom. Ashton's (1984) illustration of how this could be accomplished clearly facilitated this transfer of research findings into the accounting/auditing classroom. Although there is great potential for audit J/DM research to be used in this fashion, further examples of systematic education enhancement are hard to identify. Interestingly, audit

J/DM research seems to have found its way into training programs developed by audit firms to a greater extent than in university classes. For example, studies of auditor expertise have been used in developing training programs intended to help practicing auditors learn to make judgments and decisions that exhibit desired characteristics (e.g., consensus, stability).

As contemplated by the fifth objective (advancing nonaudit J/DM knowledge), audit J/DM research has the potential both to test generic J/DM theory and to elucidate variables germane to development of J/DM theories in other applied contexts. J/DM processes may be modeled as a function of the task/context, the processor, and the interaction of the task/context and processor. In addition, the task/context may be broken down into two components: content and structure (see Einhorn and Hogarth, 1981). Further, for purposes of discussion, it is useful to distinguish two types of tasks/contexts: generic and applied. Herein, a generic task/context is one in which structure is emphasized by the researcher and content is relatively deemphasized (e.g., book-bag and poker-chip task). An applied task/context, in contrast, is one in which both structure and content are important (e.g., employee performance evaluation in an organization). Generic tasks often are performed primarily for research purposes whereas applied tasks may occur in both natural and research settings. Further, research representations of both generic and applied tasks require both structural abstraction and content simplification. However, consistent with the structural emphasis, the level of content abstraction is greater in the case of generic tasks than for applied tasks. To illustrate, book-bag and poker-chip tasks are devoid of content but are structural representations of sequential belief-revision tasks.

We also distinguish between experienced and inexperienced processors, thereby creating a model with four task/context-processor combinations.[4] Much of the J/DM literature has employed either a generic task/context and used inexperienced subjects (e.g., students performing a book-bag and poker-chip task) or an applied task/context using experienced subjects (e.g., medical diagnosis by practicing physicians). Whereas the other two combinations (generic task performed by an expert/experienced subject and applied task performed by a novice/inexperienced subject) are not as often research foci, studies employing these task/context–processor combinations can make valuable additions to the J/DM literature by increasing knowledge about the incremental effects of tasks and processors on J/DM processes and outcomes. For example, studying inexperienced subjects (e.g., students) performing an applied J/DM task can provide a baseline for assessing the effects of experience.

Applied J/DM studies, including studies of audit J/DM, historically have provided valuable evidence about the effects of task/context structures on J/DM behavior. Many contexts have been investigated in the various applied J/DM literatures (e.g., medicine, meteorology, military). Each context has numerous structural features, many of which are shared with other contexts, but the constellation of a context's structural features distinguishes it from the others. For example, auditing has numerous individual structural features in common with other contexts, but the constellation of these features makes auditing distinctive. Salient individual structural features of auditing contexts include substantial multiperiod and multiperson (i.e., audit team) interaction and asymmetric penalties and rewards. In addition, tasks within the auditing context have varying degrees of subjectivity, usually are sequential and iterative, and generally require specialized content knowledge. Auditing tasks also are characterized by explicit risk assessments performed by persons (audit team members) who possess varying degrees of such content knowledge. Further, there are accountability requirements (see Tetlock, 1985) in the audit context that mandate that J/DM be professionally documented, legally defensible, and completed within explicit time allotments. Lastly, while there typically is no timely revelation of the true state of nature (i.e., outcome feedback) some timely feedback may be provided by reviews of documented task performance.

Structural features like those just described make audit tasks/contexts rich testing grounds for J/DM theories. To illustrate, audit J/DM research results, as discussed below, often have been consistent with generic J/DM results and with results from other applied J/DM tasks but, at times, departures have been reported (e.g., auditors' judgments generally are consistent with *less reliance* on simplifying heuristics; auditors' probabilistic judgments do *not* exhibit overconfidence). In our view, "consistent" results may demonstrate the insensitivity of J/DM theories to different task/context structures while "inconsistent" results can elucidate the extent to which such theories are sensitive to specific task/context structures and contents. Researchers interested in generic J/DM theories and those interested in theories of J/DM for applied contexts other than auditing should find value in such evidence.

Following the first three audit J/DM research objectives specified in this section, we observe that extant studies have greatly increased the storehouse of knowledge about audit J/DM. However, audit J/DM research now has reached a level of development at which it is more difficult for substantive contributions to be made. A continuing chapter theme, therefore, both for new and active audit J/DM researchers, will be the need to focus more attention on structural features of audit tasks/contexts in developing theories and hypotheses, designing tests of hypotheses, and interpreting results. Further, a companion theme will be that significantly greater attention to audit task content and to the interaction of task and processor are warranted.

History, foci, and prior reviews of audit J/DM research

There was little, if any, scientific research on audit J/DM prior to the early 1970s. Indeed, back then it was not uncommon for members of the academic community to suggest that auditing is an art and, therefore, is not amenable to scientific investigation. Looking back, three events seem to have sparked scientific research on audit judgments/decisions. First, an American Accounting Association (1972) research report introduced to accounting and auditing scholars Brunswik's lens model as a method for descriptively modeling how people make judgments/decisions with accounting information. Second, the first audit research conferences were held during 1972 and 1974 at the Universities of Kansas and Illinois, respectively. Third, in 1976 Peat, Marwick, Mitchel and Co. published *Research Opportunities in Auditing (ROA)* and concurrently established a *ROA* program that made funding, subjects, and data available to scholars interested in auditing.[5] In concert, these events stimulated a dramatic transformation in the range, quantity and quality of audit research. In a four-year time period, audit research and, in particular, audit J/DM research, went from birth to a major focus of accounting scholars.

The early audit J/DM research primarily addressed two broad questions: (1) Are the findings from the psychology literature, generally based on generic tasks performed by university student subjects, reproducible with audit tasks performed by auditor subjects? and (2) *How* and *how well* do auditors make audit judgments/decisions? Subsequently, as audit J/DM researchers became more familiar with the psychology literature and as an auditing research base began to emerge, these initial questions were augmented with other rather broad questions. One important example was how and how well do auditors (as intuitive statisticians) make judgments/decisions compared to statistical models? Specific questions investigated in the early studies would include: (1) Are auditors overconfident when formulating subjective probability judgments? (2) Are auditors conservative (relative to Bayes's rule) when revising probabilities? (3) Are an individual auditor's judgments/decisions consistent or reliable? (4) What is the level of auditors' J/DM consensus? (5) What is the level of auditors' self-insight? (6) Do auditors use heuristics and exhibit the same biases as other judges? (7) How well do auditors learn from experience? and (8) How can the quality of audit J/DM be improved? These research questions evolved in a temporal pattern similar to the nonaudit J/DM literature of the same period (e.g., Slovic and Lichtenstein, 1971; Tversky and Kahneman, 1974; Einhorn and Hogarth, 1981). Consistently, these audit J/DM studies typically treated the information processor as a "black box," only rarely digging into what transpires between information inputs and outputs. Indeed, during this period, as auditing researchers were becoming familiar with this new literature, the research had a "borrow and transfer" orientation.

Several reviews of audit J/DM research previously have been reported. Some are restricted to audit J/DM research while some include various other streams of behavioral accounting research (e.g., financial, managerial). Most of these reviews are organized on a paper-by-paper basis and all were published by the early 1980s. The reviews by Ashton (1982, 1983) are structured by theoretical framework (e.g., policy capturing, probabilistic judgment, heuristics, and biases) and type of accounting/auditing judgment and decision, while the reviews by Libby (1981) and Libby and Lewis (1977, 1982) are structured in terms of an input–process–output representation of audit judg-

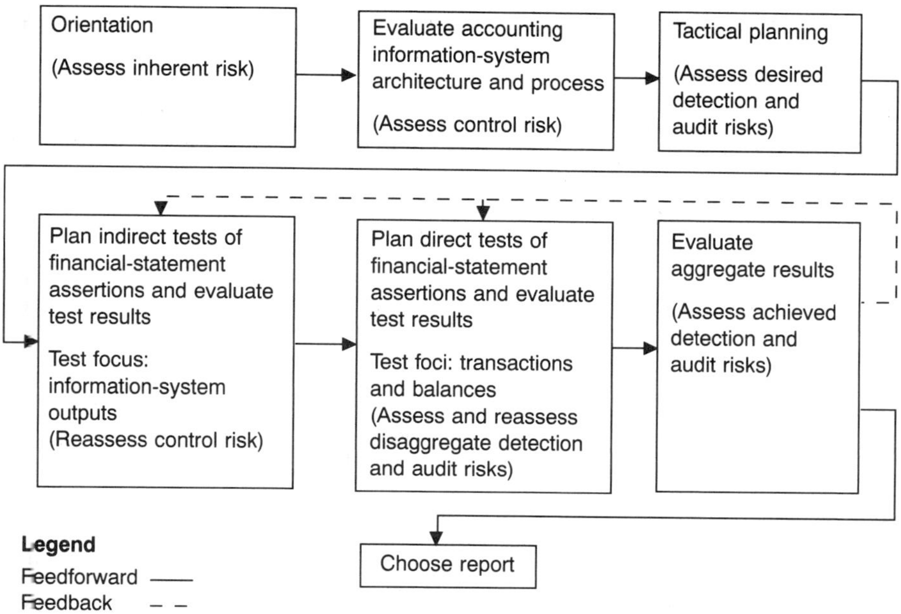

Figure 1. Audit judgment process overview.

ments/decisions and by theoretical framework. Felix and Kinney (1982) and Joyce and Libby (1982) provided reviews structured by audit tasks, issues and, importantly, by the audit judgment process. Using the audit judgment process for this purpose was significant, as it facilitated a movement from the borrow-and-transfer orientation to a "contrast-before-transfer" orientation in which greater attention began to be focussed on the distinguishing features of auditing and auditors vis-à-vis generic and other applied tasks (see Bonner and Pennington, 1991). Finally, to provide continued guidance, KPMG Peat Marwick renewed its *ROA* program (Abdel-khalik and Solomon, 1988) with Ashton et al. (1988) providing an updated agenda for audit J/DM research structured by a generic J/DM framework.

The audit process

An overview of the audit process is provided in Figure 1, which is adapted from Felix and Kinney (1982).[6] Because the primary objective of this section is to orient readers having limited familiarity with auditing, this process overview and the accompanying description have a tutorial flavor. Specifically, we have omitted (for now) many of the interesting potential departures from the "textbook approach" that may be observed in practice and are a function of general J/DM tendencies and the interaction of such tendencies with features of the audit domain. Before describing the audit process, it is important that three general features of an audit be understood. First, there is no standard set of audit procedures for every organization whose financial statements are to be audited. Indeed, in addition to producing and evaluating evidence bearing on the financial statements, a substantial portion of the audit process is directed toward determining the most effective and efficient means of producing such evidence in light of the circumstances presented by each organization.

Second, although much of our audit process description is framed from the perspective of an individual auditor, all but the smallest audits are performed by teams comprised of auditors with differing levels of experience and characterized by considerable task specialization (see Solomon, 1987). Generally, less-experienced team members carry out specific evidence-generating steps and document in "working papers" the results, while more experienced team members plan the audit procedures, supervise performance, and review the documented work (called "the review process"). More experienced members also make decisions to consult with appropriate persons about any special problems that arise.

Third, professional audit standards have increasingly led to a focus on risk assessment. Indeed, the basic purpose of an audit has recently been recast as minimizing the risk that, unknown to the auditor but subsequent to his/her efforts, the organization's financial statements contain significant departures from GAAP (see American Institute of Certified Public Accountants, 1990). This risk, called "audit risk," has been conceptualized as a function of three component risks:

Audit Risk = *f* (Inherent Risk, Control Risk, Detection Risk).[7]

Inherent risk is the risk that misstatements will arise, *control risk* is the risk that the organization's information system will fail to detect and correct misstatements, and *detection risk* is the risk that the auditor's procedures will fail to detect and correct misstatements that have arisen and were missed by the controls. From a risk perspective, an audit is the process by which evidence is produced and evaluated to allow the auditor to minimize the audit risk of reaching the erroneous conclusion that the financial statements do *not* contain misstatements. The first two risk components are characteristics of the *organization* making the financial-statement assertions (hereafter, "the auditee") and, thus, are not directly affected by the auditor. However, the latter risk component is a direct function of the audit process employed and how well it is executed. Such execution depends critically upon the quality of a myriad of judgments and decisions.

Each of the phases depicted in Figure 1 typically involves the auditor performing several tasks. The first phase is an orientation phase, the objective of which is to devise a general strategy for the audit. Key tasks performed are intended to produce knowledge with respect to the auditee's operations and its internal and external environment as inputs to a judgment of the inherent risk that misstatements have arisen in individual assertions contained in the auditee's financial statements. For example, the auditor might make inquiries regarding the demand for the auditee's products and the general financial health of the industry in which it operates. In addition, the auditor could inspect documents (e.g., contracts) that might contain cues to the presence of special pressures on the auditee's management to meet target assertion levels (e.g., a key component of the compensation of the auditee's president might be tied to net income or some derivative thereof such as earnings-per-share of common stock).

Having made an assessment of inherent risk, the auditor, during the second phase, judges the architecture of the accounting-information system to form a preliminary judgment of the control risk that if a misstatement were to arise it would *not* be detected and corrected. During this phase the auditor would read procedure manuals and make inquiries to obtain information from which he or she can document the system architecture. Subsequently, the auditor would analyze the system architecture with an eye toward identifying any significant weaknesses which may exist. Such identification requires the auditor to employ technical knowledge of information-system design. Thus, for example, the knowledgeable auditor would be concerned about a situation in which one auditee employee is authorized both to receive cash at the time a sale is made and to manually record the amount of the sale. In this situation, the employee in question could, as a part of his or her regular duties, introduce and conceal a misstatement by recording a lower quantity of goods sold than actually were sold and then pocket the cash difference.

The third phase involves tactical planning. Such planning facilitates assessment of desired detection and audit risks. In particular, conditional on what has been learned about the auditee so far, tactical planning involves deciding the most efficient and effective approach to producing evidence that will support a belief about the financial statements. An auditor can learn about the validity of a financial-statement assertion by testing the assertion directly (e.g., personally observing the existence of a fixed asset) or by studying the information system that produced the assertion (architecture and outputs) and, thus, indirectly testing the assertion. In general, the direct approach is thought to be more effective but more costly (less efficient) than the indirect approach. In a specific situation, however, the auditor must use what he or she has learned about the auditee to decide which approach or mix of approaches to use. For example, if the system architecture were judged to be relatively weak, the auditor might decide to bypass studying system outputs and concentrate on directly testing financial-statement assertions. Alternatively, if the system architecture were judged to be relatively strong, the auditor might judge it adequate to study system outputs instead of performing more costly direct tests.

Tactical planning also involves two other key tasks. First, the auditor must, in essence, ask and answer the following question: How large can a misstatement be before I want to have assurance that I will detect it? This task, called "planning materiality" assessment, requires that the auditor judge how precise the audit will be. In formulating this judgment, the auditor recognizes that financial statements and the information systems that produce them are of imperfect precision. Moreover, the auditor recognizes that the needs of financial-statement users can be met with somewhat imprecise information and that it is not cost-effective to increase precision above some level.

Second, at the tactical planning phase, the auditor typically would perform some tasks known collectively as analytical procedures to direct his or her attention to assertions that may have a relatively higher risk of misstatement. These procedures exploit interperiod or intraperiod relationships among financial-statement information. Thus, for example, if an auditor were to know that in the past, on the date the financial statements were issued, the auditee's outstanding credit sales were approximately 10% of total sales, barring any change in circumstances, the expected current outstanding credit sales would be 10% of total sales. To the extent that the financial statements indicated otherwise, conventional audit wisdom would suggest a heightened risk that the assertion concerning current outstanding credit sales is misstated. Consequently, the auditor may want to perform a direct test of that financial-statement assertion.

Next, the auditor either would plan indirect tests of financial-statement assertions and evaluate test results or would proceed directly to the fifth phase of the audit process. Assuming that the fourth phase is not bypassed, the auditor would judge if the system architecture studied earlier is actually in use by the auditee and effective at detecting and correcting misstatements. One key task, therefore, is to plan tests focussing on features of the system architecture that are expected to contribute most to this misstatement detection and correction ability. An illustration of such a test would be using the auditee's information system to process dummy transactions containing known errors to see if they are detected by the information system. In addition to planning the nature of such tests, auditors must determine their timing (i.e., when during the period covered by the financial statement or subsequently should they be performed) and extent (e.g., how many dummy transactions should be used). After performing these tests, the auditor evaluates the evidence produced and, at the conclusion of this phase, makes a reassessment of control risk.

During the fifth phase, taking into account what he or she has learned so far, the auditor makes planning judgments about the nature, timing, and extent of the direct tests of financial-statement assertions that will lead to an effective and efficient audit. An initial judgment (or reassessment) of desired detection and audit risks also will be made. Tests at this stage are focussed on the details of financial-statement assertions (e.g., confirming with creditors that accounts receivable exist) or on the interrelationships among data (e.g., analytical procedures). Subsequently, the auditor must evaluate the evidence produced by each of these tests and determine if additional procedures are required. If such procedures are performed, the auditor must interpret their results.

Evaluation of aggregate results is the focus of the sixth phase: The auditor considers interrelationships among the various individual test results and subjectively aggregates the evidence relevant to the various financial-statement assertions. In addition, the auditor makes an assessment of "achieved" detection and audit risks. The final phase of the audit process culminates with the auditor choosing a report that best communicates his or her evaluation of the totality of the evidence collected.[8] That is, the auditor formulates a global judgment (called an "opinion") about the validity of the assertions within and among the financial statements. Such judgment formulation requires a second focus on materiality. At this phase, however, the primary concern (which auditors call "reporting materiality") is the importance of detected misstatements (and others that the evidence suggests are likely) to potential users of the financial statements.

Several possibilities exist at this point. First, the auditor may judge the evidence accumulated so far to be sufficiently inconclusive that additional evidence must be collected before any global judgment is made. The dashed "feedback" lines coming out of the sixth box in Figure 1 show this possibility. Second, the auditor may judge that the accumulated evidence is sufficient to support the conclusion that no adjustment to any of the financial-statement assertions is necessary. In this case, the auditor would issue a report stating that the financial statements are valid (i.e., follow GAAP). Alternatively, if the auditor judges that at least one adjustment is necessary, the auditee will have to decide whether or not to make the adjustment.[9] If the auditee makes the requested adjustment(s), the auditor would issue a report stating that the financial statements are valid. But if the auditee disagrees with the auditor, the auditor would reconsider the initial judgment after evaluating any new evidence the auditee provides (possibly proposing a smaller adjustment and obtaining the auditee's reaction) and then decide if the report should state that the financial statements are valid or invalid.

Analytical procedures: A J/DM elaboration

This subsection highlights some of the cognitive activities that pervade the audit process by focusing on analytical procedures. Analytical procedures were chosen because they are J/DM rich. That is, while performing the various subtasks that collectively are known as analytical procedures, the auditor engages in a wide spectrum of cognitive activities including forming mental representations, generating and testing hypotheses, external and internal (i.e., in memory) information search, and information evaluation and combination. Once again, we employ a "textbook" approach that creates a tutorial flavor.

As noted earlier, analytical procedures focus on the interrelationships among data and are based on the assumption that, absent some change in circumstances, data interrelationships that have held in the past will persist. Analytical review, the process of performing such procedures, is a subjective

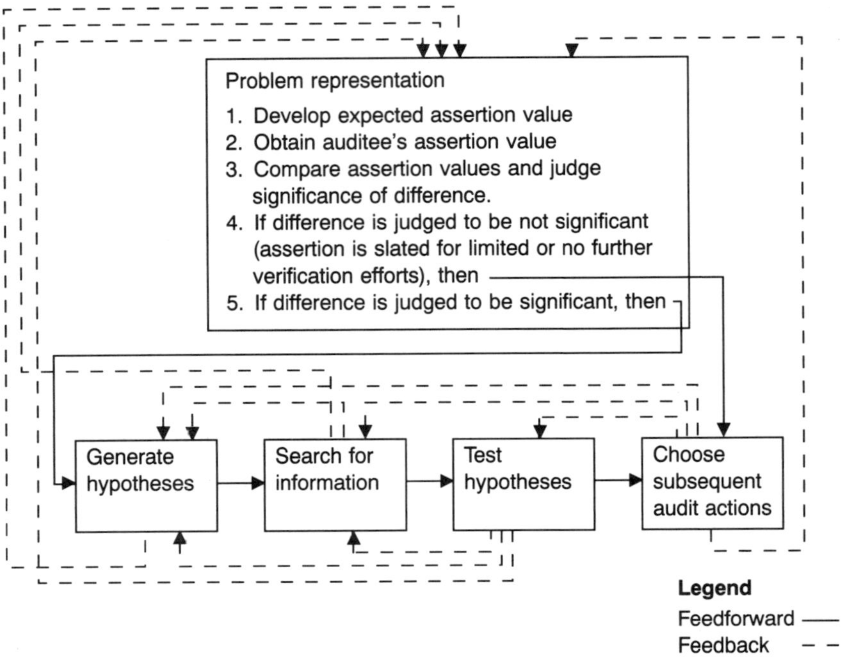

Figure 2. Judgments and decisions in analytical procedures.

process and has been characterized previously from a diagnostic–inference perspective (see Libby, 1985 and Koonce, 1992).[10] To illustrate, an auditor may wish to evaluate the reasonableness of the dollar value shown on the financial statements for uncollected credit sales (i.e., accounts receivable) by computing a ratio of the current dollar value of accounts receivable to current total sales and then comparing this ratio to a similar ratio for a prior period. As depicted in Figure 2 (adapted from Koonce, 1992), analytical review is not unlike the sequential, iterative process in which a physician engages when a patient presents symptoms and requests a diagnosis (Ashton et al., 1988; Blocher and Cooper, 1988).

The five-step analytical review process begins when the auditor decides to evaluate a financial-statement assertion (e.g., valuation of accounts receivable balances) using analytical procedures. Having made that choice, the first step is to form a mental representation of the problem. Usually, this step will involve the auditor subjectively developing an expected value for the assertion, which then will be compared subjectively with the value that the auditee intends to report. Forming such an expected value will require the auditor to retrieve from memory procedural and declarative knowledge, especially that gathered earlier in the audit, which may be indicative of changing circumstances (e.g., a change in credit policy).

To illustrate, based on prior-period data, the auditor might determine that the ratio of the current dollar value of accounts receivable to current total sales should be near 0.10. Ultimately, the "problem" facing the auditor at this time is to judge the significance of any difference between the expected assertion value and the assertion value that the auditee intends to report (which, for illustrative purposes is assumed to produce a ratio of 0.15). If the difference (0.05) were judged to be insignificant, a decision would be made to restrict or possibly to terminate further verification efforts with respect to that assertion. This possibility is depicted by the solid line from the "problem representation" box in Figure 2 to the box annotated by "choose subsequent audit actions." It is significant that dire (but delayed) consequences may arise if the latter decision were made erroneously, i.e., in a situation in which the assertion actually were significantly misstated. Specifically, the auditor may be sued for damages suffered by financial-statement users who have relied on the misstated assertions.

Alternatively, if the (0.05) difference were judged to be significant, the auditor's next step would be to generate hypotheses that may explain the observed difference. This possibility is depicted by the solid line going to the "generate hypotheses" box in Figure 2. A key activity here is retrieval from memory of hypotheses or construction of hypotheses suggested by prior year's audit activities or by the auditee during the current year's audit. For example, a hypothesis might be that circumstances (e.g., credit-granting policies) had changed, thus changing the expected ratio of outstanding credit sales to total sales. Once such a plausible hypothesis or hypothesis set is generated, the auditor searches for information specifically for hypothesis-testing purposes. This purposeful search can result in belief revision and, ultimately (perhaps after several iterations), one of the hypotheses would remain. For example, the auditor might verify that the credit-granting policy had changed and that the change was properly authorized.

Next, the auditor will choose subsequent audit actions that could include slating the assertion for intensive audit scrutiny (if the nonrejected hypothesis were that the assertion were invalid) or terminating further verification efforts (if the nonrejected hypothesis were that the assertion were valid). To continue the illustration, the auditor either would increase the intensity with which outstanding accounts receivable were audited or conclude that only minimal further efforts were needed. Again, serious consequences may arise if the latter course of action were chosen but the assertion actually was misstated. On the other hand, an auditor who erroneously chooses the former course of action could be "disciplined" by the auditee and the marketplace because of the audit-process inefficiency he or she would have introduced.

Literature review: Organizing framework

Given the present objective of communicating with readers having limited knowledge of auditing, two of the organizing principles for this section are

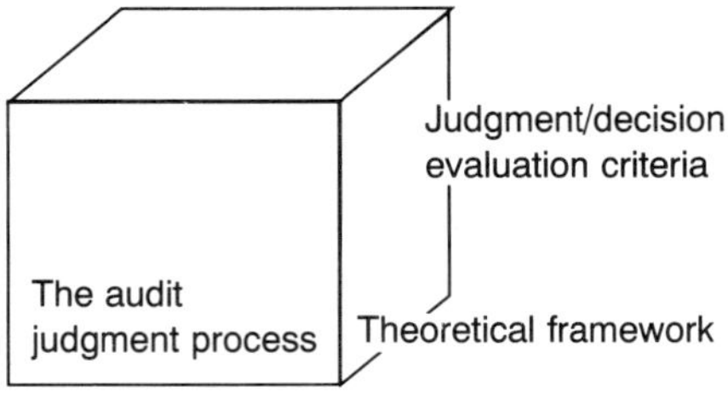

Audit judgment process	Theoretical frameworks	Judgment/Decision evaluation criteria
Orientation	Policy capturing	Consensus
Evaluate information-system architecture and process	Probabilistic judgment	Cue usage
Tactical planning	Heuristics and Biases	Stability
Plan indirect tests of financial-statement assertions and evaluate test results	Cognitive processes	Self-insight
Plan direct tests of financial-statement assertions and evaluate test results	Multiperson information processing	Accuracy
Evaluate aggregate results		Consistency
Choose report		

Figure 3. Organizing framework: The cube.

the J/DM theoretical frameworks underlying the study and the J/DM evaluation criteria employed. A third organizing principle is the stage of the audit J/DM process as discussed above. Thus, a "cube" featuring the J/DM theoretical framework, J/DM evaluation criteria, and the stage of the audit J/DM process provides the structure for the remainder of this chapter (see Figure 3). The largely descriptive orientation of this section sets the stage for critical discussion and suggestions for future audit J/DM research in subsequent sections.

Theoretical framework and judgment/decision evaluation criteria

Most of the published research on audit J/DM has used one or more of the "standard" theoretical frameworks employed in nonaudit J/DM studies. For present purposes, five frameworks are used: policy capturing, probabilistic judgment, heuristics and biases, cognitive processes, and multiperson information processing. The scope of our review is restricted to audit J/DM studies that used one or more of these frameworks. In addition, the scope is restricted to papers published in the following journals before 1992: *Accounting, Organizations and Society; Auditing: A Journal of Practice and Theory; Contemporary Accounting Research; Journal of Accounting Research;* and *The Accounting Review.* An overwhelming majority of the extant audit J/DM studies and virtually all of those studies meeting our other inclusion criteria have been published in these journals. Lastly, the scope is restricted to studies that employed practicing auditors as subjects.

Several types of audit J/DM studies employing practicing auditor–subjects are excluded from the review and evaluation. These omitted studies generally are not structured or motivated by any of the aforementioned J/DM frameworks and may be characterized as follows. First, they typically are oriented toward producing evidence on a substantive issue of immediate concern to the practicing auditing community. Second, they generally do not have theory-driven hypotheses. Third, these studies typically manipulate information about the auditee (e.g., management integrity, the compensation system), its accounting information system (e.g., its architecture), and/or a professional audit or accounting standard or procedure. Fourth, the standard for evaluation of observed judgments/decisions is strict adherence to a professional or legal standard or procedure.

Each of the studies meeting our criteria was inspected to discern the phase of the audit judgment process in which it was set, the theoretical framework underlying the study, and the J/DM evaluation criteria used. The evaluation criteria will be familiar to J/DM researchers as they have been used extensively in J/DM studies. They include cue usage, self-insight, accuracy, consensus, stability, and consistency.[11] Each of these evaluation criteria could and generally have been used to test hypotheses motivated by any of the five theoretical frameworks. Because audit J/DM researchers' operationalization of these criteria sometimes have differed from that of nonaudit J/DM researchers, we selectively describe such operationalization.

Cue usage primarily has been measured in policy-capturing studies by the significance of a cue in a statistical model (e.g., analysis of variance) or by statistics like omega-squared. In studies based on other frameworks, cue usage has been assessed as the extent to which a subject's judgment is affected by new information (i.e., a form of the pretest/posttest experimental design). *Self-insight* typically has been assessed as the correlation, over all cues, between a subject's cue usage and the importance rating subjectively attached to each cue (e.g., by allocating 100 points among the cues).

Accuracy has been used in only a few studies because, for many audit tasks, there is no unambiguous external criterion (outcome realization) against which to compare the J/DM. Instead, three operationalizations of accuracy have been used. First, in those policy-capturing studies that employed tasks having a readily observable external criterion, accuracy was measured ex post by the correlation between a judgment/decision and the realized external criterion. Second, in the probabilistic judgment studies that had a readily observable external criterion, accuracy was measured ex post in a variety of ways including calibration, extremeness, and logarithmic and quadratic scoring rules. Third, for those studies that used audit tasks in which a readily observable external criterion did not exist, a surrogate was developed using either a consensus response of a panel of experts or a simulated estimate of the "true" value of the unobservable external criterion. Accuracy then was assessed either by the policy-capturing or probabilistic judgment approaches just described.

Consensus has been the most frequently used evaluation criterion. In policy-capturing studies, it has been computed as the mean correlation between the judgments/decisions of each pair of subjects. In studies other than policy-capturing, consensus has been evaluated by reference to the level of similarity of judgments or subjective probability distributions.

Stability (or reliability) has been assessed as the correlation between a single subject's responses to the same stimuli at different points in time, ranging from repeat cases in a single experimental session to multiple sessions a few weeks apart. In contrast to the typical J/DM approach, audit J/DM studies have operationalized *consistency* (convergent validity) as the intrasubject correlation between two different judgment types. For example, one might compare an auditor's control-risk judgments with his or her judgments of required audit effort.

Policy-capturing studies

Twenty-eight experimental studies empirically modeled auditors' judgment and decision policies (Table 1, pp. 154–155). When multiple audit tasks were employed in a single study, it was placed into more than one task category.[12] The modal study used Brunswik's lens model as the empirical framework to investigate consensus and cue usage. Fewer studies examined stability, consistency, self-insight and accuracy. J/DM policies were modeled using ANOVA, discriminate analysis, conjoint measurement, and the analytical hierarchy procedure. In 14 of the 28 studies, the auditor-subjects were asked to evaluate the architecture of an auditee's accounting-information system (see expanded discussion below).

Consensus was examined in 22 studies, and the unweighted mean correlation over these studies is 0.59. Although considerable variation existed in the level of consensus across studies (mean correlations range from 0.28 to 0.93 across studies), it was greater than 0.50 (0.70) in 71% (42%) of the studies. This level of consensus is higher than that typically reported in nonaudit J/DM studies.

Cue usage was examined in 21 studies. In all of these studies, a policy-capturing model explained almost all of the variance in a subject's judgments; typically, about four to six cues were found to be significant, with considerable individual differences in cue usage across auditors. In addition, the relative importance of particular cues generally has been found to be consistent with professional auditing standards. Lastly, there has been almost no evidence of configural cue usage. The exceptions are two studies by Brown and Solomon (1990, 1991), which are discussed more fully below.

Nine studies report a total of 12 stability correlations, with an unweighted average of 0.86. There is relatively little variation across studies, as the range of correlations is 0.73 to 0.98. As in other J/DM settings, stability has been higher than consensus in the audit context. Two studies tested consistency, operationalized as the intrasubject correlation between two different, but logically related, judgments. Both reported a mean correlation of 0.82 (Gaumnitz et al., 1982; Schneider, 1985).

Self-insight into cue usage was examined in seven studies (including Ashton, 1974b, which appeared in a J/DM journal), with an unweighted mean correlation of 0.73 across settings. The level of self-insight ranged from 0.53 to 0.89 across auditor subjects and/or tasks, indicating some variation across studies. Overall, the auditor subjects have demonstrated a fairly high level of awareness of their use of information, which may stem from training and public accounting firm practices (e.g., the use of J/DM aids such as checklists).

Four studies focussed on the level of judgment accuracy. Kida (1980) and Ashton (1985) used the same cues but different auditor subjects and both report a high level of accuracy. In these two studies, the mean levels of accuracy over subjects (measured by percentage of correct judgments) were 83% and 84%, respectively. Using a similar task that was experimentally couched in terms of human selection/mechanical combination, Simnett and Trotman (1989) reported that the accuracy of auditors' business failure predictions were sensitive to cue selection and combination strategies. Specifically, subjects' predictions were not affected by the information-combination mode when cues were selected by humans; however, when cues were selected mechanically, the environmental model combined the cues to form more accurate predictions than did the humans. Lastly, Libby and Libby (1989) reported evidence that the accuracy of a judgment could be improved by mechanically combining component judgments to form a global judgment rather than directly forming a global judgment.

Several studies have analyzed the association between experience—defined as years of auditing experience—and the various J/DM evaluation criteria. However, consistent with nonaudit J/DM studies (Johnson, 1988), no obvious pattern has been reported, suggesting that cue usage, consensus, stability, or self-insight are not related to experience. Moreover, in some studies, the results have been the opposite of that predicted (e.g., less experienced auditor subjects exhibited greater self-insight or more consensus than more experienced subjects).

With a few exceptions, these audit J/DM research findings are consistent with the results of nonaudit J/DM studies. This consistency is noteworthy because the audit studies utilized trained and experienced subjects who performed experimental versions of their usual professional tasks. On the one hand, such consistency suggests that criticisms of generic J/DM studies for using student subjects may be overstated. On the other hand, the consistency suggests that the structural features of audit contexts did not affect the generalizability of J/DM theories.

Table 1. *Policy capturing studies*

	Judgment/decision evaluation criteria					
Audit process activities	Consensus	Cue usage	Stability	Consistency	Self-insight	Accuracy
1. Orientation	Colbert (1988)	Colbert (1988)	Colbert (1988)		Colbert (1988)	
2. Evaluate accounting information-system architecture	Ashton (1974a) Ashton & Brown (1980) Gaumnitz et al. (1982) Hamilton & Wright (1982) Mayper (1982) Abdel-Khalik et al. (1983) Brown (1983) Tabor (1983) Schneider (1984, 1985) Kaplan (1985) Meixner & Welker (1988) Brown & Solomon (1990)	Ashton (1974a) Ashton & Brown (1980) Hamilton & Wright (1982) Abdel-Khalik et al. (1983) Brown (1983) Schneider (1984, 1985) Kaplan (1985) Mayper et al. (1989) Brown & Solomon (1990)	Ashton (1974a) Ashton & Brown (1980) Abdel-Khalik et al. (1983) Brown (1983) Meixner & Welker (1988)	Gaumnitz et al. (1982) Schneider (1985)	Ashton & Brown (1980) Hamilton & Wright (1982) Brown (1983)	
3. Tactical planning	Brown & Solomon (1991)	Brown & Solomon (1991)				
4. Plan indirect tests and evaluate results		Libby & Libby (1989)				Libby & Libby (1989)

5. Plan direct tests and evaluate results	Joyce (1976) Gaumnitz et al. (1982) Tabor (1983) Kaplan (1985) Schneider (1985) Srindhi & Vasarhelyi (1986) Bamber & Snowball (1988) Brown & Solomon (1991)	Joyce (1976) Kaplan (1985) Schneider (1985) Brown & Solomon (1991)	Joyce (1976) Srindhi & Vasarhelyi (1986)	Gaumnitz et al. (1982) Schneider (1985)	Joyce (1976)	
6. Evaluate aggregate results						
7. Report decision	Moriarity & Barron (1979) Kida (1980) Messier (1983) Ashton (1985)	Boatsman & Robertson (1974) Moriarity & Barron (1976, 1979) Firth (1979) Kida (1980) Messier (1983)	Messier (1983)		Messier (1983)	Kida (1980) Ashton (1985) Simnett & Trotman (1989)

In 25 of the 28 experiments, cues were generated by factorial designs (mostly fractional replications) with subject's J/DM policies modeled by ANOVA, conjoint measurement or the analytical hierarchy method. A potential problem with studies using factorial designs (and attendant orthogonal cues) is inconsistency with the audit ecology. In the remaining studies, experimental cues with higher ecological validity were used and discriminant analysis was employed for policy-capturing purposes.

Only four policy-capturing studies have investigated the accuracy of auditor's judgments/decisions (Kida, 1980; Ashton, 1985; Libby and Libby, 1989; and Simnett and Trotman, 1989). The reason for this limited focus on accuracy is that most audit tasks (e.g., judging the quality of information-system architecture) do *not* have (readily observable) outcomes, making it difficult to assess accuracy. The experimental task in Kida (1980), Ashton (1985), and Simnett and Trotman (1989) was business failure prediction based on accounting information. While not inherently an audit task, as financial analysts and credit managers also predict business failure, it is sometimes performed by auditors. These three studies assessed judgment accuracy by the correspondence between an auditor's predictions and outcome realizations. An alternative approach to addressing accuracy was taken by Libby and Libby (1989), in which "truth" was surrogated by the consensus response of a panel of experts. Because unambiguous external criteria do not exist in most audit settings, most policy-capturing studies primarily relied on consensus as the measure of J/DM quality. But reliance on consensus has raised concerns about its reliability as a surrogate for accuracy because it is possible that a set of judges could have high consensus but low accuracy: their judgments/decisions are in agreement but not with external criteria (cf. Ashton, 1985; Pincus, 1990).

In response to concern about reliance on the consensus criterion, two studies investigated the relationship between accuracy and consensus. Ashton (1985) used four measures of accuracy and consensus (individual versus pairwise, absolute versus relative) for two different tasks to assess empirically the correlation between accuracy and consensus. She found the mean Pearson correlation between accuracy and consensus to be 0.84, suggesting that consensus is a good surrogate for accuracy.[13] Pincus (1990) conducted an analytical analysis of the relationship between accuracy and consensus for dichotomous choices when judges are equally competent and the prior probabilities are equal that the two alternatives are correct. Consensus was found to be a good surrogate for accuracy only when the probability that a judge will make the correct decision is at least 0.50; further increases in this probability improves the ability of consensus to surrogate for accuracy. Moreover, when prior odds are unequal, the probability that the consensus choice is accurate depends on the alternative chosen. For example, the consensus alternative is more (less) likely to be accurate when it is the alternative with the higher (lower) prior odds.

Probabilistic judgment studies

This audit research stream, rooted in behavioral decision theory, generally has focused on subjective probability assessment, probability combination, and risky choice behavior. The initial audit probabilistic judgment studies addressed the extent of differences between (a) auditors' judgments and predictions derived from statistical models and (b) judgments obtained from auditors using different elicitation methods. Once such differences were documented, researchers sought to explain and predict them. Such explanations typically have been based on heuristics and biases and, more recently, on the insights from cognitive psychology and cognitive-science research. The present subsection reviews the early studies that focused on identifying differences in individual auditors' judgment behavior and performance whereas the next two subsections review audit J/DM studies based on heuristics and biases and cognitive processes.

Seven experimental studies investigated auditor assessment of subjective probability distributions (see Table 2). The typical study was designed to test whether the probability elicitation method was associated with significant between-subject differences in subjective probability distributions. Both direct methods (fractile, bisection, fixed interval, cumulative distribution-function assessment) and indirect methods (equivalent prior sample, hypothetical future sample information) have been used. In these studies, the researchers' focus has been differences in assessed distributions, using either the consensus (Corless, 1972; Felix, 1976; Crosby, 1981; Solomon et al., 1982; Abdolmohammadi and Berger, 1986) or accuracy criterion (Abdolmohammadi and Berger, 1986; Shields et al., 1987, 1988). The early studies were devoid of theory-driven hypotheses, while some of the later studies were designed to test predictions derived from psychological theory. For example, Shields et al. (1988) used concepts from the framing literature to make predictions about how the relative accuracy of subjective probability distributions interacts with response method (probability–value or value–probability) and problem framing (dollar value of account balance or dollar error of account balance). The general results of these studies are that: (1) the response mode affects elicited probability distributions; (2) the magnitude of this effect depends somewhat on the length of the auditor's experience and the level of uncertainty about the accounting system; (3) consensus is low; (4) auditors' judgments are not as poorly calibrated as are the typical subject's judgments in nonaudit J/DM studies (see below); and (5) in contrast to the typical J/DM finding of overconfidence (see Keren, 1991), auditors' judgments have been found to exhibit underconfidence.[14]

Two studies examined whether auditors combine information and make judgments consistent with predictions derived from the axioms of decision theory. Bamber (1983) developed and tested a model of how source credibility impacts on probability revision. He found that auditor subjects overly

Table 2. *Probabilistic judgment studies*

Audit process activities	Judgment/decision evaluation criteria					
	Accuracy	Consensus	Cue usage	Stability	Self-insight	Consistency
1. Orientation						
2. Evaluate accounting information-system architecture		Corless (1972) Felix (1976) Crosby (1981) Bamber (1983)	Bamber (1983)			
3. Tactical planning						
4. Plan indirect tests and evaluate results		Corless (1972)				
5. Plan direct tests and evaluate results	Abdomohammadi and Berger (1986) Shields et al. (1987, 1988)	Solomon et al. (1982) Bamber (1983) Abdomohammadi and Berger (1986)	Bamber (1983) Shields et al. (1988)			
6. Evaluate aggregate results						
7. Report decision		Ward (1976) Newton (1977) Lewis (1980)	A. Ashton (1982)			

discounted information received from sources with low credibility compared to predictions from the model. A. Ashton (1982) reported that auditors' decisions were consistent with the irrelevance axiom, with the violation rate being lower when the classic Allais problem was cast in audit contexts rather than the original generic context.[15]

Three studies addressed issues relating to risky choice. Ward (1976), Newton (1977), and Lewis (1980) attempted to describe the shape of auditors' utility functions and to assess the level of consensus among them. Most auditor subjects were found to have utility functions for losses consistent with risk aversion. Moreover, there was a high level of consensus for loss outcomes, and consensus was higher for subjects within a particular audit firm than for subjects across different firms.

Heuristics-and-biases studies

Once differences between auditors' J/DM and predictions from statistical models were documented, audit researchers started to use the heuristics-and-biases approach developed by Tversky and Kahneman (1974); Kahneman et al., 1982) to see if it could describe auditors' probabilistic judgments. Some studies tested whether the representatives and anchoring and adjustment heuristics described auditors' judgments and others examined Hogarth and Einhorn's (1992) belief-adjustment model.[16] The studies reviewed in this section are categorized in Table 3.

Three studies tested whether the representativeness heuristic described auditors' judgments. Uecker and Kinney (1977) found that although 70% of the judgments made by auditor subjects were correct, 54% of the subjects made at least one judgment consistent with the representativeness heuristic when evaluating sample results. In addition, the level of audit experience did not significantly effect these results. Joyce and Biddle (1981b) conducted six experiments in a fraud prediction context to test for neglect of base rates and sensitivity to the reliability of information (source credibility). Four between-subject experiments indicated that most subjects' probability revisions were sensitive to base-rate information. However, the magnitude of the regression toward the base rate was insufficient relative to Bayesian revision. These results are in contrast to many J/DM results from studies also using between-subject designs (i.e., little, if any sensitivity to base rates).

Joyce and Biddle's other two experiments tested for source reliability effects and the results depended on the experimental design. When a between-subjects design was used, auditor subjects' responses did not vary depending upon source reliability. With a within-subject design, however, the subjects did adjust their responses for variation in source reliability. But, because demand effects may have influenced these results, Rebele et al. (1988) used a between-subjects design and reported that auditor subjects were sensitive to source credibility. In total, these results and Bamber (1983) suggest that, in

Table 3. *Heuristics-and-Biases Studies*

	Judgment/decision evaluation criteria					
Audit process activities	Cue usage	Accuracy	Self-insight	Consensus	Stability	Consistency
1. Orientation						
2. Evaluate accounting information-system architecture	Ashton and Ashton (1988) Butt and Campbell (1989)					
3. Tactical planning	Kinney and Uecker (1982) Biggs and Wild (1985) Rebele et al. (1988) Heintz and White (1989)					
4. Plan indirect tests and evaluate results	Uecker and Kinney (1977) Kinney and Uecker (1982) Butler (1986)					
5. Plan direct tests and evaluate results	Joyce and Biddle (1981a,b) Wright (1988) Tubbs et al. (1990)	Wright (1988)				
6. Evaluate aggregate results	Butler (1986)					
7. Report decision	Joyce and Biddle (1981a)					

contrast with J/DM research, auditors are relatively sensitive to the reliability of information sources.

Six studies tested whether auditors make judgments consistent with the anchoring and adjustment heuristic. In a series of six experiments, Joyce and Biddle (1981a) reported that, while adjustments were typically insufficient from an irrelevant anchor, many of the observed results cannot be fully accounted for by the anchoring and adjustment heuristic. Kinney and Uecker (1982) reported in two experiments that auditor judgments were affected by hypothesized anchors that were assumed to have been used. In follow-up studies with improved experimental designs, Biggs and Wild (1985) and Heintz and White (1989) reported similar results; however, Wright (1988), using a different task and design, reported a small anchoring and adjustment effect. Butler (1986) reported that student subjects anchored on information provided by the researcher whereas auditor subjects anchored on an "internal" benchmark (possibly a function of knowledge stored in memory).

Three auditing papers tested the belief-adjustment model (Hogarth and Einhorn, 1992). Ashton and Ashton (1988) performed five experiments and found no effect of information order on judgments when the information received was consistently positive or consistently negative. However, a recency effect was detected when the information received was mixed (positive and negative). These results are consistent with predictions from the belief-adjustment model. However, contrary to evidence reported in J/DM studies, less extreme revision was reported for simultaneous versus sequential receipt of information. Similar results are provided by Tubbs et al. (1990), who conducted four experiments and found no order effects on judgments with the receipt of consistent information, but recency effects were observed with mixed information. In contrast, Butt and Campbell (1989) did not detect a recency effect when their auditor subjects received mixed information.

Most of the results of heuristics-and-biases studies in which auditor subjects performed audit judgment tasks are similar to those reported for student subjects in J/DM studies using generic tasks. There are, however, certain important exceptions. Significant among the exceptions are that auditors' J/DM is more sensitive to base rates and that auditors exhibit a greater tendency to adjust beliefs in light of new information. These exceptions, which cannot be accounted for by the usual heuristics-and-biases models, as well as a desire to provide more complete and accurate audit J/DM models, motivated researchers to begin employing approaches developed in the cognitive psychology and cognitive science literatures.

Cognitive process studies

Following the J/DM literature (e.g., Payne et al., 1988), the trend in audit J/DM research has been to dig deeper into the "black box" between information inputs and outputs. Part of the impetus for this strategy seems to have been audit J/DM researchers' greater awareness of the methods and measures used by nonaudit J/DM researchers to elucidate cognitive activities.

However, part of the impetus for this research strategy also was greater recognition that explanations more deeply rooted in cognitive processes were needed if a more complete and accurate understanding of auditors' J/DM were to be forthcoming (see Birnberg and Shields, 1984). Thus, much of the focus of audit J/DM research has evolved to modeling and testing cognitive activities like problem representation (e.g., Peters, 1990), hypothesis generation (e.g., Libby, 1985), hypothesis evaluation (e.g., Frederick and Libby, 1986; Bonner and Lewis, 1990), and information search (e.g., Biggs et al., 1988) using theories and methods adapted from cognitive psychology and cognitive science. The chapter by Libby in this book (Chapter 7) provides a comprehensive review of this emerging and important area of audit J/DM research.

Multiperson information-processing studies

Some multiperson aspects of auditing were mentioned earlier (e.g., supervision of team members, review of their work as documented in working papers, and consultation with appropriate persons in connection with special problems). Recognizing these multiperson aspects, researchers have reported studies in which the focus was either group-choice shift, group versus individual policy capturing or probabilistic judgment, and "team" review processes (see Table 4). Based on the choice-shift paradigm, Schultz and Reckers (1981) investigated the risk-taking propensities of interacting groups of audit partners in comparison with that of individual partners. In addition, some groups interacted face-to-face while others interacted by telephone. The nature of the consultation (binding versus advisory) also was manipulated. Some differences were noted between the groups and individuals in propensities to make risky choices (i.e., require financial-statement disclosures) but few were statistically significant. While the nature of the consultation and the communication channel had significant effects, those results have not been pursued further by researchers.

Solomon (1982) investigated the extent to which individuals and groups of auditors assess similar subjective probabilities. Subjective probability judgments of financial-statement account values provided by individual auditors were compared with those of three-member groups of auditors interacting under different structures (e.g., nominal/interacting groups versus interacting/nominal groups). Consensus, calibration, and extremeness were employed as evaluation criteria. The results were mixed, with group judgments consistently exhibiting greater consensus and extremeness and individual judgments exhibiting better calibration. In contrast with typical J/DM results, but consistent with the earlier observation, auditor judgments did *not* exhibit overconfidence in any experimental condition.

Review as a mechanism for multiperson interaction within the audit team has received limited research attention despite the fact that much interaction occurs in the "review process" (i.e., reviewing working papers prepared by less experienced team members). Two policy-capturing studies investigating

Table 4. *Multiperson information-processing studies*

	Judgment/decision evaluation criteria					
Audit process activities	Cue usage	Consensus	Accuracy	Self-insight	Stability	Consistency
1. Orientation						
2. Evaluate accounting information-system architecture	Trotman and Yetton (1985)	Trotman and Yetton (1985)				
3. Tactical planning						
4. Plan indirect tests and evaluate results						
5. Plan direct tests and evaluate results		Solomon (1982)	Solomon (1982) Trotman (1985)			
6. Evaluate aggregate results						
7. Report decision	Schultz and Reckers (1981)					

this form of interaction are exceptions. Trotman and Yetton (1985) reported that, relative to individual judgment, the review process (operationalized as a "dispersed" group; see Hill, 1982 and Solomon, 1987) significantly increased the consensus about the reliability of an auditee's information-system architecture. Trotman and Yetton (1985) also compared the reviewed judgments with those of two-person interacting groups and two-person statistical composites and reported no significant differences. Trotman (1985) investigated the accuracy of judgments of likely assertion misstatements due to information-system architecture weaknesses made in a face-to-face review mode. These judgments were compared to those of individual auditors, two-person interacting groups and two-person statistical composites. Accuracy was found to be greater for all of the multiperson modes relative to the individuals but, again, no significant differences were detected between the reviewed judgments and judgments from the interacting groups.

Prior research: The modal cell

In this section, an in-depth discussion is provided of studies that used the policy-capturing paradigm to investigate auditor judgments of information-system architecture. Because this type of study is the modal audit J/DM study, our discussion provides a means of illustrating the development of audit J/DM studies over the past approximately twenty years (see Table 2).

The first such study was reported in 1974 by Ashton. Since it provided the impetus for so many extensions, we begin by describing several features of that study. The subjects in Ashton (1974a) were practicing auditors, generally with two to three years of experience. Their task was to evaluate the architecture of an information subsystem relating to the processing of a manufacturing firm's payroll transactions. The dependent-variable scale had 6 levels (ranging from 1 = extremely weak to 6 = adequate to strong). Six independent variables (representing features of the information-system architecture) were included at two levels each (present or absent) and were manipulated within subjects using a fractional 2^6 factorial design. As in predecessor J/DM studies (e.g., Hoffman et al., 1968), ANOVA was used to analyze the subjects' responses and to estimate individual policy-capturing models.

A number of judgment attributes were investigated, including consensus and cue usage. With the exception of the relatively high degree of consensus on the overall quality of the system architecture (mean correlation of 0.70), results generally were consistent with those reported in J/DM studies. For example, there was considerable variability in those system architecture features thought to be most important and, based on the explained variance attributable to interaction terms, little evidence of configural processing was identified.

A recent meta-analysis (Trotman and Wood, 1991) identified 16 extensions of Ashton (1974a). In addition to the issues addressed in the original Ashton paper, these studies investigated the effects of increased task complexity (Ashton and Brown, 1980) and the review process (Trotman and Yetton, 1985) on auditor J/DM. Consistent with most J/DM studies, a robust finding has been that "linear," as opposed to configural, cue processing explained almost all of the auditor subjects' judgment variance. Similar results were obtained by Ashton and Brown (1980), who increased the number of cues in their study with the intention of enhancing their ability to detect configural processing.

While Ashton and Brown attempted to detect configural processing by varying task structure, Brown and Solomon (1990) performed a detailed analysis of the content of the task in Ashton (1974a) to discern ex ante, in the context of a professional evaluation of the architecture of an information system, what types of configural processing should be *expected*. Based on this analysis, they investigated the cues used in prior studies and found that none should be expected to have been configurally processed. Brown and Solomon (1990) then designed an experiment in which specific cues would be expected to be configurally processed. While evidence of configural processing was reported in the predicted cue combinations and its magnitude was large relative to prior studies, the absolute magnitude of configural processing remained modest. However, striking evidence of configural processing was uncovered in a different task (risk assessment in connection with analytical procedures). Specifically, Brown and Solomon (1991) reported that over 90% of their auditor subjects exhibited configural processing, with the average explained variance attributed to the single predicted interaction term being almost 40%. These results were attributed to the disordinal nature of the underlying cue relationship.

Evaluation of extant research and recommendations

This section provides an evaluation of audit J/DM studies organized along the three dimensions of the cube presented in Figure 3. In addition to evaluative commentary, recommendations are presented for future audit J/DM studies. Such recommendations include the need to broaden the J/DM evaluation criteria and empirical methods used, investigate new variables and their interrelationships, and do a better job of representing within audit J/DM studies the structure and content of audit tasks/contexts as well as processor–task/context interactions.

J/DM evaluation criteria

Although a variety of evaluation criteria have been used, the most common criterion in audit J/DM studies has been consensus. The absence of an unambiguous external referent has made it difficult to evaluate auditor J/DM in terms of ex post accuracy. This characteristic of audit tasks has been especially troublesome in studies of how well auditors make judgments/decisions. It also has led to considerable interest in the relationship between accuracy and consensus in auditing contexts and to an interest in different measures of consensus. Correlational measures have been popular even though they are not influenced by absolute differences in judgments/decisions between subjects or between judgments and external criteria (see Gaumnitz et al., 1982). That is, while the judgments/decisions of two subjects could move in the same direction and be of similar magnitudes relative to each subject's mean judgment/decision, there could be significant absolute differences in their judgments/decisions.

The importance of accuracy and accuracy surrogates follows from the traditional view of auditing as a "search for truth." If auditing were viewed more from the perspective of evidence marshalling and justification (as in studies like Emby and Gibbins, 1988), other evaluation criteria would be more salient. For example, justifiability/defensibility and efficiency would be important criteria given the various accountability foci in auditing (superiors, auditees, regulators, or judges/juries). Continued attention to consensus probably is appropriate, however, because one important way to justify a judgment is to establish that other professionals would have made the same judgment.

Audit J/DM process

One theme of this chapter is that greater attention should be focused on the structural features of audit tasks (Libby, 1990). A companion theme has been the concurrent need to increase attention to audit task content. In contrast, most of the extant audit J/DM research can be characterized as testing whether generic J/DM theories apply in the auditing domain. Much of this research has focused on whether auditors process information and make judgments/decisions similar to nonauditors in nonaudit contexts. However, since, in the context of prior studies, there typically has been little reason for auditors to differ from other judges or decision makers, it is hardly surprising that most audit J/DM research results have been qualitatively similar to the results of nonaudit J/DM studies. While these foci might be appealing during the embryonic stage of audit J/DM research, they are inherently limited for latter stages of development. Fortunately, this implicit study of the auditor as processor is now being replaced by a richer approach (Bonner and Pennington, 1991) in which the foci are identifying what is different about audit tasks/contexts and how such differences might cause auditors to process information and make judgments/decisions differently from how they would be made by other judges or decision makers in other contexts.

An important part of planning an audit J/DM study, given the shift from viewing the auditor as a generic processor, is a task analysis to identify the information-processing demands for successful task completion (Newell and Simon, 1972). For example, understanding and effectively researching how an auditor verifies the potential revenue stream of a biomedical firm from a newly patented medication requires the researcher to analyze the structure and content of the problem. Such analysis would include identifying the auditor's goal (e.g., unbiased estimate of future revenues, justify the decision to the auditee or the auditor's superior, defend the decision in court), how the auditor organizes the task (e.g., information search, hypothesis testing), and the content knowledge that the auditor uses in arriving at a judgment/decision (e.g., the biochemistry of target diseases, regulations, and doctors' propensities to recommend the medication to patients).

Several implications relating to task and subject surrogation, research methods, and the scope of tasks studied are attendant with the shift from viewing the auditor as a generic information processor. Focusing first on task surrogation, a key consideration is the extent to which a study should be task rich (mirror the natural world) or lean (include only those variables explicitly part of the theory being tested). One way to enhance task richness is to incorporate more of the variables present in natural audit settings that may be expected to affect auditors' task performance. Such variables may include teams, other actors such as peers and auditee personnel, time pressure, incentive effects, and multiperiod consequences. Some recent audit research has provided rich research settings but, unintentionally brought to light a dilemma (e.g., Peters, 1990; Biggs et al., 1988). These studies have relied on task analyses and investigated auditors' information processing in rich informational settings. However, complex sets of variables and interrelationships resulted that, in turn, made it difficult to test hypotheses. Thus, on the one hand, using lean settings facilitates effective testing of hypotheses. On the other hand, since a lean environment may appear sterile or foreign, an experienced auditor's J/DM in such an environment may not be isomorphic to that in a natural environment. In this latter case, the researcher is left to ponder the value of investigating auditor J/DM that may occur only in research settings.

A more explicit organizational context (e.g., hierarchical levels, incentives, performance reviews, teams) also would improve future research. For example, while individual auditors often face time pressure and do not operate in isolation when formulating judgments, information typically would not have been provided to subjects about these matters unless a researcher had a specific interest in time pressure or multiperson issues. Because such contextual variables may have a direct influence on J/DM or an indirect effect as moderating or intervening variables, these are potentially important underspecifications of the organizational context of audits.

Field studies are one way to bring more of the organizational context into the research arena. To illustrate, Wolf (1981) used the critical-incidents method, through a series of interviews and office visits, to describe the information and decision environment of experienced audit managers. Gibbins and Wolf (1982) used a survey to identify information thought to be important at the various stages of the audit process. Subsequently, Emby and Gibbins (1988) used responses to a questionnaire to develop a description of factors that influence the extent to which auditors feel a need to justify their J/DM.

One finding of these latter studies is that, in practice, auditors seem more concerned about producing evidence to support a preferred judgment/decision and documenting that evidence so the judgment/decision can be defended than they are about the criteria J/DM researchers typically have employed to evaluate audit J/DM (see also Gibbins, 1984). Consequently, the experimental audit J/DM research may have mischaracterized the auditor's objective function as a "search for truth." This evidence justification/defensibility characterization of the auditor's objective function may be a natural development in an environment in which there is great supply-side competition, little J/DM outcome (state realization) feedback, and significant economic consequences to both the auditor–suppliers and the auditee–consumers. Irrespective of its cause, researchers may have overemphasized certain qualitative aspects of audit J/DM (e.g., accuracy and accuracy surrogates) and underemphasized others (e.g., defensibility, efficiency). Only recently have studies emerged that recognize that the audit may be less a search for truth and more an exercise in marshalling evidence to justify or defend a choice that is preferred by the auditee or by some other party to whom the auditor is accountable (e.g., Johnson and Kaplan, 1991). However, even in these studies, justifiability and defensibility are being used as independent rather than as dependent variables (i.e., not as J/DM evaluation criteria).

Field studies also can be used to identify new variables for further study in laboratory experiments. For example, Baker (1977) used the participant-observation method to develop a model of information exchanges among high-ranking auditors, thereby shedding light on the forms of multiperson structures and communication patterns that are good candidates for inclusion in laboratory experiments. Similarly, Dirsmith and Covaleski (1985) performed a field study to investigate how mentoring is used in audit firms to promote learning and socialization of inexperienced auditors. The results of this study, which suggests that expertise is acquired in the audit setting more by observing other experts than by studying firm training or textbook materials, may have important implications for laboratory experimentation on audit expertise and may suggest that multiperson experimentation can contribute to what is known about knowledge acquisition in auditing. McNair's (1991) study of how time and performance pressures interact with an "up-or-out" human resource policy to trigger tradeoffs between the cost and quality of audits is another example of how field studies can contribute. Although time pressure has been incorporated in some audit J/DM laboratory studies, no audit J/DM study has investigated the impact of an up-or-out policy. A final example of the potential contribution of field studies to laboratory studies is provided by Dirsmith and Haskins's (1991) investigation of how an audit firm's structure affects its employees' understanding of and approach to inherent-risk assessment.

Turning to task scope, considerable audit J/DM precedes or follows the audit process phases depicted in Figure 1 but, generally, have not captured audit J/DM researchers' attention (see Cushing and Loebbecke, 1986). Rather, with a few exceptions, researchers have investigated auditor J/DM in connection with tasks performed to plan specific audits and evaluate the evidence produced.[15] While there have been considerable payoffs from such studies and they should continue, we remain relatively ignorant regarding other audit tasks. As shown in Figure 4, pre-audit activities include decisions to compete for the audit of an organization's financial statements, price

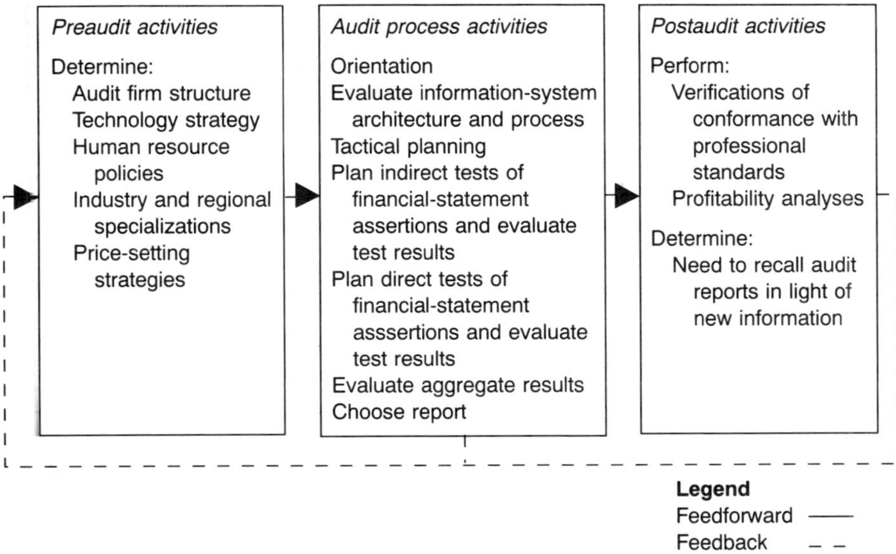

Figure 4. Expanded audit process overview.

setting in a competitive-bidding situation, and strategic choices concerning how strong a presence an audit firm desires in a particular industry, how the audit firm should be structured, how and what uses should be made of technology, and what human resource policies should be adopted. Post-audit J/DM activities include the need to recall issued audit reports upon receipt of new information, ex post verifications of conformance with professional standards (both internal and external to the audit firm—e.g., "peer reviews"), and profitability analyses of completed audits. In our view, these are important foci for J/DM studies for two reasons.

First, large consequences are associated with these decisions. For example, some audit firms did not react on a timely basis to trends in the savings and loan industry, and apparently have exposed themselves to losses of reputation and profits. Firms also may not have attended to postaudit activities on a sufficiently comprehensive and timely basis, thereby exposing themselves to additional losses from the apparent failure to recall audit reports on timely bases. Second, the outcomes of this J/DM effectively may determine (or, at least, influence) some of the contextual features of the audit J/DM process. To illustrate, how competitive bids are formulated affects how much revenue an audit will generate which, in turn, influences both how much time is likely to be budgeted and how much time pressure an auditor will face.

Subject surrogation issues include the use of students as surrogates for practicing auditors, less experienced auditors as surrogates for more experienced auditors, and experienced auditors as surrogates for expert auditors (see Ashton and Kramer, 1980). At a minimum, it would seem that greater use of more experienced and knowledgeable subjects as well as subjects with greater authority and recognized expertise would be of value. However, because considerable audit expertise seems to develop as a consequence of industry specialization, the modal context of existing audit studies (a for-profit manufacturing firm) may provide little opportunity for such subjects to demonstrate their expertise. This observation suggests that audit J/DM researchers might be more creative in choosing and designing audit tasks/contexts. Related implications include the importance of testing the extent to which manufacturing-industry experience/knowledge affects performance in audits of manufacturing firms, and whether such industry experience/knowledge (content) enhances or interferes with performance in audits of nonmanufacturing firms. Subject surrogation also is an issue because of the frequent use of nonrandom samples of auditor subjects. That is, almost all audit J/DM studies have used convenience samples of auditors, such as those attending an audit firm's training program or those "drafted" by partners from offices near the researcher's university. Nonrandom subject selection, coupled with the use of auditors from a limited number of auditing firms, may result in an appearance of greater generality than really exists, especially when there is significant between-firm variation in audit approaches and firm structure.

A final audit process issue is that researchers could better disclose the specific stage of the process in which they intend to place their subjects. We had difficulty classifying several audit J/DM studies in the sequence of audit activities because the information reported in the papers was insufficient. In addition, several studies seem to place the auditor subject at one point in terms of the J/DM required but provide the auditor subject with information that typically would not be present at that point. Greater attention to and disclosure of task features and the audit process sequence would be helpful. Improved disclosures not only would enhance a study's conformance with the audit ecology, but would also better inform subjects and readers about the exact nature of the task being investigated. Several audit process descriptions other than that employed herein have appeared in prior papers (e.g., Felix and Kinney, 1982; Bonner and Pennington, 1991). We suggest that every research task should be identified with sufficient precision that its location within the audit J/DM process is determinable in at least one of these descriptions. At a minimum, this will require enhanced disclosures of the information-processing demands of research tasks, the information set provided to the subjects, and where in the sequence of audit activities the subjects were placed when performing the research task.

Theoretical frameworks

Audit J/DM studies have tended to follow the lead of nonaudit J/DM studies with respect to theoretical framework. Thus, there has been a progression from frameworks that treat the J/DM process as a black box to those that begin to shine a light inside the box. The former would include heuristics-and-biases studies, while the latter would include those based on a cognitive process framework. An important choice now confronting audit J/DM researchers is whether, or to what extent, to continue motivating research by the theoretical frameworks in Figure 3 or by theoretical frameworks employed in cognitive psychology, cognitive science, and artificial intelligence. While this choice concerns the extent to which audit J/DM research will venture further into the black box as opposed to continuing input–output modelling, it also has implications for the methods used. For example, although almost all J/DM research is associated with laboratory experimentation, much cognitive science and artificial-intelligence research employs case studies and simulations.

Previously, we discussed the "borrow-and-transfer" character of the early audit J/DM studies and the "contrast-before-transfer" orientation of later studies. A benefit of these strategies is that audit J/DM research was grounded in well-developed theories of general J/DM behavior. However, there are two potential costs. First, some important lines of research have not been pursued. For example, when departures from the results of generic J/DM studies have been documented in audit J/DM studies, researchers typically have not systematically investigated potential causes but have only speculated ex post about them (see the next section). Second, general J/DM theories, by definition, do not incorporate the specific content and structure of any particular task/context. Thus, using either research strategy increases the risk that audit J/DM studies will focus on theories that are underspecified with respect to important features of auditing. We believe that audit J/DM researchers, alone or in concert with nonaudit J/DM researchers, can make valuable contributions by bringing evidence to bear on theories that explain J/DM behavioral nuances that seemingly are due to structure or content features of auditing.

An important choice facing audit J/DM researchers is the extent to which their theory development or testing will emphasize: (1) *tasks,* focussing on the transferability of generic J/DM theory to audit settings or testing the effects of audit tasks/contexts features on generic J/DM; (2) *processors,* focussing on how experienced auditors make audit judgments/decisions compared to other types of J/DM (e.g., A. Ashton, 1982) or the effects of experience on auditors' audit J/DM; or (3) *the interaction of task and processor.* This choice of emphasis has implications for the degree to which a study concentrates on the "cells" versus the "marginals" of the two-by-two task–processor model introduced above. Again, the dimensions of this model are processor (inexperienced or experienced) and task (generic or applied). As already discussed, structure is emphasized in generic tasks whereas content receives greater relative emphasis in applied tasks. A study intended to develop or test theory related to the task or the processor would focus on the relevant marginal of the two-by-two model. In contrast, a study intended to investigate the interaction of task and processor would focus on experienced versus inexperienced processors *and* two or more tasks (e.g., two applied tasks, two generic tasks, an applied and a generic task).

We believe that future audit J/DM research will have a greater chance to make a substantive contribution if it is more focused on the task and the task–processor interaction. There presently is some trend in this direction and, if it continues, more and more audit task/context features may emerge as independent variables in audit J/DM theories. In turn, larger and larger modifications of generic J/DM theories may be needed to fuel such audit J/DM research. These trends may be a cause or a consequence of an evolution from the borrow-and-transfer orientation to one that emphasizes an understanding of J/DM as it occurs in natural audit settings. Irrespective of their genesis, they are important signs of the development of audit J/DM research and may portend an increased ability of audit J/DM researchers to contribute to the broader field of J/DM.

Contributions to nonaudit J/DM research

In this final section, we highlight four audit J/DM findings that have the potential to contribute to revision of nonaudit J/DM theory. These findings represent departures from nonaudit J/DM research findings and, thus, could be informative of boundary conditions for J/DM theory. This section also closes the chapter by providing strategic suggestions for nonaudit applied J/DM researchers. As noted earlier, audit J/DM studies largely have used laboratory experiments in which practicing auditors performed simplified tasks and the initial studies tested whether generic theories apply in audit contexts. Recent studies have begun to broaden the incorporated features of auditing (e.g., time pressure, the review process) and auditors (e.g., domain-specific knowledge) thereby enhancing their potential to modify J/DM theories. Some of these newer studies are motivated by, and use the methods of, cognitive psychology and cognitive science. Irrespective of their motivation and method, these newer studies constitute rich sources of evidence for researchers interested in professional J/DM in informationally complex and ambiguous environments.

First, the relatively high level of consensus reported in most policy-capturing audit J/DM studies is an important departure from nonaudit J/DM studies. Little is known, however, about the causes of this departure or about factors that affect consensus levels. One might speculate that important factors include the amount and nature of formal training, industry knowledge, decision aids that add structure to the task (e.g., checklists), the nature of multiperson interaction (e.g., mentoring, performance review), and incentives. Investigating the impact of factors like these would be valuable because consensus is important in many contexts as an accuracy surrogate, either in its own right or as a determinant of justifiability/defensibility (Joyce, 1976; Emby and Gibbins, 1988).

Second, Brown and Solomon (1990, 1991) found significant configural processing of the predicted nature. One could speculate that configural processing is a skill acquired by auditors because of factors such as those just delineated to potentially explain auditors' greater consensus. Another implication is that detecting configural cue usage may require even greater attention to task content than has been paid in other applied J/DM studies. Focusing on task structure may be more pertinent to determining if the structure required for processing the content exceeds a cognitive limit. For example, when the relevant knowledge (content) for a risk judgment increases, at some point the auditor may change information-processing structures by switching from a compensatory to a noncompensatory model (Payne et al., 1988). In this sense, the content and structure of a task may interact to affect J/DM. Therefore, to understand the contingent nature of structural-information processing, task content must be considered.

Third, audit J/DM studies indicate that auditors do *not* exhibit overconfidence when they assess subjective probabilities for audit events (Solomon, 1982; Solomon et al., 1985; Tomassini et al., 1982). This finding has been cited numerous times in the J/DM literature along with the limited number of other instances in which experts have been found to assess probabilities consistent with proper calibration or underconfidence (e.g., Keren, 1991 and Yates, 1990). Although it has been speculated that auditor's culturally valued conservatism may play a role (Tomassini et al., 1982), little is known about the likely cause of auditors' superior calibration. This result is another example of the need to support stronger attributions about the reason(s) for atypical findings if the potential of audit J/DM research is to be more fully realized. Again, such attributions will require even more attention to features of the environment, and the actors within it, that distinguish auditing from other contexts.

Fourth, two findings from the audit heuristics-and-biases studies may be useful for revising generic J/DM theories. The general finding of these studies is that auditors do *not* exhibit the same *degree* of biases as has been exhibited in psychological studies (e.g., neglect of base rates). As with other departures, however, little more than speculation has occurred about the underlying reasons (Smith and Kida, 1991). The second finding of generic J/DM interest comes from studies of auditor sequential-belief revision (e.g., Ashton and Ashton, 1988; Tubbs et al., 1990). Many of the results of these studies are consistent with those of the nonaudit studies. Exceptions to J/DM results using students are that auditors apparently are more predisposed to revise beliefs upon receipt of new information and auditors place greater weight on negative versus positive information in belief revision.

Our closing suggestion to nonaudit applied J/DM researcher is to develop research programs well-grounded in the relatively rich task and process representations of experienced judges and decision makers. Looking back at the first twenty years of audit J/DM research, because of its predominant "borrow and transfer" orientation, too little attention was paid to issues such as what do experienced persons consider to require judgments/decisions in a task setting, what are the objectives of experienced persons when making judgments/decisions, and what criteria do they employ to evaluate the quality/adequacy of J/DM. Paying greater attention to these issues would seem to be a necessary condition for enhancing our understanding of both the generality/limitations of generic J/DM theory and J/DM nuances within specific applied contexts. In our view, J/DM researchers will have to spend more time out of the lab and in the field to be able to meet this challenge.

Acknowledgments

An earlier draft of this chapter was presented in the University of Illinois Judgment and Decision Research Program Seminar Series (February 1992), the May 1992 Duke University Conference on Judgment and Decision Making Research in Accounting and Auditing, and during April 1992 at the University of Missouri and Laval University. We would like to acknowledge the comments of participants in these meetings as well as comments by Bob Ashton, Jake Birnberg, Sarah Bonner, Kathryn Kadous, Don Kleinmuntz, Mark Peecher, Jim Peters, Dan Stone, and Ken Trotman.

Notes

1. Indeed, auditors have "attested" to a variety of assertions ranging from magazine circulation statistics to features of computer software to the accuracy of textbooks in representing current professional standards. In these instances, interested parties range from current and prospective advertisers to current and prospective employees and business-computer owners to current and prospective faculty and student-textbook adopters/users. Other types of audits are compliance audits and operational audits. For the latter type, the focus is on an organization's procedures and methods used to achieve articulated goals with the concern being effectiveness and efficiency. Thus, for example, the U.S. General Accounting Office may perform an audit of the Federal Drug Administration (FDA) to determine the extent to which the FDA is efficient in using funds allocated by Congress to protect the public from harm due to the sale of unsafe drugs. For compliance audits, the focus is on determining the extent to which the organization has followed prescribed procedures or rules set forth by some higher authority (see Arens and Loebbecke, 1991). To illustrate, a compliance auditor might determine the extent to which a university has complied with applicable (antidiscrimination) laws in hiring new faculty or in computing overhead charges on research contracts. Perhaps the most visible of all audits, an IRS tax audit, can be thought of as a type of compliance audit (i.e., compliance with the Internal Revenue Code in reporting an entity's tax liability).
2. Readers interested in the normative studies should refer to Cushing (1974), Kinney (1975), and Dacey and Ward (1985).
3. Some evidence that the potential of audit J/DM studies to contribute to the advancement of nonaudit J/DM knowledge has been recognized is provided by those studies that have been published in J/DM journals (e.g., Anderson and Wright, 1988; Ashton, 1974b; Ashton and Ashton, 1990; Solomon et al., 1985; Tomassini et al., 1982). These studies have relied on a variety of theoretical frameworks (e.g., heuristics and biases, probabilistic judgment, cognitive processes), have addressed wide-ranging issues (including the extent to which auditors use simplifying heuristics in revising beliefs, the prevalence of the "explanation effect" in auditor judgment formulation, and the extent and nature of auditor probabilistic judgment miscalibration). In addition, a review of the results of audit heuristics-and-biases studies which presented implications for other applied J/DM settings recently appeared in a psychology journal (Smith and Kida, 1991).
4. Some might distinguish types of processors in terms of expertise (i.e., novice versus expert)

or include more than two levels irrespective of whether the construct is experience or expertise. Though, as discussed in Davis and Solomon (1989), we are aware of the differences between expertise and experience and, for some purposes, would find defining more than two levels of each to be of value, for the present purpose of delineating audit J/DM research objectives, two levels of either expertise or experience are sufficient.

5. Currently, this large international auditing and accounting firm is called KPMG Peat Marwick.
6. The present adaptation differs from the original Felix and Kinney (1982) characterization of the audit process in two primary respects. First, we have changed some of the terminology in an effort to reduce audit jargon. Second, Felix and Kinney's nine phases have been reduced to seven by combining their "Compliance Testing" and "Evaluation of Internal Accounting Controls" phases into one phase called "Plan Indirect Tests of Financial-Statement Assertions and Evaluate Test Results" and by combining their "Opinion Formulation" and "Reporting" phases into one phase called "Choose Report."
7. Although the audit risk model has had a very significant impact on audit practice, it sometimes has been criticized by audit researchers (see Cushing and Loebbecke, 1983 and Kinney, 1989).
8. Audit standards focus the auditor's attention at this phase on control of type II inferential error, which would arise if the auditor were to conclude that materially misstated financial statements were *not* misstated. However, as noted below, it is reasonable to assume that auditors also pay attention to type I inferential errors, which would arise if the auditor were to conclude that financial statements were materially misstated when such financial statements actually were not materially misstated.
9. As discussed later, once a judgment is made that the financial statements require some adjustment, the nature and extent of the adjustment which ultimately is made (mere disclosure versus changing the reported values) may be a function of negotiation between the auditor and auditee.
10. Some aspects of analytical review may be quantified through the use of statistical approaches like regression analysis (Stringer and Stewart, 1986). Usually such approaches are directed at the formation of an "expectation" and the determination of the significance of any difference between the expectation and the value that the organization intends to report. However, even when statistical approaches are employed, many of the key inputs must be determined on a judgmental basis.
11. Some researchers might add conformance with a normative model to this list of J/DM evaluation criteria. In our view, such conformance generally is a special case of accuracy (i.e.) the external criterion to which a judgment or decision is compared is the output of a normative model). Conformance with the postulates or axioms of a normative model is another special case that has been less frequently used in audit J/DM studies.
12. In some papers, the stage of the audit is described unambiguously. Because of limited information disclosure (or ambiguity) in other papers, categorizing some studies in terms of audit process phase is difficult. When in doubt, we focused on when in the audit process the study's dependent variable judgment/decision would be made.
13. See Keasey and Watson (1989) for a similar empirical analysis with some different consensus measures applied in a nonauditing accounting context.
14. This surprising calibration result also was the subject of two auditing studies that appeared in psychology journals (Tomassini et al., 1982 and Solomon et al., 1985) and one auditing study of multiperson information processing (Solomon, 1982).
15. Several other studies that examined various aspects of probability combination are reviewed in the next two sections.
16. The focus in these studies often is conformance with a descriptive model.That is, once failure of a judgment or decision to conform with a normative model's prediction or solution has been established, the researcher's interest becomes learning about the processes used to formulate judgments and make decisions. Importantly, in these studies, judgments and decisions are compared with descriptive J/DM model (anchoring and adjustment) predictions, often with little direct concern about assessing the quality or "goodness" of the judgments and decisions.
17. Huss and Jacobs (1991) is one such exception. These authors studied auditor J/DM (risk assessments) made in connection with the task of determining if a proposed new audit client should be accepted.

7

The role of knowledge and memory in audit judgment

Robert Libby

Over the past decade, growing interest in the role of knowledge as a determinant of audit judgment performance has developed from three sources. First, observations that experienced auditors are paid more and assigned to what appear to be more demanding and important tasks (e.g., Gibbins, 1984) were not supported by consistent findings of experience-related performance differences (Wright, 1988; Bedard, 1989). This anomaly led to the realization that predicting and understanding the causes of experience effects requires more systematic analysis. In particular, it underscored the need to specify the knowledge necessary to complete different judgment tasks; when, how, and how well the knowledge would normally be acquired; and the cognitive process(es) through which the knowledge would be brought to bear on the decision task (Frederick and Libby, 1986; Abdolmohammadi and Wright, 1987). Second, increasing interest in less-structured audit judgment tasks (e.g., Einhorn, 1976; Kida, 1984; Libby, 1985; Biggs et al., 1988) such as analytical risk assessment, fraud detection, and going-concern judgments, focused attention on the role of the auditor's task-specific knowledge in problem recognition, hypothesis generation, and information search (cf. Libby, 1981, 1983; Gibbins, 1984; Waller and Felix, 1984a). Third, while the above studies focused on general knowledge of audit phenomena, other researchers (e.g., Plumlee, 1985; Moeckel and Plumlee, 1989; Frederick, 1991) addressed the fact that memory for evidence gathered during a particular engagement has important implications for decision performance. Even in situations where detailed workpapers are readily available, limitations of short-term memory require that decision makers initially refer to their long-term memory about the engagement to test the implications of further evidence. Errors in retrieval of the previously encountered information may be an important source of decision error.

Many have now concluded that a complete picture of audit judgment performance will require significant emphasis on knowledge and memory issues. Knowledge and memory studies can also provide insights related to a variety of practical questions such as:

- In what tasks can the skills of more experienced auditors be most effectively employed?
- How can university education, firm training, and experience be organized to maximize learning?
- When will different types of learning aids or decision aids be most beneficial?
- When will generalists' or specialists' performance be superior?
- Which entry-level auditors will be most successful?

While many recent contributions have been made to our understanding of the role of knowledge in audit judgment, I suggest that for this literature to add substantively to our understanding of audit judgment, we need a general model of knowledge acquisition and its impact on judgment performance that lays out and defines the key variables and the functional relations among them. It is possible to look at much of the current literature as being aimed at model building, though few studies were consciously intended to serve that purpose.[1] However, many controversies in the literature still appear to result from a lack of clarity as to the nature of the underlying model of audit judgment performance. Examples of some of the more recent controversies are:

- Is experience a proxy for or a determinant of knowledge?
- Will knowledge increase over the whole range or only a limited range of an auditor's career?
- How conducive is the audit environment to necessary learning and what kinds of learning are fostered?
- When will knowledge differences result in performance differences?

The purpose of this chapter is to construct a model of the role of knowledge in audit judgment performance (which I call "The Antecedents and Consequences of Knowledge") and then use the model to organize the existing literature to determine what we have learned about its components and what we have yet to learn. The model also provides a basis to address conceptual and methodological issues suggested by the literature, and explore future research directions. Readers are referred to other recent papers (Bedard, 1989; Choo, 1989; Colbert, 1989) for a more exhaustive, detailed review and critique of individual papers.

The chapter will be organized as follows. First, a causal model of knowledge-related determinants of audit judgment performance and a general operational approach to examining knowledge issues (the "expertise paradigm") are presented. The model is then used as a structure for integrating the literature. Following this, the model and operational approach provide a basis for discussing conceptual and methodological issues raised by the reviewed work. The next section discusses the implications of the research for

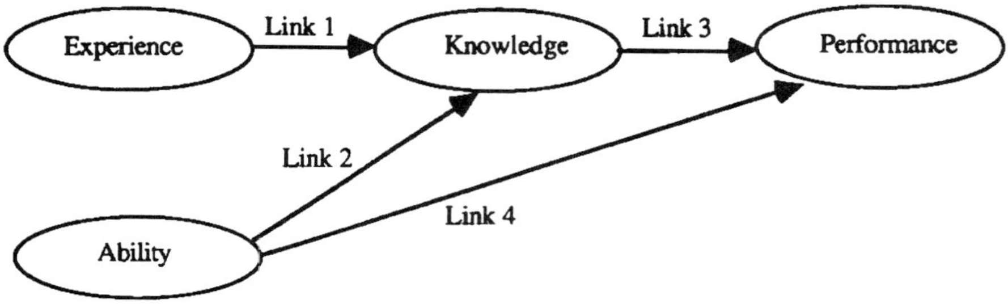

Figure 1. Antecedents and consequences of knowledge

general theories of judgment and decision making. In the final section, some directions for the future are suggested.

Audit expertise: Knowledge-related determinants of performance

Antecedents and consequences of knowledge

Judgment performance is a function of four factors presented in equation 1 (Einhorn and Hogarth, 1981a; Libby, 1983):

$$\text{Performance} = f\ (\text{Ability, Knowledge, Motivation, Environment}) \quad (1)$$

These relations are complicated further by the fact that knowledge, the independent variable in Eq. (1) of principal interest here, is itself determined by the other three factors in the performance equation, and by experience:

$$\text{Knowledge} = g\ (\text{Ability, Experience, Motivation, Environment}) \quad (2)$$

The current paper focuses on the relations among ability, knowledge, experience, and performance. To limit the discussion to manageable proportions, motivation and resulting cognitive effort will initially be assumed to be constant across individuals and above the minimum necessary for learning and task performance to be accomplished.[2] In addition, the fourth factor, environment, will only be considered when the task environment (e.g., type of task, time pressure, structure) determines the relations of knowledge and ability to performance.[3] The nature of the learning opportunities provided (e.g., type of feedback, training, learning aids) are treated as attributes of experience. Given these constraints, the antecedents and consequences of knowledge can be represented through the path diagram presented in Fig. 1. The model recognizes: (1) that there are only two classes of inputs (abilities and experiences), (2) that these two inputs cause the internal state of knowledge that is an intermediate output variable, and (3) along with the direct effects of abilities, knowledge affects performance (an output variable).[4]

In the next section, each of the principal variables in the model will be briefly defined and their relevant dimensions delineated. This is followed by a discussion of the four links between the variables as they exist in the audit environment. This environment is one where accountants complete a variety of judgment tasks that differ in the opportunities to learn relevant knowledge, and the amount and nature of the abilities and knowledge required for their successful completion. As a consequence, the key to successful study of knowledge-related determinants of performance is *specifying the knowledge needed and cognitive processes involved in performing specific audit tasks* (cf. Frederick and Libby, 1986; Bonner and Pennington, 1991).

As Alba and Hutchinson (1987) note, the related psychological literature is replete with competing theories of the relations discussed here. However, the existence of most of the relations discussed here is noncontroversial and the competing theories often predict them equally well. As a consequence, I will follow Alba and Hutchinson's practice and try to employ general explanations reflecting consensus views where possible.

Definitions of variables

In general, the diversity in both the tasks performed by auditors and the knowledge and abilities required by each requires disaggregation of the audit opinion-formulation process into individual tasks and detailed analyses of the underlying cognitive processes (Frederick and Libby, 1986, p. 289).[5] As a consequence, a separate version of Figure 1 could be constructed for each specific audit task, including only elements of experience, abilities, and knowledge relevant to that task. Further, the strength of the relations should vary across tasks. For example, Libby and Tan (1992) found that the effects of problem-solving ability on knowledge and performance (links 2 and 4) were significant in Bonner and Lewis's (1990) earnings-manipulation task but insignificant in their internal-control task. Finally, each variable has a number of relevant dimensions (cf. Gibbins et al., 1991; Bonner and Lewis, 1990). The definitions of the variables and the dimensions employed here are summarized in Table 1 and described in more detail below.[6]

Experiences. In keeping with the broad focus of the paper, experiences are defined to include the wide variety of first- and second-hand task-related encounters that provide opportunities for learning in the audit environment.[7] Such encounters include actual task completion, reviewing the work of others, receipt of review comments from superiors (process feedback), receipt of outcome feedback, discussion of other audits with colleagues, reading formal audit guides, and training.[8] In prior research, "experience" has been defined in terms ranging from the very narrow (e.g., task completion) to the very broad (e.g., all task-related encounters). A broad definition is used here because the presence or absence of various types of experiences plays an important role in determining what is learned in the audit environment. Type of encounter will determine what and how well knowledge is acquired and is thus the key dimension for partitioning experience.

Table 1. *Definitions and dimensions of variables*

Experiences – task-related encounters that provide opportunities for learning
- Type of encounter –
  - *First-hand encounters,* including task completion and reviewing the work of others, receipt of review comments from superiors (process feedback), and outcome feedback
  - *Second-hand encounters,* including discussion of other audits with colleagues, reading formal audit guides, and education and training

Knowledge – information stored in memory
- *Episodic memory* for particular experiences and *semantic memory* for concept meanings and relations
- *World knowledge, general-domain knowledge,* and *subspecialty knowledge*

Abilities – capacity to complete information-processing tasks that contribute to audit problem solving
- Type of process – *e.g., encoding, retrieval, analysis*

Performance – correspondence of the judgment to a criterion
- Component subtasks – *problem recognition, hypothesis generation, information selection, cue measurement,* etc.
- Criterion –
  - *Effectiveness – relation to environmental event* or outcome (e.g., business failure), a *statistical norm* (e.g., Bayesian updated probability), *judgments of others* (e.g., consensus, designated experts)
  - *Efficiency – time on task, cost*

The types of learning opportunities that an auditor experiences will vary from task to task. For example, firms may provide substantial training and formal audit guidance for some tasks and little for others (Bonner and Pennington, 1991). Similarly, outcome feedback may be readily available for some tasks but unavailable for others (Davis and Solomon, 1989; Ashton, 1991). Further, because many audit tasks or subtasks are normally performed at different stages of one's career (Abdolmohammadi, 1990), the nature of experience also changes over time. For example, within a particular audit task (e.g., internal-control evaluation), the less experienced auditor may measure relevant cues (the existence or lack of existence of listed controls) whereas the more experienced auditor combines the cues into a decision (e.g., level of control reliance). It is also likely that one may complete a task at one career stage and review the work of others who have completed the task during later stages.

Since all experiences are not alike, specific experiences should be viewed as opportunities to acquire specific knowledge that will be more or less relevant to the performance of different future audit tasks (Libby, 1990, p. 134). Any definition of "task-related" experience should also consider the possibility of transfer of knowledge acquired in one task to new tasks (Marchant, 1989), though findings of transfer are very limited.

Knowledge. Knowledge is information stored in memory.[9] A useful distinction often made in the memory literature is between memory for particular experiences (e.g., the controls present in XYZ Co.'s purchases subsystem) or "episodic memory" and memory for concept meanings and relations (e.g., effective controls over purchases subsystems) or "semantic memory."[10] Since knowledge of auditing in general and knowledge related to the current audit engagement are both necessary for task performance, both types of knowledge are relevant to our discussion. Alternative organizational structures for knowledge that have different functional properties have also been suggested (e.g., taxonomic and schematic structures; see Frederick, 1991). As a consequence, knowledge structure, as well as knowledge content, is an important determinant of audit judgment performance.

Since knowledge is an internal state, its characteristics cannot be directly observed. As a result, models of the content and organization of memory and the related learning and retrieval processes are treated here as useful metaphors (and not physical representations), which can only be tested indirectly. Inferences concerning content or organizational differences are made based on differences in observables such as recall, recognition, response times, concurrent verbalizations during processing, information search, judgments requiring use of the knowledge, etc.

A broad range of knowledge is relevant to performance of audit judgment tasks. Bonner and Lewis (1990) suggest three general categories of audit knowledge: world knowledge, general-domain knowledge, and subspecialty knowledge. Each phase of the audit (e.g., internal-control risk assessment) relies on a number of components from each of the three categories (e.g., statistical sampling, ideal controls, knowledge of error frequencies for this type of client, etc.; see Bonner and Pennington, 1991). As noted earlier, all elements of audit knowledge are not equally relevant to the performance of all tasks (cf. Frederick and Libby, 1986).

Abilities. Abilities are defined here as the capacity to complete information-encoding, retrieval, and analysis tasks that contribute to audit problem solving. The nature of human intelligence is among the most controversial topics in psychology. A wide variety of psychometric and computational models outlining primary mental abilities have been developed (Sternberg, 1984). Among these abilities are many that contribute to audit problem solving.

Although the linkage to studies of audit knowledge and memory issues has rarely been made,[11] the literature has long recognized that individual differences in abilities will affect learning and judgment performance (see Mock and Vasarhelyi, 1984). Like knowledge, these abilities are unobservable internal states. Their existence is normally inferred from accuracy and speed on psychometric tests. Different audit tasks presumably rely to differing degrees on various abilities.

Performance. From its earliest days, the central thrust of audit judgment research has been assessing audit judgment performance and its determinants (Libby and Lewis, 1977, 1982). Recent discussions of knowledge and memory research have reemphasized the need for a performance orientation in this area (see e.g., Bedard, 1989; Choo, 1989; Davis and Solomon, 1989; Marchant, 1990). While the conceptual definition of performance employed is not made explicit in most studies, an expected-utility definition of performance is usually implicit. It has further been recognized that performance on a specific audit judgment task can vary in effectiveness and efficiency (cf. Davis and Solomon, 1989; McDaniel, 1990).

Operationally, a criterion value is normally specified and performance is defined as the correspondence of the judgment to the criterion. Typical criterion values for assessing effectiveness are an environmental event or outcome (e.g., business failure), a statistical norm (e.g., Bayesian updated probability), or judgments of others (e.g., a professional standard, consensus with other similar judges or an "expert" panel). Minimization of time on task or cost per unit of information gained is often used as the efficiency criterion. Some measure of the relation between the judgment and criterion (e.g., correlation, hit rate) is then argued or assumed to be related, ceteris paribus, to utility.[12] The appropriate level of utility analysis (the individual auditor, audit firm, or society) and form of the relation between the measure and expected utility are rarely addressed.

Since auditors complete a wide variety of judgment tasks, audit judgment performance is task specific (cf. Frederick and Libby, 1986; Gibbins et al., 1991). Each judgment task itself involves a variety of component subtasks (e.g., cue selection, cue measurement, etc.; Bonner, 1990) and performance can vary across components. It should also be noted that success as an auditor in general requires more than successful performance of technical audit tasks, which are the focus of audit judgment research.

Linkages among the variables

Figure 1 depicts abilities and experiences as two inputs to the determination of knowledge, which is an intermediate internal state, and abilities and knowledge as determinants of performance (cf. Marchant, 1990). Task demands determine the knowledge necessary for successful task completion and the processes through which the knowledge is brought to bear on the decision problem. As noted earlier, the strength of these relations will vary across tasks. The four links among the four variables provide a basis for clarifying the major focus of existing studies, evaluating their contributions, and suggesting new research directions for the future.

Link 1: The relations between experiences and knowledge. As noted above, experiences only provide opportunities for learning (cf. Marchant, 1990), and the quality of these opportunities varies from situation to situation. Consequently, what can be learned from experience will depend not only on the number of task-related encounters, but on the type of encounters (Waller and Felix, 1984b; Bonner and Pennington, 1991). Since learning requires both recognition that there is something to learn and the means to learn (cf. Neuberg and Fisk, 1987, p. 442),[13] the quality of the learning environment can be judged by the degree to which it accurately signals the need to learn and provides the necessary means.

Some form of direct or indirect (supervisory) outcome feedback often provides the signal of the need to learn. Incomplete outcome feedback can provide an inaccurate signal. When actions are taken based on judgments, feedback is normally available only when positive actions have been taken. For example, evidence concerning the success or failure of both selected and rejected applicants is necessary to accurately assess the quality of audit firm employment decisions. Yet evidence concerning the rejected applicants is rarely available. High base rates of success, low selection ratios, and/or treatment effects can result in high positive hit rates, but many unobservable false negatives (Einhorn and Hogarth, 1978; Libby, 1981; Waller and Felix, 1984b). As a consequence, erroneous decision rules can appear effective based solely upon feedback on selected applicants (the positive hit rate). When selecting an item for action (e.g., admitting someone to a prestigious school) improves performance, both complete and incomplete outcome feedback can be biased.[14]

Even when the need to learn is evident, the auditor may lack appropriate means for error correction because it may not be evident why the error occurred or how to correct the action. As a consequence, considering the availability of process feedback is also critical to evaluating the learning environment. Bonner and Pennington's (1991) analysis of learning environments in auditing strongly suggests that instruction, professional guidance, and review feedback, which are process oriented, promote learning whereas outcome feedback alone does not. Exposure to well-organized knowledge bases appears to be necessary for maximum learning and expert performance in audit tasks, particularly when only outcome feedback is available.

Different types of first- and secondhand experiences also appear to contribute to the development of different knowledge components. For example, Marchant (1990) suggests that indirect experience (training, manuals, summary data) contributes more to the development of general knowledge and direct experience contributes more to subspecialty knowledge development. Furthermore, interactive effects are possible. Butt (1988) has examined the interactive effect of experiences with individual cases and summary data and Nelson (1993) the interactive effect of experience with event frequencies and evidence diagnosticities.

As mentioned earlier, different audit tasks are normally performed at different stages of one's career. Further, technical training is concentrated in the first five years of practice (Bonner and Pennington, 1991). Combined with the decreasing influence of additional repetitions on learning, this suggests that knowledge related to any particular task is unlikely to be acquired at a constant rate over one's career.

Link 2: The relations between abilities and knowledge. As any teacher will attest, what is learned is also a function of the individual's abilities to learn.[15] In auditing, initial entrants into the profession must surmount a three-part screening process, which includes completing the minimal academic requirements, passing the CPA examination (or non-U.S. equivalent), and obtaining employment. This process restricts the range of learning abilities represented in the entry-level population. Early stages of the promotion/retention process further limit the range. While persistent effects of abilities are still likely, this range limitation should weaken measures of the strength of this link in audit practice compared to other employment contexts where the range is greater (e.g., Schmidt et al., 1986).

Link 3: The relation between knowledge and performance. The effect of knowledge on performance will be determined by the fit of the auditor's knowledge and abilities to the particular task, component subtask, and effectiveness/efficiency facet of performance (cf. Gibbins et al., 1991). Bonner and Pennington's (1991) analysis of performance effectiveness on various audit tasks suggests that experienced auditors' performance is most effective on tasks that involve "construction processes" (cf. Choo, 1989). Construction processes include internal and external information search and comprehension, hypothesis generation, and design. Auditors also perform well when causal models or task rules are useful in hypothesis evaluation. Reduction processes, including hypothesis evaluation based on statistical rules, estimation, and selection among alternatives, are performed less well. This relation suggests that either the quality of audit knowledge related to the former category of processes is superior, the processes are more sensitive to knowledge differences, or the criterion for success is less ambiguous.

Psychological studies suggest that knowledge gained through repetition may have the greatest effect on the efficiency dimension of performance. Repetition leads to automaticity in procedures, which lessens the demands on the auditor's limited information-processing capacity. This frees resources for completion of other parts of the task, which results in efficiency gains and, where time pressure exists, effectiveness gains. As cognitive structures become more refined, judges are more able to isolate important information, elaborate on existing information, and retrieve episodic knowledge, which also increase efficiency (Alba and Hutchinson, 1987). As indicated earlier, all of these relations are contingent on the degree of match between the individual's knowledge store and that necessary for task performance.

Link 4: The relations between ability and performance. Various abilities, including verbal comprehension, numerical computation, analogical reasoning, memory capacity, and others, are potentially relevant to audit judgment performance. The sensitivity of particular audit judgment tasks to each of these ability differences will depend on the degree to which the ability is required. Further, given the restriction of range noted above for many of these abilities, all auditors may have the minimum ability necessary for completion of some tasks, and ability-associated performance differences may appear in efficiency rather than effectiveness. Finally, it should be noted that multiple methods are normally available to solve a particular judgment problem (Brunswik, 1955). For example, some problems can be solved using generic problem-solving algorithms or task-specific heuristics. As a consequence, to the degree that a particular ability allows appropriate algorithms to be employed, ability can serve as a substitute to some degree for knowledge in determining performance effectiveness. Task-specific heuristics normally offer efficiency advantages. In other circumstances, superior ability may allow inferences to be made that may substitute for incomplete knowledge. The fact that certain minimum levels of ability and knowledge may be necessary for task performance, and that at certain levels ability and knowledge may substitute for one another, presents the possibility of interactions in their effects on performance. These possibilities have not been examined in the auditing literature.

Motivation and resulting effort—an intervening variable. It was noted above that many of the relations discussed were sensitive to the auditor's level of motivation and the resulting level of effort expended on the task. Attention or cognitive effort is defined as a nonspecific input of energy to all mental activities (Kahneman, 1973). Effort expended can vary in intensity and duration. Cognitive effort will be viewed here as an intervening variable in Figure 1, which determines both the degree to which learning takes place and knowledge is successfully applied, but does not change the sign of the other relations in the model. Effort (working harder or longer) can also substitute in some tasks for lesser knowledge or ability.

Summary. The above discussion presents the following picture of the determinants of audit-judgment performance:

1 Accountants conduct a variety of judgment tasks.
2 These tasks differ in:
   a. the opportunities to learn relevant knowledge from informal and formal training and experience;
   b. the amount and nature of the abilities, knowledge, and effort required for their successful completion.
3 Each element of performance will be determined by the fit of the auditor's abilities and knowledge to those required by that element of the task at hand.

The "expertise paradigm"

Frederick and Libby (1986) suggest a series of common-sense guidelines that studies of knowledge issues should follow based on Fiedler (1982). These guidelines will be referred to here as the "expertise paradigm."

Conceptual perspective: Specifying the knowledge and cognitive processes. Given the variety of audit tasks and the differences in the amount and nature of the knowledge they require, the first guideline suggests that *hypotheses be developed in advance about the effects of specific knowledge elements or their organization on observable behavior.* This requires specification of the knowledge necessary to complete a particular task, when, how, and how well it will be acquired, and the process(es) through which it will be brought to bear on the task. Developing hypotheses on the basis of such analysis not only increases the chance for successful demonstrations of important effects, but provides a systematic basis to determine the reasons for failures to demonstrate predicted effects.

Operational perspective: Knowledge–task interactions. Knowledge is an internal mental state that cannot be directly observed. As a consequence, the second guideline suggests that *demonstrating a hypothesized knowledge difference and/or its effects on performance requires constructing an experimental task where the observable implications of using and not using knowledge* (or using different knowledge) *are different.* The failure to uncover experience effects in many prior studies was the result of having employed tasks in which more and less experienced auditors would be expected to have the same knowledge or where different knowledge would be expected to result in the same behavior (cf. Bonner, 1990). Such tasks will be referred to as *novice tasks.*

The third guideline indicates that *the rivalry between differing knowledge elements can best be established by manipulating stimuli and/or context factors* (the idea here is that context activates a knowledge element that interacts with the stimulus being evaluated) *and comparing individuals with different experiences.* If the knowledge element of interest relates to the stimuli, the stimuli must be manipulated. Alternatively, if it relates to context, then a single stimulus must be evaluated in multiple contexts. Finally, if the hypothesized knowledge relates to the interaction of the two (the interpretation of the stimuli is contingent on the context), then both must be manipulated.

The power of a design based on the third guideline lies in its ability to eliminate alternative explanations for knowledge or performance differences. An example from Frederick (1991), which examines the linkage between experience and knowledge (link 1), illustrates the power of such a design. Part of Frederick's work investigates differences in the organization of general internal-control knowledge between experienced and inexperienced auditors. His first two hypotheses suggest that training exposes both inexperienced and experienced auditors to a taxonomic structure for internal-

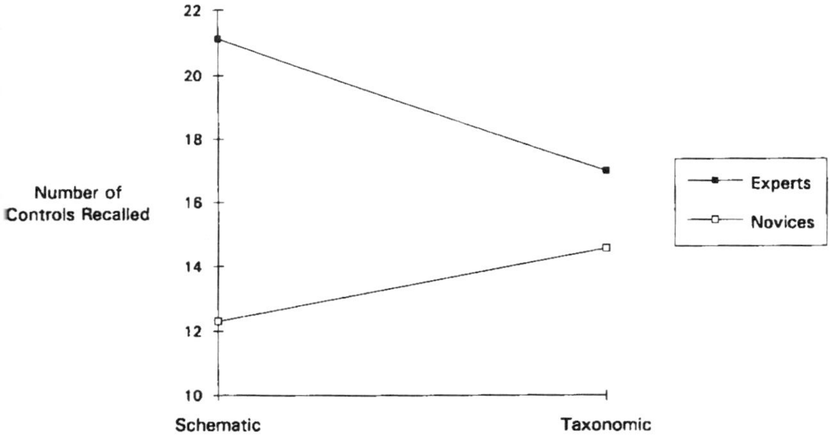

Figure 2. Number of controls freely recalled

control knowledge (organized by internal-control objectives), whereas experiencing actual systems allows only experienced auditors to acquire a schematic structure (organized by flow of transactions). He operationalizes these hypotheses based on the finding that the temporal links, which exist only in the schematic structure, act as retrieval cues aiding recall from memory. Since only experienced auditors have the schematic structure, only they should exhibit superior recall of schematically organized controls.

He tested these predictions by presenting a group of practicing auditors having 3 to 5 years of experience and a group of students having no experience with a listing of the same 33 controls over purchases and disbursements listed either taxonomically (by objective) or schematically (by flow of transactions). Since his hypothesis related to the stimuli, he varied the stimuli (organization of the information) and the subjects' experiences in a 2 × 2 between-subjects design. Participants were told to study the controls and then to recall and record them as they came to mind. He then counted the number of controls recalled in each condition. As predicted and illustrated in Figure 2, the inexperienced exhibited no significant difference in recall across organizations, but the experienced exhibited superior recall in the schematic condition.

The power of the design lies in the high degree of assurance it provides that the result was due to a difference in knowledge organization and not other subject differences or knowledge-content differences. The relative weakness of simpler designs is made evident by considering the two simpler alternatives. First, if only the schematic-structured materials had been employed, and the experienced auditors outperformed the inexperienced, two important alternative explanations for the results would not have been eliminated:

(1) experienced auditors having superior memory in general (for all stimuli) and (2) experienced auditors having greater knowledge *content* but the same *organization* (since familiarity with stimuli eases recall). In the second simple alternative design, if only experienced auditors had been asked to learn the taxonomic and schematic organized materials, superior memory for the schematic organized material could have resulted from the inherent ease of remembering the schematic ordering independent of internal-control knowledge (for example, because of its relation to a simpler mnemonic). The 2 × 2 design used by Frederick eliminates each of these alternative explanations because they would have produced parallel lines in Figure 2. Similar designs can be used to test each of the four links in the Figure 1 model.

What we know about knowledge-related effects

The analysis of the existing literature will concentrate on studies with a primary focus on one or more of the four links in the model. Within each link, the literature will be classified by audit task, except where findings are of broader applicability. In most cases, exploratory studies that do not hypothesize specific knowledge-related effects in advance are not included in the review (e.g., studies reporting general experience–performance correlations as secondary findings).

Using Figure 1 as the basis for classifying the literature presents a number of problems. First, as noted earlier, some papers are not explicit as to purpose or were designed on the basis of a different conceptual framework from that employed here. As a consequence, some classifications may appear ambiguous. Second, a common approach to addressing knowledge-related issues in the literature to date is to implicitly or explicitly assume that experience differences are reflected in knowledge differences (link 1 is valid), assess the relation between experience and performance, and attribute the findings to the relation between knowledge and performance (link 3). While I classify these studies based on their intent as tests of link 3, such tests, of course, are joint tests of the assumed experience–knowledge and the knowledge–performance relation.

A third difficulty results from the fact that the great majority of studies to date deal with the relations of ability to knowledge and ability to performance (links 2 and 4) by either controlling for ability differences or ignoring them. This limits the size of these categories. Finally, a small number of more recent studies attempt to simultaneously examine some or all of the relations and thus belong to more than one category. These studies are discussed at the end of this section.

Link (1): What do auditors know and how did they learn it?

Research discussed in this section varies greatly in purpose and approach. Three distinctions are of principal importance. First, some studies in this category are limited to documenting particular aspects of what experienced auditors know, while others also address the learning process. Second, many studies of the effects of experience on knowledge infer those relations based upon the systematic association of experience differences and judgment differences. Error in specifying the processes through which knowledge will be brought to bear on the judgment task may invalidate the inference. A smaller number of studies have employed memory tests (e.g., recall) to assess this relation. Third, the great majority of research on learning has examined the impact of the *sum of experiences* accumulated over a period on particular knowledge elements. Many fewer studies have distinguished among the effects of *particular experiences* on particular knowledge elements.

Financial statement errors. Peters et al. (1989), summarizing protocols from experienced auditors making inherent risk assessments, observed that these assessments were generated on an account-by-account basis. A useful piece of knowledge for forming inherent-risk judgments in this way is the degree to which different accounts are prone to error. Using a frequency knowledge test, Ashton (1991) found that experienced auditors could identify the few accounts most vulnerable to material error in manufacturing and retailing, but were less accurate in ranking accounts where errors were less frequent in these industries, and less accurate at all levels in natural resources and financial industries. Her results further indicate that this knowledge was accumulated early in her subjects' careers (i.e., this is a novice task). Some indication of differential learning based on particular experiences with certain industries was also in evidence.

A number of papers have examined learning of accounting error types or causes (e.g., next period's sales recorded in the current period, goods returned but not recorded, etc.). These errors[16] and various nonerror causes serve as hypotheses that guide diagnostic activity throughout the audit (Libby, 1985). Libby and Frederick (1990) demonstrated that as auditors gain experience, their knowledge of the set of potential financial statement errors becomes more complete, they learn error occurrence rates, and they organize that knowledge along dimensions, including transaction cycle. They employed a frequency test to test the first effect and a hypothesis-generation task to test the second and third in a manufacturing setting. The results indicate that this learning continued for the first five years of the subjects' careers. Following the expected decreasing influence of repetition on learning, the majority of the learning took place in the early years, and little further learning was in evidence by year five (see also Ashton, 1991). It is interesting to note that Kaplan and Reckers' (1989) results suggest that less experienced auditors are more likely to attribute a given piece of unexpected audit evidence to error versus normal activity. This is consistent with Libby and Frederick's (1990) suggestion that attention given to historic cases of fraud in auditing courses may leave students with unrealistic perceptions. This may be related to the professional-skepticism results discussed below.

Tubbs (1992) applied a free-recall task and a conditional prediction task to further examine the development of financial statement error knowledge. His results suggest that more experienced subjects were aware of more errors, had more accurate error knowledge, and were aware of more atypical errors and causally related features of errors such as the department in which the error occurred and the internal-control objective violated (though only awareness of the internal-control objective violated increased with experience). DeSarbo et al. (1994) also found evidence of both a transaction cycle and audit-objective dimension in staff auditors' free sorts of a set of 35 financial statement errors. Frederick et al. (1994), who asked students, audit staff, and managers to sort these errors by transaction cycle and audit objective violated, found that the transaction-cycle dimension developed earlier in one's career than the audit-objective dimension. These results and others described below suggest the importance of knowledge of the causal relations in the accounting and related control systems to diagnosis of financial statement errors.

Three studies have examined how particular experiences affect learning about financial statement errors. Libby's (1985) results suggest that particular recent experiences with errors affect their memorability. In that study and the others described above, experience with different errors is treated as an observed independent variable measured by a self-report because the learning of interest took place in the subjects' actual uncontrolled work environment. Two studies have attempted to examine the effects of various types of experience through experimental manipulation in the lab. Butt (1988) showed that experienced auditors' better-organized memory structures allowed them to acquire the relative frequency information used in the above tasks more effectively than novices. She also established that frequency information was acquired more effectively when it was presented case-by-case than when it was presented in summary form, which may have implications for the effectiveness of practice versus instruction. Further, the effectiveness of summary information was enhanced when it was presented in the context of other case-by-case information. Nelson (1993) examined the process of jointly learning error frequencies and the diagnosticity of financial ratios used in analytical review. His subjects again demonstrated accurate learning on a case-by-case basis.

Internal-control evaluation. A number of studies have examined experienced auditors' internal-control knowledge. Some of the studies were designed to document experienced auditors' understanding of certain internal-control concepts. Others were aimed at testing the relations between experience and knowledge. Most of the studies in both categories infer knowledge based on judgment differences. In addition, two studies have used memory measures to investigate whether more-experienced auditors have more and better organized knowledge of the characteristics of a good internal control system (Weber, 1980; Frederick, 1991).

Frederick and Libby (1986) suggested that predictions of the financial statement implications of internal-control weaknesses are based on two knowledge types: (1) knowledge of the double-entry generating process that results in the cooccurrence of certain pairs of account errors and (2) knowledge of the associations of internal-control weaknesses with particular account errors. It was further suggested that experienced auditors have both knowledge types, but novices only the former. Tversky's (1977) feature-matching model was used as a model of process to predict the effects of these knowledge differences on judgments of the conjunction of account errors. The results support the hypothesis concerning the knowledge difference. Brown and Solomon's (1991) policy-capturing study provided further evidence that account cooccurrences are well known even among inexperienced auditors. Bonner and Lewis (1990), who asked auditors with varying experiences to list two errors that could occur given an internal-control weakness for a manufacturing company, also found that general audit experience and manufacturing experience were related to knowledge of these relations.

Three studies have employed policy-capturing methods to test whether auditors understand particular relations among control features and audit risk judgments or planning decisions. Libby et al. (1985) employed the audit-risk model to generate predictions concerning the contingent or configural nature of the effects of susceptibility of accounting processes to error, the strength of control design, and the strength of related compliance tests on control-reliance decisions. A selected group of expert audit managers and partners evaluated a series of realistic cases and their decisions were consistent with the suggested relations. Libby and Libby's (1989) results for less-experienced auditors suggest that they may be less aware of these contingencies. Brown and Solomon (1990) examined knowledge of configural relations among particular controls. They tested whether auditors understood the differential effects of compensating and amplifying controls when separation-of-duties controls were strong or weak. While no comparisons were made based on level of experience, 40% of the auditors recognized this relation.

While the above studies delineate the nature of internal-control knowledge and assess its association with experience, only one paper has looked at the effects of differing types of experiences on the acquisition of internal-control knowledge. Spires (1991) examined the effects of alternative firm policies reflected in training and formal guidance in firm manuals on the perceived strengths of various compliance tests. He found that, although auditors from different firms tended to agree on the ranking of compliance tests by strength as implied by their judgments of reliance on controls (e.g., document and reperformance is a stronger test than document alone, which is a stronger test than inquiry and observation), auditors from firms requiring reperformance tests derived more assurance from them than auditors from firms that didn't. Further, auditors from firms whose policy manuals (instruction) explicitly caution that inquiry and observation are weak tests derived marginally less assurance from them than auditors from other firms.

Weber (1980) was the first to directly assess the result of a memory process (recall) and to consider relating that result to judgment differences. The approach taken in this important paper is well represented in the literature today. He was also the first to examine subspecialty knowledge. He examined whether EDP audit specialists' knowledge of computer controls was greater and better organized than that of inexperienced auditors'. EDP auditors with specialized training and experience recalled more controls than the inexperienced and there was more clustering in their recall, supporting his hypotheses.

Frederick (1991) was the first to hypothesize a specific organizational difference between more- and less-experienced auditors' knowledge. Again focusing on alternative sources of learning, he suggested that training exposes both inexperienced and experienced auditors to both a taxonomic organization of controls (where controls are related by audit objective insured), but that experience with actual systems is the primary source of learning for a schematic structure (where controls are related by the flow of transactions). As suggested earlier, the extra temporal links between controls in the schematic structure allowed only the experienced auditors to recall more information about a system when that information is presented schematically (by flow of transactions). This suggests that part of the advantage of experienced auditors is that they can better recall the attributes of an internal control system that results from having acquired the schematic knowledge structure. He tied this advantage to a particular type of memory error in a second part of the study discussed later. Biggs et al. (1987) suggested that EDP controls are evaluated by experienced auditors based on experiences with particular previous cases, again highlighting the importance of experience with actual systems. These studies suggest how the structure of semantic memory can affect the encoding and recall from episodic memory.

Substantive procedures. Parts of three studies examined auditors' knowledge of substantive tests. Brown and Solomon's (1991) policy-capturing study demonstrated that experienced auditors were aware of the compensatory nature of some substantive audit procedures. In the Biggs et al. (1988) verbal-protocol study of the role of analytical review in planning other procedures, managers better understood the links between client problems and appropriate audit procedures and objectives (e.g., that increasing accounts receivable confirmation was not relevant to collectibility problems). Similarly, in the Bonner and Lewis (1990) task in which auditor subjects were asked to list two substantive procedures useful in detecting listed financial statement errors, knowledge was correlated with both months of experience and percentage of audit work done in manufacturing.

In estimating the risk of analytical procedures, Bonner (1990, 1991) found that experience had no effect on knowledge necessary for cue measurement, but more experienced auditors had greater knowledge of factors affecting analytical-procedures risk. However, similar to Spires (1991), this latter finding was only in evidence in the firm that provided detailed instructions in their audit manual for this area.[17]

Going-concern problems. Choo and Trotman (1991) had auditors examine information about a firm after being told that the partner-in-charge suggested the firm might have a going-concern problem. They hypothesized that more experienced auditors (>3 years of experience) would have better-developed knowledge of the characteristics of a failing firm. More experienced auditors paid more attention to information *in*consistent with failure, and, in judging the probable truth of facts not previously stated about the firm, were more likely than inexperienced auditors to think that facts inconsistent with failure were true. Both experienced and inexperienced auditors, however, were more likely to think that consistent as opposed to inconsistent new facts were true. That is, given the going-concern scenario, all auditors thought that "fail" facts were more likely than "viable" facts; but more-experienced auditors were more ready to expect to encounter some "viable" facts in a firm with a going-concern problem. These findings were interpreted as supporting the existence of better-developed knowledge structures. Ricchiute's (1991) finding that causally ordered going-concern evidence had more impact than that ordered in normal working paper form further supports the importance of causal models as organizing frameworks for audit knowledge.

Professional skepticism. Auditors are supposed to display an attitude of professional skepticism, which is pervasive across audit tasks. A number of studies have addressed whether such skepticism is displayed and how it develops with experience.

One possible measure of skepticism is attention to inconsistent or contradictory information. Choo and Trotman (1991) found that more-experienced auditors recalled more information inconsistent with a going-concern hypothesis than did inexperienced auditors. Moeckel (1990) found that more-experienced auditors were better able to detect contradictions in evidence when reviewing audit workpapers.[18] Similarly, Bouwman (1984) observed that, when students and auditors reviewed financial statements, the students ignored and auditors "zeroed in on" contradictions in the presented information. The similarity of results obtained by this trio of papers is striking given that they employ very different means (a relatively abstract experiment with recall as the dependent measure, a more "naturalistic" recognition experiment, and a protocol-analysis study).

There is also a consistent set of results in judgment studies in which less-experienced auditors are more conservative or less optimistic than more-experienced auditors. In Wright et al.'s (1991) experiment 1, auditors' estimates of the probability of continuation as a going concern were higher than those provided by students. Again, in their experiment 2, more-experienced auditors estimated the probability of continuation as a going concern as higher than did less-experienced auditors. In Abdolmohammadi (1991), less-experienced auditors gave higher expected population deviation rates than more-experienced auditors when neither group had a decision aid (estimates were the same with the aid). Messier's (1983) less-experienced partners had lower materiality and disclosure thresholds than more-experienced partners. In Abdolmohammadi and Wright (1987), less-experienced auditors were more likely to qualify an opinion for uncertainty due to a land write-down, and more likely to require an adjustment.

Is this a cognitive difference, a utility-function difference, or a combination of both? There are some indications of cognitive elements: the fact that the "conservatism of the inexperienced" goes away with the decision aid in Abdolmohammadi (1991), and the evidence in Biggs et al. (1988) that less-experienced subjects use too many test procedures because they don't know which are really effective or are less conscious of efficiency issues. Further study of the cause of this persistent finding is warranted.

Link 3: What effect does knowledge have on performance?

As suggested earlier, the dominant approach to examining performance effects is to assume an experience–knowledge relationship (normally based on detailed task analysis), assess the relation between experience and performance, and attribute it to the relation between knowledge and performance (link 3). These tests are joint tests of both links 1 and 3. Though the value of using knowledge measures as independent variables has been noted (Davis and Solomon, 1989; Libby, 1990), only a few studies have separately tested link 3.

Financial statement errors. In Libby and Frederick (1990) more-experienced auditors generate more plausible and fewer implausible error causes. As indicated earlier, the more-experienced auditors produced higher scores on an error cause frequency knowledge test. They also generated more frequently occurring causes as explanations for audit findings in the hypothesis-generation task. Both of these findings indicate a possible efficiency or effectiveness advantage to the more-experienced auditors as they search for explanations for evidence. Bonner and Lewis (1990) also found that those with higher test scores on an analytical-review knowledge test were more accurate at generating error causes for unexpected fluctuations and explaining how the errors affected accounts and ratios.

A protocol study by Bedard and Biggs (1991) presented results compatible with these experiments. Auditors performed analytical review on an inventory case with a seeded error. Hypothesis generation was the stage at which most errors occurred, and the least-experienced auditors had the most difficulty at this stage. Auditors with more recent manufacturing experience and presumably more accessible knowledge were also better at generating correct hypotheses in Bedard and Biggs (forthcoming). The importance of industry-specific knowledge is supported by Johnson and Jamal (1987) and Johnson et al. (1989), where the auditor with the relevant industry experience was better at detecting an error due to fraud than auditors with either more or less overall audit experience. A similar lack of transfer was noted by Marchant (1989) who found that experience with analogous errors in different parts of the accounting system did not aid hypothesis-generation performance. However, this finding may have resulted from the dominance of knowledge obtained in practice over that acquired in the experiment.

The importance of the accessibility of available knowledge as a determinant of performance was made clear in Heiman (1990). She examined the impact of knowledge of alternative explanations for audit findings in the evaluation of error hypotheses. Providing alternatives significantly reduced auditors' probability estimates for the evaluated error. Those requested to generate their own alternatives adjusted their probability based on the number of alternatives they could recall from memory. In related work, Anderson and Wright (1988) reported that generating an explanation for an event sequence increased its perceived probability, but only for inexperienced auditors.

Internal control evaluation. More-experienced auditors have more, and better organized, knowledge of the characteristics of a good internal-control system (Weber, 1980; Frederick, 1991). However, large, reliable differences in performance of internal-control judgment tasks have not been in evidence (Wright, 1988). For example, Bonner and Lewis (1990) were able to explain only 3% of the variance in performance on their internal-control task with a combination of four experience and knowledge variables. An interesting finding in the literature may explain these findings. Note that Bonner's (1990) first experiment suggests that inexperienced auditors can *recognize* the characteristics of good control systems about as well as experienced auditors, but Weber (1980) and Frederick (1991) indicate that they cannot *recall* them as well. This suggests that the knowledge difference (e.g., stronger traces, better organization) is more critical on tasks requiring recall as opposed to recognition (cf. Libby and Lipe, 1992). The structured nature of most internal-control tasks limits reliance on recall and may thus limit the effect of knowledge on performance (cf. Libby and Frederick, 1990).

Only one study has examined the impact of the manner in which knowledge is acquired on a performance attribute. Again, the implication here is that different learning opportunities produce different levels of knowledge. Meixner and Welker (1988) tested whether repeated conduct of the task, policy feedback from superiors, learning from the norms of the work group, or the mortality of poor performers who did not employ congruent policies, provided more effective learning opportunities. Repeated conduct (familiarity) was not correlated, whereas the last three types of experience were correlated with improved consensus. This finding is consistent with Bonner and Pennington's (1991) conclusions described earlier.

Plumlee (1985) suggests a possible disadvantage of knowledge in internal-control evaluation. In his study, internal auditors who evaluated systems they participated in designing were less able to identify internal-control weaknesses than less-familiar auditors who had not. The cause of this phenomenon warrants further investigation.

Substantive procedures. Bonner and Lewis (1990) found that superior analytical-procedures knowledge, as measured by relevant CPA exam and textbook type questions and by self-ratings, was associated with superior performance on an analytical-review task similar to that used by Libby (1985) and Bedard and Biggs (1989).

Like Plumlee (1985), Moeckel and Plumlee (1989) suggested a possible disadvantage of some forms of knowledge. They studied auditors' confidence in their improper memories for prior audit evidence. In general, they found that knowledgeable auditors were highly confident in their memories when they confused their own inferences with actually observed evidence. To the degree that this confidence reflects a willingness to rely on memory rather than refer back to the workpapers, errors in judgment may result.

Going-concern indicators. Choo (1991) had auditors judge the probability of failure in the case of a firm that did fail, and write down how they would investigate further and the basis for their present judgment. More knowledge (correct statements about characteristics of failed firms and appropriate investigation procedures) was associated with better predictions [= higher *p*(fail)]. Although experience leads to greater consensus in a number of audit tasks, Wright et al. (1991) were unable to find an improvement in consensus with experience (either auditor versus student or more- versus less-experienced auditor) on going-concern judgments.

Materiality thresholds. A number of studies have examined differences in materiality thresholds based on general audit experience. Auditors' materiality judgments have greater consistency and consensus than students' judgments, in part because of cue weighting [auditors rely more on the most important cue, effect-on-net-income, than students (Krogstad et al., 1984)]. Krogstad et al. (1984) found no differences by rank among auditors; but Messier (1983) found that more-experienced partners' materiality judgments displayed more consensus, and more percentage of variance explained, than less-experienced partners' judgments. These results are generally consistent with Ashton and Kramer's (1980) study of internal-control evaluation. Carpenter and Dirsmith (1990) found that specific experiences with in-substance

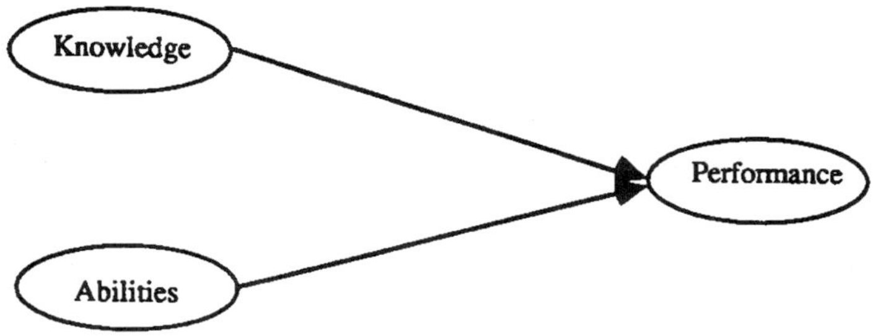

Figure 3. Model implicit in Bonner and Lewis (1990) analysis

defeasances made auditors more likely to consider them material, and (or because) such experience made auditors more likely to consider the transactions as mere earnings manipulations.

Subspecialty knowledge. Bonner and Lewis's (1990) study provided significant evidence of the importance of subspecialty knowledge as a determinant of audit performance. In their financial-instruments task, subspecialty knowledge measured by a test of knowledge of hedging transactions other than interest-rate swaps was significantly related to performance on an interest-rate swap task.

Links 2 and 4: What effect does ability have on knowledge acquisition and performance?

Individual differences in ability and the nature of audit expertise have not been jointly studied until recently (Bonner and Lewis, 1990).[19] The traditional approach in the expertise literature has been to control for differential abilities through use of the "expertise paradigm" described above (Frederick and Libby, 1986; Butt, 1988; Bonner, 1990; Frederick, 1991; Nelson, 1993) or tests to assure that abilities were not correlated with other variables of interest, such as experience (Marchant, 1989).

Bonner and Lewis (1990) recognized both the need to consider the task specificity of audit knowledge and judgment performance and the importance of assessing the role of abilities as a determinant of performance instead of controlling for them. Using experience as a proxy for unmeasured knowledge, they estimated the relative contributions of ability and knowledge to performance of four audit tasks using regression analysis.

The model implicit in their method of data analysis, which is presented in Figure 3, is different from the framework employed here, and does not allow direct estimation of the two learning links, the effects of experience and ability on knowledge (links 1 and 2). To allow estimation of links 1 and 2, as well as 3 and 4, Libby and Tan (1994) reanalyzed the correlation matrix reported in their paper using the conceptual model presented in Figure 1, which treats ability and experiences as inputs that result in the internal state—knowledge—which, along with the direct effects of ability, determine performance. LISREL 7 was employed to test the causal relations.[20]

Only one measure of ability was used in Bonner and Lewis (1990): problem-solving ability as measured by scores on GRE questions related to problem solving. The Libby and Tan (1994) reanalysis indicated that problem-solving ability significantly affected the acquisition of general business knowledge and financial-instruments knowledge (link 2). Problem-solving ability also had a significant direct positive effect on performance (link 4), both in diagnosing an accounting error based on analytical review and in uncovering earnings manipulation. The models also indicated that experience increased knowledge related to all four audit tasks.[21]

Other studies of multiple links. Three studies have jointly examined the experience–knowledge–performance relation. Libby and Frederick (1990), described above, assessed both frequency knowledge (using a test) and hypothesis-generation performance in an analytical-review task. They found that more-experienced auditors had more accurate error frequency knowledge and generated more frequently occurring errors as explanations for the analytical-review findings. Using path analysis, Heiman-Hoffman (1992) found that more-experienced auditors had knowledge of more alternative hypotheses for analytical-review findings than did the less experienced, which in turn affected their estimates of the likelihood of a target hypothesis. In the area of internal control, Frederick (1991) found that while a better-organized schematic structure for controls (possessed by more-experienced auditors) improved performance, it did not eliminate recognition failures for omitted internal controls.

As discussed above, Bonner and Lewis (1990) assess the contribution of ability and different types of knowledge in a psychometric study of the determinants of performance in four audit tasks. They suggest and demonstrate how the relative contribution of these factors will vary across tasks. This paper is particularly important because it is the first attempt to make relevant cross-task comparisons. However, as the discussion here and in Marchant (1990) suggests, it is important to emphasize that it is not appropriate to consider experience and knowledge as *competing* explanations for performance, since experience is an input to the process and knowledge is an output.

Conceptual and methodological issues

As noted earlier, a number of recent reviews have been published dealing with the nature of expertise in auditing (Libby, 1989; Bedard, 1989; Choo,

1989; Colbert, 1989; Davis and Solomon, 1989; Marchant, 1990; Bonner and Pennington, 1991). Two common concerns expressed in these papers are: (1) the need for greater precision in defining variables and relations among variables and (2) the need to continue to focus on the three themes described above. Both concerns are reflected in discussions of the meaning of the term "expertise." The model presented in Figure 1 provides a basis for clarifying the purpose of existing and future studies and suggests that studies of expertise include those that examine one or more of the linkages in the causal model. While not all studies will directly assess performance effects, defining a study's purpose in terms of the specific linkages in the model indicates its ultimate relation to some aspect of decision performance. Again in keeping with the above themes, the linkages also focus attention on the processes involved in knowledge acquisition and application to decision problems.

While the model in Figure 1 may help clarify the focus of the research, individual studies will examine different aspects of the linkages. In general, studies of links 1 and 3 will tend to focus on one of two questions (Libby, 1989; Bonner and Pennington, 1991):

1 What do people, on average, learn from training and experience and how is performance affected?
2 What particular aspects of training and experience lead to differential knowledge and performance?

Studies of links 2 and 4 focus on a third question:

3 Why do individuals with the same experiences learn and perform differently?

Different studies will then examine the relations of different abilities and/or experiences to different kinds of knowledge and then to different aspects of performance on different tasks. Once a study's research question of interest has been so categorized, the appropriateness of many operational choices can be evaluated.

Use of the framework can also facilitate resolution of many of the existing controversies in the literature. Most of the current controversies discussed in the above-mentioned reviews revolve around the question: When should one expect an experience–knowledge–performance relation and what should be its magnitude? Important subparts of this question are:

1 Is experience a proxy for or a determinant of knowledge?
2 Will knowledge increase over the whole range or a limited range of one's career?
3 How conducive is the audit environment to learning and what kinds of learning are fostered?
4 When will knowledge differences result in performance differences?

Is experience a proxy for or a determinant of knowledge?

Conceptually, task-related experience (along with ability and effort) is an input to or determinant of knowledge. Further, experience only represents the opportunity to acquire knowledge (cf. Marchant, 1990), and the quality of these opportunities will vary (cf. Davis and Solomon, 1989; Bonner and Pennington, 1991). As a consequence, its relation to knowledge will be imperfect and should be expected to vary from situation to situation and individual to individual.

In many of the studies described above, experience is employed as an *operational* proxy for knowledge. Its appropriateness as a proxy will depend on the expected strength of the experience–knowledge relation, which will be determined by the factors described above. Nevertheless, assuming no differences in measurement error, measures of knowledge actually acquired must be more closely related to performance than measures of opportunities to learn (experience) because of the additional step in the relation.[22] Use of more direct measures of knowledge to test knowledge–performance relations has been strongly encouraged by Choo (1989), Davis and Solomon (1989), and Libby (1989) and implemented by Bonner and Lewis (1990). However, both studies of the relations between experience and knowledge (link 1) and studies of the relations between knowledge and performance (link 3) are necessary to our understanding of the nature of expertise.

The appropriate approach to measuring experience has also received much attention in the above-mentioned reviews. Except in the rare studies where experience is manipulated in the lab (Butt, 1988; Nelson, 1993), experience is an observed variable measured using self-reports. Months of audit experience or rank are the most commonly used measures. Bonner and Pennington (1991) point out that, for months of experience to be closely related to performance, an auditor must have the opportunity to acquire the necessary knowledge over the period measured and the knowledge must be somewhat general, in that almost everyone practicing as an auditor must have the opportunity to acquire a standardized body of knowledge. They further point out that since most of the studies described above have examined audit knowledge and judgment tasks that meet these conditions (cf. Libby, 1987), using these general measures was an appropriate starting point.

More general measures of task-related experience must by their nature be less closely associated with knowledge than more specific measures of task-related experience. However, this does not suggest that only more specific measures are appropriate or of interest, because the appropriateness of the selected measure must be evaluated on the basis of the purpose of the study. Research on more common audit-decision problems that auditors must solve in the conduct of nearly every audit will necessarily focus on more general measures of experiences. Studies of decision problems in which those who can validly be called experts are few in number, (as are the number of situations in which their expertise will be called upon) will naturally focus on more specific measures.

Will knowledge increase over the whole range or a limited range of an auditor's career?

As noted earlier, many audit tasks are normally completed at different career stages (Abdolmohammadi and Wright, 1987). This fact combined with the decreasing effect of repeated exposure on learning, makes choosing relevant points on the experience scale, where further learning can be expected, a critical design issue. Using less-specific measures of experience will normally add only random measurement error, which decreases the power of tests; choosing the wrong points on the experience scale may result in examination of inconsequential differences in actual experience. Ashton (1991) illustrates both points. In her examination of knowledge of account error frequencies in specialized industries, she demonstrated how more-specific measures of experience were more closely related to knowledge. At the same time, she established that knowledge of the accounts most frequently containing error in manufacturing companies (accounts receivable and payable and inventories), which can be learned from an auditing text, was not associated with any measure of experience (this was a "novice task"). Similarly, when audit managers were asked to estimate error cause frequencies, as a consequence of the decreasing effect of exposure on learning, months of experience beyond five years was again unrelated to knowledge. In the latter two cases, all subject groups had achieved nearly asymptotic levels of knowledge.

Rarely should experience be expected to produce continuous improvement in knowledge or performance. Appropriate matching of the experience measure, points selected along the experience continuum, and task are critical to both developing and testing hypotheses concerning knowledge effects.

Measurement error also limits one's ability to make comparisons across accounting tasks and between accounting and nonaccounting tasks. When task difficulty differs or differing levels of error exist in measurement of experience, knowledge, or performance across tasks (Marchant, 1990), direct comparisons across tasks of levels of knowledge, performance, or associations among the three variables are inappropriate. Since most experiments do not sample tasks and cases randomly from the environment (they do not employ a "representative design"), they are generally ill-suited for parameter estimation or parameter comparisons such as these. Experiments using systematic designs are generally more suited for testing for the existence and direction of effects, not their magnitudes.

How conducive is the audit environment to learning and what kinds of learning are fostered?

The nature of the learning environment is only now being discussed in detail and experimental studies of learning have focused only on frequency learning (Butt, 1988; Nelson, 1993) or multiple-cue-probability learning (Ashton, 1990). Bonner and Pennington (1991) surveyed partners and managers concerning the portion of knowledge related to different tasks learned from experience or training and examined training schedules, professional guidance, and review materials used in large auditing firms. They concluded that instruction, professional guidance, and process (review) feedback are significantly related to performance, but outcome feedback is not. The most effective form of feedback is supervisory review, which promotes the learning of causal relations. Concerning the roles of instruction versus practice, they concluded that learning is promoted when one is first provided with a causal model through instruction, which is then followed by practice.

Bonner and Pennington's (1991) analysis suggests that the quality of the learning environment in auditing varies dramatically from task to task. Questions concerning the quality of the learning environment in auditing are clouded further by the level of aggregation that is assumed. For example, from the individual staff auditor's perspective, learning what behaviors lead to positive reviews by superiors may be of greatest importance, independent of the effects the behavior may have on the cost or effectiveness of error detection. The detailed review procedures followed by most firms should promote this type of learning. Similarly, for the individual senior auditor, subsequent substantive tests provide outcome feedback relevant to evaluating their internal-control judgments, which again should promote learning. However, at the firm level, the effects of audit-strategy changes on costs and frequencies of incorrect acceptance and incorrect rejection errors are very difficult to assess. More ambiguities are added at the societal level. A better understanding of the nature of learning environments in auditing will require a great deal of additional analysis. Both the Butt (1988) and Nelson (1992a) experiments and Bonner and Pennington's (1991) multimethod study are important steps in this direction.

When will knowledge differences result in performance differences?

The effect of knowledge differences on performance will be a function of the match between the knowledge and the task, the sensitivity of the judgment component of interest, and the performance criterion of interest. Since knowledge is task specific, auditors who know more in general may not have more knowledge or even the correct knowledge relevant to the task at hand. Johnson and Jamal's (1987) description of the case where a partner with more experience and presumably more general audit knowledge is outperformed by a less-experienced partner with relevant specialty knowledge illustrates this possibility well.[23]

Einhorn (1976) and Libby (1985) suggest that certain components of less-structured tasks, including hypothesis generation, will be particularly sensitive to knowledge differences. Bonner (1990, 1991) also demonstrates the differential sensitivity of various components of typical multiple-cue combination tasks to knowledge differences. Bonner and Pennington's (1991) analysis further suggests this differential sensitivity. The discussion presented here indicates that one must also consider whether efficiency, as opposed to effectiveness, results should be expected. This again reinforces the need to analyze the knowledge necessary to complete a task, when, how, and how well it will be acquired, and the processes through which it will be brought to bear on the judgment task.

Contributions to the theory of judgment and decision making

While most accounting and auditing studies are not designed to compare the validity of competing theories of cognition, the field of auditing provides opportunities to test the generalizability of findings from basic research to complex tasks learned over an extended period. In auditing, a large number of similar individuals with similar training and experience perform a similar series of increasingly complex and important tasks over a period of 20 years or more within the same organizational structure. As a consequence, the audit context provides a nearly unique laboratory for the study of the long-term development of expertise. Our practical interest in the nature of expertise also leads to investigations of relations that have not been examined in the basic social science literature. A few examples follow.

As Solomon and Shields (Chapter 6, this volume) note, most of the findings from studies of nonaccounting judgment tasks generalize to accounting and auditing tasks. However there are exceptions that suggest the limits of current theories. Of particular note in the research reviewed here are Butt (1988), Nelson (1993), Anderson and Wright (1988), and Frederick (1991).

Butt found that the structure of auditors' knowledge of financial statement errors affected frequency learning. In particular, instances of closely associated errors resulted in overestimation of the perceived frequency of occurrence of both errors. The fact that subjects' natural category structure imposed itself on frequency learning brings into question the completeness of theories suggesting complete automaticity of such learning, since automatic processes should be insensitive to prior knowledge (Hasher and Zacks, 1984; see also Libby, 1985, Ashton, 1991, and Nelson, 1994 for discussions). Such findings also suggest that tests of the accuracy of frequency learning will be sensitive to the fit of the category structure implicit in the measuring instrument and the subjects' natural category structures (see Frederick et al., 1992 for a description of the natural category structure for financial statement errors).

Nelson (1993) found that Medin and Edelson's (1988) discovery of an inverse base rate effect (a particular type of inaccurate application of frequency information learned from experience) did not generalize to the learning of financial statement error frequencies. Interestingly, similar findings were in evidence for both experienced auditors and naive subjects, suggesting that the results were not due to a knowledge difference. Alternatively, in Anderson and Wright's (1988) study of the explanation effect in an audit setting, they were able to replicate the psychology result with naive subjects, but not with experienced auditors, suggesting a knowledge effect.

Frederick's (1991) study of detection of omitted controls was the first test of output interference with complex stimuli and knowledgeable subjects. He found that the existence of a well-formed schematic memory structure eliminated output interference between categories. But, contrary to the predictions of schema theory, output interference within categories was not eliminated by a schematic memory structure.

Although the above-mentioned studies test the limits of current theories, other auditing studies have examined new phenomena that naturally occur in the learning and decision environment of auditing. Notable is Butt's (1988) examination of learning of event frequencies from joint presentation of individual instances and summary data. Whereas even experienced subjects were unable to accurately learn from summary data alone, the addition of the individual-instance data allowed them to learn from the summary data. Studies such as this may lead to both expansion of psychological theory and practical guidance for the training of auditors.

Conclusion

The literature examining relations among ability, experience, knowledge, and performance is the fastest growing segment of audit-judgment research. Significant additions to our understanding have been made by research employing a wide variety of approaches including policy capturing, probabilistic judgment, learning and memory, problem solving, psychometrics, and archival-data analysis. This diversity is an important strength of the literature. Broader psychometric approaches (e.g., Bonner and Lewis, 1990) and deeper, more narrowly focused memory studies that examine single links or pairs of links (e.g., Frederick, 1991) have different strengths and weaknesses and can both make important contributions to the study of the nature of audit expertise. Similarly, studies that examine learning based on experience in the lab and those that assess the effects of experiences accumulated in practice also contribute different pieces of the expertise puzzle. Different research approaches that focus on different individual linkages or sets of linkages are necessary to produce the complete picture of the nature of audit expertise.

It is critical to recognize that an understanding of each of the links in Figure 1 is equally important to understanding the nature of expertise in auditing. This point is best illustrated by the fact that, even if experience–performance relations have been adequately demonstrated, we cannot understand their implications for decision improvement without understanding the knowledge differences that produce the performance differences. Hogarth (1991) makes a similar point when he suggests that one cannot determine how to improve performance without understanding the process.

Future research must then consider the effects of motivation, which itself is a function of the environment. An auditor's effort (cognitive or physical) is affected by factors such as justifiability of the act, accountability, and reward structure in the audit environment (Gibbins, 1984). These factors may affect the knowledge or level of attention brought to bear on a task, thereby affecting performance (Libby and Lipe, 1992).

Regardless of the issues addressed or the approach taken, there are two keys to successful study of the nature of audit expertise. The first is precision in conceptual definition of variables and their relations. The conceptual model in Figure 1 will hopefully aid in developing such precision. The guidelines in the "expertise paradigm" provide the second key. Successful studies of these issues must develop hypotheses in advance based on specification of the knowledge necessary to complete a particular task, when, how, and how well the knowledge will be acquired, and the process(es) through which it will be brought to bear on the task. They must then test these hypotheses using subjects who can reasonably be expected to have different knowledge and experimental tasks in which the knowledge differences have observable implications. As was suggested above, the failure to uncover experience effects in many prior studies was the result of having employed tasks in which more- and less-experienced auditors would be expected to have the same knowledge or in which different knowledge would be expected to result in the same behavior. Other results are suspect because of the failure to provide the control for alternative explanations accorded by the expertise paradigm. Only through more careful conceptual and empirical analysis will we increase our understanding of auditor expertise.

Acknowledgments

This chapter is based in part on Libby and Luft (1993). I am grateful to Bob Ashton, Sarah Bonner, Bill Kinney, Joan Luft, Mark Nelson, Ken Trotman, and Bill Wright for helpful comments on earlier versions.

Notes

1. Most notably, Bonner and Lewis (1990) employ a model of auditor performance and Bonner and Pennington (1991) further explore some of the relations in the model.
2. Further discussion of motivational issues is provided in a later section of the chapter.
3. Readers are referred to Libby and Luft (1993), Solomon and Shields (Chapter 6, this volume) and Messier (Chapter 8, this volume) for more extensive discussion of these issues.
4. Other variables such as effort, which are not the focus of this paper, also affect learning and performance.
5. Felix and Kinney (1982) and Solomon and Shields (Chapter 6, this volume) provide such a disaggregation of the audit process and Bonner and Pennington (1991) analyze the cognitive processes involved at each stage.
6. The listing of dimensions presented below is not exhaustive, but represents what I believe to be most relevant to modeling knowledge-related phenomena in audit judgment.
7. This is similar to Alba and Hutchinson's (1987) definition of familiarity.
8. Performance and resulting feedback also indirectly affect the experiences that the individual will be exposed to in the future (e.g., early promotion changes future assignments).
9. Information may be perceived or inferred.
10. Other distinctions, such as that between declarative knowledge of facts and attributes versus procedural knowledge of rules and procedures to operate on the declarative knowledge (see Waller and Felix, 1984b; Choo, 1989), are also made in the psychological literature but have not played a major role in the audit-judgment literature.
11. Bonner and Lewis (1990) is a notable exception.

12. Problems faced in measuring different elements of audit judgment performance and the usefulness of different operational measures have only occasionally been discussed in the literature (e.g., Libby, 1981; Gaumnitz et al., 1982; Ashton, 1985; Trotman and Yetton, 1985).
13. These conditions assume adequate motivation and apply to learning that does not occur automatically.
14. The controversy over the scarcity/abundance of outcome feedback in auditing will be discussed in a later section. Much of this controversy, like others, stems from failure to define variables and specify a model of the knowledge-related determinants of performance or expertise.
15. As noted above, learning is also a function of effort, which will be discussed later in this section.
16. From this point on the term "errors" will be used to include both unintentional errors and irregularities.
17. Notably, as in Frederick and Libby (1986), Bonner (1990) controlled for subject differences other than experience with a second similarly structured task in which experience differences were expected to have lesser effects.
18. Assigning of responsibility may also improve detection (Moeckel and Plumlee, 1990).
19. However, Dickhaut (1973) investigated these relations in a different accounting setting.
20. Both Bonner and Lewis (1990) and Marchant (1990) suggest this general approach for future research.
21. This included the above two tasks and the internal-control and financial-instruments tasks.
22. If measures of experience contain more measurement error than measures of knowledge, this problem will be exacerbated.
23. However, the failure to employ a control task in this illustration leaves open a number of important alternative explanations for the result, including the possibility that the less-experienced audit partner was superior at all tasks.

8

Research in and development of audit decisions aids

William F. Messier, Jr.

The auditor's judgment process has been subjected to extensive study since Ashton's seminal work in 1974.[1] In general, the results of audit judgment research are consistent with those of prior psychological research, including findings related to the lens model, heuristics and biases,[2] memory, and expertise. The chapters in this book by Solomon and Shields (Chapter 6) and Libby (Chapter 7) discuss this literature. Much of this research suggests that audit judgment can be improved through the use of decision aids. The purpose of the present chapter is to review and analyze the research in and development of decision aids in auditing.

The chapter is organized as follows. The first section provides a background for the ensuing discussions. The second section discusses motivations for developing or using decision aids. The third section discusses potential effects of audit decision aids on individual judgment and auditing firms. The fourth section categorizes the types of audit decision aids, while the fifth section reviews research on audit decision aids. The sixth section discusses the development of decision aids by auditing firms. The last section proposes areas for future research.

Background

Auditing is the process by which an auditor accumulates and evaluates evidence about quantifiable information (e.g., financial statements) related to an economic entity for the purpose of reporting on the correspondence between the entity's quantifiable information and some established criteria (e.g., generally accepted accounting principles) (American Accounting Association, 1973). Solomon and Shields' (Chapter 6, this volume) Figure 1 depicts the audit process as containing seven stages: (1) orientation, (2) evaluating accounting information system architecture and process, (3) tactical planning, (4) plan indirect tests of financial statement assertions and evaluate test results, (5) plan direct tests of financial statement assertions and evaluate test results, (6) evaluate aggregate results, and (7) choose report.

The decision-making process followed by the auditor in completing these activities is consistent with the model of decision making proposed by Einhorn and Hogarth (1981c). It contains three phases: information acquisition, information evaluation, and action/choice. For example, suppose an auditor wishes to determine whether the entity's internal control structure over sales transactions is sufficiently reliable to prevent material misstatements of sales and accounts receivable. The information-acquisition phase involves discussing with the entity's employees the control procedures present in the sales system and may also include examining a sample of sales transactions that have been processed through the system. The information-evaluation phase entails assessing the reliability and diagnosticity of the resulting evidence vis-à-vis the hypothesis that the internal-control structure prevents material misstatements. The third phase involves the auditor's choosing to rely or not rely on the entity's internal control structure. Various types of decision aids are used by auditors to support all activities in this decision-making process.

Rohrmann's (1986, p. 365) definition of a decision aid is adopted in this chapter because it is broad enough to apply to a wide array of decision aids. He defines a decision aid as:

> . . . any explicit procedure for the generation, evaluation and selection of alternatives (courses of action) that is designed for practical application and multiple use. In other words: a [decision aid] is a *technology* not a theory. (emphasis added)

This broad definition is refined for the auditing setting later in the chapter.

Motivations for developing or using audit decision aids

Decision aids have a long history in auditing. Examples include audit programs, internal control questionnaires, decision tables, and various types of checklists. Referring to the internal control example in the previous section, a questionnaire might be used during the information-acquisition phase to gather evidence on control procedures that are present in the accounting system. Similarly, a decision table might be used to evaluate the various combinations of control procedures for preventing material misstatements. Based on the evidence gathered and evaluated using these decision aids and other sources of evidence, the auditor chooses to rely or not rely on the client's internal control structure.

Audit researchers and practitioners recently have focused considerable efforts on the study of audit decision aids. Part of this increased interest is due to the transition by auditing firms from experience-based to research-based audit approaches (Ashton and Willingham, 1989). In the past, decision aids were developed somewhat informally based on practicing auditors' perceptions of how to solve a particular practice-related problem.[3] More recently, various aspects of the audit process have been rigorously examined by audit researchers and practitioners, and decision aids proposed as possible solutions for some of the problem areas identified. Thus, more recently developed decision aids tend to result more from systematic research efforts than from auditors' on-the-job experiences (Elliott, 1983).

Early judgment research in auditing pointed out potential shortcomings of *unaided* audit judgment. For example, lens model research often found a lack of consensus among auditors (i.e., different auditors evaluating the same evidence often made different judgments). Additionally, other studies indicated that auditors often are not sufficiently sensitive to base rate information and do not fully understand the inverse relationship between sample size and sample variability. As Ashton and Willingham (1989, p. 2) state, "the ultimate goal of this [audit decision-making] research is to provide a scientific basis for improving audit decisions, thus favorably impacting the efficiency and/or effectiveness of audits." Given the shortcomings identified by audit-judgment research, the emphasis shifted from simply documenting judgment biases, errors, and inconsistencies to the development of decision aids that might improve unaided judgment.

Two additional factors have motivated auditing firms to develop decision aids that offer the potential for improving the *effectiveness* and *efficiency* of audits. First, competitive pressures, brought about in part by changes in the AICPA's Code of Professional Conduct (e.g., elimination of the prohibition on competitive bidding and advertising), have motivated auditing firms to find ways of conducting audits more efficiently. Second, recent investigations by Congressional committees into auditor involvement in the much publicized savings and loan failures (United States General Accounting Office, 1991), as well as the Government Accounting Office's report on the quality of audits of governmental units, have raised questions about the effectiveness of audits.

Effects of audit decision aids

While decision aids have been proposed as a way of improving audit judgment, it does not necessarily follow that they will be cost effective. Additionally, decision aids may have both positive and negative effects on an auditor's judgments and an auditing firm's activities (Ashton and Willingham, 1989). The discussion in this section initially focuses on alternatives to decision aids. This is followed by a discussion of the potential effects of decision aids on individual judgment and auditing firms.

Decision aids versus alternatives

Decision aids are not the only possible solution to the presence of inconsistencies, biases, and errors in auditors' decision making. Fischhoff (1982, p. 424) suggests that, in general, the source of bias or inconsistency should determine the appropriate strategy for debiasing. He proposes that the appropriate strategy depends on whether the bias results from faulty tasks, faulty judges, or a mismatch between judge and task.[4]

When the source of the bias is a faulty task, it is unlikely that a decision aid will overcome the problem. In such cases, it may be more appropriate to clarify the instructions for the judge or demonstrate the impossibility of solving the task. When the problem lies with the judge, and the judge is "perfectible," extensive training with the task is an appropriate strategy. If the judge is "incorrigible," however, some type of decision aid may be more appropriate. When there is a mismatch between the task and the judge, then the "person–task system" should be restructured or extensive training is needed. Restructuring can involve the use of a decision aid. Thus, a decision aid is likely to be preferable to training when the task can be restructured to better match the judge's information-processing capabilities, or when the success of training is uncertain (Ashton and Willingham, 1989, p. 8).

An important consideration in the choice between additional training and decision aids is the relative cost and effectiveness of the two alternatives. As Ashton and Willingham (1989) have pointed out, we know very little about the relative costs and effectiveness of training versus decision aids in auditing. This issue is discussed further in the section of this chapter that addresses areas for future research.

Effects of decision aids on individuals' judgments

Many decision aids are based on the premise that it is more effective for the individual to make a series of "smaller" judgments related to a problem rather than to make an overall global judgment. These smaller judgments typically serve as input to a decision aid that produces a decision or recommendation for the larger problem. This decomposition approach has potential implications for audit judgment when decision aids are used to support individual auditors.[5] Ashton and Willingham (1989) cite the following effects:

- An increased emphasis on judgment
- An increase in the structure of judgment inputs
- Increased *or* decreased judgment consistency
- A need to justify the decision aid's output
- Circumvention of the decision aid by the auditor

Increased emphasis on judgment. Using a decision aid to combine the auditor's input judgments does not reduce the need for sound professional judgment. When an audit decision aid is used to combine several input judgments, the auditor's responsibility is to provide those inputs. For example, the nonstatistical sample size equation and tables provided by the *Audit Sampling* guide (American Institute of Certified Public Accountants (AICPA), 1983b) require the auditor to provide three input judgments (degree of desired assurance, tolerable error, and error expectation) instead of one judgment for sample size. An implication of decomposing holistic judgments in this fashion is that auditing firms may need to train their auditors in the proper formulation of the relevant input judgments. Moreover, this increased emphasis on input judgments may cause auditors to view their task as mechanical and not devote enough attention to each of the "smaller" judgments (Ashton and Willingham, 1989).

Structuring input judgments. The use of decision aids will likely lead to an increase in the structure of input information. Prior research suggests that information processing is improved when the input information is congruent with the decision model employed. For example, Einhorn (1972) suggested that decision makers are good at identifying important input cues, but that inconsistencies arise when those inputs are combined to reach a judgment. Einhorn (1972) suggested using experts to identify and measure inputs, but using a mechanical combination rule (or decision aid) instead of human combination. The use of structured input judgments may lead to greater judgment consistency because it may be easier for the decision maker to use the decision aid.

Increasing versus decreasing consistency. One of the purposes of using decision aids is to increase judgment consistency (both consensus and stability). Much of the audit-judgment research discussed earlier indicates relatively low consensus among auditors for many tasks (e.g., internal-control structure assessment and audit materiality judgments). The decomposition approach, which requires the auditor to make several judgments instead of one, is expected to result in increased consistency. However, there is evidence that the use of audit decision aids based on decomposition may *decrease* consistency.[6] For example, Kachelmeier and Messier (1990) find that the nonstatistical sample size equation and tables provided with the *Audit Sampling* guide (AICPA, 1983b) lead to higher variability (less consensus) in sample size judgments than intuitive sample size judgments. Libby and Libby (1989), however, find that when component judgments in an internal-control setting are familiar to subjects who have been specifically trained in the task, increased consistency results. Their study suggests that positive effects result if the input judgments are properly structured.

Justifying decision aid output. Part of the auditor's decision process involves justifying decisions that are made (Gibbins and Emby, 1984; Messier and Quilliam, 1992). Research in auditing and elsewhere suggests that justification leads to increased consistency (Ashton, 1990, 1992; Hagafors and Brehmer, 1983; Johnson and Kaplan, 1991). Ashton and Willingham (1989) discuss the tradeoff between using a decision aid or explicitly requiring justification of the decision. They consider this to be important since "the cost of an increased emphasis on justification is likely to be considerably less than the cost of developing and maintaining decision aids" (p. 14). However, a number of questions need to be considered in situations in which a decision aid has already been implemented into a firm's practice. Will the output from the decision aid be sufficient justification for the decision or will additional documentation be needed? Who should be authorized to override the output from a decision aid, and under what (perhaps predefined) circumstances will this be allowed?

Circumventing the decision aid. Auditors may be able to circumvent decision aids in some instances. For example, the sample size formula and tables provided by the *Audit Sampling* guide (AICPA, 1983b) can be circumvented by "working backwards" (Kachelmeier and Messier, 1990). That is, the auditor can decide on the desired sample size and then select input judgments to yield the desired sample size. Kachelmeier and Messier's (1990) results supported the working backwards hypothesis. Minimizing this possibility is an important consideration for an auditing firm interested in implementing decision aids.

Effects of decision aids on auditing firms

Decision aids may have a number of important effects on auditing firms. The following discussion focuses on three possible effects:

- An increase in the structure of the firm's audit methodology
- Organizational effects related to development and implementation
- Legal liability issues[7]

Increased structure of the firm's audit methodology. Implementation of audit decision aids is likely to increase the structure of an auditing firm's audit methodology. Cushing and Loebbecke (1986) examined the audit manuals of 15 audit firms and concluded that their audit technologies could be classified along a structured-unstructured continuum. Kinney (1986), who examined the voting patterns of the firms on auditing standards that affected the structured nature of the audit process, found that firms with relatively structured technologies tended to favor standards that increased structure while firms with relatively unstructured technologies did not favor such standards.

Since the research by Cushing and Loebbecke (1986) and Kinney (1986), audit technology has been shown to affect client disclosure patterns (Morris and Nichols, 1988), control and coordination mechanisms between audit team members (Bamber and Snowball, 1988), perceptions of organizational characteristics and role stress (Bamber et al., 1989), use of a decision aid (Kachelmeier and Messier, 1990), and inherent risk judgments (Dirsmith and Haskins, 1991). If the increased use of decision aids increases the structure of audit methodologies, as seems likely, then further effects on such variables may occur.

Organizational effects. If decision aids are viewed as a technology (Rohrmann, 1986), then there are likely to be numerous additional effects on the organization (Cooper and Zmud, 1990; Markus and Robey, 1988; Weiss and Birnbaum, 1989). Unfortunately, as Markus and Robey (1988) reported in their review of the literature on information technology and organizational change, reliable generalizations about the relationships between technology and organizational change are rarely available. In auditing, little or no research exists on this issue. As a result, the discussion that follows is speculative and based on research from the information systems and organizational literature. Much of this research has been conducted in corporate settings. Since auditing firms are partnerships, and therefore subject to different operating and legal liability constraints, the findings should be considered only suggestive.

Technology (e.g., decision aids) can be viewed as an "exogenous force which determines or strongly constrains the behavior of individuals and organizations" (Markus and Robey, 1988, p. 585). Weiss and Birnbaum (1989) indicate that little is known about how to implement a technology strategy. However, Cooper and Zmud (1990) have proposed a model of the information technology implementation process. It consists of six stages: initiation, adoption, adaptation, acceptance, routinization, and infusion. Organizational issues related to the implementation of information technology arise at each of stage of the model.

Implementing a technology such as a decision aid can have both "top-down" and "bottom-up" effects. It is generally assumed that some level of management authority approves the introduction of a decision aid and that it will be adopted by the end-users. For example, the executive office of an auditing firm may develop a decision aid for a specific audit task. After appropriate testing in field settings, the firm may place the decision aid in each office of the firm, giving rise to a number of potentially important issues.

First, what is the best approach to implementing new technology such as a decision aid in an auditing firm? Should the firm's executive office mandate the use of the decision aid, or should the aid simply be made available to end-users who are allowed to use or not use the decision aid? Both approaches would seem to have advantages and disadvantages.[8] One advantage of mandating the use of the decision aid is greater consensus within the firm. However, requiring the firm's auditors to use it may lead to dysfunctional behavior such as circumvention, as discussed earlier (see Kachelmeier and Messier, 1990).

Second, in implementing a decision aid, it is important for the auditing firm to manage the political dimension of the effort (Dyer and Page, 1988; Page and Dyer, 1990; Weiss and Birnbaum, 1989). The auditing firm needs to recognize and manage the diverse interests of the firm's employees who may be affected by the successful implementation of the aid (Cooper and Zmud, 1990). For example, if the decision aid appears to be a replacement for tasks performed by certain employees, they may attempt to undermine the firm's implementation efforts. Another example of possible political consequences may involve the use of an expert auditor to develop an expert system. If the expert auditor views the future implementation of the expert system as a threat to his or her job or as a reduction of his or her influence (power) within the firm, the expert may not fully cooperate in the system's development.

Legal liability. The use of decision aids and, in particular, expert systems may raise legal liability issues for auditing firms. For example, if an auditing firm makes an expert system available to its auditors and an auditor chooses not to use it, will the auditor and firm be held liable if some related aspect of the audit is later found defective? Or, suppose an auditor overrides a decision aid's recommendation. Will this be viewed as evidence of a lack of due professional care? Finally, suppose an expert system makes an incorrect decision. Who is liable and what standard should be used to measure the performance of the expert system? Frank (1988, p. 63) has commented that technology will remove many cognitive tasks from human control and thus alter the assumptions underlying the current legal systems. This will pose a significant challenge to the institutions responsible for creating the law.

Types of audit decision aids

A broad definition of decision aids was provided earlier in this chapter (Rohrmann, 1986). Decision aids in auditing range from simple worksheets for calculating sample size (Elliott, 1983) to complex computer-based expert systems like Risk Advisor (Graham et al., 1991). For discussion purposes, decision aids are categorized into three types in this section: simple or deterministic aids, decision support systems, and expert systems. Simple or deterministic decision aids, which may or may not be computerized, include any tools that aid judgment in a straightforward algorithmic manner. A decision support system has been defined as "a computer-based system used by managers as an aid to decision making in semi-structured decision tasks through direct interaction with data and models" (Benbasat and Nault, 1990, pp. 203–204). Decision support systems are based on limited, specialized knowledge. Expert systems are defined as computer programs that use specialized (rather than general-purpose) knowledge about a particular problem area, use symbolic reasoning rather than only numerical calculations, and perform at a level of competence that is better than nonexpert humans (Luconi et al., 1986).

Abdolmohammadi (1987) and Messier and Hansen (1984, 1987) use similar approaches to classifying types of decision aids. They categorize decision aids by the type (complexity) of task and the decision-making activities required for that complexity. The complexity of the task is classified into three categories: structured, semistructured, and unstructured. The decision phases follow the Einhorn and Hogarth's (1981c) model: information acquisition,

Table 1. *Relationships between the task, decision making phases, and type of decision aid*

Decision making phases	Task: Structured	Semistructured	Unstructured
Information acquisition	Well defined	Reasonably defined	Ill defined
Information evaluation	Little uncertainty	Some uncertainty	High uncertainty
Action/choice	Little judgment	Some judgment	Extensive judgment
Expertise level	Low	Moderate	High
Type of decision aid	Simple/deterministic	Decision-support system	Expert systems

information evaluation, and action/choice.[9] As the complexity of the task increases from structured to semistructured to unstructured, more expertise with the task is required. Similarly, the complexity of the decision aid also increases. These relationships are shown in Table 1.

In a structured problem domain, information acquisition is usually well defined, little uncertainty exists about the evidence to be evaluated, little judgment is involved in the action/choice, and the expertise necessary for such decisions is usually low. A simple decision aid based on some type of algorithm is generally most appropriate for such tasks. When the task is semistructured, information acquisition is reasonably defined, some uncertainty exists about the evaluation of the evidence, some judgment is required for the decision, and a moderate level of expertise is necessary. Decision support systems appear to be appropriate for those tasks. The unstructured task may be best served by an expert system. Here, information acquisition is ill-defined, high uncertainty exists about the evidence to be evaluated, the action/choice involves extensive judgment, and a high level of expertise is required for the decision. This categorization of the types of decision aids is used in the following sections as a framework for discussing research and development of audit decision aids.

Research into audit decision aids

While the documented shortcomings of human judgment have led researchers to propose decision aids as one means of improving decision making, there has been surprisingly little research into the effects of audit decision aids. Further, the majority of research that has been conducted has focused on simple or deterministic decision aids. This section reviews studies that have examined the effects of simple decision aids and provides a summary of selected research on expert systems.

Simple decision aids

Most simple decision aids follow a decomposition strategy. The proposed benefits of the decomposition approach to decision aiding are (1) it forces the decision maker to consider all relevant information, (2) it helps the decision maker to combine the relevant information correctly, and (3) it reduces the cognitive strain on the decision maker (Jiambalvo and Waller, 1984). Several auditing studies have examined decomposition approaches in various settings.

The audit risk model,[10] cited in SAS No. 47 (AICPA, 1983a) as a model for planning the audit, decomposes the auditor's assessment of audit risk into three components: inherent risk, control risk, and detection risk.[11] This model can be viewed as a decision aid that assists auditors in deciding on the appropriate level of audit testing. Three studies have examined the effectiveness of the audit risk model as a decision aid. In these studies, the audit risk model is viewed as an algorithmic rule for combining the auditor's assessments of the individual components of audit risk.

Jiambalvo and Waller (1984) compared two groups of auditors' assessments of the audit risk model components for four accounts receivable cases. One group made a holistic assessment for test of details risk. The other group made assessments of audit risk, control risk, and analytical procedures risk in addition to the assessment of test of details risk. The results showed no difference in test of details risk between the group using holistic assessment and the assessment of test of details risk made by the group using the decomposition approach. There was, however, a difference between the decomposition group's intuitive assessment of test of details risk and the test of details risk resulting from the algorithmic combination of their assessments of the three input components. The intuitive assessments were significantly lower than the assessments using the algorithmic combination, suggesting that auditor's intuitive combination of the risk components does not correspond with the audit risk model.

Daniel (1988) extended Jiambalvo and Waller's study by including a separate component for inherent risk as suggested by SAS No. 47.[12] Auditors were asked to assess audit risk for accounts receivable using a self-selected audit engagement and to decompose the audit risk assessment into the various risk components. Daniel (1988) found that the audit risk assessments using either the formula from SAS Nos. 39 or 47 were lower than the auditors' holistic (intuitive) assessment of audit risk. This confirms Jiambalvo and Waller's findings that auditor's holistic risk judgments are not consistent with the audit risk model.[13] Thus, the divide and conquer strategy does not appear to be effective in the case of the audit risk model.

Libby and Libby (1989) point out two problems with these studies. First, the subjects were unfamiliar with one or more of the component judgments and no training was provided. Second, the components were assessed as probabilities, which may have been particularly difficult for the subjects. Libby and Libby (1989) examined the effectiveness of a technique that closely resembled Einhorn's (1972) expert measurement/mechanical combination approach, i.e., having the decision maker measure the cues and then using a model for combining those measurements into a global judgment. Libby and Libby (1989) applied Einhorn's approach to a control reliance decision by developing a mechanical model (i.e., a decision aid) based on data gathered from a panel of internal control experts (Libby et al., 1985) and a committee consisting of two audit partners and a senior manager from the participating public accounting firm. The auditors were divided into two groups: (1) an expert measurement/mechanical combination group and (2) a global judgment group. The global judgment group made an overall reliance judgment on an accounting cycle. The expert measurement/mechanical combination group made component judgments of control strength and test strength for each process in the cycle, and these component judgments were combined using the mechanical model. Both groups received training on the components of the audit risk model and how the components might be applied in practice. The expert measurement/mechanical combination group also received training on the use of the response scales for the component judgments. The subjects evaluated six case versions adapted from Libby et al. (1985).

The results indicated that the expert measurement/mechanical combination group produced control reliance decisions that were closer to those of the firm's experts than were the decisions of the global judgment group. Libby and Libby (1989) attribute the difference in their results from the prior studies (Jiambalvo and Waller, 1984; Daniel, 1988) to two factors. First, the selection of the components and their presentation more closely matched the firm's workpaper format and the subjects received training in the unfamiliar aspects of the task. Second, they used a linear combination rule, whereas the prior studies used normative models that were multiplicative and thus may have had amplified response errors.

Butler (1985) hypothesized that auditors may find the assessment of sampling risk for a substantive test of details to be cognitively complex and subject to bias. He constructed a simple four question decision aid based on Kahneman and Tversky's (1979a) debiasing procedure. The questions focused the auditors' attention on distributional information (i.e., a reference class) and their ability to make judgmental assessments of sampling risk. Two groups of auditors made risk assessments for eight cases related to accounts receivable confirmations. The control group made the assessments without the decision aid while the experimental group used the four-question decision aid. The auditors' judgments were compared to a statistically determined risk assessment based on a multinomial dollar-unit sampling program. The results showed that the auditors who utilized the decision aid made judgments that were closer to those of the sampling program, and also made more correct accept/reject decisions about the account balance, than the control group auditors.

Kachelmeier and Messier (1990) examined the effects on auditor's sample-size judgments of the nonstatistical decision aid included in the AICPA's *Audit Sampling* guide (1983b). Three issues were addressed. First, they examined whether the use of the decision aid removed the "belief in law of small numbers" bias[14] (Tversky and Kahneman, 1971) by forcing the auditors to concentrate on three components of the decision aid rather than directly on the global judgment (sample size). The components of the decision aid require the auditor to assess the amount of audit assurance placed on the test, the amount of error expected in the population, and the amount of tolerable error for the account balance. Second, they examined whether auditors circumvented the decision aid by starting with a desired (intuitive) sample size and then forcing the component judgments to justify that sample size. Finally, they examined whether the use of the decision aid affected the variability of the sample size decisions.

Three groups of senior auditors selected a nonstatistical sample for testing inventory. One group provided a sample size decision without the decision aid. The second group calculated sample size using the decision aid. The third group provided only the input parameters for the components of the decision aid, and the researchers calculated the resulting sample size. The results indicated that (1) the decision aid led to larger sample sizes, (2) there was evidence that the auditors "worked backwards," and (3) the decision aid led to greater variability across subjects' judgments.[15] Kachelmeier and Messier (1990) concluded that these results support Ashton and Willingham's (1989) comments that decision aids can have negative effects.

Ashton (1990) also showed that using a decision aid can be associated with negative effects on decision making when the aid's positive effects are undermined by task characteristics that, by themselves, often lead to better performance. Ashton's framework has two tenets. First, task characteristics such as financial incentives, performance feedback, and decision justification can either increase or decrease performance by strengthening the pressure on a decision maker to perform well. Second, the presence of such characteristics can offset the positive effects of decision aids by changing the nature of the task so that the decision maker believes "risky" decision strategies are necessary for successful performance. Pursuing "risky" strategies can, in turn, lead decision makers to decrease their reliance on mechanical decision aids, and performance can fall.

This framework was tested by having senior auditors predict ratings assigned by Moody's Investors Service to bonds issued by 16 industrial corporations. The subjects were provided with three financial ratios that were correlated with the Moody's ratings. The auditors were assigned to one of eight groups: one group made the bond ratings without the decision aid, financial incentive, performance feedback, or justification; three groups made the ratings without the decision aid but received either incentives, feedback, or justification; one group made the bond ratings with a decision aid but without incentives, feedback, or justification; three groups used the decision aid and received either incentives, feedback, or justification. The results showed that when the decision aid was combined with the presence of either incentives, feedback, or justification, performance was lower than when the aid was *not* combined with these task characteristics.

In a related study, Ashton (1992) compared a group with access to a decision aid with a control group (having no decision aid) and a group that was required to provide written justifications for their judgments. Justification is, of course, an integral part of the audit process (Gibbins and Emby, 1984; Messier and Quilliam, 1992). The results show that the auditors who had the decision aid available, and those required to justify their judgments, were more accurate and consistent than the control group. Justification led to an improvement in accuracy and consistency of 60% and 89%, respectively, of the improvement associated with the decision aid. However, as Ashton points out, the costs of developing, maintaining, and updating such aids is also likely to exceed the costs associated with justification.

Expert systems

Researchers have two different motivations for developing expert systems (Messier and Hansen, 1987). One is to develop a cognitive simulation based on one (or a few) expert(s). Following this approach, the researcher tries to capture the processes followed and the decisions made by the expert. The other motivation is to develop a system that performs the task as well as experts, with little concern for mimicking the underlying decision processes.[16]

Studies by Biggs et al. (1993), Merservy et al. (1986), and Peters (1990) are examples of the cognitive-simulation approach. Expert systems developed by Boritz and Wensley (1990, 1992), Dungan and Chandler (1985), Hansen and Messier (1986a,b; Messier and Hansen, 1992), and Steinbart (1987) are examples that are concerned with performing the task well.[17] The knowledge-acquisition approaches for developing these systems have utilized a number of different methods including questionnaires, interviews, protocol analysis, expert systems shells, and rule-induction methods. The remainder of this section reviews two examples of each approach.

Merservy et al. (1986) constructed an expert system, ARISC (Auditor Response to Identified Systems Controls), which models an auditor's internal-control evaluation process in the purchasing cycle. A computational model of one audit manager (whose firm identified him as an expert) was developed using protocol analysis, interviews, and textbooks. The ARISC model was refined by processing prototype internal control cases through the system in collaboration with the expert. Verification involved comparing the model's processes and decisions with those of the expert and three additional audit managers. Data analysis concentrated on the completeness, effectiveness, and agreement of the system and the auditors in five areas: hypothesis generation, problem-solving processes, cue usage, lines of reasoning, and outcomes. The results support Merservy et al.'s (1986, p. 71) conclusion that "the model appears to simulate the processes of expert auditors, particularly the auditor after whom it was modeled."

Peters (1990) developed a cognitive, computational model of the risk hypothesis generation process for audit planning. The system was programmed in LISP. The underlying model specifies the domain knowledge used by auditors to generate risk hypotheses, the processes used to apply the knowledge, and the form and content of the risk hypotheses. Various data-gathering techniques were used to develop the model in three phases. The first phase included a literature review, observation of two audit-planning meetings, and open-ended interviews. Nine auditors from two Big Six firms participated in this phase. In the second phase, Peters conducted structured interviews with six auditors from two Big Six firms. The interviews included reenactment of risk decisions and simulated client transfer discussions[18] to identify factors that auditors associated with audit risk. The final phase required that each of two audit managers select one client and reconstruct the processes used to identify audit risk. These data were combined with the information gathered in the other two phases to build the initial computer program of the risk hypothesis generation process.

The model's processes were tested by having two audit managers solve aloud a new case developed by Peters based on a public company. Concurrent verbal protocols were gathered and broken into episodes (i.e., pauses or breaks in the subject's expressions). The model's processes were compared to the two audit managers' protocols to test the model's seven major predictions.[19] In this case, testing the predictions is basically equivalent to testing the model underlying the process. The evidence provides moderate support for the predictions: (1) the protocol analysis indicated that the auditors used decision deferral, backtracking, and default values to reduce uncertainty related to missing information or data; (2) the auditors generated expected balances for accounts and relationships among accounts; (3) the auditors used inherent, control, and detection risk information in generating risk hypotheses, and (4) the analysis of the auditors' protocols did not find any direct evidence of probabilistic assessments for risk hypotheses.

The model was also tested by having three audit managers (one manager from a firm used in the development work and two managers from two additional Big Six firms) answer an open-ended questionnaire for the two real-world cases used to develop the model and the new case developed by Peters. The subjects completed the questionnaire by providing a detailed critique of the model's analyses of the cases. Simple frequency counts were made of the number of times the model and subjects disagreed on the analysis of the individual financial statement accounts. Intersubject disagreement was also computed. The results show very little agreement on the decisions either between the subjects or between the model and the subjects. Peters (1990, p. 99) suggests that the lack of consistency is probably due to the complex and ill-structured nature of the task.[20]

Dungan and Chandler (1985) developed an expert system (AUDITOR) that assists an auditor in assessing the adequacy of a client's allowance for bad debts. The system was developed in two stages: (1) initial modeling of the system's goal, rules, and rule weights and (2) refinement of the system using expert auditors who operated the system interactively.

The system was validated using two procedures. First, an auditor (not involved in the development of AUDITOR) served as a judge by comparing AUDITOR's judgment of the allowance for bad debts with the actual judgments made by auditors in the field. The expert system's conclusions were considered acceptable in nine of ten cases. The second procedure was a "blind" validation. In this instance, an auditor rated the acceptability of AUDITOR's judgments and those made in the field without knowing their source. The system's judgments were considered acceptable in ten of eleven cases.[21] The best results were achieved where the decision was to reserve all or nothing of the accounts receivable balance, i.e., in the most extreme (and easiest) cases for the allowance. The system's performance was poorer when a partial reserve was required.

Hansen and Messier (1986a,b) developed EDP-XPERT, an expert system intended to assist computer audit specialists (CASs) in making judgments of the reliability of controls in advanced computer environments. It is a rule-based system that uses the AL/X shell. The initial knowledge base was refined with the help of a senior CAS and resulted in a system containing 133 rules structured into four goals: the reliability of supervisory, input, processing, and output controls.

A preliminary investigation (Hansen and Messier, 1986b) of the quality of the system's judgments was undertaken using 17 auditors participating in an initial CAS training program. The subjects used EDP-XPERT to evaluate the EDP controls on a hypothetical case company. They also completed a questionnaire that gathered attitudinal data on expert systems and EDP-XPERT. The subjects' evaluations of EDP-XPERT across nine criteria were reasonable, given the state of development of the system. For three of the four goals, the auditors' control judgments were consistent with EDP-XPERT's conclusions.

The system's rule base was later expanded to include controls for on-line real-time systems and data base management systems (Messier and Hansen, 1992). The prior rules and the basic goal structure were revised to accommodate the new additions. The rule base was again refined with the assistance of a senior CAS, resulting in three major goals: supervisory, data base management, and application controls.

This version of the system was tested on two major cases and on clients selected by the participating senior CASs. The judgments made by EDP-XPERT were compared to the senior CASs unaided judgments. There was a 14.3% misclassification rate on the two cases using this criterion.[22] The system performed less favorably on the real-world clients selected by the subjects, as the misclassification rate was 42.8% for these companies. Messier and Hansen (1992) conclude that EDP-XPERT's knowledge base contains a substantial amount of knowledge about auditing advanced computer systems, but that the system's performance could be improved if a more suitable expert system shell were used or if the system were reprogrammed using an AI language.

Development of audit decision aids

Examples of audit decision aids that have been developed by auditing firms are discussed in this section. The discussion provides an overview of the firms' development efforts. Detailed reviews of audit decision aids can be found in Abdolmohammadi (1987), Ashton and Willingham (1989), Boritz (1992), Brown (1991), Brown and Murphy (1990), Murphy and Brown (1992), and Messier and Hansen (1987).

Simple/deterministic decision aids

The use of statistical sampling techniques and other statistical tools is evidence of the development of simple decision aids by the auditing profession (AICPA, 1983b). For example, discriminant analysis models have been used for assisting going-concern decisions (Kida, 1980; Mutchler, 1985), and regression analysis and time series models, e.g., STAR – Statistical Techniques for Analytical Review (Stringer, 1975), have also been used to assist auditors with analytical procedures (Kinney, 1983). Although many other audit decision aids have been relatively simple "memory joggers," such as questionnaires and checklists, research has recently led a number of auditing firms to accelerate the development of decision aids. For example, based on the Mock and Turner (1981) study of auditors' nonstatistical sample size decisions, KPMG Peat Marwick developed a one-page workpaper to help their auditors reach greater firm-wide consensus on sample size decisions (Libby, 1981). The AICPA (1983b) suggested a similar type of decision aid for nonstatistical sampling decisions.

The development of the microcomputer has allowed public accounting firms to automate much of the workpaper documentation that previously was completed manually. This has also made it possible to place the various aids in the field in computerized form.

Decision support systems/expert systems

The distinction between a decision support system and expert system is not always clear (Abdolmohammadi, 1987; Murphy and Brown, 1992).[23] For example, Murphy and Brown (1992) report that because there is not full agreement on the definition of an expert system, they had to rely on the individual public accounting firm's terminology to classify a system as an expert system, in their survey. As a result, some systems that might be considered decision support systems by some firms may be called expert systems in this classification. This is particularly true of systems that automate time-consuming manual processes normally performed by staff and that do not require a high level of expertise. Some of these systems are more appropriately called "intelligent questionnaires," "expert databases," or decision support systems (Murphy and Brown, 1992), as little expertise is associated with their use.

Research and development of audit expert systems is in the formative stages. However, explosive growth has occurred in the development of expert systems by auditing firms in the last decade. The early research on expert systems was started by academics (Dungan and Chandler, 1985; Hansen and Messier, 1986a,b; Messier and Hansen, 1984; Steinbart, 1987). All of the these systems were primitive prototypes and would have required considerable developmental effort to be used by practicing auditors. The first expert systems developed by auditing firms were Coopers and Lybrand's ExperTAX (Shpilberg and Graham, 1986) and KPMG Peat Marwick's Loan Probe (Kelly et al., 1986). ExperTAX helps auditors and tax professionals gather and review data for tax accrual and tax planning purposes. Loan Probe assists auditors in establishing appropriate reserves for potential losses on bank loans. More recently, Price Waterhouse has developed a series of expert systems that are being integrated into the firm's practice. This includes PLANET (Delisio et al., 1993), which can be used for audit risk assessment and planning, and SAVILLE (Hamscher, 1992), which models the internal control structure of accounting systems.

Most of the expert systems developed by auditing firms for auditing purposes[24] fall into several practice areas: work-program development, risk analysis, internal control evaluation, tax accrual and deferral, disclosure compliance, and technical support (Boritz, 1992; Brown, 1991). Table 2, based on Boritz (1992), Brown (1990), and Murphy and Brown (1992), classifies these systems as they relate to three practice areas studied extensively by audit researchers. The "other" column contains some of the expert systems discussed previously. Of course, other expert systems about which auditing firms are unwilling to release information may also exist.

Areas for research on audit decision aids

The development of audit decision aids can be a research activity. For example, one might be interested in constructing an expert system to solve a particular task. The process of developing the relevant knowledge base involves acquiring an understanding of the general problem domain. Protocol analysis may be used to acquire knowledge from a few experts and this may result in a detailed understanding of the problem domain (cf. Biggs et al., 1987). Such knowledge can point the way to important issues related to the task. Academics can contribute to research in audit decision aiding, including (1) simple decision aids, (2) expert systems versus alternatives, (3) validating expert systems, and (4) knowledge acquisition.

Table 2. *Examples of decision support systems/expert systems developed or used by auditing firms*

Firm	Work-program development	Risk analysis	Internal-control evaluation	Other
Arthur Andersen & Company	EASY			
Coopers & Lybrand	Expertest	Risk Advisor	C&L Control Risk Assessor	ExperTAX ExempTAX Sample Sizer
Deloitte-Touche	Audit Planning Advisor		Internal Control Expert	
Ernst & Young	EY Decision Support		FLOW EVAL CCR/36 Advisor	VATIA PANIC
KPMG Peat Marwick				Bank Failure Prediction Loan Probe
Price Waterhouse	APEX 2	PLANET	SAVILLE Systematic AS/400 Expert	Professional Disclosure Requirements CROSBY

SOURCE: Boritz (1992), Brown (1991) and Murphy and Brown (1992).

Simple decision aids

In an earlier section, research related to decision aids that decomposed the problem into components was discussed. A decomposition strategy seems to be prevalent in most simple decision aids. Although most of the audit research studies discussed showed negative effects from such a strategy, Libby and Libby (1989) have shown that with proper structure and training, auditors' decisions can be improved. More research is needed to establish the conditions under which a decomposition strategy improves auditors' judgments.

A long-standing controversy exists in the psychology literature on the use of clinical versus statistical judgment (e.g., Bunn and Wright, 1991; Dawes et al., 1989; Einhorn, 1988; Garb, 1989; Hammond et al., 1987; Kleinmuntz, 1982, 1990; Ravinder, et al., 1988). Research typically shows the superiority of statistical over clinical judgment (Dawes et al., 1989), but few clinical practitioners rely on statistical techniques (Garb, 1989; Kleinmuntz, 1990).[25] Audit practitioners seem to be prone to the same problem. Various statistical techniques are available to auditors, yet they are seldom used in practice (Biggs and Wild, 1984). Future research should examine why this phenomenon occurs.

Expert systems versus alternatives

As discussed earlier, the costs of developing and maintaining expert systems could exceed their benefits. For example, one auditing firm has indicated that they spent over $1 million to develop one of their systems. This amount does not include the additional expenditures necessary to maintain the system. Ashton and Willingham (1989) call for evidence that expert systems are more effective than training or the use of less costly and simpler decision aids. For example, mechanical combination models similar to Libby and Libby (1989) may be more cost beneficial than expert systems.[26] Examining the tradeoff between expert systems and alternatives should be a fruitful area for future research.

One of the benefits cited for implementing expert systems is to make expertise in the problem domain available to nonexpert members of the firm (Elliott and Keilich, 1985). However, such a strategy could actually inhibit the development of future experts in the problem domain if current personnel overrely on the expert system. Or the expert system, rather than the domain environment, may shape the development of their expertise. This could result in problems when the environment changes and the expert system is slow to adapt to the changes. Future research should examine the possible effects of expert systems on the development of expertise.

Validating expert systems

There is no correct answer for most audit decisions (Ashton, 1982; Libby, 1981). As a result, researchers have not been able to use accuracy as a measure of audit judgment quality. Instead, consensus has been used. Analogously, the usual approach to validating expert systems in auditing is to compare their output against the solution proposed by the expert or team of experts.

Little information is available on the extent to which expert systems developed by auditing firms or auditing researchers have been rigorously validated. While the systems have clearly undergone some testing, published accounts suggest that testing has been mainly of a "trial and error" nature (e.g., Kelly, et al., 1986; Graham et al., 1991; Shpilberg and Graham, 1986). Joint projects between academics and practitioners that investigate alternative criteria for validating expert systems' performance might prove especially fruitful.[27] Since expert systems developed by auditing firms are used on "real-world" clients, future research might track the performance of such systems over time.

Knowledge acquisition

A key issue in the development of expert systems is acquisition of the expert's knowledge (Messier and Hansen, 1987). Numerous techniques have been used by researchers to capture the knowledge and rules that experts use to solve a task. However, the most popular technique, verbal protocol analysis, is extremely time consuming and cumbersome to use. There are also questions concerning the ability of protocol analysis to access the expert's decision processes (Ericsson and Simon, 1980; Nisbett and Wilson, 1977).

Recent advances in a subarea of artificial intelligence referred to as machine learning offer the potential for overcoming some of these difficulties. Algorithms have been developed that extract decision rules from a series of examples taken from the problem domain, and some have been applied in audit settings. For example, Messier and Hansen (1988) showed that one such algorithm (ID3) produced decision rules that outperformed both bank loan officers and discriminant models of them in predicting loan default. In another study, Hansen et al. (1993) demonstrated that two induction algorithms outperformed LOGIT in predicting going-concern opinions. Related work in the use of artificial neural networks has produced similar results (Bell et al., 1990; Hansen and Messier, 1991). Additional research along these lines may prove useful in identifying ways to capture experts' knowledge.

Acknowledgments

The author would like to thank M. Abdolmohammadi, R. Ashton, S. Biggs, D. Kleinmuntz, J. Dickhaut, and the participants at the Duke Conference and accounting workshops at the universities of Connecticut and Florida for their helpful comments on earlier versions of this chapter. The author was supported by a summer research grant from the Fisher School of Accounting.

Notes

1. Detailed reviews of this research can be found in Ashton (1982, 1983), Ashton et al. (1988), Joyce and Libby (1982), and Libby (1981).
2. Some of the findings for heuristics and biases are at odds with the basic psychology findings. In their analysis of heuristics and biases in auditing, Smith and Kida (1991, p. 485) conclude that "although the evidence indicates that the heuristics and biases common to many experiments using student subjects and generic tasks are also present in the judgment of professional auditors performing familiar, job-related tasks, the nature of these heuristics or the extent of their presence is often notably different."
3. There was little or no published evidence that such aids were subjected to a systematic development process or rigorous testing procedures. Thus, it is not possible to determine if such decision aids were developed based on sound research methodologies or whether it was merely assumed that trial-and-error use of the decision aid by auditors in the field would validate the aid's effectiveness.
4. See Ashton and Willingham (1989) and Fischhoff (1982) for a more detailed discussion of the issues briefly covered here.
5. The view taken here is that decision aids are used to support audit judgment rather than replace it.
6. Research conducted outside of auditing has produced mixed results on the effect of decomposition aids on accuracy or consistency. Cornelius and Lyness (1980) and Lyness and Cornelius (1982) find increased accuracy and consistency, while Burns and Pearl (1981) and Chakravarti et al. (1979) find the opposite.
7. Ashton and Willingham (1989) cite four other effects that are not discussed here: (1) sub-

stitution of capital for labor, (2) accepting error, (3) increased competition from nonaccountants, and (4) security considerations.

8. It is normally assumed that managers influence the extent to which technology is adopted and used by subordinates. Leonard-Barton and Deschamps (1988) found, however, that managerial influence is not perceived equally by all subordinates. Their research shows that subordinates who are inclined to adopt new technology (e.g., those having personal innovativeness and task-related skills) will do so *without* management support. Subordinates who do not possess these characteristics may wait for a management directive before adopting the new technology.
9. Abdolmohammadi (1987) uses Simon's (1960) model, which contains three phases: intelligence, design, and choice. These phases are analogous to the phases proposed by Einhorn and Hogarth (1981c). Einhorn and Hogarth's model is used here because it has served as the basis for extensive protocol analysis research conducted to aid in constructing expert systems (e.g., Biggs et al., 1987).
10. The audit risk model (AR = IR × CR × DR) components are defined as: Audit risk (AR) is the risk that the auditor may unknowingly fail to appropriately modify misstated financial statements. Inherent risk (IR) is the susceptibility of an assertion to a material misstatement, assuming there are no related internal-control structure policies or procedures. Control risk (CR) is the risk that a material misstatement that could occur in an assertion will not be prevented or detected on a timely basis by the entity's internal-control structure policies and procedures. Detection risk (DR) is the risk that the auditor will not detect a material misstatement that exists in an assertion.
11. Detection risk can be divided further into analytical procedures risk (APR) and test of details risk (TDR) (AICPA, 1981), where analytical procedures risk is the risk that analytical procedures (e.g., simple comparisons and ratio analyses) and other relevant substantive tests would fail to detect material misstatements in an assertion, and test of details risk is the risk that substantive tests of details would fail to detect material misstatement in an assertion.
12. Jiambalvo and Waller (1984) used the SAS No. 39 formulation of the audit risk model (AR = CR × APR × TDR). Inherent risk was assumed equal to 1.0 in this formulation and not formally included in the model. Daniel (1988) explicitly included the inherent risk component, to be consistent with the changes in the model resulting from SAS No. 47.
13. Boritz et al. (1987) report similar findings when comparing Canadian auditors' judgments to the U.S. audit risk model and a Bayesian form of the model.
14. This bias suggests that individuals exaggerate the informativeness of small samples. In other words, individuals understate the extent to which statistical power diminishes as sample sizes are reduced, with a tendency to attribute too much power to a relatively small sample.
15. It is possible that the greater variability found results from the fact that the subjects were not trained in the use of the decision aid (Libby and Libby, 1989).
16. In practice, this distinction is sometimes blurred. To develop an expert system that performs the task well usually requires capturing domain specific knowledge and identifying decision rules used by individual experts.
17. See Boritz (1992), Brown (1991), Brown and Murphy (1990), and Messier and Hansen (1987) for reviews of other expert systems in auditing.
18. Client transfer discussions occur when an audit manager rotates off an engagement and briefs the incoming audit manager on client-specific audit issues.
19. The predictions involved issues such as risk hypothesis generation stages, the order of information search, procedures used to reduce uncertainty, the use of qualitative and quantitative data, items affecting expectations, characteristics of the internal control environment, and causal explanation for sources of risk.
20. See Messier (1990) for a more detailed commentary on Peters' model.
21. Dungan and Chandler (1985) do not report the results of the validator's judgments of the field auditor's judgments.
22. The analysis for both the cases and client data was based on the judgments for each of the three goals examined by the system.
23. Abdolmohammadi (1987) classifies decision aids such as regression models and linear programming as decision support systems. Because of their algorithmic nature and the definition used here for decision support systems, I have chosen to classify such tools as simple decision aids.
24. Expert systems have also been developed for taxation, consulting, management accounting,

and computer suppcrt purposes. See Armitage and Boritz (1991), Brown (1991), and Michaelsen and Messier (1987).

25. Blattberg and Hoch (1990) have shown that an equal weighting of model and manager increased the accuracy of managerial forecasting over either the model or manager in isolation.
26. See Carroll (1987) and Schwartz et al. (1989) for an interesting exchange on the issue of expert systems versus simple linear models.
27. See O'Keefe et al. (1987) and O'Leary (1988) for a more detailed discussion of issues related to validating expert systems.

Part IV
Conclusion

9

Twenty years of judgment research in accounting and auditing[1]

Michael Gibbins and Robert J. Swieringa

And that's the way it is.
Walter Cronkite

An accountant, in preparing the financial statements for a financial institution, must assess whether it is probable that certain loans are impaired, in part because that assessment is required under generally accepted accounting principles.

Several corporate executives are meeting with auditors from the company's independent accounting firm to try to settle a dispute about how to account for the recent divestiture of a subsidiary. The contending proposed accounting treatments will have significantly different effects on the company's expected reported earnings and financial position in the current year and subsequent years. Both parties must judge what is appropriate and fair in the circumstances. The executives are very sensitive to potential effects on the company's share price and their compensation arrangements. The auditors are very sensitive to potential effects on their exposure to legal liability.

The partner in charge of an audit is under pressure from the client to reduce the audit fee and is considering whether the introduction of some new audit software plus proposed changes in the client's accounting system will permit the fee to be reduced without impairing the quality of the audit.

The general manager of a manufacturing plant under severe competitive pressure is using accounting information to help determine the plant's production and marketing strategies. Related accounting information is used by the manager to calculate performance bonuses for the manager's senior subordinates and by head office to measure the plant's, and therefore the manager's, performance.

Introduction

The four examples above describe settings that require judgment. They reflect uncertainty, strategy, technology, expertise, feedback, evidence evaluation, and other factors that are of interest to judgment researchers generally, and that are central to the practical context in which professionals must cope. They include a mix of internal experience, external rules, and frustrating ambiguity when the experience and rules are incomplete, contradictory, inapplicable or plain absent. They are the stuff of judgment research in accounting and auditing, and they form the contextual background for this final chapter.

We have been asked to comment on the research reviewed in the preceding chapters. That request provides an opportunity for retrospective sense-making (Weick, 1979). Our comments draw on the observations and summaries in those chapters and use the above examples to emphasize connections and trends. Our comments are somewhat selective: we do not provide a literature review, because the preceding chapters and other articles and books provide useful reviews of a large and diverse literature.[2] However, we acknowledge that our comments may reflect some excess baggage from literature reviews we have provided in the past (Dyckman et al., 1978; Gibbins, 1977; Gibbins and Newton, 1987; Gibbins and Mason, 1988; Swieringa and Weick, 1982). We also do not repeat the overview that is presented in the first chapter. Instead, we comment on issues that interest us and that we hope interest others. Our perspective is personal at times, so we will try to make our points of reference clear and trust that variations from views expressed in other chapters will add to the reader's interest and will emphasize our general conclusion: judgment research in accounting and auditing is diverse and shows no signs yet of settling down to a standard paradigm or the sum of accepted wisdom.

The title of this chapter encodes four essential components of the perspective developed in the chapter.

Accounting

Accounting can be defined as the identifying, measuring, recording, and communicating of financial information associated with economic events. Accounting provides a broad platform for the study of information production, verification, dissemination, and use; for the effects of the information on individuals, organizations, markets, and society; for the effects of each of these on the information; for interactions of every kind; and for all sorts of specific inquiry into economic, psychological, statistical, fiscal, contractual, strategic, technical, and other phenomena. Accounting research also is a very broad field that includes judgment research and a host of other research approaches and interests. The preceding chapters demonstrate a liberal, inclusive view of what judgment research is and of relevant accounting problems.

Auditing

General-purpose financial statements are often audited by independent accountants (auditors) for the purpose of enhancing confidence in the reliability of those financial statements. The most common group of people whose judgments are studied in judgment research in accounting and auditing includes the partners and professional staff of public accounting firms who audit those financial statements. Though the preceding chapters comment on the judgments of business managers, stock market participants, management accountants, and others, most of the replicated and substantiated body of findings focuses on auditors. Indeed, judgment research is the most common approach used in studying auditing and auditors, perhaps equalling all other approaches combined in the number of studies published on that topic. As a result, the reference to "judgment research in accounting and auditing" in the title to this chapter may be somewhat misleading because that research has focused more on auditing than on accounting.

Twenty years

Judgment research in accounting and auditing is only about 20 years old. Though some experimental and survey studies of decisions made in accounting were undertaken in the 1950s and 1960s, judgment research blossomed in the mid-1970s, in part because of the joint development of auditing as a subject of academic research and of useful approaches in psychology (the Brunswik Lens, heuristics and biases, and information-processing analyses of problem solving, to mention some of those more important to accounting and auditing). Reviews of experimental and survey studies in accounting and auditing that were undertaken in the late 1960s and early 1970s expressed concerns about a lack of theoretical emphasis, a lack of ties to the work of others, and a lack of rigor (American Accounting Association, 1974; Dyckman et al., 1978; Gibbins, 1977). A review of experiments published from 1970–1981 concluded that progress was being made in overcoming those concerns (Swieringa and Weick, 1982).

The preceding chapters provide a snapshot of judgment research in accounting and auditing as of early 1992. That research has made real progress and more progress is expected. Significant literatures now exist in the areas represented in this book and in related fields and disciplines. More is now demanded from individual studies, in part because of the progress that has been made. Progress also creates ambiguity and uncertainty. Frameworks and methods change, there is impatience with the pace of progress, and some nagging concerns about practical significance continue.

Judgment research

Judgment research in accounting and auditing is similar to general judgment research in that its intellectual wellspring is psychology and the typical study tends to be theory driven – a cognitive or interpersonal theory provides the motivation and hypotheses. However, judgment research in accounting and auditing differs from general judgment research in its strong motivation to understand and capture essential features of the applied setting. The research design used in general judgment research often depends on theory (for example, a theory of order effects or memory structures) but is not particularly dependent on the specific problem setting or group of participants.

Judgment research in accounting and auditing is both theory driven and setting sensitive. The research chooses theory partly for its potential for assisting in understanding judgments in applied setting. It focuses on incentives, constraints, tasks, structures, and other characteristics of applied settings as potential modifiers or determinants of human judgment processes. It focuses on the participants who exercise judgment, including their experience, expertise, professional goals, career concerns, and so on, and it seeks to improve participants' judgments in those settings by developing decision aids and other assistance and by exploring the implications of the research for the participants and others.

Those components and the preceding chapters suggest that judgments in accounting and auditing are embedded in the context of the judgment task and the setting in which people exercise judgment. Understanding that context therefore requires specifying various relations between judgment processes and numerous contextual factors. This is a major goal of the research. In the sections that follow, we focus on the task, the setting, and the people who exercise judgment. We then conclude with some observations about relationships between judgment research in accounting and auditing and general judgment research, other accounting and auditing research, developments and concerns in the accounting profession and business community generally, and the general enterprise of academic research and scholarly analysis.

The task

By its very nature, judgment research is task-oriented. Judgment is studied in the context of specific judgment tasks. Research includes task description and analysis, and the results may shed just as much light on the components of the task as on the judgment processes of the people performing it (Hogarth, 1991).[3]

Judgment research in accounting and auditing is intimately connected with accounting's practical techniques and technologies, such as double-entry bookkeeping, computer-based information processing, and manuals and other decision aids. That research has contributed significantly to our understanding of several tasks, including internal-control analysis and evaluation, audit evidence sampling and aggregation, financial analysis for bank loan and credit evaluation, and management-performance analysis and evaluation. More extensive task analysis is needed and is underway in a number of areas. The examples at the beginning of this chapter all refer to judgment tasks that have not been studied extensively.

The specific task for judgments in accounting and auditing is inevitably subjective and complex, and the potential costs of an erroneous judgment are high. Consider the first example of the accountant who is assessing whether it is probable that certain loans are impaired and by how much they are impaired. No matter how thorough the accountant's investigation is, there is no way of knowing with certainty which loans are impaired and by how much at interim points during the life of the loan. Moreover, since many financial institutions such as banks and thrifts hold large loan portfolios, the costs of inadequate loan-loss provisions can be very high. Many financial institutions and their public accounting firms are currently being sued by governmental agencies and others because of alleged material understatements of loan-loss provisions.

Evaluating loans and determining the adequacy of the provision for loan losses are complex processes. The accountant typically obtains information about existing loans from a variety of systems. For example, the accountant obtains information from internally generated listings such as "watch lists," past-due reports, nonperforming-loan reports, overdraft listings, listings of loans to insiders, management reports of total loan amounts by borrowers, historical loss experience by type of loan, loan files that lack current financial data, borrowers that are experiencing problems such as operating losses, marginal working capital, inadequate cash flow, or business interruptions, and loans to borrowers in industries that are experiencing economic instability. The information obtained is then used as part of a systematic process to designate individual loans that warrant monitoring and a specific loss provision is further designated as loss, doubtful, substandard, or special mention. Different predicted loss rates are then associated with each classification.

The task in judgment research in accounting and auditing presents an interesting paradox. Judgment studies are based on a particular task (such as loan evaluation, internal-control evaluation, product profitability measurement, financial accounting and disclosure choices, tax planning, or others). Judgment studies take the laboratory to the participants in the sense that the participants are expected to continue to do what they normally would do anyway, except they are expected to do it under closer scrutiny with more structure imposed on the stimuli. Participants remain largely on their own turf and use well-rehearsed routines that they impose on materials that resemble their normal inputs.

However, the task used in judgment studies is a simplified representation of the natural task. Moreover, considerable control often is exerted over the information and displays presented to participants and the focus is on relatively limited responses to those presentations. As a result, the accountants and auditors who are participants in judgment studies may not be as familiar or comfortable with the simple representation as they are with the natural task, and they are often cut off from the factors such as decision aids, consultations, and reviews that assist them in performing the natural task. Winkler and Murphy (1973) make a similar argument about the correspondence of the experiment and the applied task.

Concerns are sometimes expressed that the tasks used in judgment studies bear little resemblance to natural tasks. Swieringa and Weick (1982) observe that if experimental events and tasks are believed, attended to, and taken seriously (experimental realism), there may be little, if any, need for judgment tasks to be similar to real-world events (mundane realism). They note that the basic advantage of the use of a simplified representative task is that it may allow for direct tests of theory or for theory construction; the theory is the basis for generalization back to the natural task. The basic advantage of the use of a complex representative task is that it may allow for tests of complex theories or tasks that have vivid situated meanings; the complex theories or situated meanings are the basis for generalization back to the natural task.

The preceding chapters describe the tasks that have been used in judgment research in accounting and auditing. A large proportion of the judgment studies have used simplified representative tasks to test or develop theories. This use is particularly true for studies of management incentives [Waller (Chapter 2) and Young and Lewis (Chapter 3)], auditor expertise [Solomon and Shields (Chapter 6) and Libby (Chapter 7)], and decision aids [Messier (Chapter 8)]. For examples and comments on task effects and task analysis, see Bedard and Biggs (1991), Bédard and Chi (1993), Bonner and Lewis (1990), Bonner and Pennington (1991), Gibbins and Jamal (1993), Heiman (1990), Moeckel (1991), Peters (1990), and Swieringa and Weick (1982); also see Bedard (1989) for an archival analysis of an auditing task.

The preceding chapters suggest that judgment researchers have underexploited financial accounting judgments. The first two examples at the beginning of this chapter focus on typical judgments in financial accounting. Different accountants frame those judgments differently and different accounting treatments result, sometimes for ostensibly similar circumstances.

The first example focuses on judgments about loan losses and is typical of judgments about losses on other assets that are not expected to be recovered through operations and of judgments about obligations incurred because of product warranties, the risk of uninsured losses, pending or threatened litigation, or actual or possible claims and assessments. Generally accepted accounting principles require that estimated losses be accrued if information available prior to the issuance of financial statements indicates that it is probable that an asset had been impaired or a liability had been incurred at the date of the financial statements and the amount of the loss can be reasonably estimated. Different people interpret the words "probable," "had been impaired," "had been incurred," and "reasonably estimated" differently and hold different views about what the objective of the assessment is and how loan losses should be measured.

The second example focuses on how to account for the recent divestiture of a subsidiary. The accounting treatment for specific transactions and events such as a divestiture often depends on how those transactions and events are viewed and whether they are linked with other transactions and events. For example, the accounting treatment of the divestiture is different if it is viewed as a disposal of a segment or as a disposal of part of a line of business or class of service. That treatment also is different if the subsidiary was recently acquired as part of a larger business combination and was expected to be sold shortly after that combination was completed.

Judgments in financial accounting are becoming more prevalent and more difficult as transactions and events increasingly take place in the context of contract relations instead of simple contracts. Accounting judgments are easier to frame and make when transactions and events occur in the context of contracts that are simple, discrete, of short duration, and reflect limited relations among parties, and when precise measures exist for objects of exchange, no future cooperation is anticipated, and no sharing arrangements are assumed. Those judgments are more difficult to frame and make when transactions and events occur in the context of contract relations that are complex, of long duration, and reflect close relations among the parties, and when some objects of exchange cannot be measured currently, some future cooperation is anticipated, sharing relations exist, some troubles are anticipated, and interactions are assumed. Complex contract relations exist for parent and subsidiary relations, financial instruments, contributions to nonprofit organizations, and a variety of compensation arrangements.

Those contract relations also confront accountants with difficult measurement judgments. Accounting for retiree health care arrangements requires estimates of health care cost trend rates and discount rates over periods in excess of 80 years. Similarly, estimates are required in accounting for reclamation costs for extractive activities and for decommissioning costs for nuclear power plants. Accounting for some financial instruments and for certain deferred-compensation arrangements also requires estimates of uncertain future outcomes. In addition, accounting for basket purchases or sales of entities (leveraged buyouts) or of complex financial instruments relies heavily on estimates of uncertain future outcomes. The need to make estimates of uncertain future outcomes raises questions not only about how those estimates should be made, but also about which future events should be anticipated and reflected in accounting measurements.

Judgments in financial accounting increasingly resemble experimental tasks. In framing and making those judgments, accountants access the literature of generally accepted accounting principles through search-and-retrieval computer software. That literature may provide guidance either directly or indirectly by analogy. Technical-inquiry services provided by public accounting firms and by other professional organizations (e.g., the Financial Accounting Standards Board or American Institute of Certified Public Accountants) also can be accessed by written or telephone inquiries and those services may access previous inquiries through search-and-retrieval computer software in providing guidance about the judgment task.

Judgment researchers also have underexploited certain audit judgments. The third example at the beginning of this chapter focuses on an auditor who is considering ways to reduce the audit fee without impairing the quality of the audit. Over the years, significant resources have been devoted to obtaining a better understanding of audit process activities and audit risk and its components of inherent, control, and detection risk [see Figure 1 in Solomon and Shields (Chapter 6)] and to developing a better technology for conducting an audit. Judgment research in auditing has contributed to obtaining that understanding and to developing that technology.

Yet, almost no attention has been devoted to certain key judgments that precede audit-process activities and influence the context for audit judgments. Solomon and Shields (Chapter 6) observe that judgments about how strong a presence an auditing firm desires in a particular industry, whether to compete for contracts to audit a particular organization's financial statements, how high or low to set the price in a competitive bidding situation, and so forth, have large consequences associated with them and use the example of the savings and loan industry to make their point.

Auditing firms that had a presence in the savings and loan industry experienced a significant change in their "audit exposure," a term that is sometimes used to refer to the negative consequences – such as economic losses, litigation, or an impaired reputation – that might result from issuing a technically inappropriate audit opinion or from being sued (Sullivan et al., 1985). Many auditing firms are currently reassessing their concentration of audit exposure in various industries. Research about how auditors make judgments about audit exposure and how those judgments influence audit process activities and audit risk could make a significant contribution to our understanding of judgments in auditing.

Another area that judgment researchers have underexploited is judgments in taxation, including those by taxpayers, tax advisors, and tax agencies or assessors. Alm (1991) provides a perspective on research about taxpayer reporting that includes some judgment research as well as experimental market studies and other experiments on taxpayer compliance and other actions. Other recent judgment research in taxation includes cognitive modeling work by Marchant et al. (1989) and laboratory market studies by Anderson et al. (1990).

We suggest and expect that more effort will be devoted to task analysis, including analysis of the task as embedded in the economic, organizational and professional contexts described below. As Hogarth (1991) commented, accounting and auditing researchers have a comparative advantage and greater intrinsic interest in such task analysis than other judgment researchers. This greater use of accounting researchers' "institutional" knowledge about accounting and auditing will strengthen the field's contribution to accounting and auditing problems and should also provide a variety of task–context settings interesting to judgment researchers generally. Applied studies of medical and legal judgment have informed judgment research in accounting and auditing, and the process also should work in the opposite direction as judgment research in accounting and auditing becomes more strongly based in its applied context.

The setting

Judgment tasks are performed in larger settings that reflect economic forces important to the individual and the organization in which the individual works, the organization's structure, culture, and internal incentives, and the professional standards and structures that surround accounting and auditing. Embedding the study of judgment into the larger setting has been a continuing challenge for judgment researchers in accounting and auditing, both because they have tended to see this as an important part of their contribution and because the understanding of those larger settings has been continuously expanded by research using other methods to study accounting and auditing, particularly analytical economic modeling, empirical investigations of capital markets, and analysis of behavior in organizations.

The fourth example at the beginning of this chapter focuses on the use of accounting information to help determine a plant's production and marketing strategies and to measure performance. That example reflects two important roles of accounting information [see Waller (Chapter 2)]. One role is in helping the plant manager determine those strategies. That role is what Demski and Feltham (1976) refer to as the "decision facilitating" role of accounting information. Accounting information is provided to a decision maker before a decision is made to help resolve some form of uncertainty in the decision problem at hand. The other role is in measuring performance and in calculating performance bonuses. That role is what Demski and Feltham (1976) refer to as the "decision-influencing" role of accounting information. Accounting information is provided to a decision maker after a decision has been made and implemented to evaluate the decision maker's performance, with the purpose of motivating action selection. Most important, the decision-facilitating and decision-influencing roles of accounting information are not independent; they interact. The accounting information the plant manager uses to determine production and marketing strategies may be driven by the accounting information that is used to measure performance. Those two roles and interactions between them are why judgment research in accounting and auditing is and should be setting-sensitive.

Economic forces

Myriad economic forces surround people who make judgments. Competitive and other economic pressures seem to be ever-increasing. Assessments of loan losses are affected by general economic conditions. Accounting choices are affected by perceived effects on assessments of individual and organizational performance. Auditing choices are affected by the competitive market for audit services and by efforts by clients to reduce costs, including auditing costs. Managers are affected by competitive markets in formulating strategies and in measuring and assessing performance.

Judgment research in accounting and auditing has dealt with economic forces mainly in two ways. The first, adapted from behavioral decision research and present since the field began, is to build those forces into judgment problems at the individual level by expressing choices as financial or economic gambles, varying the payoffs for those choices, eliciting implied-utility functions under conditions promoting risk aversion, and following economic principles (such as expected utility or Savage's axioms of rational choice) in specifying "appropriate" responses to choices. The focus has generally been on understanding the judgment process rather than on development of the economic assumptions. Waller (Chapter 2) and Solomon and Shields (Chapter 6) comment on this research. The results of that research have been largely consistent with those of general judgment research, perhaps because simplified research settings and student participants have often been used. But somewhat more adherence to the assumptions of rationality has been found in that research than in general judgment research.

The second way that judgment research in accounting and auditing has dealt with economic forces has been to model judgment settings using the tools of economics and then to examine the ability or willingness of participants to respond to the incentives, costs, and other factors specified by the economic models. This research has been more sophisticated in its use of economics, has followed the development of economic models elsewhere, and has been more normative in its orientation than has the first kind. [See Waller (Chapter 2), Young and Lewis (Chapter 3), and Berg, Dickhaut, and McCabe (Chapter 5).] The results of that research have been quite varied, partly due to the variety of types and complexities of the economic models used, and perhaps also due to the use of student participants in it. But it has been clear that the economic factors play a large role in participants' responses.

Researchers who study judgment in accounting and auditing have not been particularly eager to build economic variables into their work until recently, perhaps because there have been so many psychological and task variables to occupy their attention, and because economic models have not until recently been well-enough developed to support empiricism beyond basic rationality and consistency investigations. However, the interest in employing economic models to make behavioral predictions or to suggest variables likely to be significant in the applied setting has been growing, and the increased sophistication associated with this may be responsible for the virtual disappearance of studies in accounting and auditing that use simple scenarios of the "heuristics and biases" sort.[4]

As is argued by Waller (Chapter 2), the improved integration of economics and judgment perspectives is a very positive development and shows promise for a significant contribution of judgment research in accounting and auditing back to the general judgment and economics fields. There are two economics-related areas of study that are still in embryonic stages in accounting and auditing judgment research but which we hope and expect to become more prevalent. One area is the study of judgment as strategic behavior using the experimental economic paradigm (see Dopuch and King, 1991, and the January 1992 *Accounting Review* "forum" on laboratory markets and auditing research). The second area is the integration of individual-level judgment with studies of aggregate organizational and market behavior [see Berg, Dickhaut, and McCabe (Chapter 5)]. The impetus for treating judgments as strategic comes, for example, from developments in game theory and contract (agency) theory, both of which have had a large effect in other areas of research in accounting and auditing, from the large recent growth in experimental markets and other experimental economics studies, and from studies of auditing (including economic models of auditors' relations with clients and behavioral studies of management fraud), which treat the auditor's problem as one of dealing with a strategic opponent in addition to being a technical-evidence evaluator (King and Wallin, 1990; Jamal, 1991).

Organizational factors

For many years, it has been recognized in several fields of research that individuals make judgments and decisions as members of groups, firms, professions, or other organizations. Though some judgments are traceable solely to independent individual preferences and payoffs, most judgment problems in accounting and auditing are set within organizations, in which the individuals' preferences and payoffs are modified by the collective.

All of the individuals in the four examples at the beginning of this chapter work with or within organizations, so we might expect all of them to be at least partially responsive to factors such as career advancement, bonuses and other incentives, power, status, and the organization's practices for dealing with other people inside and outside the organization. The accountant who assesses loan losses may report directly to or indirectly through an internal-audit function, which in turn may report to an examining committee or to an audit committee of the board of directors. Accounting choices are approved by executives at various levels within the organization and within the public accounting firm. The decisions of partners in public accounting firms and of managers in organizations are subject to approval and evaluation.

Judgment research in accounting and auditing has generally treated judgment problems as separable from the organization, and research participants have been treated as independent actors, so few organizational factors have been addressed in depth so far. Intraorganizational economic incentives have been modeled and examined empirically to some extent [see Young and Lewis (Chapter 3)], following the developments described in the preceding section, and there was some interest in the 1970s in group phenomena such as the risky shift.

The main attention to organizational variables has followed from an interest in differential expertise or authority in making judgments that may go with the individual's rank in the organization. The principal focus here has been in categorizing public accountants (auditors) as being partners, audit managers, supervisors, or juniors, and there has been some similar interest in the organizational level of corporate managers who demand or use management-accounting information. [Rank is often included as a blocking variable in experiments and surveys: see also Dillard and Ferris (1989) for studies specifically interested in differences among individuals.] A large number of judgment differences that correlate with rank have been observed, but there has been little investigation by judgment researchers into the reasons for those differences or their stability. Organizational behavior-oriented studies of managers' budget-related behavior, "contingency theory" analyses of the internal role of accounting systems, and some social psychological studies of accountants and auditors were influential during the seventies but have become rare in more recent years. It has been conventionally observed that auditors and executives make decisions in groups, but the process behind those decisions has seldom been investigated using judgment approaches. Solomon (1987) reviews the small auditing literature and Gibbins and Mason (1988) report a field-questionnaire study of judgment in financial reporting that attended to group and organizational issues.

Recently, a few judgment studies in accounting and auditing have treated organizational variables as more central to the process, though judgment has been viewed as essentially an individual process mediated by group or organizational influences rather than as an organizational phenomenon. Two examples are studies of the effects of audit firm structure (e.g., McDaniel, 1990; Spires, 1991) and a burgeoning group of studies on auditors' accountability to others, especially others hierarchically above them, for their judgments (e.g., Ashton, 1990; Johnson and Kaplan, 1991; Lord, 1992; Messier and Quilliam, 1992).

Attention to organizational variables is welcome in moving judgment research closer to the "reality" experienced by accountants, auditors, managers, and others as is the similar attention to economic variables noted above. By uprooting participants from their day-to-day setting and studying them in constrained laboratory or training conditions, researchers may have severed connections that are instrumental to an understanding of how judgment works in the field. There have been some suggestions in recent work on accountability (e.g., Messier and Quilliam, forthcoming), on auditors' experience of errors (Ashton, 1991) and on the role of justification in audit firms (Emby and Gibbins, 1988; Ashton, 1992) that this severing has meant that some earlier results were misleading, but only further organizationally sensitive research will confirm that.

Professional context

Public accountants are mostly Certified Public Accountants and therefore explicitly members of a profession and subject to various professional standards. Corporate managers also exhibit many of the trappings of professionals, so the professional context is likely to have a powerful effect on their judgments as well (Gibbins et al., 1992, Chapter 4). Since, in our society, professionals are granted some authority and responsibility to exercise judgment, judgment processes may also have a powerful effect on the professional context and on the nature and value of the choices made by professionals.

An assessment of loan losses, for example, is required under generally accepted accounting principles and under various governmental regulations that have been established for loan accounting and reporting. Accounting choices are made within the context of generally accepted accounting principles and often are subject to Securities and Exchange Commission and stock exchange regulations about financial disclosure. Auditing choices are made within the context of generally accepted auditing standards.

The professional context potentially distinguishes accounting and auditing situations from the generic situations studied in other judgment research and provides both a reason for that research to be differently focused and a setting of interest to scholars concerned with the behavior of other professionals such as physicians and attorneys.

Judgment research in accounting and auditing has been sensitive to, and in some respects directed by, the nature and existence of professional standards. From the beginning, important studies examined the role of standards in judgment and such related topics as consensus on the application of standards, both from the point of view of the preparers and auditors of the information [see Solomon and Shields (Chapter 6)] and that of the users of it [see Maines (Chapter 4)]. Some research, such as that on audit risk and evidence evaluation, has been influential in the setting of professional standards (see Kinney and Uecker, 1982). Judgment research in accounting and auditing constitutes probably the largest body of results on the operation of judgment in a standards-constrained environment, though the standards have usually been taken as given rather than as a variable of interest. Studies commonly compare auditors' judgments to applicable professional standards, with the objective of evaluating the judgments against the standards [see e.g., Bédard (1991)]. Some attention recently has been devoted to studying the effects of standards on tax compliance judgments and the effects of financial accounting standards on financial accounting (Mason and Gibbins,

1991). The discussion in Messier (Chapter 8) is relevant to this issue as well, because standards can be considered to be decision aids to the extent they communicate appropriate ways of dealing with judgment problems (see also Gibbins and Mason, 1988, Chapter 5).

The people who exercise judgment

Developments in cognitive psychology and many researchers' concern with understanding whether individual accountants and auditors are making good judgments have led to a surge in "expertise" research in auditing, generally focusing on memory processes and knowledge structures and connected to improved task analyses [see Libby (Chapter 7)]. Referring to the examples at the beginning of this chapter, what expertise do the various people bring to the situations, how have their experiences equipped (or failed to equip) them to cope with the tasks and settings, and do their judgments measure up to external criteria of quality?

Over the 20 years of its life, judgment research in accounting and auditing has undergone a shift in psychological basis from social psychology and behavioral decision theory to more cognitive, task-oriented approaches. For example, in the early to mid-1970s, several studies of probability elicitation were motivated by decision-theory ideas about the role of probability in judgment (e.g., Corless, 1972; Chesley, 1975). Later, studies based on the heuristics-and-biases research by Tversky and Kahneman were prominent (e.g., Swieringa et al., 1976; Joyce and Biddle, 1981a). More recently, studies oriented to memory processes and cognitive structures have been prominent (e.g., Bedard and Biggs, 1991; Bonner, 1990; Choo and Trotman, 1991; Frederick, 1991; Frederick and Libby, 1986; Jamal, 1991; Moeckel, 1990; Peters, 1990; Rennie, 1991). This evolution was a natural one, because the interaction between cognition and task was always of interest to researchers in accounting and auditing, prompting a great deal of enthusiasm in the seventies about "policy-capturing" studies, most using the Brunswik Lens, to provide statistical descriptions of auditors' and accountants' apparent use of information (e.g., Ashton, 1974a,b).

Research that specifically focuses on people who use accounting reports is reported in Maines (Chapter 4). However, there has been little judgment research about individual differences among auditors. Judgment studies in auditing tend to focus on task or cognitive issues that either are proposed to be applicable across auditors of various personality or other types, or are just not developed with individual differences in mind. The result is that judgment research in accounting and auditing has focused more on the task and setting than on the people who exercise judgment.

Descriptive research now tends to focus more on tasks and cognitive processes (e.g., Bedard and Biggs, 1991; Jamal, 1991; Peters, 1990), and studies of older issues [such as that by Emby (1991) of probability elicitation] also are more likely to focus on cognitive processes. However, this trend to focus on cognitive processes is still based largely on the experimental method: the research approaches of behavioral decision theory and cognitive psychology are dominant in the field as compared to protocol analyses and the other less experimental approaches used in problem solving, computing, and information-processing studies (Hogarth, 1991).

Observations

General judgment research

Judgment research in accounting and auditing has paralleled the more general judgment research, though it has been more applied. Similar development of methods and data analysis (particularly within-subject designs to maximize the benefit obtained from the time of practitioner and manager subjects) has occurred and the applied orientation has led to somewhat more focus on task. The accounting and auditing implications of such general topics as points of reference (framing), probability, confirmation bias, choice processes, memory structures, and bounded rationality have been examined in some depth.

Accounting and auditing research, as the preceding chapters have demonstrated, has tested large numbers of judgment hypotheses in contexts of interest and has broadened the understanding and the contribution of the theories those hypotheses are based upon.

The strong preference for using as participants people having significant task-relevant experience and expertise (auditors, business managers, financial analysts, bankers, and others related to accounting-information preparation and use) has helped to produce a body of findings about "real people" and "real tasks" that is impressive. Few of those findings are dramatically different from those in other literatures, but they are useful to extend and help generalize basic findings, and the differences that have been found provide a useful criticism of some general assumptions. For example, it appears that auditors have a higher degree of self-insight than do the student participants of many general studies (Ashton, 1983), which may reflect a more cognitively obtrusive professional environment in which one is expected to know how one's choices were made, and which may suggest that labeling self-insight as coincidental (Nisbett and Ross, 1980) may not be generally valid. The professional context produces a strong demand for justification of choices (Ashton, 1992; Emby and Gibbins, 1988; Gibbins and Mason, 1988), and that demand provides both another motivation for choice than the basic rationality and cognitive consistency criteria popular in general judgment studies and an additional bridge to such general fields of study as accountability (Tetlock, 1985).

The study of auditors and managers also helps in the criticism and improvement of methods generally used in judgment research. One example is the use of simplified economic or statistical models to guide the research.

That use is increasingly viewed as problematic by judgment researchers in accounting and auditing because the simplifications violate the applied conditions that make accounting and auditing settings interesting. Those concerns may be a warning that contextual factors may affect the validity of other research using simplified settings.

A second example is in the use of deception in judgment research. Deception of participants who are skeptical by nature, who are members of firms and other communicating groups, and who, wearing other hats, have a say in the allocation of resources to research and to other activities dear to the researchers, is a particularly controversial issue.[5] Significant deception of research participants has been largely avoided by judgment researchers in accounting and auditing, who have developed ways of working with practitioners and of motivating their attention to the research that may be of interest to other judgment researchers.[6]

Other accounting and auditing research

The relation between judgment research and other accounting and auditing research potentially operates in both directions. The effects of judgment research on other research are weak so far. While there have been glimmers of recognition of judgment research findings in the writings of other researchers (e.g., Hand, 1990, on functional fixation in capital markets), it seems fair to say that auditing and other judgment work has had little impact on other accounting and auditing research. This is due to a difference in emphasis. Judgment research is more applied and is more focused on empirical science than most other accounting and auditing research, which tends to be more concerned with examining hypotheses generated from largely economics-based normative theory, and with descriptive research using archival data. Moreover, the judgment-research field has, as noted already, not yet made sufficient progress on some issues other researchers consider important, such as incentives, organizational structures, or aggregate behavior, to facilitate connections to those researchers. In our view, judgment research is moving in a direction that will improve those connections [see Waller (Chapter 2), Young and Lewis (Chapter 3), Maines (Chapter 4), and Berg, Dickhaut, and McCabe (Chapter 5)], but at present there is more potential than accomplishment.

The effects of other areas of accounting and auditing research on judgment research are much stronger. Generally, the findings of nonbehavioral research, such as manufacturing-variance analysis, statistical-quality control, executive compensation, the nature of the auditing industry, statistical sampling of evidence, and capital-market impact of accounting regulations, have been reflected in judgment studies, usually in helping to create the experimental situations in which the research participants work. A major challenge for judgment research is to incorporate the rich understanding of accounting and auditing contexts that is rapidly being developed by other researchers.

Incorporation of that understanding is a normal part of the preamble and motivation of judgment studies, so the challenge is being recognized by researchers.

We note two ways in which improved connections among judgment and other accounting and auditing research would work for the benefit of all researchers. One would be increased effort in joint development of theory. Judgment theories tend to be more detailed and less overarching than the economic and organizational theories used in other areas. The judgment perspective may thus help bring other theories closer to the empirical domain, and the larger perspective of the others may help to knit the judgment theories together into a more coherent whole. A second improvement would be to seek nonbehavioral, or at least nonjudgmental, corroboration of judgment-research findings, thus helping to connect the perspectives. An example is the work on financial disclosure by Gibbins et al. (1990), which was based on interviews and archival data and found evidence of framing effects and various apparent perceptual mechanisms on the part of people involved in making disclosures. The findings are consistent with judgment research results. Another example is the theoretically broad examination of audit technology and structure offered by Dirsmith and Haskins (1991), which supports and extends the judgment-research findings in the same area (e.g., McDaniel, 1990; Spires, 1991).

Professional and business concerns

Judgment research in accounting and auditing is applied, so it might naturally be expected to contribute to the improvement of judgment and decisions by practitioners and business people. One area in which that contribution has been specifically sought is in the development of decision aids, as described by Messier (Chapter 8). That contribution is improving as the research becomes more effectively embedded in the applied context, so that the decision aids become more applicable to that context. As Ashton (1990) showed, decision aids may have complex effects. In that study, an aid reduced judgment performance, apparently because the participants took its presence as an indication that the task was harder than they thought and so they did not apply their normal expertise to it. Ashton's study is an example of an approach that seems likely to increase in frequency: researching the value of decision aids rather than just developing such aids. Other studies include McDaniel's (1990) demonstration that structuring the audit process can reduce, rather than increase, the effectiveness of the audit if time pressure is a factor, Emby's (1991) study of the use of a decision aid (graphical presentation of probabilities) to overcome alleged human information-processing shortcomings, and a large body of "accounting education" research on use of computers and other pedagogical aids.

Generally, we expect that improved task and context analysis in judgment research will bring natural improvements in the contribution to practice and business. The practical contribution that the memory and mental representation part of judgment research can make is probably some distance in the future, because the understanding of cognitive structures applicable to accounting and auditing tasks is still rudimentary, but there is a significant potential, particularly because there are natural connections between this research and computer-based research on such aids as expert systems and artificial intelligence [see Messier (Chapter 8)].

More broadly, accounting and auditing research overall has been criticized for its alleged lack of application to the concerns of the "real world." A typical complaint is that accounting research tends to examine issues after they have happened rather than provide predictive advice to practitioners. Judgment studies are not as dependent upon archival data as are many other accounting and auditing studies, so they may naturally be less subject to this criticism. Judgment studies often have been motivated by currently important business or practice issues, such as improving the effectiveness of internal-control evaluation or other audit techniques, or understanding the behavior of managers faced with preparing or being evaluated by budgets. Moreover, judgment studies can be used to address "what if" questions. They can be used to explore alternatives and to create conditions that have no existing counterparts outside the laboratory (see Swieringa and Weick, 1982).

A heavily attended session at the 1991 annual conference of the American Accounting Association generally was very critical of the lack of contribution of accounting and auditing research to practice. However, judgment research in auditing was specifically noted as having succeeded more than most fields in making a useful contribution. One area of accomplishment is that the philosophical basis of auditing (Mautz and Sharaf, 1961) has been examined more deeply using judgment-research methods than by other approaches, through various experiments on the nature of internal controls, the choice of verification procedures, the structuring of the audit approach, and other topics.

The academic enterprise

Judgment research in accounting and auditing has contributed to the general body of academic research. It has contributed in understanding such general topics as the effectiveness of business management, the quality of external auditing and other professional services, the role of the auditing industry in business and society, measurement and disclosure in financial reporting, standard-setting, and professional education. The contribution of judgment research in accounting and auditing has perhaps been reduced by a tendency to shift from topic to topic as interests in the underlying general judgment discipline have evolved and practical problems and enthusiasms have changed. However, the field's refusal to get caught in dead ends and its tendency to incorporate contemporary issues may also be part of its strength.

A critical mass of findings may take longer to assemble, given the dynamism of the field, but they may have more staying power.

Conclusion

Accounting and auditing judgment research has produced a large and interesting set of findings. The field's challenge is to apply rigorous research techniques to tasks that are dynamic, complex and embedded in important and onerous settings. That challenge is recognized by researchers, but ultimately, success will depend on the researchers' skill in identifying important tasks and examining them in ways that preserve the organizational, economic, institutional, and technical features that make them important to the accountants and auditors who perform them and to the people who rely on the results. We expect the *next* 20 years of judgment research in accounting and auditing to be even more strongly focused on the judgment tasks and the settings in which they are performed.

Notes

1. Expressions of individual views by members of the FASB and its staff are encouraged. The views expressed in this chapter are those of the authors. Official positions of the FASB on accounting matters are determined only after extensive due process and deliberations.
2. In addition to those in the other chapters of this book, useful recent literature review comments are included in Abdolmohammadi and Wright (1987), Ashton et al. (1988), Bédard (1989), Bédard and Chi (1993), Bonner and Lewis (1990), Bonner and Pennington (1991), Choo (1989), Davis and Solomon (1989), Dillard and Ferris (1989), Gibbins and Mason (1988), Hogarth (1991), Johnson et al. (1989), Libby (1990), and Solomon (1987). Others are mentioned as specific issues are raised below.
3. Research on auditor individual differences and other such "person" variables has also demonstrated task effects: see e.g., Dillard and Ferris (1989) and Pincus (1990).
4. An example of this sort of scenario is from the authors' own research (Swieringa et al., 1976). See Ashton (1984) for a set of suggested heuristics-and-biases scenarios adapted for auditing settings.
5. During a recent auditing-research conference, a long and acrimonious argument broke out about the use of deception with professional participants because of its potential to impair the relationship between the professional community and accounting academics more generally. Some accounting and auditing researchers believe that such deception should be banned or very severely restricted. See Gibbins (1992).
6. The dangers of working too closely with participants and perhaps creating demand effects have also been examined. See, e.g., Pany & Reckers (1987).

References

Abarbanell, J., & Bernard, V. (1992). Tests of analysts' overreaction/underreaction to earnings information as an explanation for anomalous stock price behavior. *The Journal of Finance, 47,* 1181–1207.

Abdel-khalik, A.R. (1973). The effects of aggregating accounting reports on the quality of the lending decison: An empirical investigation. *Journal of Accounting Research, 11,* 104–138.

Abdel-khalik, A.R. (1974a). The entropy law, accounting data, and relevance to decision making. *The Accounting Review, 49,* 271–283.

Abdel-khalik, A.R. (1974b). On the efficiency of subject surrogation in accounting research. *The Accounting Review, 49,* 743–750.

Abdel-khalik, A.R., & El-Sheshai, K. (1980). Information choice and cue utilization in an experiment on default prediction. *Journal of Accounting Research, 18,* 325–342.

Abdel-khalik, A.R., & Keller, T.F. (1979). *Earnings or cash flows: An experiment on functional fixation and the valuation of the firm.* Studies in Accounting Research No. 16. Sarasota, FL: American Accounting Association.

Abdel-khalik, A.R., Snowball, D.A., & Wragge, J.H. (1983). The effects of certain internal audit variables on the planning of external audit programs. *The Accounting Review, 58,* 215–227.

Abdel–khalik, A.R., & Solomon, I. (Eds.) (1988). *Research Opportunities in Auditing: The Second Decade.* Sarasota, FL: American Accounting Association.

Abdolmohammadi, M.J. (1987). Decision support and expert systems in auditing: A review and research directions. *Accounting and Business Research, 17,* 173–185.

Abdolmohammadi, M.J. (1990). A taxonomy of audit task complexity and experience requirements in auditing: Implications for audit research and practice. Working Paper, Bentley College.

Abdolmohammadi, M.J. (1991). Error frequency utilization in tests of controls: Decision aid and experience effects. Working Paper, Bentley College.

Abdolmohammadi, M.J., & Berger, P.D. (1986). A test of the accuracy of probability assessment techniques in auditing. *Contemporary Accounting Research, 3,* 149–183.

Abdolmohammadi, M.J., & Wright, A. (1987). An examination of the effects of experience and task complexity on audit judgments. *The Accounting Review, 62,* 1–13.

Acland, D. (1976). The effects of behavioral indicators on investors' decisions: An exploratory study. *Accounting, Organizations and Society, 1,* 133–142.

Affleck-Graves, J., Davis, L., & Mendenhall, R. (1990). Forecasts of earnings per share: Possible sources of analyst superiority and bias. *Contemporary Accounting Research, 6,* 501–517.

Akerlof, G., & Yellen, J. (1985). Can small deviations from rationality make significant differences to economic equilibria? *The American Economic Review, 75,* 708–720.

Alba, J., & Hutchinson, J.W. (1987). Dimensions of consumer expertise. *Journal of Consumer Research, 13,* 411–454.

Alchian, A.A. (1950). Uncertainty, evolution, and economic theory. *Journal of Political Economy, 58,* 211–221.

Aldag, R.J., & Power, D.J. (1986). An empirical strategy for implementing a decision support analysis. *Decision Sciences, 17,* 572–588.

Alm, J. (1991). A perspective on the experimental analysis of taxpayer reporting. *The Accounting Review, 66,* 577–593.

Altman, E.I. (1983). Multidimensional graphics and bankruptcy prediction: A comment. *Journal of Accounting Research, 21,* 297–299.

Altman, E.I., & McGough, T.P. (1974). Evaluation of a company as a going concern. *The Journal of Accountancy, 143,* 50–57.

American Accounting Association (1972). Report of the committee on accounting valuation bases. *The Accounting Review, 47* (Supplement), 534–573.

American Accounting Association (1973). Committee on basic auditing concepts. *A Statement of Basic Auditing Concepts.* Studies in Accounting Research No. 6. Sarasota, FL: Author.

American Accounting Association (1974). Report of the committee on the relationship of behavioral science and accounting. *The Accounting Review, 49* (Supplement), 127–139.

American Institute of Certified Public Accountants (1981). *Audit Sampling.* Statement on Auditing Standards No. 39. New York: Author.

American Institute of Certified Public Accountants (1983a). *Audit Risk and Materiality in Conducting an Audit.* Statement on Auditing Standards No. 47. New York: Author.

American Institute of Certified Public Accountants (1983b). *Audit Sampling.* Audit and Accounting Guide. New York: Author.

American Institute of Certified Public Accountants (1990). *Statements on Auditing Standards AU Section 312. Audit risk and materiality in conducting an audit.* AICPA Professional Standards: Statements on Auditing Standards. New York: Author.

Anderson, M. (1988). A comparative analysis of information search and evaluation of professional and non-professional financial analysts. *Accounting, Organizations and Society, 13,* 431–446.

Anderson, M., Anderson, U., Helleloid, R., Joyce, E., & Schadewald, M. (1990). Internal revenue service access to tax accrual workpapers: A laboratory investigation. *The Accounting Review, 65,* 857–874.

Anderson, U., & Wright, W.F. (1988). Expertise and the explanation effect. *Organizational Behavior and Human Decision Processes, 42,* 250–269.

Antle, R., & Smith, A. (1986). An empirical investigation of the relative performance evaluation of corporate executives. *Journal of Accounting Research, 24,* 1–39.

Arens, A.A., & Loebbecke, J.K. (1991). *Auditing: An Integrated Approach.* (Fifth edition). Englewood Cliffs, N.J.: Prentice Hall.

Arkes, H. R. (1991). Costs and benefits of judgment errors: Implications for debiasing. *Psychological Bulletin, 110,* 486–498.

Arkes, H.R., Dawes, R.M., & Christensen, C. (1986). Factors influencing the use of a decision rule in a probabilistic task. *Organizational Behavior and Human Decision Processes, 37,* 93–110.

Armitage, H.M., and Boritz, J.E. (1991). *Decision–support and expert systems for management accountants.* Hamilton, Ontario: The Society of Management Accountants of Canada.

Arrow, K. (1985). The economics of agency. In J. Pratt & A. Zeckhauser (Eds.), *Principals and Agents: The Structure of Business* (pp. 37–51). Cambridge, MA: Harvard Business School Press.

Ashton, A.H. (1982). The descriptive validity of normative decision theory in auditing contexts. *Journal of Accounting Research, 20,* 415–428.

Ashton, A.H. (1985). Does consensus imply accuracy in accounting studies of decision making? *The Accounting Review, 60,* 173–185.

Ashton, A.H. (1991). Experience and error frequency knowledge as potential determinants of audit expertise. *The Accounting Review, 66,* 218–239.

Ashton, A.H., & Ashton, R.H. (1988). Sequential belief revision in auditing. *The Accounting Review, 63,* 623–641.

Ashton, R.H. (1974a). An experimental study of internal control judgments. *Journal of Accounting Research, 12,* 143–157.

Ashton, R.H. (1974b). Cue utilization and expert judgments: A comparison of independent auditors with other judges. *Journal of Applied Psychology, 59,* 437–444.

Ashton, R.H. (1974c). The predictive-ability criterion and user prediction models. *The Accounting Review, 49,* 719–732.

Ashton, R.H. (1975). User prediction models in accounting: An alternative use. *The Accounting Review, 50,* 710–722.

Ashton, R.H. (1976). Cognitive changes induced by accounting changes: Experimental evidence on the functional fixation hypothesis. *Journal of Accounting Research, 14* (Supplement), 1–17.

Ashton, R.H. (1981a). A descriptive study of information evaluation. *Journal of Accounting Research, 19,* 42–61.

Ashton, R.H. (1981b). Some observations on the auditing research environment. In J.O. Mason (Ed.), *1981 Accounting Research Convocation* (pp. 85–96). Tuscaloosa, AL: University of Alabama.

Ashton, R.H. (1982). *Human information processing in accounting.* Studies in Accounting Research No. 17. Sarasota, FL: American Accounting Association.

Ashton, R.H. (1983). *Research in audit decision making: Rationale, evidence, and implications.* Research Monograph No. 6. Vancouver: Canadian Certified General Accountants Research Foundation.

Ashton, R.H. (1984). Integrating research and teaching in auditing: Fifteen cases on judgment and decision making. *The Accounting Review, 59,* 78–97.

Ashton, R.H. (1990). Pressure and performance in accounting decision settings: Paradoxical effects of incentives, feedback, and justification. *Journal of Accounting Research, 28* (Supplement), 148–180.

Ashton, R.H. (1992). Effects of justification and a mechanical aid on judgment performance. *Organizational Behavior and Human Decision Processes, 52,* 292–306.

Ashton, R.H. (1994). Decision research in taxation: Review, analysis, and recommended research agenda. Manuscript in Preparation.

Ashton, R.H., & Ashton, A.H. (1990). Evidence-responsiveness in professional judgment: Effects of positive versus negative evidence and presentation mode. *Organizational Behavior and Human Decision Processes, 46,* 1–19.

Ashton, R.H., & Brown, P.R. (1980). Descriptive modeling of auditors' internal control judgments: Replication and extension. *Journal of Accounting Research, 18,* 269–277.

Ashton, R.H., Kleinmuntz, D.N., Sullivan, J.B., & Tomassini, L.A. (1988). Audit decision making. In A.R. Abdel-khalik & I. Solomon (Eds.), *Research Opportunities in Auditing: The Second Decade* (pp. 95–132). Sarasota, FL: American Accounting Association.

Ashton, R.H., & Kramer, S.S. (1980). Students as surrogates in behavioral accounting research: Some evidence. *Journal of Accounting Research , 18,* 1–15.

Ashton, R.H., & Willingham, J.J. (1989). Using and evaluating audit decision aids. In R.P. Srivastava & J.E. Rebele (Eds.), *Auditing Symposium IX: Proceedings of the 1988 Touche Ross/University of Kansas Symposium on Auditing Problems* (pp. 1–25). Lawrence, KS: University of Kansas.

Awasthi, V., & Pratt, J. (1990). The effects of monetary incentives on effort and decision performance: The role of cognitive characteristics. *The Accounting Review, 65,* 797–811.

Bailey, C.D. (1990). CIAs and CPAs: Do they agree on internal accounting controls? *Internal Auditor,* 46–49.

Bailey, K.E., Bylinski, J., & Shields, M. (1983). Effect of audit report wording changes on the perceived message. *Journal of Accounting Research, 21,* 355–369.

Bailey, W. (1981). The effects of audit reports on chartered financial analysts' perceptions of the sources of financial-statement and audit-report messages. *The Accounting Review, 56,* 882–896.

Baiman, S. (1982). Agency research in managerial accounting: A survey. *Journal of Accounting Literature, 1,* 154–213.

Baiman, S. (1990). Agency research in managerial accounting: A second look. *Accounting, Organizations and Society, 15,* 341–371.

Baiman, S., & Evans, J.H. (1983). Pre-decision information and participative management control systems. *Journal of Accounting Research, 21,* 371–395.

Baiman, S., & Lewis, B. (1989). An experiment testing the behavioral equivalence of strategically equivalent employment contracts. *Journal of Accounting Research, 27,* 1–20.

Baker, C.R. (1977). Management strategy in a large accounting firm. *The Accounting Review, 52,* 576–586.

Bamber, E.M. (1983). Expert judgment in the audit team: A source reliability approach. *Journal of Accounting Research, 21,* 396–412.

Bamber, E.M., & Snowball, D. (1988). An experimental study of the effects of audit structure in uncertain task environments. *The Accounting Review, 63,* 490–504.

Bamber, E.M., Snowball, D. & Tubbs, R.M. (1989). Audit structure and its relation to role conflict and role ambiguity: An empirical investigation. *The Accounting Review, 64,* 285–299.

Bar-Hillel, M. (1990). Back to base rates. In R. Hogarth (Ed.), *Insights in Decision Making: A Tribute to Hillel J. Einhorn* (pp. 200–223). Chicago, IL: University of Chicago Press.

Barefield, R.M. (1972). The effect of aggregation on decision making success: A laboratory study. *Journal of Accounting Research, 10,* 229–242.

Barrett, M.E. (1971). Accounting for intercorporate investments: A behavioral field experiment. *Journal of Accounting Research, 9,* 50–65.

Beaver, W. (1973). What should be the FASB's objectives? *The Journal of Accountancy, 136,* 49–56.

Becker, G.S. (1976). *The Economic Approach to Human Behavior.* Chicago, IL: University of Chicago Press.

Becker, S., & Green, D. (1962). Budgeting and employee behavior. *Journal of Business, 35,* 392–402.

Bédard, J. (1989). Expertise in auditing: Myth or reality? *Accounting, Organizations and Society, 14,* 113–131.

Bédard, J. (1991). Expertise and its relation to audit decision quality. *Contemporary Accounting Research, 8,* 198–222. In French on pp. 223–252.

Bédard, J., & Chi, M.T.H. (1993). Expertise in auditing. *Auditing: A Journal of Practice & Theory, 12* (Supplement), 21–45.

Bedard, J.C. (1989). An archival investigation of audit program planning. *Auditing: A Journal of Practice & Theory, 8,* 57–71.

Bedard, J.C., & Biggs, S.F. (1991). Pattern recognition, hypotheses generation, and auditor performance in an analytical task. *The Accounting Review, 66,* 622–642.

Bedard, J.C., & Biggs, S.F. (forthcoming). The effect of domain-specific experience on evaluation of management representations in analytical procedures. *Auditing: A Journal of Practice & Theory.*

Belkaoui, A. (1983–84). The effects of diagnostic and redundant information on loan officers' predictions. *Accounting and Business Research, 14,* 249–256.

Bell, D.E., Raiffa, H., & Tversky, A. (Eds.) (1988). *Decision Making: Descriptive, Normative, and Prescriptive Interactions.* Cambridge, UK: Cambridge University Press.

Bell, T.B., Ribar, G.S., & Verchio, J.R. (1990). Neural nets vs. logistic regression: A comparison of each model's ability to predict commercial bank failures. In R.P. Srivastava (Ed.), *Auditing Symposium X: Proceedings of the 1990 Deloitte & Touche/University of Kansas Symposium on Auditing Problems* (pp. 29–53). Lawrence, KS: University of Kansas.

Bell, T.B., & Wright, A. (Eds.) (forthcoming). *Auditing Practice, Research, and Education: A Productive Collaboration.* New York: American Institute of Certified Public Accountants.

Benbasat, I., & Nault, B.R. (1990). An evaluation of empirical research in managerial support systems. *Decision Support Systems, 6,* 203–226.

Berg, J. (1990). The impact of controllability and informativeness on the use of public information in contracting: An experimental investigation. Working Paper, Washington University.

Berg, J., Coursey, D., & Dickhaut, J. (1990). Experimental methods in accounting: A discussion of recurring issues. *Contemporary Accounting Research, 6,* 825–849.

Berg, J., Daley, L., Dickhaut, J., & O'Brien, J. (1986) Controlling preferences for lotteries on units of experimental exchange. *Quarterly Journal of Economics, 101,* 281–306.

Berg, J., Daley, L., Dickhaut, J., & O'Brien, J. (1992). Moral hazard and risk sharing:

Experimental evidence. In M. Isaac (Ed.), *Research in experimental economics* (Vol. 5, pp. 1–34). Greenwich, CT: JAI Press.

Berg, J., Daley, L., Gigler, F., & Kanodia, C. (1990). *The value of communication in agency contracts: Theory and experimental evidence.* Vancouver: Canadian Certified General Accountants Research Foundation.

Berg, J., Dickhaut, J., & Kanodia, C. (1992). Information asymmetry and escalation: Can you make a case? Working Paper, University of Iowa and University of Minnesota.

Berg, J., Dickhaut, J., & Kanodia, C. (1993). The role of information asymmetry in escalation phenomena: Empirical evidence. Working Paper, University of Iowa and University of Minnesota.

Berg, J., Dickhaut, J., & McCabe, K. (1992). Risk preference instability across institutions: A dilemma. Working Paper, University of Iowa and University of Minnesota.

Berliner, J.S. (1956). A problem in Soviet business administration. *Administrative Science Quarterly, 1,* 86–101.

Bernard, V., & Thomas, J. (1989). Post-earnings-announcement drift: Delayed price response or risk premium? *Journal of Accounting Research, 27* (Supplement), 1–36.

Bernard, V., & Thomas, J. (1990). Evidence that stock prices do not fully reflect the implications of current earnings for future earnings. *Journal of Accounting and Economics, 13,* 305–340.

Bettman, J., & Weitz, B. (1983). Attributions in the board room: Causal reasoning in corporate annual reports. *Administrative Science Quarterly, 28,* 165–183.

Biggs, S.F. (1979). An empirical investigation of the information processes underlying four models of choice behavior. In T. Burns (Ed.), *Behavioral Experiments in Accounting II* (pp. 35–81). Columbus, OH: Ohio State University Press.

Biggs, S.F. (1984). Financial analysts' information search in the assessment of corporate earning power. *Accounting, Organizations and Society, 9,* 313–324.

Biggs, S.F., Bedard, J.C., Gaber, B.G., & Linsmeier, T.J. (1985). The effects of task size and similarity on the decision behavior of bank loan officers. *Management Science, 31,* 970–987.

Biggs, S.F., Messier, W.F., & Hansen, J.V. (1987). A descriptive analysis of computer audit specialists' decision-making behavior in advanced computer environments. *Auditing: A Journal of Practice & Theory, 6,* 1–21.

Biggs, S.F., & Mock, T.J. (1983). An investigation of auditor decision processes in the evaluation of internal controls and audit scope decisions. *Journal of Accounting Research, 21,* 234–255.

Biggs, S.F., Mock, T. & Watkins, P. (1988). Auditors' use of analytical review in audit program design. *The Accounting Review, 63,* 148–161.

Biggs, S.F., Selfridge, M., and Krupka, G.R. (1993). A computational model of auditor knowledge and reasoning processes in the going–concern judgment. *Auditing: A Journal of Practice & Theory, 12* (Supplement), 82–99.

Biggs, S.F., & Wild, J.J. (1984). A note on the practice of analytical review. *Auditing: A Journal of Practice & Theory, 3,* 68–79.

Biggs, S.F., & Wild, J.J. (1985). An investigation of auditor judgment in analytical review. *The Accounting Review, 60,* 607–633.

Binmore, K., Shaked, A., & Sutton, J. (1985). Testing noncooperative bargaining theory: A preliminary study. *The American Economic Review, 75,* 1178–1180.

Binmore, K., Shaked, A., & Sutton, J. (1988). A further test of noncooperative bargaining theory: Reply. *The American Economic Review, 78,* 837–839.

Birnberg, J.G., & Shields, J.F. (1989). Three decades of behavioral accounting research: A search for order. *Behavioral Research in Accounting, 1,* 23–74.

Birnberg, J.G., & Shields, M.D. (1984). The role of attention and memory in accounting decisions. *Accounting, Organizations and Society, 9,* 365–382.

Birnberg, J.G., Shields, M.D., & Young, S.M. (1990). The case for multiple methods in empirical management accounting research (with an illustration from budget setting). *Journal of Management Accounting Research, 2,* 33–66.

Birnberg, J.G., & Slevin, D. (1976). A note on the use of confidence interval statements in financial reporting. *Journal of Accounting Research, 14,* 153–157.

Blattberg, R.C., & Hoch, S.J. (1990). Database models and managerial intuition: 50% model + 50% manager. *Management Science, 36,* 887–899.

Blaug, M. (1980). *The methodology of economics.* Cambridge, UK: Cambridge University Press.

Blocher, E., & Cooper, J. (1988). A study of auditors' analytical review performance. *Auditing: A Journal of Practice and Theory, 7,* 1–28.

Boatsman, J.R., & Robertson, J.C. (1974). Policy-capturing on selected materiality judgments. *The Accounting Review, 49,* 342–352.

Bolton G. (1991). A comparative model of bargaining: Theory and evidence. *The American Economic Review, 81,* 1096–1136.

Bonner, S.E. (1990). Experience effects in auditing: The role of task-specific knowledge. *The Accounting Review, 65,* 72–92.

Bonner, S.E. (1991). Is experience necessary in cue measurement?: The case of auditing tasks. *Contemporary Accounting Research, 8,* 253–269.

Bonner, S.E., Davis, J.S., & Jackson, B.R. (1992). Expertise in corporate tax planning: The issue identification stage. *Journal of Accounting Research, 30* (Supplement), 1–28.

Bonner, S.E., Hastie, R., & Young, S.M. (1993). Incentive Effects on Cognition and Behavior. Work in Progress, University of Southern California.

Bonner, S.E., & Lewis, B.L. (1990). Determinants of auditor expertise. *Journal of Accounting Research, 28* (Supplement), 1–20.

Bonner, S.E., & Pennington, N. (1991). Cognitive processes and knowledge as determinants of auditor expertise. *Journal of Accounting Literature, 10,* 1–50.

Boritz, J.E. (1992). The use of artificial intelligence in auditing. Presentation at the XIV World Congress of Accountants, Washington, D.C., October 11–14.

Boritz, J.E., Gaber, B., and Lemon, W.M. (1987). An experimental study of review of preliminary audit strategy by external auditors. Toronto: Canadian Academic Accounting Association.

Boritz, J.E., and Wensley, A.K.P. (1990). Structuring the assessment of audit evidence – an expert systems approach. *Auditing: A Journal of Practice & Theory, 9* (Supplement), 49–87.

Boritz, J.E., and Wensley, A.K.P. (1992). Evaluating expert systems with complex outputs: The case of audit planning. *Auditing: A Journal of Practice & Theory, 11,* 14–29.

Bouwman, M. (1982). The use of accounting information: Expert versus novice behavior. In G. Ungson & D. Braunstein (Eds.), *Decision Making: An Interdisciplinary Inquiry* (pp. 134–167). Boston, MA: Kent.

Bouwman, M.J. (1984). Expert vs. novice decision making in accounting: A summary. *Accounting, Organizations and Society, 9,* 325–327.

Bouwman, M., Frishkoff, P., & Frishkoff, P. (1987). How do financial analysts make decisions?: A process model of the investment screening decision. *Accounting, Organizations and Society, 12,* 1–30.

Brinker, B.J. (1990). *Emerging Practices in Cost Management.* Boston, MA: Warren, Gorham & Lamont.

Brown, C. (1981). Human information processing for decisions to investigate cost variances. *Journal of Accounting Research, 19,* 62–85.

Brown, C. (1983). Effects of dynamic task environment on the learning of standard cost variance significance. *Journal of Accounting Research, 21,* 413–431.

Brown, C., & Solomon, I. (1990). Auditor configural information processing in control risk assessment. *Auditing: A Journal of Practice and Theory, 9,* 17–38.

Brown, C., & Solomon, I. (1991). Configural information processing in auditing: The role of domain-specific knowledge. *The Accounting Review, 66,* 100–119.

Brown, C.E., & Murphy, D.S. (1990). The use of auditing expert systems in public accounting. *Journal of Information Systems, 5,* 63–72.

Brown, C.E. (1991). Expert systems in public accounting: Current practice and future directions. *Expert Systems with Applications: An International Journal, 3,* 3–18.

Brown, P.R. (1983). Independent auditor judgment in the evaluation of internal audit functions. *Journal of Accounting Research, 21,* 444–455.

Brown, R.V., & Lindley, D.V. (1982). Judgment by reconciling incoherence. *Theory and Decision, 14,* 113–132.

Brownell, P. (1982). Participation in the budgetary process: When it works and when it doesn't. *Journal of Accounting Literature, 1,* 124–153.

Brunswik, E. (1952). *The Conceptual Framework of Psychology.* Chicago: University of Chicago Press.

Brunswik, E. (1955). Representative design and probabilistic theory in a functional psychology. *Psychological Review, 62,* 193–217.

Buchman, T. (1985). An effect of hindsight on predicting bankruptcy with accounting information. *Accounting, Organizations and Society, 10,* 267–286.

Bulmer, M. (1984). *The Chicago School of Sociology.* Chicago, IL: University of Chicago Press.

Bunn, D., & Wright, G. (1991). Interaction of judgmental and statistical forecasting methods: Issues & analysis. *Management Science, 37,* 501–518.

Burgstahler, D., & Sundem, G.L. (1989). The evolution of behavioral accounting research in the United States, 1967–1988. *Behavioral Research in Accounting, 1,* 75–108.

Burns, M., & Pearl, J. (1981). Causal and diagnostic inferences: A comparison of validity. *Organizational Behavior and Human Performance, 28,* 379–394.

Butler, S.A. (1985). Application of a decision aid in the judgmental evaluation of substantive test of details samples. *Journal of Accounting Research, 23,* 513–526.

Butler, S.A. (1986). Anchoring in the judgmental evaluation of audit samples. *The Accounting Review, 61,* 101–111.

Butt, J. (1988). Frequency judgments in an audit-related task. *Journal of Accounting Research, 26,* 315–330.

Butt, J., & Campbell, T.L. (1989). The effects of information order and hypothesis-testing strategies on auditors' judgments. *Accounting, Organizations and Society, 14*, 471–479.

Camerer, C. (1981). General conditions for the success of bootstrapping models. *Organizational Behavior and Human Performance, 27*, 411–422.

Camerer, C. (1987). Do biases in probability judgment matter in markets?: Experimental evidence. *The American Economic Review, 77*, 981–997.

Camerer, C. (1989). An experimental test of several generalized utility theories. *Journal of Risk and Uncertainty, 2*, 61–104.

Camerer, C. (1990). Behavioral game theory. In R.M. Hogarth (Ed.), *Insights in Decision Making: A Tribute to Hillel J. Einhorn*. Chicago, IL: University of Chicago Press.

Camerer, C. (1992). The rationality of prices and volume in experimental markets. *Organizational Behavior and Human Decision Processes, 51*, 237–272.

Camerer, C., & Kunreuther, H. (1984). Linking individuals and markets through behavioral decision theory: An experimental approach. Working Paper, University of Pennsylvania.

Camerer, C., Loewenstein, G., & Weber, M. (1989). The curse of knowledge in economic settings. *Journal of Political Economy, 97*, 1232–1254.

Camerer, C., & Weigelt, K. (1991). Information mirages in experimental asset markets. *The Journal of Business, 64*, 463–493.

Caplan, E.H. (1966). Behavioral assumptions of management accounting. *The Accounting Review, 61*, 496–509.

Caplan, E.H. (1971). *Management Accounting and Behavioral Science*. Reading, MA: Addison-Wesley.

Carpenter, B.W., & Dirsmith, M.W. (1990). Materiality, qualitative considerations and professional standards: The relationship between the nature of debt extinguishment transactions and the boundedly rational materiality judgments of auditors. Working Paper, Pennsylvania State University.

Carroll, B. (1987). Expert systems for clinical diagnosis: Are they worth the effort? *Behavioral Science, 32*, 274–292.

Casey, C. (1980a). The usefulness of accounting ratios for subjects' predictions of corporate failure: Replication and extensions. *Journal of Accounting Research, 18*, 603–613.

Casey, C. (1980b). Variation in accounting information load: The effect on loan officers' predictions of bankruptcy. *The Accounting Review, 55*, 36–49.

Casey, C. (1983). Prior probability disclosure and loan officers' judgments: Some evidence of the impact. *Journal of Accounting Research, 21*, 300–307.

Casey, C., & Selling, T. (1986). The effect of task predictability and prior probability disclosure on judgment quality and confidence. *The Accounting Review, 61*, 302–317.

Chakravarti, D., Mitchell, A., & Staelin, R. (1979). Judgment based marketing decision models: An experimental investigation of the decision calculus approach. *Management Science, 25*, 251–263.

Chalos, P. (1985). Financial distress: A comparative study of individual, model and committee assessments. *Journal of Accounting Research, 23*, 527–543.

Chalos, P., & Haka, S. (1989). Participative budgeting and managerial performance. *Decision Sciences, 20*, 334–347.

Chalos, P., & Haka, S. (1990). Transfer pricing under bilateral bargaining. *The Accounting Review, 65*, 624–641.

Chalos, P., & Pickard, S. (1985). Information choice and cue use: An experiment in group information processing. *Journal of Applied Psychology, 70,* 634–641.

Chernoff, H., & Rizvi, M. (1975). Effect of classification error on random permutations of features in representing multivariate data by faces. *Journal of the American Statistical Association, 70,* 548–554.

Chesley, G.R. (1975). Elicitation of subjective probabilities: A review. *The Accounting Review, 50,* 325–337.

Chew, S.H., & Waller, W.S. (1986). Empirical tests of weighted utility theory. *Journal of Mathematical Psychology, 30,* 55–72.

Chewning, E., & Harrell, A. (1990). The effect of information load on decision makers' cue utilization levels and decision quality in a financial distress decision task. *Accounting, Organizations and Society, 15,* 527–542.

Choo, F. (1989). Expert-novice differences in judgment/decision making research. *Journal of Accounting Literature, 8,* 106–136.

Choo, F. (1991). An analysis of auditor's scriptal knowledge content and judgments. Working Paper, University of New South Wales.

Choo, F., & Trotman, K.T. (1991). The relationship between knowledge structures and judgments for experienced and inexperienced auditors. *The Accounting Review, 66,* 464–485.

Chow, C. (1983). The effects of job standard tightness and compensation scheme on performance: An exploration of linkages. *The Accounting Review, 58,* 667–685.

Chow, C., Cooper, J., and Haddad, K. (1991a). The effects of pay schemes and ratchets on budgetary slack and performance: A multiperiod experiment. *Accounting, Organizations and Society, 16,* 47–60.

Chow, C., Cooper, J., and Haddad, K. (1991b). Participative budgeting: The multiperiod incentive effects of pay schemes and ratchets under state uncertainty. In S. Moriarity (Ed.), *Accounting, Communication and Monitoring* (pp. 65–79). Norman, OK: The University of Oklahoma Center for Economic and Management Research.

Chow, C., Cooper, J., and Waller, W. (1988). Participative budgeting: Effects of a truth-inducing pay scheme and information asymmetry on slack and performance. *The Accounting Review, 63,* 111–122.

Chow, C., and Haddad, K. (1991). Relative performance evaluation and risk taking in delegated investment decisions. *Decision Sciences, 22,* 583–593.

Chow, C., McNamee, A., and Plumlee, D. (1987). Practitioners' perceptions of audit step difficulty and criticalness: Implications for audit research. *Auditing: A Journal of Practice & Theory, 6,* 123–133.

Chow, C., Shields, M.D., and Chan, Y.K. (1991). The effects of management controls and national culture on manufacturing performance: An experimental investigation. *Accounting, Organizations and Society, 16,* 209–226.

Colbert, J. (1988). Inherent risk: An investigation of auditors' judgments. *Accounting, Organizations and Society, 13,* 111–121.

Colbert, J. (1989). The effect of experience on auditors' judgments. *Journal of Accounting Literature, 8,* 137–149.

Committee on Accounting Valuation Bases (1972). Report of the committee on accounting valuation bases. *The Accounting Review, 48* (Supplement), 535–573.

Cooper, R., & Kaplan, R.S. (1991). *The design of cost management systems: Text, cases, and readings.* Englewood Cliffs, NJ: Prentice-Hall.

Cooper, R.B., & Zmud, R.W. (1990). Information technology implementation research: A technological diffusion approach. *Management Science, 36,* 123–139.

Corless, J.C. (1972). Assessing prior distributions for applying Bayesian statistics in auditing. *The Accounting Review, 47,* 556–566.

Cornelius, E.T., and Lyness, K.S. (1980). A comparison of holistic and decomposed judgment strategies in job analysis by job incumbents. *Journal of Applied Psychology, 65,* 155–163.

Coutts, K.J. (1987). Average cost pricing. In J. Eatwell, M. Milgate & P. Newman (Eds.), *The new palgrave: A dictionary of economics* (pp. 158–159). London: Macmillan.

Cox, J.C., & Isaac, R.M. (1986). Experimental economics and experimental psychology: Ever the twain shall meet? In A.J. MacFayden and H.W. MacFayden (Eds.), *Economic psychology: Intersections in Theory and Applications* (pp. 647–669). Dordrecht, Netherlands: North-Holland.

Craik, F.I.M., & Tulving, E. (1975). Depth of processing and the retention of words in episodic memory. *Journal of Experimental Psychology: General, 104,* 268–294.

Crosby, M.A. (1981). Bayesian statistics in auditing: A comparison of probability elicitation techniques. *The Accounting Review, 56,* 355–365.

Cushing, B.E. (1974). A mathematical approach to the analysis and design of internal control systems. *The Accounting Review, 49,* 24–41.

Cushing, B.E., & Loebbecke, J.K. (1983). Analytical approaches to audit risk: A survey and analysis. *Auditing: A Journal of Practice and Theory, 3,* 23–41.

Cushing, B.E., & Loebbecke, J.K. (1986). *Comparison of audit methodologies of large accounting firms.* Studies in Accounting Research No. 26. Sarasota, FL: American Accounting Association.

Cyert, R.M., & March, J.G. (1963). *A Behavioral Theory of the Firm.* Englewood Cliffs, NJ: Prentice-Hall.

Dacey, R., & Ward, B. (1985). On the fundamental nature of professional opinions: The traditional, Bayesian, and epistemic methods of attestation. In A.R. Abdel-khalik & I. Solomon (Eds.), *Audit Research Symposium 1984* (pp. 63–91). Urbana, IL: University of Illinois.

Dalton, M. (1959). *Men Who Manage.* New York: Wiley.

Daniel, S.J. (1988). Some empirical evidence about the assessment of audit risk in practice. *Auditing: A Journal of Practice & Theory, 7,* 174–181.

Danos, P., Holt, D., & Imhoff, E. (1984). Bond raters' use of management financial forecasts: Experiment in expert judgment. *The Accounting Review, 59,* 547–573.

Danos, P., Holt, D., & Imhoff, E. (1989). The use of accounting information in bank lending decisions. *Accounting, Organizations and Society, 14,* 235–246.

Davis, D., & Holt, C. (1993). *Experimental Economics.* Princeton, NJ: Princeton University Press.

Davis, J., & Solomon, I. (1989). Experience, expertise, and expert-performance research in public accounting. *Journal of Accounting Literature, 8,* 150–164.

Davis, J., & Swenson, C. (1988). Role of experimental economics in tax policy research. *The Journal of the American Taxation Association, 10,* 40–59.

Davis, L. (1989). Report format and the decision makers' task: An experimental investigation. *Accounting, Organizations and Society, 14,* 495–508.

Dawes, R.M. (1979). The robust beauty of improper linear models in decision making. *The American Psychologist, 34,* 571–582.

Dawes, R.M., Faust, D., & Meehl, P.E. (1989). Clinical versus actuarial judgment. *Science, 243,* 1668–1674.

DeBondt, W., & Thaler, R. (1985). Does the stock market overreact? *The Journal of Finance, 40,* 793–807.

DeBondt, W., & Thaler, R. (1987). Further evidence on investor overreaction and stock market seasonality. *The Journal of Finance, 42,* 557–581.

DeBondt, W., & Thaler, R. (1990). Do security analysts overreact? *The American Economic Review, 80,* 52–57.

DeJong, D., & Forsythe, R. (1992). A perspective on the use of laboratory market experimentation in auditing research. *The Accounting Review, 67,* 157–170.

DeJong, D., Forsythe, R., & Uecker, W. (1985). The methodology of laboratory markets and its implications for agency research in accounting and auditing. *Journal of Accounting Research, 23,* 753–793.

Delisio, J., McGowan, M., and Hamscher, W. (1993). PLANET: An expert system for audit risk assessment and planning. PW-TR-No. 30, Price Waterhouse Technology Centre.

DeLong, J., Shleifer, A., Summers, L., & Waldmann, R. (1991). The survival of noise traders in financial markets. *The Journal of Business, 64,* 1–20.

Demsetz, H. (1982). *Economic, Legal, and Political Dimensions of Competition.* Amsterdam: North-Holland.

Demski, J.S. (1980). *Information Analysis* (2nd Edition). Reading, MA: Addison-Wesley.

Demski, J.S., & Feltham, G.A. (1976). *Cost Determination: A Conceptual Approach.* Ames, IA: Iowa State University Press.

Demski, J.S., & Feltham, G.A. (1978). Economic incentives in budgetary control systems. *The Accounting Review, 53,* 336–359.

Demski, J.S., & Kreps, D.M. (1982). Models in managerial accounting. *Journal of Accounting Research, 20* (Supplement), 117–148.

DeSanctis, G., & Jarvenpaa, S. (1989). Graphical presentation of accounting data for financial forecasting: An experimental investigation. *Accounting, Organizations and Society, 14,* 509–525.

DeSarbo, W.S., Libby, R., & Jedidi, K. (1994). Catscale: A new stochastic multidimensional scaling methodology for the spatial analysis of sorting data and the study of stimulus categorization. *Computational Statistics and Data Analysis, 18,* 165–184.

Dickhaut, J. (1973). Alternative information structures and probability revision. *The Accounting Review, 48,* 61–79.

Dickhaut, J.W., & Lere, J.C. (1983). Comparison of accounting systems and heuristics in selecting economic optima. *Journal of Accounting Research, 21,* 495–513.

Dillard, J.F., & Ferris, K.R. (1989). Individual behavior in professional accounting firms: A review and synthesis. *Journal of Accounting Literature, 8,* 208–234.

Dillard, J.F., & Fisher, J.G. (1990). Compensation schemes, skill level and task performance: An experimental examination. *Decision Sciences, 21,* 121–137.

Dirsmith, M., & Covaleski, M. (1985). Informal communications, nonformal communications and mentoring in public accounting firms. *Accounting, Organizations and Society, 10,* 149–169.

Dirsmith, M., & Haskins, M.E. (1991). Inherent risk assessment and audit firm technology: A contrast in world theories. *Accounting, Organizations and Society, 16,* 61–90.

Dopuch, N., & King, R.R. (1991). *Experimental tests of auditing as a credibility generating mechanism.* Research Monograph No. 19. Vancouver: Canadian Certified General Accountants Research Foundation.

Dopuch, N., & Ronen, J. (1973). The effects of alternative inventory valuation methods: An experimental study. *Journal of Accounting Research, 11,* 191–211.

Dorward, N. (1987). *The Pricing Decision: Economic Theory and Business Practice.* London: Harper & Row.

Doupnik, T., & Rolfe, R. (1989). The relevance of aggregation of geographic area data in the assessment of foreign investment risk. In *Advances in Accounting* (Vol. 7, pp. 51–65). Greenwich, CT: JAI Press.

Duh, R., & Sunder, S. (1986). Incentives, learning and processing of information in a market environment: An examination of the base-rate fallacy. In S. Moriarity (Ed.), *Laboratory Market Research* (pp. 50–79). Norman, OK: University of Oklahoma, Center for Economic and Management Research.

Dungan, C.W., and Chandler, J.S. (1985). AUDITOR: A microcomputer-based expert system to support auditors in the field. *Expert Systems, 2,* 210–221.

Dybvig, P., & Ross, S. (1987). Arbitrage. In J. Eatwell, M. Milgate, & P. Newman (Eds.), *The New Palgrave: A Dictionary of Economics* (Vol. 1, pp. 100–106). London: Macmillan.

Dyckman, T.R. (1964). On the investment decision. *The Accounting Review, 39,* 285–295.

Dyckman, T.R., Gibbins, M., & Swieringa, R.J. (1978). Experimental and survey research in financial accounting: A review and evaluation. In A.R. Abdel-khalik & T.F. Keller (Eds.), *The Impact of Accounting Research on Practice and Disclosure* (Part 2, pp. 48–105). Durham, NC: Duke University Press.

Dyckman, T.R., Hoskin, R.E., & Swieringa, R.J. (1982). An accounting change and information processing changes. *Accounting, Organizations and Society, 7,* 1–12.

Dyer, W.G., & Page, R.A. (1988). The politics of innovation. *Knowledge in Society, 1,* 23–41.

Ebert, R., & Kruse, T. (1978). Bootstrapping the security analyst. *Journal of Applied Psychology, 63,* 110–119.

Eggertsson, T. (1990). *Economic Behavior and Institutions.* Cambridge, UK: Cambridge University Press.

Einhorn, H.J. (1972). Expert measurement and mechanical combination. *Organizational Behavior and Human Performance, 7,* 86–106.

Einhorn, H.J. (1976). A synthesis: Accounting and behavioral science. *Journal of Accounting Research, 14* (Supplement), 196–206.

Einhorn, H.J. (1980). Learning from experience and suboptimal rules in decision making. In T. Wallsten (Ed.), *Cognitive Processes in Choice and Decision Behavior* (pp. 1–20). Hillsdale, NJ: Erlbaum.

Einhorn, H.J. (1988). Diagnosis and causality in clinical and statistical prediction. In D.C. Turk & P. Salovey (Eds.), *Reasoning, Inference and Judgment In Clinical Psychology* (pp. 51–70). New York: Free Press.

Einhorn, H.J., & Hogarth, R.M. (1978). Confidence in judgment: Persistence of the illusion of validity. *Psychological Review, 85,* 395–416.

Einhorn, H.J., & Hogarth, R.M. (1981a). Rationality and the sanctity of competence. *The Behavioral and Brain Sciences, 4,* 334–335.

Einhorn, H.J., & Hogarth, R.M. (1981b). Behavioral decision theory: Processes of judgment and choice. *Annual review of psychology, 32,* 53–88.

Einhorn, H.J., & Hogarth, R.M. (1981c). Behavioral decision theory: Processes of judgment and choice. *Journal of Accounting Research, 19,* 1–41.

Einhorn, H.J., & Hogarth, R.M. (1985). A contrast/suprise model for updating beliefs. Working Paper, University of Chicago.

Einhorn, H.J., Kleinmuntz, D., & Kleinmuntz, B. (1979). Linear regression and process-tracing models of judgment. *Psychological Review, 86,* 465–485.

Elias, N. (1972). The effects of human asset statements on the investment decision: An experiment. *Journal of Accounting Research, 10,* 215–233.

Elliott, R.K. (1983). Unique audit methods: Peat Marwick International. *Auditing: A Journal of Practice and Theory, 2,* 1–12.

Elliott, R.K., & Jacobson, P.D. (1987). Audit technology: A heritage and a promise. *The Journal of Accountancy, 166,* 198–218.

Elliott, R.K., & Kielich, J.A. (1985). Expert systems for accountants. *The Journal of Accountancy, 164,* 126–134.

Emby, C. (1991). Sequential belief revision and subjective probability: An experiment in auditing judgment. Working Paper, Simon Fraser University.

Emby, C., & Gibbins, M. (1988). Good judgment in public accounting: Quality and justification. *Contemporary Accounting Research, 4,* 287–313.

Enis, C. (1988). The impact of current-value data on the predictive judgments of investors. *Accounting, Organizations and Society, 13,* 123–145.

Epstein, S. (1992). Testing principal-agent theory. In M. Isaac (Ed.), *Research in Experimental Economics* (Vol. 5, pp. 35–60). Greenwich, CT: JAI Press.

Ericsson, K.A., & Simon, H.A. (1980). Verbal reports as data. *Psychological Review, 87,* 215–251.

Estes, R., & Reimer, M. (1977). A study of the effect of qualified auditors opinions on bankers' lending decisions. *Accounting and Business Research, 28,* 250–259.

Estes, R., & Reimer, M. (1979). An experimental study of the differential effect of standard and qualified auditors' opinions on investors' price decisions. *Accounting and Business Research, 9,* 157–162.

Felix, W.L. (1976). Evidence on alternative means of assessing prior probability distributions for audit decision making. *The Accounting Review, 51,* 800–807.

Felix, W.L., & Kinney, W.R. (1982). Research in the auditor's opinion formulation process: The state of the art. *The Accounting Review, 57,* 245–271.

Feltham, G.A. (1972). *Information evaluation.* Studies in Accounting Research No. 5. Evanston, IL: American Accounting Association.

Fiedler, K. (1982). Causal schemata: Review and criticism of a popular construct. *Journal of Personality and Social Psychology, 42,* 1001–1013.

Financial Accounting Standards Board (1978). *Objectives of financial reporting by business enterprises.* Statement of Financial Accounting Concepts No. 1. Stamford, CT: Financial Accounting Standards Board.

Firth, M. (1979). Consensus views and judgment models in materiality decisions. *Accounting, Organizations and Society, 4,* 283–295.

Fischhoff, B. (1982). Debiasing. In D. Khaneman, P. Slovic, & A. Tversky (Eds.), *Judgment under Uncertainty: Heuristics and Biases* (pp. 422–444). New York: Cambridge University Press.

Forsythe, R. (1986). The application of laboratory methods to testing theories of resource allocation under uncertainty. In B. Gilad & S. Kaish (Eds.), *The Handbook of Behavioral Economics* (pp. 19–60). Greenwich, CT: JAI Press.

Forsythe, R., Horowitz, J., Savin, N.E., & Sefton, M. (1989). Replicability, fairness, and pay in experiments with simple bargaining games. Working Paper, University of Iowa.

Forsythe, R., & Lundholm, R. (1990). Information aggregation in an experimental market. *Econometrica, 58,* 309–347.

Forsythe, R., Nelson, F., Neumann, G., & Wright, J. (1992). Anatomy of an experimental political stock market. *The American Economic Review, 82,* 1142–1161.

Forsythe, R., Palfrey, T., & Plott, C. (1982). Asset valuation in an experimental market. *Econometrica, 50,* 537–567.

Forward, J. (1969). Group achievement motivation and individual motives to achieve success and to avoid failure. *Journal of Personality, 37,* 297–309.

Francis, J., & Philbrick, D. (1993). Analysts' decisions as products of a multi-task environment. *Journal of Accounting Research, 31,* 216–230.

Frank, S.J. (1988). What AI practitioners should know about the law, part I. *AI Magazine, 9,* 63–75.

Frazer, J. (1922). *The Golden Bough: A Study in Magic and Religion* (Vol. 22, pp. 12–43, 58–69). New York: Macmillan.

Frederick, D.M. (1991). Auditors' representation and retrieval of internal control knowledge. *The Accounting Review, 66,* 240–258.

Frederick, D.M., Heiman-Hoffman, V., & Libby, R. (1994). The structure of auditors' knowledge of financial statement errors. *Auditing: A Journal of Practice & Theory, 13,* 1–21.

Frederick, D.M., & Libby, R. (1986). Expertise and auditors' judgments of conjunctive events. *Journal of Accounting Research, 24,* 270–290.

Frederickson, J.R. (1992). Relative performance information: The effects of common uncertainty and contract type on agents' effort levels. *The Accounting Review, 67,* 647–669.

Friedman, M. (1953). *Essays in Positive Economics.* Chicago, IL: University of Chicago Press.

Frishkoff, P., Frishkoff, P.A., & Bouwman, M.J. (1984). Use of accounting data in screening by financial analysts. *Journal of Accounting, Auditing and Finance, 8,* 44–53.

Ganguly, A., Kagel, J., & Moser, D. (1994). The effects of biases in probability judgments on market prices. *Accounting, Organizations and Society, 19,* 675–700.

Garb, H.N. (1989). Clinical judgment, clinical training, and professional experience. *Psychological Bulletin, 105,* 387–396.

Gaumnitz, B.R., Nunamaker, T.R., Surdick, J.J., & Thomas, M.F. (1982). Auditor consensus in internal control evaluation and audit program planning. *Journal of Accounting Research, 20,* 745–755.

Gibbins, M. (1977). A behavioral approach to auditing research. In *Symposium on Auditing Research* 2 (pp. 141–186). Champaign, IL: University of Illinois.

Gibbins, M. (1984). Propositions about the psychology of professional judgment in public accounting. *Journal of Accounting Research, 22,* 103–125.

Gibbins, M. (1992). Deception: A tricky issue for behavioral research in accounting and auditing. *Auditing: A Journal of Practice & Theory, 11,* 113–126.

Gibbins, M., & Emby, C. (1984). Evidence on the nature of professional judgment in public accounting. *In Auditing Research Symposium 1984* (pp. 181–212). Champaign, IL: University of Illinois.

Gibbins, M., & Jamal, K. (1993). Problem-centred research and knowledge-based theory in the professional accounting setting. *Accounting, Organizations and Society, 18,* 451–466.

Gibbins, M., & Mason, A.K. (1988). *Professional judgment in financial reporting.* Toronto: Canadian Institute of Chartered Accountants.

Gibbins, M., & Newton, J. (1987). Behavioral research, reporting standards and the usefulness of information. In P.A. Griffin (Ed.), *Usefulness to Investors and Creditors of Information Provided by Financial Reporting* (2nd edition, pp. 85–114). Stamford, CT: Financial Accounting Standards Board.

Gibbins, M., Richardson, A., & Waterhouse, J. (1990). The management of corporate financial disclosure: Opportunism, ritualism, policies, and processes. *Journal of Accounting Research, 28,* 121–143.

Gibbins, M., Richardson, A., & Waterhouse, J. (1992). *The Management of Financial Disclosure: Theory and Perspectives.* Vancouver: Canadian Certified General Accountants Research Foundation.

Gibbins, M., Shaver, J.M., & Emby, C. (1991). Framed activation: A cognitive model for the application of individual and group professional knowledge to an auditing task. Working Paper, University of Alberta.

Gibbins, M., & Wolf, F.M. (1982). Auditors' subjective decision environment: The case of a normal external audit. *The Accounting Review, 57,* 105–124.

Gilad, B., & Kaish, S. (Eds.). (1986). *Handbook of behavioral economics.* (Vols 1a and 1b). Greenwich, CT: JAI Press.

Goldberg, L. (1968). Simple models or simple processes? Some research on clinical judgments. *The American Psychologist, 23,* 483–496.

Gonedes, N. (1972). Efficient capital markets and external accounting. *The Accounting Review, 47,* 11–21.

Gonedes, N., & Dopuch, N. (1974). Capital market equilibrium, information production, and selecting accounting techniques: Theoretical framework and review of empirical work. *Journal of Accounting Research, 12* (Supplement), 48–129.

Graham, L.E., Damens, J., & VanNess, G. (1991). Developing risk advisor[sm]: An expert system for risk identification. *Auditing: A Journal of Practice & Theory, 10,* 69–96.

Green, P.E., Robinson, P.J., & Fitzroy, P.T. (1967). *Experiments on the Value of Information in Simulated Marketing Environments.* Boston, MA: Allyn and Bacon.

Gresik, T., & Satterthwaite, M. (1989). The rate at which a simple market converges to efficiency as the number of traders increases: An asymptotic result for optimal trading mechanisms. *Journal of Economic Theory, 48,* 304–332.

Grether, D.M. (1980). Bayes rule as a descriptive model: The representativeness heuristic. *The Quarterly Journal of Economics, 95,* 537–557.

Grether, D.M., & Plott, C.R. (1979). Economic theory of choice and the preference reversal phenomenon. *The American Economic Review, 69,* 623–638.

Griffin, P. (1987). *Usefulness to Investors and Creditors of Information Provided by Financial Reporting* (2nd edition). Stamford, CT: Financial Accounting Standards Board.

Groves, T. (1973). Incentives in teams. *Econometrica, 41,* 617–631.

Groves, T., & Loeb, M. (1979). Incentives in a divisionalized firm. *Management Science, 25,* 221–230.

Guth, W., Schmittberger, R., & Schwarze, B. (1982). An experimental analysis of ultimatum bargaining. *Journal of Economic Behavior and Organization, 3,* 367–388.

Hagafors, R., & Brehmer, B. (1983). Does having to justify one's judgments change the nature of the judgment process? *Organizational Behavior and Human Decision Processes, 31,* 223–232.

Hall, R.L., & Hitch, C.J. (1939). Price theory and business behavior. *Oxford Economic Papers, 2,* 12–45.

Haltiwanger, J., & Waldman, M. (1985). Rational expectations and the limits of rationality: An analysis of heterogeneity. *The American Economic Review, 75,* 326–340.

Hamilton, R.E., & Wright, W.F. (1982). Internal control judgments and effects of experience: Replications and extensions. *Journal of Accounting Research, 20,* 756–765.

Hammond, K.R., Hamm, R.M., Grassia, J. & Pearson, T. (1989). Direct comparison of the efficacy of intuitive and analytical cognition in expert judgment. *IEEE Transactions on Systems, Man, and Cybernetics, 17,* 753–770.

Hamscher, W. (1992). Modeling accounting systems to support multiple tasks: A progress report. *Proceedings of the 10th National Conference on Artificial Intelligence,* 519–524.

Hand, J.R.M. (1990). A test of the extended functional fixation hypothesis. *The Accounting Review, 65,* 739–763.

Hand, J.R.M., & Maines, L. (1994). The role of cognitive biases in individuals' ability to forecast typical quarterly EPS series. Unpublished Working Paper, Duke University.

Hansen, J.V., Koehler, G.J., Messier, Jr., W.F., & Mutchler, J.R. (1993). Developing expert system knowledge structures: A comparison of inductively generated rules and LOGIT. *Decision Support Systems, 9,* 235–243.

Hansen, J.V., & Messier, W.F. (1986a). A knowledge based, expert system for auditing advanced computer systems. *European Journal of Operational Research, 26,* 371–379.

Hansen, J.V., & Messier, W.F. (1986b). A preliminary investigation of EDP-XPERT. *Auditing: A Journal of Practice & Theory, 6,* 109–123.

Hansen, J.V., & Messier, W.F. (1991). Artificial neural networks: Foundations and application to a decision problem. *Expert Systems With Applications: An International Journal, 3,* 135–141.

Harper, R.M., Mister, W.G., & Stawser, J.R. (1987). The impact of new pension disclosure rules on perceptions of debt. *Journal of Accounting Research, 25,* 327–330.

Harre, R., & Secord, P.F. (1972). *The Explanation of Social Behaviour.* Oxford, UK: Basil Blackwell.

Harrison G., & McCabe K. (1992a). Testing non-cooperative bargaining in experiments. In M. Isaac (Ed.), *Research in Experimental Economics* (Vol. 5, pp. 137–169). Greenwich, CT: JAI Press.

Harrison G., & McCabe K. (1992b). Expectations and fairness in a simple bargaining experiment. Working Paper, University of South Carolina and University of Minnesota.

Harvey, D., Rhode, J., & Merchant, K. (1979). Accounting aggregation: User preferences and decision making. *Accounting, Organizations and Society, 4,* 187–210.

Hasher, L., & Zacks, R.T. (1984). Automatic processing of fundamental information: The case of frequency of occurrence. *The American Psychologist, 39,* 1372–1378.

Hayek, F.A. (1948). The meaning of competition. In *Individualism and Economic Order* (pp. 92–106). Chicago, IL: University of Chicago Press.

Heiman, V.B. (1990). Auditors' assessments of the likelihood of error explanations in analytical review. *The Accounting Review, 65,* 875–890.

Heiman-Hoffman, V.B. (1992). Experience effects in analytical review: The relation between knowledge and judgment. Working Paper, University of Pittsburgh.

Heintz, J.A. (1973). Price-level restated financial statements and investment decision making. *The Accounting Review, 48,* 679–689.

Heintz, J.A., & White, G.B. (1989). Auditor judgment in analytical review: Some further evidence. *Auditing: A Journal of Practice & Theory, 8,* 22–39.

Hendricks, J. (1976). The impact of human resource accounting information on stock investment decisions: An empirical study. *The Accounting Review, 51,* 292–305.

Hill, G.W. (1982). Group versus individual performance: Are N+1 heads better than one? *Psychological Bulletin, 91,* 517–539.

Hilton, R.W. (1980). Integrating normative and descriptive theories of information processing. *Journal of Accounting Research, 18,* 477–505.

Hilton, R.W., & Swieringa, R.J. (1981). Perception of initial uncertainty as a determinant of information value. *Journal of Accounting Research, 19,* 109–119.

Hilton, R.W., & Swieringa, R.J. (1982). Decision flexibility and perceived information value. *Decision Sciences, 13,* 357–379.

Hilton, R.W., Swieringa, R.J., & Hoskin, R. (1981). Perception of accuracy as a determinant of information value. *Journal of Accounting Research, 19,* 86–108.

Hilton, R.W., Swieringa, R.J., & Turner, M.J. (1988). Product pricing, accounting costs, and use of product-costing systems. *The Accounting Review, 53,* 195–215.

Hite, P. (1987). An application of meta-analysis for bankruptcy prediction studies. *Organizational Behavior and Human Decision Processes, 39,* 155–161.

Hoffman E., McCabe K., Shachat, K., & Smith V. (1992). Fairness or right: A reexamination of bargaining experiments. Working Paper, University of Minnesota and University of Arizona.

Hoffman, E., & Spitzer, M.L. (1982). The Coase theorem: Some experimental results. *Journal of Law & Economics, 25,* 73–98.

Hoffman, E., & Spitzer, M.L. (1985). Entitlements, rights, and fairness: An experimental examination of subjects' concepts of distributive justice. *Journal of Legal Studies, 14,* 259–297.

Hoffman, P.J., Slovic, P., & Rorer, L.G. (1968). An analysis-of-variance model for the assessment of configural cue utilization in clinical judgment. *Psychological Bulletin, 69,* 338–349.

Hofstedt, T. (1972). Some behavioral parameters of financial analysis. *The Accounting Review, 47,* 679–692.

Hogarth, R.M. (1991). A perspective on cognitive research in accounting. *The Accounting Review, 66,* 277–290.

Hogarth, R.M. (1993). Accounting for decisions and decisions for accounting. *Accounting, Organizations and Society, 18,* 407–424.

Hogarth, R.M., Gibbs, B.J., McKenzie, C.R.M., & Marquis, M.A. (1991). Learning from feedback: Exactingness and incentives. *Journal of Experimental Psychology: Learning, Memory and Cognition, 17,* 734–752.

Hogarth, R.M., & Einhorn, H.J. (1992). Order effects in belief updating: The belief-adjustment model. *Cognitive Psychology, 24,* 1–55.

Hogarth, R.M., & Reder, M.W. (Eds.). (1986). *Rational choice: The Contrast Between Economics and Psychology.* Chicago, IL: University of Chicago Press.

Hogarth, R.M., & Reder, M.W. (1986). The behavioral foundations of economic theory. *The Journal of Business, 59* (Supplement).

Hopwood, A. (1976). *Accounting and Human Behavior.* Englewood Cliffs, NJ: Prentice-Hall.

Houghton, K. (1983–84). Audit reports: Their impact on the loan decision process and outcome: An experiment. *Accounting and Business Research, 14,* 15–20.

Houghton, K. (1984). Accounting data and the prediction of business failure: The setting of priors and the age of data. *Journal of Accounting Research, 22,* 361–368.

Houghton, K., & Messier, W. (1991). The wording of audit reports: Its impact on the meaning of the message communicated. In S. Moriarity (Ed.), *Accounting, Communication and Monitoring* (pp. 85–106). Norman, OK: University of Oklahoma.

Houghton, K., & Sengupta, R. (1984). The effect of prior probability disclosure and information set construction on bankers' ability to predict failure. *Journal of Accounting Research, 22,* 768–775.

Huss, H.F., & Jacobs, F.A. (1991). Risk containment: Exploring auditor decisions in the engagement process. *Auditing: A Journal of Practice & Theory, 10,* 16–32.

Ijiri, Y., Jaedicke, R., & Knight, K. (1966). The effects of accounting alternatives on management decisions. In R. Jaedicke (Ed.), *Research in Accounting Measurement* (pp. 186–199). New York: American Accounting Association.

Iselin, E. (1991). Individual versus group decision-making performance: A further investigation of two theories in a bankruptcy prediction task. *Journal of Business Finance and Accounting, 18,* 191–208.

Jacoby, J., Kuss, A., Mazursky, D., & Troutman, T. (1985). Effectiveness of security analyst information accessing strategies: A computer interactive assessment. *Computers in Human Behavior, 1,* 95–113.

Jamal, K. (1991). *Detecting framing effects in audit judgment.* Unpublished Ph.D. Dissertation, University of Minnesota.

Janakiraman, S., Lambert, R., & Larcker, D. (1992). An empirical investigation of the relative performance evaluation hypothesis. *Journal of Accounting Research, 30,* 53–69.

Jensen, R. (1966). An experimental design for study of effects of accounting variations in decision making. *Journal of Accounting Research, 4,* 224–238.

Jiambalvo, J., & Waller, W. (1984). Decomposition and assessments of audit risk. *Auditing: A Journal of Practice and Theory, 3,* 80–88.

Johnson, D., & Pany, K. (1984). Forecasts, auditor review and bank loan decisions. *Journal of Accounting Research, 22,* 731–743.

Johnson, D., Pany, K., & White, R. (1983). Audit reports and the loan decision: Actions and perceptions. *Auditing: A Journal of Practice and Theory, 2,* 38–51.

Johnson, E. (1988). Expertise and decision under uncertainty: Performance and process. In M. Chi, R. Glaser & M. Farr (Eds.), *The Nature of Expertise* (pp. 209–228). Hillsdale, NJ: Erlbaum.

Johnson, E., Camerer, C., Sen, S., & Rymon, T. (1991). Behavior and cognition in sequential bargaining. Working Paper, University of Pennsylvania.

Johnson, E., Payne, J., Schkade, W., & Bettman, J. (1988). Monitoring information processing and decisions: The MOUSELAB system. Working Paper, Fuqua School of Business, Duke University.

Johnson, P.E., & Jamal, K. (1987). Human judgment: Limitations and opportunities for research. In A. Bailey (Ed.), *Auditor Productivity in the Year 2000: Proceedings of the 1987 Arthur Young Professors' Roundtable* (pp. 83–98). Reston, VA: Arthur Young.

Johnson, P.E., Jamal, K., & Berryman, R.G. (1989). Audit judgment research. *Accounting, Organizations and Society, 14,* 83–99.

Johnson, V.E., & Kaplan, S.E. (1991). Experimental evidence on the effects of accountability on auditor judgments. *Auditing: A Journal of Practice & Theory, 10,* 96–107.

Johnson, W.B. (1983). Representativeness in judgmental predictions of corporate bankruptcy. *The Accounting Review, 58,* 78–97.

Jordan, J. (1989). The economics of accounting information systems. *American Economic Review, 79,* 140–145.

Jordan, J. (1990). Accounting based divisional performance measurement: Incentives for profit maximization. *Contemporary Accounting Research, 6,* 903–921.

Joyce, E.J. (1976). Expert judgment in audit program planning. *Journal of Accounting Research, 14* (Supplement), 29–60.

Joyce, E.J., & Biddle, G.C. (1981a). Anchoring and adjustment in probabilistic inference in auditing. *Journal of Accounting Research, 19,* 120–145.

Joyce, E.J., & Biddle, G.C. (1981b). Are auditors' judgments sufficiently regressive? *Journal of Accounting Research, 19,* 323–349.

Joyce, E.J., & Libby, R. (1982). Behavioral studies of audit decision making. *Journal of Accounting Literature, 2,* 103–123.

Joyce, E.J., Libby, R., & Sunder, S. (1982). Using the FASB's qualitative characteristics in accounting policy choices. *Journal of Accounting Research, 20,* 654–675.

Kachelmeier, S., Limberg, S., & Schadewald, M. (1991). Fairness in markets: A laboratory investigation. *Journal of Economic Psychology, 12,* 447–464.

Kachelmeier, S., & Messier, W.F. (1990). An investigation of the influence of a non-statistical decision aid on auditor sample size decisions. *The Accounting Review, 65,* 209–226.

Kahneman, D. (1973). *Attention and Effort.* Englewood Cliffs, NJ: Prentice-Hall.

Kahneman, D., Knetsch, J., & Thaler, R. (1986). Fairness as a constraint on profit seeking: Entitlements in the market. *American Economic Review, 76,* 728–741.

Kahneman, D., Slovic, P., & Tversky, A. (Eds.). (1982). *Judgment under Uncertainty: Heuristics and Biases.* Cambridge, UK: Cambridge University Press.

Kahneman, D., & Tversky, A. (1979a). Intuitive prediction: Biases and corrective procedures. *TIMS Studies in Management Science, 12,* 313–327.

Kahneman, D., & Tversky, A. (1979b). Prospect theory: An analysis of decision under risk. *Econometrica, 47,* 263–291.

Kaish, S., & Gilad, B. (Eds.). (1991). *Handbook of Behavioral Economics* (Vols 2a and 2b). Greenwich, CT: JAI Press.

Kanodia, C., Bushman, R., & Dickhaut, J. (1989). Escalation errors and the sunk cost effect: An explanation based on reputation and information asymmetries. *Journal of Accounting Research, 27,* 59–77.

Kaplan, A., Dirlam, L., & Lanzillotti, R. (1958). *Pricing in Big Business.* Washington, D.C.: Brookings.

Kaplan, R.S. (1975). The significance and investigation of cost variances: Survey and extensions. *Journal of Accounting Research, 13,* 311–337.

Kaplan, R.S. (1977). The roles for research and development in auditing. In *Symposium on Auditing Research II* (pp. 3–11). Champaign, IL: University of Illinois.

Kaplan, R.S. (1983). Measuring manufacturing performance: A new challenge for management accounting research. *The Accounting Review, 58,* 686–705.

Kaplan, S.E. (1985). The effect of combining compliance and substantive tasks on auditor consensus. *Journal of Accounting Research, 23,* 871–877.

Kaplan, S.E., Pourciau, S., & Reckers, P.M.J. (1990). An examination of the effect of the president's letter and stock advisory service information on financial decisions. *Behavioral Research in Accounting, 2,* 63–93.

Kaplan, S.E., & Reckers, P.M.J. (1989). An examination of information search during initial audit planning. *Accounting, Organizations and Society, 14,* 539–550.

Keasey, K., & Watson, R. (1989). Consensus and accuracy in accounting studies of decision making: A note on a new measure of consensus. *Accounting, Organizations and Society, 14,* 337–345.

Kelly, K.P., Ribar, G.S., & Willingham, J.J. (1986). Interim report on the development of an expert system for the auditor's loan loss evaluation. In R.P. Srivastava & N.A. Ford (Eds.), *Auditing Symposium VIII: Proceedings of the 1986 Touche Ross/University of Kansas Symposium on Auditing Problems* (pp. 167–181). Lawrence, KS: University of Kansas.

Kennedy, J. (1993). Debiasing audit judgment with accountability: A framework and some experimental results. *Journal of Accounting Research, 31,* 231–245.

Kennedy, J. (1995). Debiasing the curse of knowledge in audit judgment. *The Accounting Review, 70,* 249–274.

Keren, G. (1991). Calibration and probability judgments: Conceptual and methodological issues. *Acta Psychologia, 77,* 217–273.

Kessler, L., & Ashton, R.H. (1981). Feedback and prediction achievement in financial analysis. *Journal of Accounting Research, 19,* 146–162.

Keys, D. (1978). Confidence interval financial statements: An empirical investigation. *Journal of Accounting Research, 16,* 389–399.

Kida, T. (1980). An investigation into auditors' continuity and related qualification judgments. *Journal of Accounting Research, 18,* 506–523.

Kida, T. (1984). The impact of hypothesis testing strategies on auditors' use of judgment data. *Journal of Accounting Research, 22,* 332–340.

King, R.R., & Wallin, D.E. (1990). The effects of antifraud rules and ex post verifiability on managerial disclosures. *Contemporary Accounting Research, 6,* 859–892.

Kinney, W.R. (1975). A decision theory approach to the sampling problem in auditing. *Journal of Accounting Research, 13,* 117–132.

Kinney, W.R. (1983). Quantitative applications in auditing. *Journal of Accounting Literature, 2,* 187–204.

Kinney, W.R. (1986). Audit technology and preference for auditing standards. *Journal of Accounting and Economics, 8,* 73–89.

Kinney, W.R. (1989). Achieved audit risk and the audit outcome space. *Auditing: A Journal of Practice & Theory, 8* (Supplement), 67–84.

Kinney, W.R., & Uecker, W.C. (1982). Mitigating the consequences of anchoring in auditor judgments. *The Accounting Review, 57,* 55–69.

Kirzner, I.M. (1973). *Competition and Entrepreneurship.* Chicago, IL: University of Chicago Press.

Kirzner, I.M. (1979). *Perception, Opportunity, and Profit.* Chicago, IL: University of Chicago Press.

Klammer, T., & Reed, S. (1990). Operating cash flow formats: Does format influence decisions? *Journal of Accounting and Public Policy, 9,* 217–235.

Kleinmuntz, B. (1982). Computational and noncomputational clinical information processing by computer. *Behavioral Science, 27,* 164–175.

Kleinmuntz, B. (1990). Why we still use our heads instead of formulas: Toward an integrative approach. *Psychological Bulletin, 107,* 296–310.

Kleinmuntz, D., & Schkade, D. (1993). Information displays and decision processes. *Psychological Science, 4,* 221–227.

Knez, P., Smith, V., & Williams, A. (1985). Individual rationality, market rationality, and value estimation. *American Economic Review, 75,* (Proceedings) 397–402.

Koonce, L. (1992). A cognitive characterization of audit analytical review. *The Accounting Review, 67,* 59–76.

Kren, L., & Greenstein, S. (1991). In S. Moriarity (Ed.), *Accounting, Communication and Monitoring* (pp. 84–95). Norman, Oklahoma: The University of Oklahoma Center for Economic and Management Research.

Kren, L., & Liao, W.M. (1988). The role of accounting information in the control of organizations: A review of the evidence. *Journal of Accounting Literature, 7,* 280–309.

Kreps, D. (1990). *Game Theory and Economic Modelling.* Oxford, UK: Clarendon Press.

Kreps, D., Milgrom, P., Roberts, J., & Wilson, R. (1982). Rational cooperation in the finitely repeated prisoners' dilemma. *Journal of Economic Theory, 27,* 245–252.

Krogstad, J.L, Ettenson, R.T., & Shanteau, J. (1984). Context and experience in auditors' materiality judgments. *Auditing: A Journal of Practice and Theory, 4,* 54–73.

Lakonishok, J., Shleifer, A., Thaler, R., & Vishny, R. (1991). Window dressing by pension fund managers. *American Economic Review, 81,* 227–231.

Langer, E. (1982). The illusion of control. In D. Kahneman, P. Slovic & A. Tversky (Eds.), *Judgment under Uncertainty: Heuristics and Biases* (pp. 231–238). Cambridge, UK: Cambridge University Press.

Langlois, R.N. (1986). *Economics as a Process.* Cambridge, UK: Cambridge University Press.

Larcker, D., & Lessig, V.P. (1983). An examination of the linear and retrospective process tracing approaches to judgment modeling. *The Accounting Review, 58,* 58–77.

Lawler, E., & Rhode, J.G. (1976). *Information and Control in Organizations.* Pacific Palisades, CA: Goodyear.

Leonard-Barton, D., & Deschamps, I. (1988). Managerial influence in the implementation of new technology. *Management Science, 34,* 1252–1265.

Lere, J.C. (1986). Product pricing based on accounting costs. *The Accounting Review, 61,* 318–324.

Levinthal, D. (1988). A survey of agency models of organizations. *Journal of Economic Behavior and Organization, 9,* 153–185.

Lewis, B.L. (1980). Expert judgment in auditing: An expected utility approach. *Journal of Accounting Research, 18,* 594–602.

Lewis, B.L., Patton, J.M., & Green, S.L. (1988). The effects of information choice and information use on analysts' predictions of municipal bond rating changes. *The Accounting Review, 63,* 270–282.

Lewis, B.L., Shields, M.D., & Young, S.M. (1983). Evaluating human judgments and decision aids. *Journal of Accounting Research, 21,* 271–285.

Libby, R. (1975a). Accounting ratios and the prediction of failure: Some behavioral evidence. *Journal of Accounting Research, 13,* 150–161.

Libby, R. (1975b). The use of simulated decision makers in information evaluation. *The Accounting Review, 50,* 475–489.

Libby, R. (1976a). Man versus model of man: Some conflicting evidence. *Organizational Behavior and Human Performance, 16,* 1–12.

Libby, R. (1976b). Man versus model of man: The need for a nonlinear model. *Organizational Behavior and Human Performance, 16,* 23–26.

Libby, R. (1976c). Discussion of cognitive changes induced by accounting changes: Experimental evidence on the functional fixation hypothesis. *Journal of Accounting Research, 14,* 18–24.

Libby, R. (1979a). The impact of uncertainty reporting on the loan decision. *Journal of Accounting Research, 17,* 35–57.

Libby, R. (1979b). Bankers' and auditors' perceptions of the message communicated by the audit report. *Journal of Accounting Research, 17,* 99–122.

Libby, R. (1981). *Accounting and Human Information Processing: Theory and Applications.* Englewood Cliffs, NJ: Prentice-Hall.

Libby, R. (1983). Determinants of performance in accounting decisions. In K.R. Bindon (Ed.), *1983 Accounting Research Convocation* (pp. 77–88). Tuscaloosa, AL: University of Alabama.

Libby, R. (1985). Availability and the generation of hypotheses in analytical review. *Journal of Accounting Research, 23,* 648–667.

Libby, R. (1987). Discussant's comments: Human judgment: Limitations and opportunities for research. In A. Bailey (Ed.), *Auditor Productivity in the Year 2000: Proceedings of the Arthur Young Professors' Roundtable* (pp. 99–103). Reston, VA: Arthur Young.

Libby, R. (1990). Experimental research and the distinctive features of accounting settings. In T. Frecka (Ed.), *The State of Accounting Research as We Enter the 1990s* (pp. 126–147). Urbana, IL: University of Illinois.

Libby, R., Artman, J.T., & Willingham, J.J. (1985). Process susceptibility, control risk, and audit planning. *The Accounting Review, 60,* 212–230.

Libby, R., & Blashfield, R. (1978). Performance of a composite as a function of the number of judges. *Organizational Behavior and Human Performance, 21,* 121–129.

Libby, R., & Frederick, D.M. (1990). Experience and the ability to explain audit findings. *Journal of Accounting Research, 28,* 348–367.

Libby, R., & Lewis, B.L. (1977). Human information processing research in accounting: The state of the art. *Accounting, Organizations and Society, 2,* 245–268.

Libby, R., & Lewis, B.L. (1982). Human information processing research in accounting: The state of the art in 1982. *Accounting, Organizations and Society, 7,* 231–285.

Libby, R., & Libby, P.A. (1989). Expert measurement and mechanical combination in control reliance decisions. *The Accounting Review, 64,* 729–747.

Libby, R., & Lipe, M. (1992). Incentives, effort, and the cognitive processes involved in accounting-related judgments. *Journal of Accounting Research, 30,* 249–273.

Libby, R. & Luft, J. (1993). Determinants of judgment performance in accounting settings: Ability, knowledge, motivation, and environment. *Accounting, Organizations and Society, 18,* 425–450.

Libby, R., & Tan, H.T. (1994). Modeling the determinants of audit expertise. *Accounting, Organizations and Society, 19,* 701–716.

Libby, R., Trotman, K., & Zimmer, I. (1987). Member variation, recognition of expertise, and group performance. *Journal of Applied Psychology, 72,* 81–87.

Liebenstein, H. (1976). *Beyond Economic Man: A New Foundation for Microeconomics.* Cambridge, MA: Harvard University Press.

Liebenstein, H. (1987). *Inside the Firm: The Inefficiencies of Hierarchy.* Cambridge, MA: Harvard University Press.

Loasby, B.J. (1990). *Equilibrium and Evolution.* Manchester, UK: Manchester University Press.

Locke, E.A., & Latham, G.P. (1990). *Goal Setting and Task Performance.* New York: McGraw-Hill.

Locke, E.A., Saari, L.M., Shaw, K.N., & Latham, G.P. (1981). Goal setting and task performance: 1969–1980. *Psychological Bulletin, 90,* 125–152.

Locke, E.A., & Schweiger, D.M. (1979). Participation in decision-making: One more look. In B.M. Staw (Ed.), *Research in Organizational Behavior* (pp. 265–339). Greenwich, CT: JAI Press.

Lord, A.T. (1992). Pressure: A methodological consideration for behavioral research in auditing. *Auditing: A Journal of Practice & Theory, 11,* 89–108.

Luconi, F.L., Malone, T.W., & Scott Morton, M.S. (1986). Expert systems: The next challenge for managers. *Sloan Management Review, 27,* 7–14.

Luft, J. (1992). Bonus and penalty incentives: Contract choice by employees. *Journal of Accounting and Economics, 18,* 181–206.

Lundholm, R. (1991). What affects the efficiency of a market? Some answers from the laboratory. *The Accounting Review, 66,* 486–515.

Lyness, K.S., & Cornelius, E.T. (1982). A comparison of holistic and decomposed judgment strategies in a performance rating simulation. *Organizational Behavior and Human Performance, 29,* 21–38.

Machlup, F. (1946). Marginal analysis and empirical research. *The American Economic Review, 36,* 519–554.

Magee, R.P. (1977). The usefulness of commonality information in cost control decisions. *The Accounting Review, 52,* 869–880.

Magee, R.P., & Dickhaut, J.W. (1978). Effect of compensation plans on heuristics in cost variance investigations. *Journal of Accounting Research, 16,* 292–314.

Maines, L.A. (1990). The effect of forecast redundancy on judgments of a consensus forecast's expected accuracy. *Journal of Accounting Research, 28* (Supplement), 29–47.

Maines, L.A. (1994). The role of behavioral accounting research in financial accounting standard setting. Working Paper, Duke University. Forthcoming in *Behavioral Research in Accounting.*

March, J.G. (1978). Bounded rationality, ambiguity, and the engineering of choice. *Bell Journal of Economics, 9,* 587–608.

March, J.G. (1988). *Decisions and Organizations.* Oxford, UK: Basil Blackwell.

March, J.G., & Olsen, J.P. (1976). *Ambiguity and Choice in Organizations.* Bergen, Norway: Universitetsforlaget.

March, J.G., & Sevon, G. (1988). Behavioral perspectives on theories of the firm. In W.F. Van Raaij, G.M. vanVeldhoven, & K.E. Warneryd, (Eds.), *Handbook of Economic Psychology* (pp. 368–402). Dordrecht, Netherlands: Kluwer.

March, J.G., & Shapira, Z. (1987). Managerial perspectives on risk and risk taking. *Management Science, 33,* 1404–1418.

March, J.G., & Shapira, Z. (1992). Variable risk preferences and the focus of attention. *Psychological Review, 99,* 172–183.

March, J.G., & Simon, H.A. (1958). *Organizations.* New York: Wiley.

Marchant, G. (1989). Analogical reasoning and hypothesis generation in auditing. *The Accounting Review, 64,* 500–513.

Marchant, G. (1990). Discussion of determinants of audit expertise. *Journal of Accounting Research, 28* (Supplement), 21–28.

Marchant, G., Robinson, J.R., Anderson, U., & Schadewald, M.S. (1989). A cognitive model of tax problem solving. *Advances in Taxation, 2,* 1–20.

Marchant, G., Robinson, J.R. Anderson, U., & Schadewald, M.S. (1991). Analogical transfer and expertise in legal reasoning. *Organizational Behavior and Human Decision Process, 48,* 272–290.

Markus, M.L., & Robey, D. (1988). Information technology and organizational change: Causal structure in theory and research. *Management Science, 34,* 583–598.

Mason, A.K., & Gibbins, M. (1991). Judgment and U.S. accounting standards. *Accounting Horizons, 5,* 14–24.

Mautz, R., & Sharaf, H. (1961). *The Philosophy of Auditing.* Sarasota, FL: American Accounting Association.

Mayper, A.G. (1982). Consensus of auditors' materiality judgments of internal accounting control weaknesses. *Journal of Accounting Research, 20,* 773–783.

Mayper, A.G., Doucet, M.S., & Warren, C.S. (1989). Auditors' materiality judgments of internal accounting control weaknesses. *Auditing: A Journal of Practice & Theory, 9,* 72–86.

McCabe, K.A. (1989). Fiat money as a store of value in an experimental market. *Journal of Economic Behavior and Organization, 12,* 215–231.

McDaniel, L.S. (1990). The effects of time pressure and audit program structure on audit performance. *Journal of Accounting Research, 28,* 267–285.

McIntyre, E. (1973). Current cost financial statements and common stock investment decisions. *The Accounting Review, 48,* 575–585.

McKelvey, R.D., & Palfrey, T.R. (1990). An experimental study of the centipede game. Working Paper, California Institute of Technology.

McNair, C.J. (1991). Proper compromises: The management control dilemma in public accounting and its impact on auditor behavior. *Accounting, Organizations and Society, 16,* 635–653.

Mear, R., & Firth, M. (1987a). Cue usage and self-insight of financial analysts. *The Accounting Review, 62,* 176–182.

Mear, R., & Firth, M. (1987b). Assessing the accuracy of financial analyst security return predictions. *Accounting, Organizations and Society, 12,* 331–340.

Mear, R., & Firth, M. (1988). Risk perceptions of financial analysts and the use of market and accounting data. *Accounting and Business Research, 18,* 335–340.

Mear, R., & Firth, M. (1990). A parsimonious description of individual differences in financial analyst judgment. *Journal of Accounting, Auditing and Finance, 5,* 501–526.

Medin, D.L., & Edelson, S.M. (1988). Problem structure and the use of base-rate information from experience. *Journal of Experimental Psychology: General, 117,* 68–85.

Meehl, P. (1954). *Clinical versus Statistical Prediction: A Theoretical Analysis and a Review of the Evidence.* Minneapolis, MN: University of Minnesota Press.

Meixner, W.F., & Welker, R.B. (1988). Judgment consensus and auditor experience: An examination of organizational relations. *The Accounting Review, 63,* 505–513.

Meservy, R.D., Bailey, A.D., & Johnson, P.E. (1986). Internal control evaluation: A computational model of the review process. *Auditing: A Journal of Practice & Theory, 6,* 44–74.

Messier, W.F. (1983). The effect of experience and firm type on materiality/disclosure judgments. *Journal of Accounting Research, 21,* 611–618.

Messier, W.F. (1990). Discussion of a cognitive computational model of risk hypothesis generation. *Journal of Accounting Research, 28* (Supplement), 104–109.

Messier, W.F., & Hansen, J.V. (1984). Expert systems in accounting and auditing: A framework and review. In E. Joyce & S. Moriarity (Eds.), *Decision Making and Accounting: Current Research* (pp. 182–202). Norman, OK: University of Oklahoma.

Messier, W.F., & Hansen, J.V. (1987). Expert systems in auditing: The state of the art. *Auditing: A Journal of Practice and Theory, 7,* 94–105.

Messier, W.F., & Hansen, J.V. (1988). Inducing rules for expert systems development: An example using default and bankruptcy data. *Management Science, 34,* 1403–1416.

Messier, W.F., & Hansen, J.V. (1992). A case study and field evaluation of EDP-XPERT. *International Journal of Intelligent Systems in Accounting, Finance and Management, 1,* 173–185.

Messier, W.F., & Quilliam, W.C. (1992). The effect of accountability on judgment: Development of hypotheses for auditing. *Auditing: A Journal of Practice & Theory, 11* (Supplement), 123–138.

Messier, W.F., & Schneider, A. (1988). A hierarchical approach to the external auditor's evaluation of the internal auditing function. *Contemporary Accounting Research, 4,* 337–353.

Michaelsen, R.H., & Messier, W.F. (1987). Expert systems in taxation. *The Journal of the American Taxation Association, 8,* 7–21.

Mock, T.J., & Turner, J.L. (1981). *Internal accounting control evaluation and auditor judgment.* Audit Research Monograph No. 3. New York, AICPA.

Mock, T.J., & Vasarhelyi, M.A. (1978). A synthesis of the information economics and lens models. *Journal of Accounting Research, 16,* 414–423.

Mock, T.J., & Vasarhelyi, M.A. (1984). Context, findings, and method in cognitive style research: A comparative study. In S. Moriarity & E.J. Joyce (Eds.), *Decision Making and Accounting: Current Research.* Norman, OK: University of Oklahoma.

Moeckel, C. (1990). The effects of experience on auditors' memory errors. *Journal of Accounting Research, 28,* 368–387.

Moeckel, C. (1991). Two factors affecting an auditor's ability to integrate audit evidence. *Contemporary Accounting Research, 8,* 270–292.

Moeckel, C., & Plumlee, R.D. (1989). Auditors' confidence in accurate and inaccurate recognition of audit evidence. *The Accounting Review, 64,* 653–666.

Moeckel, C., & Plumlee, R.D. (1990). The effect of explicit assignment of responsibility and the quality of workpaper reviews. Working Paper, Arizona State University.

Moriarity, S. (1979). Communicating financial information through multidimensional graphics. *Journal of Accounting Research, 17,* 205–224.

Moriarity, S., & Barron, F.H. (1976). Modeling the materiality judgments of audit partners. *Journal of Accounting Research, 14,* 320–341.

Moriarity, S., & Barron, F.H. (1979). A judgment-based definition of materiality. *Journal of Accounting Research, 17* (Supplement), 114–147.

Morris, D., & Noreen, E. (1991). *Beyond mk I ABC systems.* Working Paper, INSEAD.

Morris, M.H., & Nichols, W.D. (1988). Consistency exceptions, materiality judgments and audit firm structure. *The Accounting Review, 63,* 237–254.

Moser, D. (1989). The effects of output interference, availability, and accounting information on investors' predictive judgments. *The Accounting Review, 64,* 433–448.

Murphy, D., & Brown, C.E. (1992). The use of advanced information technology in audit planning. *International Journal of Intelligent Systems in Accounting, Finance and Management, 1,* 189–193.

Mutchler, J. (1985). A multivariate analysis of the auditor's going-concern opinion decision. *Journal of Accounting Research, 23,* 668–682.

Nagel, E. (1963). Assumptions in economic theory. *The American Economic Review, 53,* 211–219.

Neelin, J., Sonnenschein, H., & Spiegel, M. (1988). A further test of noncooperative bargaining theory. *The American Economic Review, 78,* 824–836.

Nelson, M.W. (1993). The effects of error frequency and accounting knowledge on error diagnosis in analytical review. *The Accounting Review, 68,* 803–824.

Nelson, M.W. (1994). The learning and application of frequency knowledge in audit judgment. *Journal of Accounting Literature, 13,* 185–211.

Nelson, R.R., & Winter, S.G. (1982). *An Evolutionary Theory of Economic Change.* Cambridge, MA: Belknap.

Neuberg, S., & Fiske, S. (1987). Motivational influences on impression formation: Outcome dependency, accuracy-driven attention, and individuating processes. *Journal of Personality and Social Psychology, 53,* 431–444.

Newell, A., & Simon, H. (1972). *Human Problem Solving.* Englewood Cliffs, N.J., Prentice-Hall.

Newton, L.K. (1977). The risk factor in materiality decisions. *The Accounting Review, 52,* 97–108.

Nicholson, W. (1983). *Intermediate Microeconomics and Its Applications.* Chicago, IL: Dryden.

Nilsson, L. (1987). Motivated memory: Dissociation between performance data and subjective reports. *Psychological Research, 49,* 183–188.

Nisbett, R.E., & Wilson, T.D. (1977). Telling more than we can know: Verbal reports on mental processes. *Psychological Review, 84,* 231–259.

Nisbett, R.E., & Ross, L. (1980). Human inference: Strategies and shortcomings of social judgment. Englewood Cliffs, NJ: Prentice-Hall.

O'Brien, J., & Srivastava, S. (1990). Arbitrage and informational efficiency: Theory and experimental evidence. Working Paper, Carnegie-Mellon University.

O'Brien, J., & Srivastava, S. (1993). Liquidity and persistence of arbitrage in experimental options markets. In D. Friedman & J. Rust (Eds.), *The Double Auction Market: Proceedings of the Santa Fe Institute Conference on Price Dynamics in Auction Markets* (pp. 397–419). Reading, MA: Addison-Wesley.

O'Keefe, R.M., Balci, O., & Smith, E.P. (1987). Validating expert system performance. *IEEE Expert, 2,* 81–89.

O'Leary, D.E. (1987). Validation of expert systems – with applications to auditing and accounting expert systems. *Decision Sciences, 18,* 468–486.

Oliver, B. (1972). A study of confidence interval financial statements. *Journal of Accounting Research, 10,* 154–166.

Onsi, M. (1973). Factor analysis of behavioral variables affecting budgetary slack. *The Accounting Review, 48,* 535–548.

Oskamp, S. (1965). Overconfidence in case-study judgments. *Journal of Consulting Psychology, 29,* 261–265.

Page, R.A., & Dyer, W.G. (1990). The politics of radical technical innovations. In L.R. Gomez-Mejia & M.W. Lawless (Eds.), *Organizational Issues in High Technology Management.* Greenwich, CT: JAI Press.

Pankoff, L., & Virgil, R. (1970). Some preliminary findings from a laboratory experiment on the usefulness of financial accounting information to security analysts. *Journal of Accounting Research, 8,* 1–48.

Pany, K., & Reckers, P.M.J. (1987). Within- vs. between-subject experimental designs: A study of demand effects. *Auditing: A Journal of Practice & Theory, 7,* 39–53.

Pany, K., & Smith, C.H. (1982). Auditor association with quarterly financial information: An empirical test. *Journal of Accounting Research, 20,* 472–481.

Paquette, L., & Kida, T. (1988). The effect of decision strategy and task complexity on decision performance. *Organizational Behavior and Human Decision Processes, 41,* 128–142.

Payne, J.W., Bettman, J.R., & Johnson, E.J. (1988). Adaptive strategy selection in decision making. *Journal of Experimental Psychology: Learning, Memory, and Cognition, 14,* 534–552.

Payne, J.W., Bettman, J.R., & Johnson, E.J. (1992). Behavioral decision research: A constructive processing perspective. *Annual Review of Psychology, 43,* 87–131.

Peat, Marwick, Mitchell & Co. (1976). *Research Opportunities in Auditing.* New York: Author.

Peters, J.M. (1990). A cognitive computational model of risk hypothesis generation. *Journal of Accounting Research, 28* (Supplement), 83–103.

Peters, J.M., Lewis, B.L., & Dhar, V. (1989). Assessing inherent risk during audit planning: The development of a knowledge-based model. *Accounting, Organizations and Society, 14,* 359–378.

Pincus, K.V. (1990). Audit judgment consensus: A model for dichotomous decisions. *Auditing: A Journal of Practice & Theory, 9,* 1–20.

Pincus, K.V. (1990). Auditor individual differences and fairness of presentation judgments. *Auditing: A Journal of Practice & Theory, 9,* 150–166.

Pitz, G.F. (1970). On the processing of information: Probabilistic and otherwise. *Acta Psychologica, 34,* 201–213.

Plott, C. (1982). Industrial organizational theory and experimental economics. *Journal of Economic Literature, 20,* 1485–1527.

Plott, C., & Sunder, S. (1988). Rational expectations and the aggregation of diverse information in laboratory security markets. *Econometrica, 56,* 1085–1118.

Plumlee, D. (1985). The standard of objectivity for internal auditors: Memory and bias effects. *Journal of Accounting Research, 23,* 683–699.

Porter, D., & Smith, V. (1989). The scope of bubbles in experimental asset markets. Working Paper: University of Arizona.

Prasnikar, V., & Roth, A. (1989). Perceptions of fairness and considerations of strategy: Some experimental data. Working Paper: University of Pittsburgh.

Rapoport, A., & Wallsten, T.S. (1972). Individual decision behavior. *Annual Review of Psychology, 23,* 131–176.

Ravinder, H.V., Kleinmuntz, D.N., & Dyer, J.S. (1988). The reliability of subjective probabilities obtained through decomposition. *Management Science, 34,* 186–199.

Rebele, J.E., Heintz, J.S., & Briden, G.E. (1988). Independent auditor sensitivity to evidence reliability. *Auditing: A Journal of Practice & Theory, 8,* 43–52.

Rennie, M. (1991). Internal control system knowledge and mental models. Working Paper, University of Regina.

Ricchiute, D. (1992). Working-paper order effects and auditors' going concern decisions. *The Accounting Review, 67,* 46–58.

Richardson, A.J., & Gibbins, M. (1988). Behavioral research on the production and use of financial information. In K. Ferris (Ed.), *Behavioral Accounting Research: A Critical Analysis* (pp. 15–45). Columbus, OH: Century VII Publishing.

Roberts, J. (1987). Perfectly and imperfectly competitive markets. In J. Eatwell, M. Milgate, & P. Newman (Eds.), *The New Palgrave: A Dictionary of Economics* (pp. 837–841). London: Macmillan.

Rockness, H. 1977. Expectancy theory in a budgetary setting: An experimental examination. *The Accounting Review, 52,* 893–903.

Rohrmann, B. (1986). Evaluating the usefulness of decision aids: A methodological perspective. In B. Brehmer, H. Jungermann, P. Lourens, & G. Sevon (Eds.), *New Directions in Research on Decision Making* (pp. 363–381). Amsterdam: North-Holland.

Ronen, J., & Livingston, J. (1975). An expectancy theory approach to the motivational impact of budgets. *The Accounting Review, 50,* 671–685.

Ross, S. (1973). The economic theory of agency: The principal's problem. *The American Economic Review, 63,* 134–139.

Ross, S. (1976a). The arbitrage theory of capital asset pricing. *Journal of Economic Theory, 13,* 341–360.

Ross, S. (1976b). Return, risk, and arbitrage. In I. Friend & J. Bicksler (Eds.), *Risk and Return in Finance* (pp. 189–218). Cambridge, MA: Ballinger.

Roth, A. (1986). Laboratory experimentation in economics. *Economics and Philosophy, 2,* 245–273.

Roth, A. (1987). *Laboratory Experimentation in Economics: Six Points of View.* Cambridge, MA: Cambridge University Press.

Roth, A. (1988). Laboratory experimentation in economics: A methodological overview. *The Economic Journal, 98,* 974–1031.

Roth A. (1991). Bargaining experiments. *Handbook of Experimental Economics,* forthcoming.

Roy, D. (1952). Quota restriction and goldbricking in a machine shop. *The American Journal of Sociology, 57,* 427–442.

Roy, D. (1954). Efficiency and 'the fix': Informal intergroup relations in a piecework machine shop. *The American Journal of Sociology, 60,* 255–266.

Rubenstein, A. (1982). Perfect equilibrium in a bargaining model. *Econometrica, 50,* 97–109.

Russell, T., & Thaler, R. (1985). The relevance of quasi-rationality in competitive markets. *The American Economic Review, 75,* 1071–1081.

Sami, H., & Schwartz, B. (1992). Alternative pension liability disclosure and the effect on credit evaluation: An experiment. *Behavioral Research in Accounting, 4,* 49–62.

Savage, L.J. (1954). *The Foundations of Statistics.* New York: Wiley.

Savich, R. (1977). The use of accounting information in decision making. *The Accounting Review, 52,* 642–652.

Schepanski, A. (1983). Tests of theories of information processing behavior in credit judgment. *The Accounting Review, 58,* 581–599.

Schiff, M., & Lewin, A.Y. (1970). The impact of budgets on people. *The Accounting Review, 45,* 259–268.

Schipper, K. (1991). Analysts' forecasts. *Accounting Horizons, 5,* 105–121.

Schmidt, F.L., Hunter, J.E., & Outerbridge, A.N. (1986). Impact of job experience and ability on job knowledge, work sample performance, and supervisory ratings of job performance. *Journal of Applied Psychology, 71,* 432–439.

Schneider, A. (1984). Modeling external auditors' evaluations of internal auditing. *Journal of Accounting Research, 22,* 657–678.

Schneider, A. (1985). The reliance of external auditors on the internal audit function. *Journal of Accounting Research, 23,* 911–919.

Schoemaker, P.J.H. (1982). The expected utility model: Its variants, purposes, evidence and limitations. *Journal of Economic Literature, 20,* 529–563.

Schultz, J.J., & Reckers, P.M.J. (1981). The impact of group processing on selected audit disclosure decisions. *Journal of Accounting Research, 19,* 482–501.

Schum, D., & Martin, A. (1982). Formal and empirical research on cascaded inference in jurisprudence. *Law & Society Review, 17,* 105–151.

Schumpeter, J.A. (1976). *Capitalism, Socialism and Democracy,* (5th Edition). London: George Allen & Unwin. Originally published in 1934.

Schwartz, R. (1988). *Equity Markets: Structure, Trading, and Performance.* New York: Harper and Row.

Schwartz, S., Griffin, T., & Fox, J. (1989). Clinical expert systems versus linear models: Do we really have to choose? *Behavioral Science, 34,* 305–311.

Selling, T., & Shank, J. (1989). Linear versus process tracing approaches to judgment modelling: A new perspective on cue importance. *Accounting, Organizations and Society, 14,* 65–77.

Selto, F.H., & Cooper, J.C. (1990). Control of risk attitude in experimental accounting research. *Journal of Accounting Literature, 9,* 229–264.

Sevcik, G., Shapiro, B., & Waller, W. (1995). *Cost-plus pricing in experimental markets: Effects of full versus variable costing on profits and survival.* Research in Progress, University of Arizona.

Shafer, G. (1985). Conditional probability. *International Statistical Review, 53,* 261–277.

Sharda, R., Barr, S.H., & McDonnell, J.C. (1988). Decision support system effectiveness: A review and an empirical test. *Management Science, 34,* 139–159.

Shields, M.D. (1983). Effects of information supply and demand on judgment accuracy: Evidence from corporate managers. *The Accounting Review, 73,* 429–442.

Shields, M.D., Chow, S., & Whittington, O.R. (1989). The effects of state risk and controllability filters on compensation contract and effort choice. *Abacus, 25,* 39–55.

Shields, M.D., Solomon, I., & Waller, W.S. (1987). Effects of alternative sample space representations on the accuracy of auditors' uncertainty judgments. *Accounting, Organizations and Society, 12,* 375–388.

Shields, M.D., Solomon, I., & Waller, W.S. (1988). Auditors' usage of unaudited book values when making presampling audit value estimates. *Contemporary Accounting Research, 5,* 1–18.

Shields, M.D., & Waller, W.S. (1988). An experimental labor market study of accounting variables in employment contracting. *Accounting, Organizations and Society, 13,* 581–594.

Shields, M.D., & Young, S.M. (1993). Antecedents and consequences of participative budgeting: Evidence on the effects of asymmetrical information. *Journal of Management Accounting Research, 5,* 265–280.

Shpilberg, D., & Graham, L.E. (1986). Developing ExperTAX: An expert system for corporate tax accrual and planning. *Auditing: A Journal of Practice and Theory, 6,* 75–94.

Simnett, R., & Trotman, K. (1989). Auditor versus model: Information choice and information processing. *The Accounting Review, 64,* 514–528.

Simon, H.A. (1955). A behavioral model of rational choice. *Quarterly Journal of Economics, 69,* 99–118.

Simon, H.A. (1956). Rational choice and the structure of the environment. *Psychological Review, 63,* 129–138.

Simon, H.A. (1957). *Models of Man.* New York: Wiley.

Simon, H.A. (1959). Theories of decision making in economics and behavioral science. *The American Economic Review, 49,* 253–283.

Simon, H.A. (1960). *The New Science of Management.* New York: Harper and Row.

Simon, H.A. (1976a). From substantive to procedural rationality. In S.J. Latsis (Ed.), *Method and Appraisal in Economics* (pp. 129–148). Cambridge, UK: Cambridge University Press.

Simon, H.A. (1976b). *Administrative Behavior: A Study of Decision-making Processes in Administrative Organization.* New York: Free Press. First published in 1945.

Simon, H.A. (1978a). Rationality as process and as product of thought. *The American Economic Review, 68,* 1–16.

Simon, H.A. (1978b). On how to decide what to do. *The Bell Journal of Economics, 9,* 494–507.

Simon, H.A. (1979). Rational decision making in business organizations. *The American Economic Review, 69,* 493–513.

Simon, H.A. (1982). *Models of Bounded Rationality: Behavioral Economics and Business Organization.* Cambridge, MA: MIT Press.

Simon, H.A. (1983). *Reason in Human Affairs.* Oxford, UK: Basil Blackwell.

Simon, H.A. (1986). Rationality in psychology and economics. *The Journal of Business, 59,* 209–224.

Simon, H.A. (1987a). Behavioral economics. In J. Eatwell, M. Milgate, & P. Newman, (Eds.), *The New Palgrave: A Dictionary of Economics* (pp. 221–225). London: Macmillan.

Simon, H.A. (1987b). Bounded rationality. In J. Eatwell, M. Milgate, & P. Newman (Eds.), *The New Palgrave: A Dictionary of Economics* (pp. 266–267). London: Macmillan.

Slovic, P. (1969). Analyzing the expert judge: A descriptive study of a stockbroker's decision processes. *Journal of Applied Psychology, 53,* 255–263.

Slovic, P., Fleissner, D., & Bauman, W. (1972). Analyzing the use of information in investment decision making: A methodological proposal. *The Journal of Business, 45,* 283–301.

Slovic, P., & Lichtenstein, S. (1971). Comparison of Bayesian and regression approaches to the study of information processing in judgment. *Organizational Behavior and Human Performance, 6,* 649–744.

Smith, J.F., & Kida, T. (1991). Heuristics and biases: Expertise and task realism in auditing. *Psychological Bulletin, 109,* 472–489.

Smith, V.L. (1981). An empirical study of decentralized institutions of monopoly restraint. In G. Horwich & J. Quirk (Eds.), *Essays in Contemporary Fields of Economics* (pp. 83–106). W. Lafayette, IN: Purdue University Press.

Smith, V.L. (1982). Microeconomic systems as an experimental science. *The American Economic Review, 72,* 923–955.

Smith, V.L. (1989). Theory, experiment, and economics. *Journal of Economic Perspectives, 3,* 151–169.

Smith, V.L. (1991). *Papers in Experimental Economics.* Cambridge, UK: Cambridge University Press.

Smith, V.L. (1991). Rational choice: The contrast between economics and psychology. *Journal of Political Economy, 99,* 877–897.

Smith, V.L., Schatzberg, J., & Waller, W. (1987). Experimental economics and auditing. *Auditing: A Journal of Practice and Theory, 7,* 71–93.

Smith, V.L., Suchanek, G., & Williams, A. (1988). Bubbles, crashes, and endogenous expectations in experimental spot asset markets. *Econometrica, 56,* 1119–1151.

Snapper, K.J., & Peterson, C.R. (1971). Information seeking and data diagnosticity. *Journal of Experimental Psychology, 87,* 429–433.

Solomon, I. (1982). Probability assessment by individual auditors and audit teams: An empirical investigation. *Journal of Accounting Research, 20,* 689–710.

Solomon, I. (1987). Multi-auditor judgment/decision making research. *Journal of Accounting Literature, 6,* 1–25.

Solomon, I., Ariyo, A., & Tomassini, L.A. (1985). Contextual effects on the calibration of probabilistic judgments. *Journal of Applied Psychology, 70,* 528–532.

Solomon, I., Krogstad, J.L., Romney, M.B. & Tomassini, L.A. (1982). Auditors' prior probability distributions for account balances. *Accounting, Organizations and Society, 7,* 27–42.

Solomon, I., & Shields, M.D. *Judgment and decision-making research in auditing.* Chapter 6, this volume.

Spires, E. (1991). Auditors' evaluation of test-of-control strength. *The Accounting Review, 66,* 259–276.

Srinidhi, B.N., & Vasarhelyi, M.A. (1986). Auditor judgment concerning establishment of substantive tests based on internal control reliability. *Auditing: A Journal of Practice & Theory, 5,* 64–76.

Stahl, I. (1972). *Bargaining Theory.* Stockholm, Sweden: Stockholm School of Economics.

Stallman, J. (1969). Toward experimental criteria for judging disclosure improvement. *Journal of Accounting Research, 7,* 29–43.

Staw, B. (1976). Knee-deep in the big muddy: A study of escalating commitment to a chosen course of action. *Organizational Behavior and Human Performance, 16,* 27–44.

Staw, B., McKechnie, P., & Puffer, S. (1983). The justification of organizational performance. *Administrative Science Quarterly, 28,* 582–600.

Stedry, A.C. (1960). *Budget Control and Cost Behavior.* Englewood Cliffs, NJ: Prentice-Hall.

Steinbart, P. (1987). Materiality: A case study using expert systems. *The Accounting Review, 62,* 97–116.

Sternberg, R. (1984). Toward a triarchic theory of human intelligence. *The Behavioral and Brain Sciences, 7,* 269–315.

Stigler, G.J. (1957). Perfect competition, historically contemplated. *Journal of Political Economy, 65,* 1–17.

Stigler, G.J. (1987). Competition. In J. Eatwell, M. Milgate, & P. Newman (Eds.), *The New Palgrave: A Dictionary of Economics* (pp. 531–536). London: Macmillan.

Stock, D., & Watson, C. (1984). Human judgment accuracy, multidimensional graphics, and humans versus models. *Journal of Accounting Research, 22,* 192–206.

Strawser, J.R. (1991). The role of accountant reports in users' decision-making processes: A review of empirical research. *Journal of Accounting Literature, 10,* 181–208.

Stringer, K.W. (1975). A statistical technique for analytic review. *Journal of Accounting Research, 13* (Supplement), 1–9.

Stringer, K.W., & Stewart, T.R. (1986). *Statistical Techniques for Analytic Review in Auditing.* New York: Wiley.

Sullivan, J.D., Gnospelius, R.A., Defliese, P.L., & Jaenicke, H.R. (1985). *Montgomery's Auditing* (10th Edition). New York: Wiley.

Sundem, G.L. (1981). Future directions in management accounting research. *Accounting Research Convocation.* Tuscaloosa, AL: University of Alabama.

Swieringa, R.J., Dyckman, T.R., & Hoskin, R. (1979). Empirical evidence about the effects of an accounting change on information processing. In T. Burns, (Ed.), *Behavioral Experiments in Accounting II* (pp. 225–259). Columbus, OH: Ohio State University Press.

Swieringa, R.J., Gibbins, M., Larsson, L., & Sweeney, J.L. (1976). Experiments in the heuristics of human information processing. *Journal of Accounting Research, 14* (Supplement), 159–187.

Swieringa, R.J., & Weick, K.E. (1982). An assessment of laboratory experiments in accounting. *Journal of Accounting Research, 20* (Supplement), 56–101.

Tabor, R.H. (1983). Internal control evaluations and audit program revisions: Some additional evidence. *Journal of Accounting Research, 21,* 348–354.

Taylor, F.W. (1967). The Principles of Scientific Management. New York: W.W. Norton. First Published in 1911.

Terborg, J.R., & Miller, H.E. (1978). Motivation, behavior, and performance: A closer examination of goal setting and monetary incentives. *Journal of Applied Psychology, 63,* 29–39.

Tetlock, P.E. (1985). Accountability: The neglected social context of judgment and choice. *Research in Organizational Behavior, 7,* 297–332.

Thaler, R.H. (1992). *The Winner's Curse: Paradoxes and Anomalies of Economic Life.* New York: Free Press.

Tomassini, L.A., Solomon, I., Romney, M.B., & Krogstad, J.L. (1982). Calibration of auditors' probabilistic judgments: Some empirical evidence. *Organizational Behavior and Human Performance, 29,* 391–406.

Trotman, K.T. (1985). The review process and the accuracy of auditor judgments. *Journal of Accounting Research, 23,* 740–752.

Trotman, K.T., & Wood, R. (1991). A meta-analysis of studies on internal control judgments. *Journal of Accounting Research, 29,* 180–192.

Trotman, K.T., & Yetton, P.W. (1985). The effect of the review process on auditor judgments. *Journal of Accounting Research, 23,* 256–267.

Tubbs, R.M. (1992). The effect of experience on the auditor's organization and amount of knowledge. *The Accounting Review, 67,* 783–801.

Tubbs, R.M., Messier, W.F., & Knechel, W.R. (1990). Recency effects in auditors' belief-revision processes. *The Accounting Review, 65,* 452–460.

Turner, M.J., & Hilton, R.W. (1989). Use of accounting product-costing systems in making production decisions. *Journal of Accounting Research, 27,* 297–312.

Tversky, A. (1977). Features of similarity. *Psychological Review, 84,* 327–352.

Tversky, A., & Kahneman, D. (1971). Belief in the law of small numbers. *Psychological Bulletin, 76,* 105–110.

Tversky, A., & Kahneman, D. (1974). Judgment under uncertainty: Heuristics and biases. *Science, 185,* 1124–1131.

Tversky, A., & Kahneman, D. (1987). Rational choice and the framing of decisions. In R. Hogarth & M. Reder (Eds.), *Rational Choice: The Contrast Between Economics and Psychology* (pp. 67–94). Chicago, IL: University of Chicago Press.

Tversky, A., & Sattath, S. (1979). Preference trees. *Psychological Review, 86,* 542–578.

Uecker, W.C. (1978). A behavioral study of information system choice. *Journal of Accounting Research, 16,* 169–189.

Uecker, W.C. (1980). The effects of knowledge of the user's decision model in simplified information evaluation. *Journal of Accounting Research, 18,* 191–213.

Uecker, W.C., & Kinney, W.R. (1977). Judgmental evaluation of sample results: A study of the type and severity of errors made by practicing CPAs. *Accounting, Organizations and Society, 2,* 269–275.

United States General Accounting Office. (1991). *Failed Banks: Accounting and Auditing Reforms Urgently Needed.* (GAO/AFMD-91–43, April 1991).

van Breda, M., & Ferris, K. (1992). A note on the effect of prior probability disclosure and information representativeness on subject predictive accuracy. *Behavioral Research in Accounting, 4,* 140–151.

Waller, W.S. (1988). Slack in participative budgeting: The joint effect of a truth-inducing pay scheme and risk preferences. *Accounting, Organizations and Society, 13,* 87–98.

Waller, W.S. (1992). Decision research in managerial accounting: Return to behavioral economics foundations. Chapter 2, this volume.

Waller, W.S. (1994). Behavioral-economics approach to probability assessment: An application in professional auditing. Working Paper, University of Arizona.

Waller, W.S., & Bishop, R. (1990). An experimental study of incentive pay schemes, communication, and intrafirm resource allocation. *The Accounting Review, 65,* 812–836.

Waller, W.S., & Chow, C. (1985). The self-selection and effort effects of standard-based employment contracts: A framework and some empirical evidence. *The Accounting Review, 60,* 458–476.

Waller, W.S., & Felix, W.L. (1984a). Cognition and the auditor's opinion formulation process: A schematic model of interactions between memory and current audit evidence. In S. Moriarty & E.J. Joyce (Eds.), *Decision Making and Accounting: Current Research* (pp. 27–48). Norman, OK: University of Oklahoma.

Waller, W.S., & Felix, W.L. (1984b). The auditor and learning from experience: Some Conjectures. *Accounting, Organizations and Society, 9,* 383–406.

Waller, W.S., & Jiambalvo, J. (1984). The use of normative models in human information processing research in accounting. *Journal of Accounting Literature, 3,* 201–226.

Waller, W.S., & Mitchell, T.R. (1984). The effects of context on the selection of decision strategies for the cost variance investigation problem. *Organizational Behavior and Human Performance, 33,* 397–413.

Waller, W.S., & Mitchell, T.R. (1991). Conditional probability judgments: Effects of imagining vs. experiencing the conditioning event. *Organizational Behavior and Human Decision Processes, 49,* 302–325.

Ward, B.H. (1976). An investigation of the materiality construct in auditing. *Journal of Accounting Research, 14,* 138–152.

Watts, R., & Zimmerman, J. (1990). Positive accounting theory: A ten year perspective. *The Accounting Review, 65,* 131–156.

Weber, R. (1980). Some characteristics of the free recall of computer controls by EDP auditors. *Journal of Accounting Research, 18,* 214–239.

Weick, K.E. (1979). *The Social Psychology of Organizing* (2nd Edition). Reading, MA: Addison-Wesley.

Weiss, A.R., & Birnbaum, P.H. (1989). Technological infrastructure and the implementation of technological strategies. *Management Science, 35,* 1014–1026.

Weitzman, M. (1976). The new soviet incentive model. *Bell Journal of Economics, 7,* 251–257.

Weitzman, M. (1980). The 'ratchet principle' and performance incentives. *Bell Journal of Economics, 11,* 302–308.

Whyte, W.F. (1955). *Money and Motivation: An Analysis of Incentives in Industry.* New York: Harper and Brothers.

Wilkins, T., & Zimmer, I. (1983). The effect of leasing and different methods of accounting for leases on credit evaluation. *The Accounting Review, 63,* 749–764.

Williamson, O.E. (1975). *Markets and Hierarchies: Analysis and Antitrust Implications.* New York: Free Press.

Williamson, O.E. (1985). *The Economic Institutions of Capitalism.* New York: Free Press.

Winkler, R.L., & Murphy, A.H. (1973). Experiments in the laboratory and the real world. *Organizational Behavior and Human Performance, 21,* 252–270.

Wolf, F.M. (1981). The nature of managerial work: An investigation of the work of the audit manager. *The Accounting Review, 56,* 861–881.

Wolfson, M. (1985a). Empirical evidence of incentive problems and their mitigation in oil and gas tax shelter programs. In J.W. Pratt & R.J. Zeckhauser (Eds.), *Principals and Agents: The Structure of Business* (pp. 101–125). Cambridge, MA: Harvard Business School Press.

Wolfson, M. (1985b). Tax, incentive, and risk-sharing issues in the allocation of property rights: The generalized lease-or-buy problem. *The Journal of Business, 58,* 159–171.

Wright, A. (1988). The impact of prior working papers on auditor evidential planning judgments. *Accounting, Organizations and Society, 13,* 595–605.

Wright, P.M. (1989). Test of the mediating role of goals in the incentive-performance relationship. *Journal of Applied Psychology, 74,* 699–705.

Wright, W.F. (1977a). Financial information processing models: An empirical study. *The Accounting Review, 52,* 676–689.

Wright, W.F. (1977b). Self-insight into the cognitive processing of financial information. *Accounting, Organizations and Society, 2,* 323–332.

Wright, W.F. (1979). Properties of judgment models in a financial setting. *Organizational Behavior and Human Performance, 23,* 73–85.

Wright, W.F. (1988). Audit judgment consensus and experience. In K.R. Ferris (Ed.), *Behavioral Accounting Research: A Critical Analysis* (pp. 305–328). Columbus, OH: Century VII Publishing.

Wright, W.F., & Aboul-Ezz, M.E. (1988). Effects of extrinsic incentives on the quality of frequency assessments. *Organizational Behavior and Human Decision Processes, 41,* 143–152.

Wright, W.F., Ho, J., & Davis, E.B. (1991). Limited consensus of going concern judgments. Working Paper, University of California-Irvine.

Yates, J.F. (1990). *Judgment and Decision Making.* Englewood Cliffs, NJ: Prentice-Hall.

Yates, J.F., McDaniel, L., & Brown, E. (1991). Probabilistic forecasts of stock prices and earnings: The hazards of nascent experience. *Organizational Behavior and Human Decision Processes, 49,* 60–79.

Young, S.M. (1985). Participative budgeting: The effects of risk aversion and asymmetric information on budgetary slack. *Journal of Accounting Research, 23,* 829–842.

Young, S.M. (1992). A framework for successful adoption and performance of Japanese manufacturing practices in the United States. *Academy of Management Review, 17,* 677–700.

Young, S.M., Fisher, J., & Lindquist, T. (1993). Manufacturing performance in workgroups: The effects of varying competitive feedback and cooperation on slack and output. *The Accounting Review, 68,* 466–481.

Young, S.M., & Selto, F. (1991). New manufacturing practices and cost management: A review of the literature and directions for research. *Journal of Accounting Literature, 10,* 265–297.

Young, S.M., Shields, M.D., & Wolf, G. (1988). Manufacturing controls and performance: An experiment. *Accounting, Organizations and Society, 13,* 607–618.

Zimmer, I. (1980). A lens study of the prediction of corporate failure by bank loan officers. *Journal of Accounting Research, 18,* 629–636.

Zimmer, I. (1981). A comparison of the prediction accuracy of loan officers and their linear-additive models. *Organizational Behavior and Human Performance, 27,* 69–74.

Index